YELLOW

YELLOW

Race in America Beyond
Black and White

FRANK H. WU

BASIC
BOOKS

A Member of the Perseus Books Group

Copyright © 2002 by Frank H. Wu

Hardcover published by Basic Books, A Member of the Perseus Books Group
First paperback edition published in 2003 by Basic Books

Designed by Jeff Williams

Library of Congress Cataloging-in-Publication Data
Wu, Frank H., 1967–
  Yellow : Race in America Beyond Black and White / Frank H. Wu.
    p. cm.
  Includes bibliographical references and index.
  ISBN 0–465–00639–6 (hc.); ISBN 0-465-00640-x (pbk.)
1. Asian Americans—Race identity. 2. Asian Americans—Social conditions. 3. Asian
Americans—Civil rights. 4. United States—Race relations I. Title.

E184.O6 W84 2001
305.895'073—dc21
                                                                                              2001043266

DHSB   03 04 05   10 9 8 7 6 5 4 3 2 1

For my wife, Carol L. Izumi

Contents

YELLOW

East Is East, East Is West

Asians as Americans

The problem of the twentieth century is the problem of
the color-line,—the relation of the darker to the lighter
races of men in Asia and Africa, in America and the islands
of the sea.

—W. E. B. Du Bois, *The Souls of Black Folk*

When I Was Johnny Sokko

I remember when I was Johnny Sokko.

Johnny Sokko was the Asian boy who shared title billing with his Giant
Flying Robot on an old black-and-white television series. He was the star of
one of many science fiction shows imported from Japan. I was a devoted fan
growing up in the early 1970s when mine was the only "Oriental" family in
our suburban neighborhood outside Detroit.

Every afternoon, I walked home from school. My parents were pleased
that, after they had picked the just-opened suburb and then their empty lot,
Winchester Elementary was built right across Sunnydale Lane. They had
bought a brand-new, two-story colonial based on the model, virtually identical with many of the other units in the subdivision development. The
neighborhood children used to play inside the wooden shells of the new

houses. The kid who lived behind us once suggested that we dig our way down to China. We started on the project, only to tire after shoveling a hole a few feet deep.

I was among the first students to attend the new school when it opened its doors. Our driveway practically lined up with its driveway. I liked being so close to school that I could feel it was mine. I have fond memories of school days: the red-headed girl who helped me tie my shoelaces; cupcakes mothers would bring to class to celebrate their children's birthdays; the smell of crayons, paste, and construction paper in art class, the materials used to make turkey silhouettes and Pilgrim hats for Thanksgiving; the cacophony of a dozen children trying to draw out harmonies on plastic recorders in music class while others sang off-key; the bustling "hot dog day" in the cafeteria, with steam coming out of the paper packaging of the frankfurters and an assortment of condiments, a break from the usual fare that our mothers had packed in lunchboxes, and the miniature cartons of milk we bought for a nickel; scrapes from falling off the monkey bars or flying from the swingsets; swimming lessons at the high school pool in the summer, until the movie *Jaws* made it unsafe to set foot in the water; holistic reading and new math; and field trips downtown to an automobile manufacturing plant and a shop that sold supplies for magicians.

Within a minute of the end of class, I would dash home, pausing just long enough to look both ways before crossing the street. After saying hello to my mother, who was in the kitchen preparing dinner—usually a steamed whole fish garnished with ginger and immersed in soy sauce—I would close the curtains in the family room, settle into my red beanbag chair, and turn on the television.

I was allowed an hour of entertainment. Then I had to sit down at the piano with a kitchen timer serving as an excruciatingly slow metronome to guarantee I practiced for the allotted half hour. I also had to do extra homework consisting mainly of long division problems my mother made up on scrap computer printout paper, extra-long, fan-folded sheets with green and white stripes, which my father had brought back from the office. I always tried to finish too quickly, and double-checking would show my careless mistakes. My hobbies were building model cars from kits, the type you glued piece by piece painstakingly, not the type that could be snapped together, and collecting baseball cards, which came in those wax packages with their cardboard-like chewing gum.

After a commercial break and station identification, I was focused on *Johnny Sokko,* which was in a limited run before he was replaced by the

Three Stooges. In the premiere, viewers learned that Johnny had been a passenger on a cruise ship, which sank after being attacked by the sea monster
Dracolon. Along with Jerry Monno, a secret agent who belonged to Uni-
corn, an international peacekeeping force, he washed up on the shore of a
deserted island. Spider, a criminal mastermind, and his Gargoyle Gang kept
their headquarters there. Emperor Guillotine from outer space had landed
there, too. While the bad guys collaborated on nefarious plans, having kid-
napped the scientist who designed the towering robot, Johnny chanced
upon this creation that became his companion. Because the robot fortu-
itously heard Johnny's voice before any other when his electronic brain was
activated, he had to obey the boy. Johnny wore a wristwatch that doubled
as his radio link with the robot. He summoned the robot whenever there
was trouble.

In the first episode, a nuclear explosion brought the machine to life to
fight for justice. His face was fixed, with glowing eyes beneath a mock Egypt-
ian headdress. His movements were haltingly mechanical martial arts gestures, the clanking armor a hint of his strength. He was able to take to the
air, with the wind visibly rushing by. He would carry Johnny in his hands,
shielding him and following his directions. He would set Johnny down in a
safe place while he defeated one after another of their archenemies: the
gigantic claw; the starfish; the sand creature; Opticon the humongous eyeball;
Torozonn the space mummy; and Drakulan, a vampire leading the undead.

Over the course of a month, I enjoyed all two dozen installments of the
serial. I could imagine myself as Johnny. I could not do that with the stars of
any other rerun, even though I liked the *Brady Bunch* well enough. I could
hum our theme song; I knew the weapons at our disposal. I choked up when
in the melodramatic finale the robot sank beneath the sea as a martyr for
humankind.

There were other Asian characters on the television networks. None of
them was as real as Johnny. Ultra Man was less thrilling than the Giant Flying Robot, because anybody could tell he was just an actor wearing a glit-
tering jumpsuit and a bug-eyed helmet. Like all superheroes, he had an origin
story. He was born when Science Patrol officer Hayata crashed into Ultra
Man's space craft. Hayata was killed, and Ultra Man felt guilty. He revived
Hayata by becoming a single being with him. By holding up the Beta Cap-
sule, Hayata would undergo a metamorphosis into Ultra Man. The light on
his chest would blink as his powers were expended, bringing him close to
death again. I used to watch him with a freckled tomboy of a girl. I even
kissed her before her parents said we couldn't be friends anymore.

The animated figures from *Speed Racer*, including Speed seated behind the wheel of his Mach 5, his father Pops in the garage, his girlfriend Trixie cheering him on, and even their pet monkey Chim Chim with his antics, were all ambiguously Asian. I wondered about their constantly wide-eyed expressions and upturned noses. Only the enigmatic Racer X was an exception. His features were hidden behind a black mask.

The only Asian woman who was a regular cast member of an American show was Mrs. Livingston, played by Miyoshi Umeki, of the old Bill Bixby program, *The Courtship of Eddie's Father*. One of my earliest memories is of tuning in to it with my parents. I can still whistle the theme song about "my best friend."

The Asians on the silver screen were even less appealing to a first-grader. The whole cast of the *Godzilla* movies, which were featured in a marathon "monster" weekend, consisted of panicking Asians fleeing Tokyo before the rampage. Our adversaries in war epics such as *Tora! Tora! Tora!* were both Asian and yet foreign. My father told my brothers and me that it wasn't good to yell, "Kill the Japs!" He wasn't able to explain why.

Johnny Sokko may have been my hero, but my classmates did not welcome him. They must have known Johnny, to be able to pick out his reasonable facsimile in the daily games of dodgeball in the gym. At home, I watched Johnny, failing to notice the bad editing, poor dubbing, and obvious special effects that marked the show. At school, I wondered why I was called "Johnny," oblivious to the looks, manners, and eccentricities that marked me.

Even though I understood soon enough that I could not help but turn into Johnny during recess, I never understood what was wrong about being him. As Johnny, I was a child with greater wisdom than adults. All of us six-year-olds could relate to that predicament. I was a hero, even if my powers came from my control over a metal automaton. My life was full of adventure as I battled the forces of evil that were threatening world conquest, even though I was allowed to ride my bike only around the block and not beyond to the busy roads that ran through the nearby fields toward the city.

My hero was the other children's enemy. Even if I did not consciously see him—or myself—as Asian, they saw it clearly. They saw me as both more and less than Johnny. To my surprise, I learned I was not white. By birth, I was yellow. My aliases included Chinaman, chink, jap, gook, or even wog in the worldly epithet spoken by the naughty student visiting from France. (I found out later that "wog" was the derogatory acronym used by the British Foreign Office for "Westernized Oriental Gentleman.") I was a joke, the object of a ubiquitous sing-song chant that meant everything and nothing, "Chinese,

Japanese, dirty knees, what are these?" It was shouted with fingers pulling back eyes into slits by classmates running in a circle around me, laughing so hard that they would fall down, as their parents supervised the playground. They dared me to fight in kung fu matches, hissing and scowling more than punching and kicking. They asked me, "How can you see with eyes like that?" My babysitter asked me if my parents were communists. My teacher looked at me expectantly when she played a documentary about China. My parents could not answer my question satisfactorily: "Why are we Chinese?"

I was unable to disguise myself. Standing there in a polyester print shirt my mother had sewn together to save money, discount store bell-bottom blue jeans, and sneakers that were a knockoff of the popular brands, with straight black hair cut at home though not with a bowl, thick glasses, and buck teeth, I was repeatedly recognized as one of many. Alongside Johnny, I could turn around and find myself transformed into Genghis Khan, Tojo, Charlie Chan, Fu Manchu, Hop Sing, Mr. Sulu, Kato, Bruce Lee, Arnold on *Happy Days*, Sam on *Quincy, M.E.* I was the Number One Son, intoning "Ah so," bending at the waist and shuffling backwards out of the room, with opium smoking, incense burning, and ancestor worshipping, the regular goings-on in the background, accompanied by an obedient wife, helpless with her bound feet. I could deliberately mishear the lyrics of Johnny Rivers's television theme song, "Secret Agent Man" as "Secret Asian Man"— "who leads a life of danger" and who "to everyone he meets . . . stays a stranger"—but I knew there could be no such mysterious hero.

As I became older, I was given many masks to wear. I could be a laborer laying railroad tracks across the continent, with long hair in a queue to be pulled by pranksters; a gardener trimming the shrubs while secretly planting a bomb; a saboteur before the day of infamy at Pearl Harbor, signaling the Imperial Fleet; a kamikaze pilot donning his headband somberly, screaming "Banzai" on my way to my death; a peasant with a broad-brimmed straw hat in a rice paddy on the other side of the world, stooped over to toil in the water; an obedient servant in the parlor, a houseboy too dignified for my own good; a washerman in the basement laundry, removing stains using an ancient secret; a tyrant intent on imposing my despotism on the democratic world, opposed by the free and the brave; a party cadre alongside many others, all of us clad in coordinated Mao jackets; a sniper camouflaged in the trees of the jungle, training my gunsights on G.I. Joe; a child running with a body burning from napalm, captured in an unforgettable photo; an enemy shot in the head or slaughtered by the villageful; one of the grooms in a mass wedding of couples, having met my mate the day before through our cult leader; an orphan in the last airlift out of a collapsed capital, ready to be adopted into the good life; a black belt martial artist breaking cinderblocks with his head, in an advertisement for Ginsu brand knives with the slogan "but wait—there's more" as the commercial segued to show another free gift; a chef serving up dog stew, a trick on the unsuspecting diner; a bad driver swerving into the next lane, exactly as could be expected; a horny exchange student here for a year, eager to date the blonde cheerleaders; a tourist visiting, clicking away with his camera, posing my family in front of the monuments and statues; a ping pong champion, wearing white tube socks pulled up too high and batting the ball with a wicked spin; a violin prodigy impressing the audience at Carnegie Hall, before taking a polite bow; a teen computer scientist, ready to make millions on an initial public offering before the company stock crashes; a gangster in sunglasses and a tight suit, embroiled in a turf war with the Sicilian mob; an urban greengrocer selling lunch by the pound, rudely returning change over the counter to the black patrons; a businessman with a briefcase of cash bribing a congressman, a corrupting influence on the electoral process; a salaryman on my way to work, crammed into the commuter train and loyal to the company; a shady doctor, trained in a foreign tradition with anatomical diagrams of the human body mapping the flow of life energy through a multitude of colored points; a calculus graduate student with thick glasses and a bad haircut, serving as a teaching assistant with an incomprehensible accent, scribbling on the chalkboard; an automobile enthusiast who customizes an imported car with a supercharged engine and Japanese decals in the rear window, cruising the boulevard looking for a drag race; an illegal alien crowded into the cargo hold of a smuggler's ship, defying death only to crowd into a New York City tenement and work as a slave in a sweatshop.

My mother and my girl cousins were Madame Butterfly from the mail order bride catalog, dying in their service to the masculinity of the West, and the dragon lady in a kimono, taking vengeance for her sisters. They became the television newscaster, look-alikes with their flawlessly permed hair.

Through these indelible images, I grew up. But when I looked in the mirror, I could not believe my own reflection because it was not like what I saw around me. Over the years, the world opened up. It has become a dizzying kaleidoscope of cultural fragments, arranged and rearranged without plan or order.

Asian-ness comes and goes as fad and fashion.[1] Tattoos of dragons entangled around Chinese ideograms are all the rage. Feng-shui consultants divine the best arrangements of furniture inside a house and plantings outside for design magazines. Miniature Zen gardens and bonsai from no-fuss kits adorn offices. Acupuncturists stick their profusion of delicate needles into even the family pet. Japanese animation becomes a staple of mainstream children's television and Japanese *anime* gains a following among more mature viewers. Imported goods from Asia develop into high-quality competition, whether toys, cars, stereos, appliances, computers, or anything else digital and miniaturized. Readers are mesmerized by Arthur Golden's 1997 best-seller, the faux *Memoirs of a Geisha*.[2] Spiritualist Deepak Chopra dispenses advice for stressed-out Westerners. Indian body painting with henna (mehndi) is copied by rock stars such as Madonna, who are then copied by adolescent white girls. Children are captivated by the home-grown Barney and the British Teletubbies only until they are old enough to learn about Pokemon, Nintendo, and Playstation.

Today, the UHF channel that broadcast *Johnny Sokko* is off the air; the series is not in syndication anywhere else; and video stores that specialize in cult classics do not carry any of the tapes, although there is a glossy magazine catering to a younger generation of hip Asian Americans that pays homage to the Giant Flying Robot by taking his name as its title. The other day, a newspaper reader wrote to the local question-and-answer columnist to ask if the show had ever existed or if he had dreamed it up during his youth.

Yes, Virginia, there was a Johnny Sokko.

I was Johnny Sokko well before I had any other personality. I have missed Johnny in the quarter century since then. The robot is long gone. I remain not only a stranger in a familiar land but also a sojourner through my own life.

Writing Race

I'd like to be as honest as possible in explaining why and how race matters, because it shapes every aspect of my life—and everyone else's. I'd like to do so in a manner that allows my white relatives and my white friends to understand and empathize.

I have learned how naïve I was to have supposed that children grew out of their race and to have expected that adults could not possibly be racist. The lives of people of color are materially different than the lives of whites, but in the abiding American spirit we all prefer to believe that our individualism is most important.

As a member of a minority group everywhere in my country except among family or through the self-conscious effort to find other Asian Americans, I alternate between being conspicuous and vanishing, being stared at or looked through. Although the conditions may seem contradictory, they have in common the loss of control. In most instances, I am who others perceive me to be rather than how I perceive myself to be. Considered by the strong sense of individualism inherent to American society, the inability to define one's self is the greatest loss of liberty possible. We Americans believe in an heroic myth from the nineteenth century, whereby moving to the frontier gives a person a new identity. Even if they do not find gold, silver, or oil, men who migrate to the West can remake their reputations. But moving to California works only for white men. Others cannot invent themselves by sheer will, because no matter how idiosyncratic one's individual identity, one cannot overcome the stereotype of group identity.

Sometimes I have an encounter that demonstrates how easily people can be transfixed by a racial stereotype. In a casual aside, a business colleague, who I thought knew me well enough to know better, may make an earnest remark revealing that his attempt to connect with me can come only through race. Although they rarely mention their personal lives, people always will make it a point to tell me about the hit movie they saw last night or the museum exhibit they toured over the weekend if it had a vaguely Asian theme, whether Chinese, Japanese, Korean, Vietnamese, or whatever, because, "It reminded me of you." They tell me I resemble the cellist Yo-Yo Ma or their five-year-old son's friend in school. Or in a passing instant, a white boy or a black boy, whom I would credit with childhood innocence, can rekindle my memory of the ordinary intolerance of days past. At an airport or riding on a subway, boys will see me and suddenly strike a karate pose, chop at the air, throw a kick, and utter some sing-song gibberish, before turning around and running away. Martin Luther King Jr. asked to be judged by the content of his character rather than the color of his skin, but in these surreal episodes I am not judged by the content of my character because the dealings have no content except for the racial image. Worse, it is as trivial for others as it is traumatic to me. I may as well be a stage prop. University of California at Berkeley literature professor Elaine Kim has recounted being told by a white friend who'd read Maxine Hong Kingston's *The Woman Warrior*, one of the earliest works of Asian American fiction to become a staple of literature courses, that only through the book did she come to understand Kim.[3] The fictional character becomes more believable than a real person, as though it is easier to know Asian Americans through the representation than through the reality.

At other times, I will have another type of encounter in the anonymous rush of contemporary life, one that confirms that people can be oblivious to folks who don't resemble them.[4] To present an analogy, most motorcyclists and bicyclists who ride regularly on city streets are accustomed to the situation in which they will make prolonged eye contact with a driver, who then blithely proceeds to cut off the bike or turn directly in front of it. The person behind the wheel may have seen the rider but responds only to vehicles like her own; anything else doesn't register. Likewise, waiting in line, I am amazed when a white person, sometimes well-dressed and distinguished looking and sometimes not, cuts in front of me or expects to be given VIP treatment. I am galled by not only the action but also the sense of entitlement that this person radiates. I want to say, "Hello? Did you not see the rest of us back here, or did you take it for granted that you were more important?" Of course, sometimes people are momentarily distracted or generally impolite. It happens often enough, however, in cases where it is fair to surmise that race and gender are involved. When whites are disrespected by other whites—for example, when they are ushered to a deserted area of the restaurant near the kitchen—they generally are not plagued by the suspicion that it is for racial reasons. It is easier for them to write off an incident as the consequence of incivility rather than another indication of something worse. Even if people of color are spurned for reasons other than race, the maltreatment harkens back to race because of the uncertainty of the matter. People of color are held to a double standard. Asian Americans are impudent if we presume to behave as others have done without doubting their right; what is assertive and commanding when it comes from a white male is bossy and presumptuous from an Asian American female. Ralph Ellison's grand novel *Invisible Man* is based on this phenomenon. Radical writer bell hooks speaks of being overtaken by a "killing rage" during these moments.[5]

I suspect I have it much easier than many others. Asian Americans are stereotyped in a manner that is at least superficially positive. I enjoy a life of the mind. I realize how much worse the problems I see must become if they are magnified by the daily difficulties of less fortunate circumstances. I do not go hungry at night.

I'd like to give some examples of our race problem. They are vexing exactly because they are minor. They are revealing and they point toward much more. In Ellis Cose's *The Rage of a Privileged Class: Why Are Middle Class Blacks Angry? Why Should America Care?* and Lena Williams's *It's the Little Things: The Everyday Interactions that Get Under the Skin of Blacks and Whites,*[6] the two journalists explain how many middle-class African Americans, who are most like white Americans, are infuriated by what seem to be petty slights. As race becomes less significant socioeconomically, it can become more important symbolically and politically. The more two individuals are alike in other respects, the more are glaring any race-based differences in the treatment accorded them. Social psychologists have established again and again that in these matters everything is relative, across and within racial groupings. During World War II, on average African American soldiers stationed in the North had lower morale than those stationed in the South. The effect could be documented regardless of whether individual servicemen had come from the North or the South. The cause was the point of comparison. Even though segregation laws and practices were far better in the North than in the South at the time, the black GIs in the North could see that black civilians were doing much better than they were, but black GIs in the South felt that black civilians under Jim Crow racial segregation were doing much worse than they were.[7] Race also is asymmetrical. What seems like benign childish jokes to the majority can seem like an endlessly recurring nightmare to a minority.

In 2001, two different military accidents each provoked a diplomatic crisis between the United States and an Asian nation. In February, an American nuclear submarine inadvertently sank a Japanese fishing boat during a drill. Nine of the 35 passengers on the boat died. In April, an American surveillance plane flying in international airspace collided with a Chinese jet fighter that had been tailing it belligerently. The American plane made an emergency landing on a Chinese island, where the crew was held hostage. The Chinese pilot was presumed dead.

In each case, as politicians on both sides demanded apologies and became increasingly hostile, the anti-Asian emotions of the public flared up. In isolated instances, commentators used racial terms such as "chink" and argued that loyal Americans should stop eating at Chinese restaurants. At least one radio deejay reportedly proposed that Chinese in the United States be rounded up for internment camps and another suggested that Chinese be deported[8]; none of the people involved seemed to realize that their comments affected and appeared to include loyal Americans. The internment camp supporter and others called up people with Chinese names and harassed them on the air.

Author John Derbyshire, who wrote the critically acclaimed novel *Seeing Calvin Coolidge in a Dream*, published an essay in *Chronicles* magazine in which he argues sincerely for internment of Chinese Americans "in the increasingly thinkable event of a war between China and the United

States."[9] He dismisses the critiques of the Japanese American internment, saying, "I must say, I never thought it was a very deplorable thing to do." Using anecdotes about beauty parlors and Kabuki theaters in the camps and Japanese loyalists who muttered about Japan winning, he echoes the internment supporters of the past: "The interned Japanese-Americans argued that they were not security threats. I am sure that most of them were not; I am equally sure that some of them were." He "guarantees" that the new camps for Chinese Americans will be established, "whatever the ACLU—or even the Supreme Court—thinks about it." Declaring "a responsible U.S. government really has no choice in the matter," he notes that he—an Englishman who has not applied to naturalize as an American "partly from a lingering sentimental attachment to my own country"—will accompany his Chinese-born wife and their two children as they are herded into such a camp.

The antagonism toward Asians may be excusable. Asian Americans cannot seem to convince non-Asian Americans that when we ask not to be blamed for what Asians have done, we are not even discussing the substance of any dissension between Americans and Asians. Foreign governments and foreign companies may well be wrong and deserving of censure, for all sorts of reasons. But conflict with Asia makes Asian Americans vulnerable, because there has been a history of anti-Asian moods leading to anti-Asian American actions. If ordinary people were to act out their aggressions toward Asia, they would hurt not Asians but Asian Americans. They cannot reach Asia, but they can easily hit Asian Americans. Other than race, there is no relationship between a Japanese American living in the United States and the Japanese clamoring for prosecution of the submarine commander. Without racial reasoning, there is no cause for presuming that a Chinese immigrant restaurateur supports China over the United States. (China took the opposite tack of assuming that Asian Americans were loyal to the United States, detaining several Chinese-born American citizens and permanent residents on trumped-up charges of espionage just after its spy plane disgrace.[10])

Even without misfortune overseas, Asian Americans are associated with one another. Every month or so, I find myself waiting in line behind or in front of another Asian American or an Asian family. Half the time, when my turn comes the clerk or the salesperson will treat us as if we were all together and will be startled to find out that we have nothing to do with one another. By itself, this racial coincidence causes a second of confusion or embarrassment and nothing more than that. However, it means that I can disregard other Asian Americans only at my peril. I may pride myself on being an independent American, but I am inextricably bound to people with whom I have nothing in common except skin color.

I don't hear it often anymore—I am too much a "race man," to borrow the phrase—but from time to time I have been told, "Oh, I think of you as white," or "Oh, I don't think of you as Asian."[11] The white people who say these things may intend them as the ultimate compliment, but the more admiring they are the worse their way of thinking. They are trying to reach out, but they are implying that it is better to be white than Asian American and they like best the Asian Americans who are most like whites. They are distinguishing between the good minority individual, at the expense of the bad minority group.

Nor need I pay any attention to race for others to show they are obsessed with it. The ordinary encounters of daily life, which should have nothing to do with race, can easily turn into unnerving incidents that are racially charged. Many Asian Americans are familiar with those awful moments when, in a dispute over who was in line first at the cash register, where dogs can be walked, who bumped into whom, or in declining to give money to a panhandler, a person who is white or black suddenly shouts something about "go back to where you came from" or mutters an aside meant to be overheard about "all these damn foreigners." In these instances, Asian Americans must decide whether they can and should disregard the racial tone. I find that when I respond, even if I try to reason with someone, people sometimes become implacable, and the effort to engage them is futile. They insist more hotly that they are right, not racist. They were merely claiming the parking space they saw first, and even if they said "you know, this is the way we do it in America" or asked "how long have you been in this country, anyway," it wasn't a veiled racial reference and I shouldn't take it as such.

In May 2001, a major study[12] that included a national telephone survey and focus groups of highly educated individuals in New York City, Los Angeles, and Chicago showed that about one-third of all Americans agree that Chinese Americans probably have too much influence in high technology and are more loyal to China than the United States. Almost half believed that Chinese Americans passing secret information to China was a problem, and one-quarter thought that Chinese Americans were taking too many jobs from other Americans. They balked at the idea of an Asian American president, corporate CEO, or boss more than they did at someone African American, Jewish, or female in any of those roles. More than two-thirds forecast that China would be a menace to the United States. Their views about China correlated with their views of Chinese Americans. The findings can be generalized, because it turns out that few Americans distinguish between Chinese Americans and other Asian Americans.

The study was sponsored by the Committee of 100, a nonpartisan group of Chinese American leaders such as the Priztker-Prize winning architect I. M. Pei, which has sought to increase the political participation of Chinese Americans and foster cooperation between China and the United States. It hired independent firms that have done corresponding work for the Anti-Defamation League over the years. The survey and focus groups were conducted before the spy plane crisis, so the negative results also cannot be attributed to any specific tensions. At the Committee of 100's annual conference, where it released the results, many observers were perplexed by the negative figures. Other surveys, however, have shown the same patterns of other Americans disliking or feeling threatened by Asian Americans.

Almost imperceptibly something strange has happened. As a nation, we have become so seemingly triumphant at vilifying racists that we have induced denial about racism. [13] Regarding racism, before the civil rights revolution many whites believed that what was, should be; now, in a post-civil rights era, they believe that what should be, already is. This profound change makes it harder than ever to communicate. What was once overt and thought to be right is now thought to be wrong but has become covert. Most people have become what social scientists John F. Dovidio and Samuel L. Gaertner have dubbed "aversive racists," conditioned to regard racism as reprehensible but also reflexively following racial impulses. [14] We also forget that white society used to subjugate African Americans and other people of color quite openly. In the segregated South, many whites were forthright and unabashed in articulating and acting on their conviction that blacks were a lesser breed of human being. In the North, some whites would have conceded that whites below the Mason-Dixon line or those afflicted by ignorance were enthralled by racism even if they would not admit it of themselves.

The evidence of such racism is expunged. Novelist Jack London, whose dispatches from Asia for the Hearst newspapers helped popularize the term "yellow peril," also wrote an essay of that title warning of the "menace" to the Western world from "millions of yellow men" (Chinese) under the management of "the little brown man" (Japanese). [15] His rejoinder to fellow socialists who admonished him for these attitudes toward Asians was "What the Devil! I am first of all a white man and only then a Socialist." [16] His belief in Anglo-Saxon supremacy was fervent and formed "a dominant note throughout all his writing," according to his daughter, as was his conviction that "the world has ever belonged to the pure breed, and has never belonged to the mongrel," in his own words. He is thought, for example, to have originated the phrase "great white hope" to describe heavyweight boxer Jim Jeffries, the idea being that Jeffries would knock out the reigning champion, the African American Jack Johnson, and win racial redemption in the ring.[17] Yet even though his classic works such as *Call of the Wild, White Fang,* and *To Build a Fire* have been selected among the best American novels in the Modern Library series, his *Yellow Peril* has been expurgated from the canon. The 1904 essay is not included or even mentioned in his collected works as gathered for the definitive Library of America edition.[18]

Race becomes ephemeral. A comic book publisher refused to give permission to editors of a scholarly collection of primary documents on Japanese Americans to reprint any part of a *Superman* serial in which the Man of Steel visits an internment camp. Clark Kent and Lois Lane learn that the government has "done all but lean over backwards in its desire to be humane and fair," unlike the Japanese vis-à-vis their prisoners of war. The ungrateful Japanese Americans, however, are planning to break out and seize Lois Lane as a hostage. Despite the historical significance of the popular portrayal of the internment camps, the publisher was the lone hold-out in refusing to allow its hero to be shown as its artists had in fact depicted him.[19]

People nowadays concur that racism is wrong. Almost all of us swear that we do not practice it. We have fooled ourselves into believing that if we vow we aren't doing it then it cannot persist. Instead of pleading with people that racial thinking is wrong, we have to struggle to show ourselves that it occurs. I marvel at the number of people who would try to wash their hands of race by simply not talking about it. The Committee of 100 survey, for example, showed that even though many non-Asian Americans were themselves being prejudiced, they still believed that Asian Americans don't face prejudice.

The dilemma of progressive denial is foreshadowed by the mindset of labor organizer Samuel Gompers, president of the AFL-CIO. At the turn of the twentieth century, he co-wrote an essay, "Meat versus Rice: American Manhood Against Asiatic Coolieism—Which Shall Survive," arguing that "while there is hardly a single reason for the admission of Asiatics, there are hundreds of good and strong reasons for their absolute exclusion."[20] On other occasions, he warned of "the menace of a possible overwhelming of our people by hordes of Asiatics."[21] He explained that "the Caucasians . . . are not going to let their standard of living be destroyed by negroes, Chinamen, Japs, or any others."[22] Despite the AFL having promised to unite working people "irrespective of creed, color, sex, nationality, or politics," Gompers forbade locals from accepting Chinese or Japanese members.[23]

Gompers was not like other anti-Asian agitators, however, who were anti-Asian with no compunction about the matter. He wanted to be known as open minded. He insisted that he had no grudge against Asian immigrants but was acting as he did because of his experiences and observations. He said in his autobiography, "it is my desire to state emphatically that I have no prejudice against the Chinese people" but only "profound respect for the Chinese nation." He said in the very next paragraph, "I have always opposed Chinese immigration not only because of the effect of Chinese standards of life and work but because of the racial problem created when Chinese and white workers were brought into the close contact of living and working side by side."[24] These contradictory comments were not exceptional. He had said earlier that that once the Chinaman comes, he has either dominated or been driven out, for "the Chinaman is a cheap man." He then added, as if he had regrets for his hatred, "the American people do not object to the Chinese because they are Chinese," but because of all the ills they would bring to the country.[25] (He had the same views toward all other Asian workers as well, especially Japanese and Korean.)

It never occurred to Gompers that Asian immigrants were not inherently any different than other laborers, but were scabs because of the situation. He did not think that he could organize them to strengthen all workers, and he did not recognize that he was contributing to the very racial problem he blamed for the inability to join forces. For him, race was crucial and exclusion was preferable to cooperation. Yet he recognized, however dimly, that it would be wrong to act out of prejudice even if he refused to recognize his own feelings as prejudice.

For me the dilemma, then, is figuring out what to do. I would like to be proactive rather than reactive and alter attitudes. I evaluate the possible responses by their persuasiveness. The most meaningful message may depend on the circumstances. It cannot be words in a formula or a display of despair. Sometimes, I am relieved that asking people, "what were you thinking?" is disarming enough to make them change their mind.

It would be as impossible to laugh off everything racial while suppressing the howl of anger as it would be inappropriate to take on all offenders and immediately call them the worst bigots. People who have committed offenses—and it is more than that they are offensive—may well wish to be color blind. They probably would be shocked if they were told they had treated people differently based on race even though thinking of themselves as polite. They might even be indignant as liberals who consider themselves-supportive of civil rights. I do not want these people to dismiss me as a whiner who is overly sensitive, nor would I want them to misconstrue me as a malcontent telling them that they must follow a fickle racial etiquette. I would rather explain that goodwill is not enough than condemn them for bad faith, modulating my tone so as not to be strident, because a dispassionate conversation may be more conducive to changing minds than a direct attack. In this process, I am not content to persuade people that their racial language may be offensive. Even if I win them over to that view, I have only suggested to them that they should use the words when I am not there to hear them, that words are more important than actions, and that race is a matter solely of subjective emotions. I am willing to cut them some slack, however. All people everyone make an occasional mistake, which does not indicate their true characters. Sensitivity also is overrated. People may tell their children to be sensitive about introducing their new boyfriends or girlfriends to their grandparents, because they don't want to upset the elders with the sight of a white or black date. Or they may turn their concerns against Asian Americans, as when an administrator at the University of California Santa Cruz in 1988 made the bizarre decision to cancel a Filipino "college night" scheduled for December 7 so that Asian Americans celebrating with food and cultural events on Pearl Harbor Day would not offend others. (The administrator later sued for libel, alleging that the individuals who protested his decision had defamed him as "racist.")[26]

So I write. I have been writing this book since adolescence, starting off typing on an old Smith-Corona when I was in high school. I have been able to maintain my good humor even as I am frustrated regularly, because I tell myself that everything is material for this book. I have been told often by white teachers who were indifferent to injustice to say to tormentors even in high school, "Sticks and stones may break my bones, but words can never hurt me." As Georgetown law professor Mari Matsuda has argued, those teachers were wrong.[27] Sticks and stones can wreak flesh wounds that will heal; words embody powerful ideas that can permanently mar or mend the psyche.

Through these pages, I start to come to terms with what it means to live as an Asian American and to consider what it might mean for the United States to thrive as a multiracial nation. I am optimistic about understanding. As a lawyer, I like to argue, but as a teacher, I aspire to provoke people to think for themselves rather than persuade them to agree with me. I am a skeptic who has doubts about my own viewpoints. I profess ignorance and ask questions, but I do not preach and can give no answers. I am seeking the best course for myself, not dictating it to others. I most respect those individuals with whom I disagree who are open-minded, willing to be convinced, and proceed on principles they will declare in public, much more than the individuals with whom I agree who are small-minded, willfully uninformed of facts, and deceitful about their genuine motivations.

I believe that we can engage in dialogue, listening to one another and the voices of our own better selves. I also am confident that we Americans can make our practices live up to the democratic promise in the great experiment of our country. In the childhood game "Ghost," each player must add a letter to the string in progress without completing the spelling of a word; likewise, participants in democratic dialogue succeed when they are able to offer an opening for the next person to have a say and not when they are able to have the last word. At the threshold, we must all be willing participants and equal players.

I would like to stimulate dialogue. My project can be published only in an unfinished form. It must be tentative and provisional, and it may be even inconsistent and speculative. Like the protection of any rights, the protection of civil rights is an ongoing process, not a finished product. If we suppose that we can achieve it as an outcome for all time, we will be disillusioned. The American Civil Liberties Union and the National Rifle Association do not wait for the First Amendment or the Second Amendment, respectively, to be secured once and for all. It is like the well-being of individuals: People who exercise until they are in good shape must continue to work out. They cannot stop and decree themselves healthy.

My success depends on cooperation with you, the reader, who undoubtedly will have a response. I anticipate robust reactions, and I would be disappointed if I did not generate dissent. The vigor of the interchange improves it. These are dangerous subjects. I make mistakes like anybody else. I am sure of only this: My book can spark discussion. As much as I agree that in a democracy none of us should dictate how to lead the good life to our fellow citizens, I also agree that we ought to be able to ask ourselves and one another what might make up the many different good lives and how best to pursue them. Believing that everyone has the right to free speech does not require believing that we are all right in our speech.[28]

Toward that end, I have written for my friends, Asian American and non-Asian American alike. I have in mind the Asian Americans who are more ethnic as well as those who are more assimilated, along with the white Americans and African Americans who are more radical and more moderate. For all of them, I have divided this volume into three sections.

I begin by considering the model minority myth and the perpetual foreigner syndrome. The myth and the syndrome are defined by the remarks, respectively, "You Asians are all doing well," and the question, "Where are you really from?" Some of us, but not all of us, are well-off, recent arrivals, or both. We are all people, most of us are Americans, but there is little else that can be said categorically that is not an oversimplification. To talk about Asian Americans requires throwing off the names assigned to us against our will. We must defy these labels, for stereotypes are scripts we are given to follow. We must compose our own lives, in which we take responsibility for the lyricism and the dissonance. Above all, our freedoms guarantee that each of us has the right to write the story of his own life.

I then address problems. Our changing society faces issues of immigration, with a movement to close the borders, and affirmative action, with backlash toward racial remedies. We are tested by cultural diversity and the temptations of racial profiling. On each of these divisive topics, Asian American examples can enhance our awareness of the color line between black and white, rather than devalue the anguish of African Americans, because Asian Americans stand astride the very color line and flag its existence for all to see. If the color line runs between whites and people of color, Asian Americans are on one side; if the color line runs between blacks and everyone else, Asian Americans are on the other side. The line, however, is drawn in part by Asian Americans, and in turn can be erased by us. Asian Americans can be agents of our own destinies, insisting that we are ourselves and refusing to be either black or white. Asian Americans meet the moral choices of honorary whiteness. I may even have been guilty of perpetuating the problems of race.

I end with resolutions. We all can find hope in the mixed race movement, which represents our future. Together we can reform coalitions, which have been the source of democratic strength in the past. Asian Americans can play a unique role in achieving racial justice. We are out-marrying at extraordinary rates, and Asian children are being adopted into white families, making up an American race by no means envisioned by early prophets of the New World. To be an Asian American is to embrace the union among diverse peoples, a group that is vital and dynamic even if artificial and fragile.

Literal Yellow, Figurative Gray

My premise is straightforward. Race is more than black and white, literally and figuratively. Yellow belongs. Gray predominates. I advance these arguments together, and they are mutually reinforcing. Being neither black nor white, Asian Americans do not automatically side with either blacks or whites. Columbia University professor Gary Okihiro once asked, "is yellow black or white?"[29] Chang-Lin Tien, who was the first Asian American to head a major research university, recalled arriving in the United States in 1956. He says that when he was a graduate student, "I never rode the city buses" in Louisville, Kentucky. He was humiliated when he boarded one and saw that "whites rode in the front and 'coloreds' rode in the rear." He asked, "Just where exactly did an Asian fit in?" He did not wish to be consigned to the back of the bus, but neither did he believe that even if he dared to sit down in the front of the bus, he could stay there in good conscience.[30] Theirs are the best type of question, because they have no answers.

The answers are erratic. On the only occasion when the Supreme Court considered whether Asian Americans were subject to the strictures of racial segregation, it reasoned in 1927 that if separate schools could be established for white pupils and black pupils, "we cannot think that the question is any different or that any different result can be reached . . . where the issue is as between white pupils and the pupils of the yellow races."[31] Blacks and Asian Americans were equivalent and interchangeable; in legal parlance, they were "fungible." Yet now it is common to refer to an "Anglo-Asian" overclass in contrast to an African American-Hispanic underclass. Iconoclast Michael Lind, who has promoted the idea of the rise of an "overclass" as a successor to "the Establishment," includes Asian Americans as possibly—but not definitely—members of such a dominant body. Journalist Dan Walters introduced the notion in his 1986 book on the new California, writing that "the high level of Asian education and economic achievement . . . has led many demographers to see them as part of an Anglo-Asian overclass that will dominate California's two-tier society of the 21st century."[32]

Asian Americans are more inconsistent than protean. During World War II, writer Roi Ottley reported "a humorous anecdote . . . of the Chinese laundryman who, in self-defense on the night of the Harlem riot, hurriedly posted a sign on his store window which read: 'Me Colored Too'."[33] Filmmaker Spike Lee later used the same scenario in his 1989 movie, *Do The Right Thing,* a moment-by-moment cinematic study of a day in the Bed-Sty neighborhood of New York City finishing in explosive racial conflict, updating it with a Korean shopkeeper as the would-be African American. The Korean shopkeeper escapes unscathed because the chorus of African American elders in the neighborhood, who have watched over him throughout the story, vouch for him in the end: "Korea man is OK. Let's leave him alone."[34] Yet in 1969, UCLA sociologist Harry Kitano remarked in the opening pages of an influential monograph: "'Scratch a Japanese American and find a white Anglo-Saxon Protestant' is a generally accurate statement." More recently, political theorist Frances Fukuyama has made a similar claim, namely that Asian Americans have assimilated into a standard that consequently cannot be considered white any longer.[35]

In race matters, numbers matter.[36] The 2000 Census shows change that is accelerating so rapidly it is hard even for Asian Americans to keep track of ourselves and grasp the meaning of the new demographics. There are now more than 10 million individuals who are Asian American, constituting between 3 and 4 percent of the nation's population.

The Asian American population has experienced staggering growth, driven by immigration. Between 1990 and 2000, the Asian American population nationwide grew by 48 percent, trailing only Latinos. The Asian American population in California grew by more than one-third to about 3.7 million (plus another half million of mixed descent that includes Asian), slightly ahead of Latinos. The Asian American population of New York City is half again as large as it was ten years ago, and Asian Americans make up one in ten residents, as the city itself continues a comeback based on Asian American and Latino immigration (the African American population stayed the same and the white population continued to decrease).

Ethnically, the largest Asian American group in the United States is Chinese American (2.4 million), followed by Filipino American (1.9 million), Asian Indian American (1.7 million), Vietnamese American (1.1 million), Korean American (1.0 million), and Japanese American (800,000). Geographically, Asian American populations are appearing outside cities that traditionally have had Asian American concentrations. The substantial Southeast Asian populations in Minnesota and Wisconsin, for example, are composed primarily of people who have arrived within the past twenty-five years; the Asian American population of Nevada tripled in a decade; and the number of Asian Indians in the Washington, D.C., metropolitan area doubled in a decade, making them the largest Asian ethnicity in the area.

In race matters, words matter, too. Asian Americans have been excluded by the very terms used to conceptualize race. People speak of "American" as if it means "white" and "minority" as if it means "black." In that semantic formula, Asian Americans, neither black nor white, consequently are neither American nor minority. I am offended, both as an academic and as an Asian American. Asian Americans should be included for the sake of truthfulness, not merely to gratify our ego. Without us—and needless to say, without many others—everything about race is incomplete.

It isn't easy to call people on their unconscious errors. If I point out that they said "American" when they meant "white," they will brush it off with, "Well, you know what I mean," or "Why are you bringing up race?" Yet it is worth pondering exactly what they do mean. What they have done through negligence, with barely any awareness, is equate race and citizenship. They may even become embarrassed once the effect is noticed. Asian Americans were upset when the MS-NBC website printed a headline announcing that "American beats out Kwan" after Tara Lipinsky defeated Michelle Kwan in figure skating at the 1998 Winter Olympics.[37] Like gold medalist Lipinsky, Kwan is an American. By implying that Kwan was a foreigner who had been defeated by an "American," the headline in effect announced that an Asian American had been defeated by a white American in a racialized contest. If two white Americans compete against each other in a sporting event—say, rivals Nancy Kerrigan and Tonya Harding—it would be preposterous for the result to be described as one of them defeated by an "American." If Kwan had won, it also would be unlikely for the victory to be described as "American beats out Lipinsky" or "Asian beats out white." Movie producer Christopher Lee recalls that when studio executives were considering making a film version of *Joy Luck Club*, they shied away from it because "there are no Americans in it." He told his colleagues, "There are Americans in it. They just don't look like you."[38]

If I point out that people said "minority" when they meant "black," they sometimes will say again, "Well, you know what I mean," or "Why should we allow foreigners to claim they are minorities?" Yet it is worth pondering exactly what they mean as well. What they have done through negligence, with barely any awareness, is to equate race and socioeconomic class. They may even become embarrassed once the effect is noticed. Asian Americans were upset when in 1999 the College Board sponsored a study of educational achievement that specifically excluded Asian Americans from the definition of "minority."[39] By any dictionary definition, Asian Americans are a minority. Even if they have or are alleged to have done well in school, they remain a minority. Any claim to the contrary must be based on unstated conditions that control what it means to be a minority. "Minority" may mean underrepresented minority or disadvantaged minority, not numerical minority, in some situations and for good reasons. But not until such implicit assertions are turned into explicit premises can they be discussed, and then they may turn out to be dubious. Even when Asian Americans try to be "minorities," they are turned into outsiders. In 2001, when U.S. Representative David Wu went to the U.S. Department of Energy to deliver a speech for Asian American Heritage Month, he was denied entrance because guards did not believe he was a citizen. They even rejected his congressional identification as possibly fake. After a friend of Wu's, another House member who was white, tested the system and had no difficulty gaining entrance, officials said the Wu incident was only a mix-up.[40]

Words also show us the paramount importance of context. Race is meaningless in the abstract; it acquires its meanings as it operates on its surroundings. With race, the truism is all the more apt that the same words can take on different meanings depending on the speaker, the audience, the tone, the intention, and the usage. The modern convenience of e-mail reminds us regularly how much of communication is nonverbal. "Oh, you Asians all look so young—I can't tell how old you are," can be flattering or insulting, depending on whether the context suggests that it is meant to compliment a person on her youthful countenance or to doubt her position of authority.

As useful as role reversals can be for demonstrating the illogic of race, the technique is not perfect for thinking about all the issues of race. Some comparisons are inapt, because race is not experienced evenhandedly. The reversal of one facet of life does not create mirror image lives. What seems to be the same on the surface can be significantly different upon inspection. I have never been called a "nigger" or a "kike."[41] I know that "nigger" and "kike" are ugly and dirty, but my knowledge is abstract and secondhand rather than concrete and personal. If someone were to use those words to refer to me, I would regard that person as a bigot—but a misguided bigot, who is ignorant even in his ignorance. I might flinch, but I would not be hurt. The words don't resonate with me as do "chink" and "jap," astonishing me with their ability to harm; they don't hit me with the force that they likely would strike an African American or a Jewish American. I was once appalled to hear an Asian American woman explain nonchalantly that "jap" stood for "Jewish American Princess" and thus was an acceptable abbreviation; she had learned this new "jap" in college and returned home on break to tell her parents it was okay because it was distinct from the "jap" they had been called. Although there are offensive terms for various white ethnic groups or based on class distinctions, there is no term seriously used about whites in general that is a counterpart to the racial epithets used for people of color. Calling a white man "honky" would probably elicit more laughs than tears. The term "wigger" exemplifies the problem. Formed by adding "w" to the "n" word and meaning white teenagers with a bad attitude who are copying black culture (or their rendition of black culture), "wigger" is simultaneously complimentary to the whites who use it to express rebellion but derogatory to African Americans for what it implies about their way of life.

Our sensibilities properly depend on the situations. I am disgusted that Idaho officials refuse to rename the landmark "Chink's Peak" and Houston officials desire to keep "Jap Road." The historical record shows that these designations are racial and few can claim to be uninformed about their hateful meaning. There is no compelling reason to keep the names other than to show who wields power and who does not. The very absence of Chinese Americans who remain around to object in Idaho (it has been Japanese Americans for the most part who have done so) only reinforces the point that words signal who is unwanted. If the desire on the part of the recalcitrant is to recognize the past, I agree with them to the extent that "Chink's Peak" or "Jap Road" should continue to be printed on maps so that there is no forgetting what went before. Yet I never much minded lawyers saying "build a Chinese Wall" to refer to limiting access to confidential materials for ethical reasons. "Chinese Wall" refers to an object with a specific cultural reference, but it has no subtext. But I wonder what businesspeople—usually, businessmen—in Silicon Valley and elsewhere are thinking when they say "open the kimono" to refer to full disclosure of information when negotiating a deal. "Open the kimono" has a sexual subtext, and I doubt a white male businessman would say that to an Asian American woman who was sitting across the conference table as the representative for another firm. "Chinese fire drill" is just downright puzzling to me. I have no idea why teenagers who stop their car at an intersection, all jump out, run around, and jump in again, having switched seats, would make anyone think of Chinese or fire drills.

Yet race often is coded, racism symbolic. Discussions about tax policy, for example, often are based on unstated assumptions about who receives government benefits. The image of an African American "welfare queen" who gives birth to more children to increase her welfare hand-outs is the most obvious of such stereotypes, as erroneous as they are powerful.[42] When foes of immigration rallied in Iowa as the state considered trying to attract new residents in 2001, speaking of preserving "the integrity of the community," they did not need to say that it was the "integrity of the (white) community" that was not to be sullied, much as the block-busting tactics of real estate agents relied on the phrase, "there goes the neighborhood" to mean "there goes the (white) neighborhood."[43] Instead of opposing integration of schools and contact between whites and African Americans, whites opposed "forced busing." Social science experiments designed to discern underlying attitudes, however, find that anti-black feelings and anti-busing feelings are one and the same.[44] I understand how a few words strung together in a sentence can seem innocuous to the person talking and odious to the person listening. A comparison of an Asian American man to a monkey can be playful; a comparison of an African American man to a monkey becomes sinister. A white person who says, "Look at me when I'm talking to you" to an Asian American woman may be obeyed, because it is a request; the same person who repeats that line to an African American woman may be sued, because it is a command reminiscent of the orders to slaves or maid. "You're from New York City, aren't you?" can be a means of disapproving conduct with the insinuation, "You're Jewish, aren't you?"

I have seen William Shakespeare's magical *A Midsummer Night's Dream* performed on stage twice by a traveling troupe called the Shenandoah Shakespeare Express, which takes up summer residence at the Folger Library in Washington, D.C. Their festive romp through this most delightful of the bard's comedies ends with a play-within-a-play farce, as the band of mechanicals stages the myth of Pyramus and Thisbe with heartfelt ineptitude, their entertainment concluding the triple wedding ceremony.

In the Shenandoah company performance, a member of the audience is recruited to play "the wall" that separates the frustrated lovers. The only action on his part is to display the "chink" between his bricks, through which Pyramus and Thisbe are able to spy one another, whisper, and kiss. This use of "chink" for crevice is wholly decent and unrelated to the racist "chink" Asian Americans know well. I cannot help but think to myself, though, that I am glad I have not been asked up there to reveal my "chink" and that no other Asian American has been readily available for the impromptu casting. Through nobody's fault, an Asian American wall with his proud chink would bring racial ruin to the evening or at least an unintended and humiliating racial reference, cueing the mischievous Puck to hurry up with his afterword apologizing "if we shadows have offended . . . ."

It is for these reasons that as an Asian American I had mixed feelings when in 1999 a white aide to Washington, D.C., mayor Anthony Williams was called to task for using "niggardly" in the sense of "cheap" and was forced to resign.[45] Williams himself was already being unfairly derided within the black community as an outsider without street credibility, who was not "black enough," with his accountant's penchant for fiscal responsibility, acerbic self-depreciating humor, and neat bowties. After a black aide complained about the comment, which referred to the city budget, Williams allowed the white aide to leave. (He later rehired him.)

In the ensuing national controversy, I was sympathetic toward the white aide, bewildered that his extensive vocabulary had not paid off but instead led to an official reprimand along with baseless assertions that he was a closet racist. But I also was sensitive to the upset that could be caused to African Americans by a term that has no etymological relationship to the foul racial label whatsoever but that sounds as if it must, especially when right-wing radio deejays belittled blacks for their linguistic deficiencies, as if the deejays regularly scanned the *Oxford English Dictionary* and blacks were predictably dumb. They "makest waste in niggarding," as Shakespeare said in his first sonnet. (There is a bilingual variation on this: The Mandarin Chinese words that can be translated "that one" sound like the n-word; it is not unheard of for Chinese immigrants to create a problem for themselves by saying "that one" within earshot of African Americans, especially if they are pointing toward something near a black person.)

I am chagrined that whites sometimes discern these nuances if they are affronted by what they deem a snub. I have been told by a few whites that I am race-baiting, because I only use examples of white racists rather than including black racists and Asian American racists, and that hurts them because they feel they are blamed by unfair association with white supremacists. I have had a few whites also inform me solemnly that I must be a racist, because I use the terms "Asian Americans" and "African Americans," but only "whites" with a lowercased "w." To be sure, I would like to treat the objections seriously and be considerate of whites' emotions because they verify our touchiness about race. I am taken aback, however, by the inference that I mean to cast aspersions on all whites by discussing some whites. Perhaps if they consider discussions of racism to be accusations directed at them even if there has been no mention of their own names, they will sympathize with people of color who take an indictment of a wrongdoer as the impeachment of a minority group. Calling whites "white" actually connotes aspirations to a preferred status and includes the tacit suffix of "American." It is comparable to asking for the designation of "Asian American" or "African American" as a substitute for slurs. "European American" is awkward and mannered, but if parallel construction would assuage readers' feelings, they should amend "white" to "European American." (Throughout the book, to avoid an "us" versus "them" dichotomy and emphasize that Asian Americans are in fact Americans, I use "we" and "us" to refer both to Asian Americans and all Americans except where I am referring to distinct individuals or groups of which I am not a part or when I speak of stereotypes. The context makes clear which sense of "we" is intended.)

Some people of color may make generalizations about whites as a group, but few whites impute moral responsibility to whites as a group. After the terrible mass murder of fifteen at Columbine high school in 1999, there was widespread speculation about the motives of the killers, who shot themselves in the head at the end of their rampage. There were distraught deliberations about whether their parents were legally culpable or whether violence in the mass media could be properly blamed. But by and large the shooters were depicted as troubled rather than typical. By no means was there a sense that white children had an instinctive propensity toward such deadly sadism or that whites in toto were guilty.

Even books about race have relegated Asian Americans and immigrants to the margins and footnotes. The stereotype of Asian Americans has become all the more powerful because Asian Americans are at once highly visible in popular culture and virtually invisible in serious discourse, allowing popular culture to define serious discourse. Even though Asian Americans and Hispanics alternated as the fastest-growing racial minority group during the 1990s, it is still easy to find books about race with almost no mention of either Asian Americans or Hispanics or ones in which we are assumed to be identical to whites or blacks (sometimes, identical to whites on one page and identical to blacks on the next page, without any explanation). In his best-selling *Two Nations: Black, White, Separate, Hostile, Unequal,*[46] a comprehensive compilation of data on race, Queens College sociologist Andrew Hacker omits Asian Americans from impartial analysis. His survey is excellent, but it is for scientific reasons that the absence of Asian Americans makes the work less rigorous in its methodology not to mention less credible as a depiction of reality. In the oral histories of *Black, White, Other: Biracial Americans Talk About Race and Identity,*[47] journalist Lise Funderberg interviews nobody with Asian ancestry, notwithstanding her expansive title and the rates of intermarriage by Asians. The omission in breakthrough work indicates that Asian Americans fall outside the scope of even "other." Even in 2001, the *New York Times* series on "how race is lived in America," later published as a book, included a major survey about racial attitudes that showed significant racial differences—among blacks and whites. Latinos and Asian Americans were not displayed separately, even though African Americans were "oversampled" to obtain statistically significant results and other surveyors have been able to make the effort to study non-black minority groups.

The disappearance of Asian Americans and others who are neither black nor white is recent and mystifying. At the turn of the century, Asian Americans (with the caveat that it is anachronistic to use any of our current terms) were considered very much part of the race problem, alongside African Americans, Latinos, Native Americans, and whites who were not part of the Anglo-Saxon Protestant old stock. W. E. B. Du Bois, who was prescient in calling out "the problem of the twentieth century" as "the problem of the color-line," typically is quoted out of context. In the oft-cited passage from *The Souls of Black Folk*, given as the epigraph to this chapter,[48] he recognizes that the color line separates whites from "the darker to the lighter races of men in Asia and Africa, in America and the islands of the sea." He is able to balance that international sense of the color line with his particular concern about the "unasked question" of the Negro, "how does it feel to be a problem?"[49]

Born in Great Barrington, Massachusetts, three years after the end of the Civil War and dying in Accra, Ghana, on the eve of the 1963 March on Washington, Du Bois had a career not likely to be surpassed for its impact on race relations. Often congratulated on having been the first black to receive a doctorate from Harvard, he is said to have replied, "Believe me, the honor was entirely Harvard's." The original public intellectual, he helped found the NAACP, and he edited its magazine, *Crisis*. He debated the great accommodator, Booker T. Washington, on the best strategy for African Americans, insisting that "the Talented Tenth" would be able to lead a people toward equality in every respect, economic, political, cultural, and social, and rejecting the accommodationist approach of enduring racial segregation while striving for self-improvement. Although Du Bois would become dogmatic later in life, his early work on Reconstruction and the Philadelphia Negro establishes him among the greatest intellects to have come from his country. Published at the turn of the last century and never out of print since then, *Souls of Black Folk* blends candid autobiography, journalistic reporting, and scholarly research. Du Bois and what he called his "little book" stand as an example of how to overwhelm racism, facing the facts with conscience.

Following Du Bois's lead, we must be conscious of black and white to transcend black and white. We can acquire such a consciousness by raising Asian Americans out of the background. Asian American perspectives modify the overall picture by supplementing other perspectives and not replacing them. The addition of Asian Americans becomes crucial for more than their own benefit. They can contribute to resolutions of the problem that carries over from the twentieth century into the twenty-first.

Serious thinkers are starting to recognize that it is important to talk about race both broadly and deeply, but bringing all of us into the picture has turned out to be more demanding in practice than in theory. Deciding that everyone should be included is necessary but not sufficient. Metaphors of "building bridges" can be trite. It could amount to nothing better than consensus without content, settling on a slogan at a high level of generalization and a low level of meaning. There is a real risk, however, that inserting non-black people of color into debates over race could make them a wedge group that divides rather than unites in the clash identified by author Jack Miles as "blacks versus browns" in his influential article of that title.[50] It is easy enough to placate an internal minority by scapegoating another one as an external enemy: African Americans can be shown Asian Americans as the "blood-suckers" who are bleeding them dry. It also is all too easy to prefer a new minority over an old one: Predominantly white institutions can become racially diverse by including Asian Americans without becoming racially integrated with African Americans.

Yet racism against African Americans, more than other forms of racial discrimination, requires our attention as a community. Acknowledging non-black racial minority groups, rather than detracting from the urgency of addressing racism against African Americans, may aid our insight into that crisis. Looking at Asian immigrants, for example, shows the inconsistencies between the color blindness that is invoked against affirmative action and the color consciousness that becomes apparent in the denunciation of immigration. The inconsistencies expose the expediency, if not the hypocrisy, of the essentially political arguments that have been deployed in the different debates.

The figurative sense of transcending black and white also becomes imperative. We can prefer ambivalence and even ambiguity. We need the opposite of a panoramic view or utilitarian philosopher Jeremy Bentham's panopticon. A panoramic view uses a single vantage point to look out at the 360 degrees of the world. We need to look from the infinite vantage points of the 360 degrees of the world at each racial event. Bentham proposed a prison based on his panopticon: The guards sat in a central tower, ringed by level after level of the prisoners in their cells, so that a single guard could observe every prisoner easily. The collective views of the many prisoners, not the single guard, provide the better picture.[51]

Race relations, like bad relationships of any type, can become fixed and unchanging. Parties use accusatory absolutes. "Never" and "always" rule out a range of options and prevent mutual and free exchanges of information and ideas. One side becomes the villain, the other the victim. As crude caricatures, both give up free will and neither can claim moral responsibility.

Many Americans react so vehemently to the charge of "racism," often countering it with the claim of "political correctness," that we lose the shades that distinguish types of racial thinking. Many assumptions and attitudes can be *racial* without necessarily being *racist*. There are gradations, intellectual and social, from the unrepentant white supremacist who agitates to remove people of color from the country, to the respectful segregationist who counsels that everyone is better off among their own, to the unwitting racialist who without malice relies on generalizations about strangers. For this reason, even as we try to use "racism" sparingly, it is necessary to speak of race more profusely.

Asian Americans may allow whites and blacks to express themselves through intermediaries. Asian Americans can identify with blacks who are outraged by some whites' insistence on countering complaints of racial discrimination with the clever argument from a hypothetical case. Demagogues say, "Aren't blacks just as racist, too?" and set the prerequisite that, before they will agree that racial discrimination against blacks is wrong, blacks must agree that racial discrimination against whites is wrong. They devise a false moral equivalence, as if whites and blacks as groups actually experience the same racial discrimination on a regular basis. Asian Americans also can identify with whites who are exasperated by some blacks' refusal to accept that others also can be oppressed. Demagogues say, "Only whites can be racist," and spurn conciliatory measures, unless whites confess that they are at fault for everything lamentable in the lives of blacks. They set up an extreme ideology, as if they would rather exacerbate hatreds. Few of us benefit if we are consigned to an "everyone does it" mentality. We would race to the bottom.

The multiple scenarios pertaining to Asian Americans may provide the means for distinguishing among forms of discrimination, between what can conceivably happen and what regularly happens. Individual whites might be subjected to blatant discrimination in anomalous instances, but blacks as a group are burdened by systematic discrimination in many more cases. Most African Americans lack socioeconomic status and political power, but there are circumstances in which blacks have one or the other, relatively and absolutely. As University of California at Berkeley ethnic studies professor Michael Omi has written, "Some scholars and activists have defined racism as 'prejudice plus power.' Using this formula, they argue that people of color can't be racist because they don't have power. But things aren't that simple." Omi points out that some people of color have "carved out a degree of power in select urban areas—particularly with respect to administering social services and distributing economic resources." He names Miami and Oakland as two cities where blacks and Hispanics compete over education, economic opportunities, and political power.[52] Some things are similar, but not all things are the same. The beating of black motorist Rodney King at the hands of white Los Angeles police officers in 1991 and the beating of white trucker Reginald Denny in 1992 following the King trial verdict at the hands of black rioters were both horrific. The graphic record of each makes it easy to replay the videotapes of the incidents endlessly. Yet as heinous as each is in isolation, their significance may not be the same in totality.

One is an action taken by officials of the government with a lengthy history of abusing people on the basis of race. The Los Angeles Police Department had killed more than a dozen African American men through the use of chokeholds; its chief, Darryl Gates, defended the consequences by arguing that blacks had different bodies than "normal" people, so their arteries didn't open properly. The other is an action by renegades who are not entrusted to protect and serve the community. As lawyer Johnnie Cochran argued in representing Denny in a lawsuit against the city, even though it was African Americans who were directly responsible for attacking Denny (and four African Americans who rescued him), the formal response to the urban unrest abandoned predominantly minority areas. Everyone in those areas, including Asian American shopkeepers (and Takao Hirata, a Japanese immigrant, who was assaulted along with Denny), was left in jeopardy.

The cruelty of the attack on Denny, dragged from his big rig and bashed in the head with a brick, cannot be denied and must not be diminished. Yet failing to consider why some African Americans spread false rumors that Denny had used a racial slur before being set upon, or how many identified with his assailants as having had not just the book but "the whole bookcase" thrown at them, is to preclude full understanding.

When considering Asian Americans it is easier to realize that people can be both perpetrators and victims of racial discrimination. We can simultaneously play both roles, inferior to one, superior to the other. Asian Americans can feel ostracized by whites and terrorized by blacks. Asian Americans can even simultaneously play both roles in relation to the same group, regarding either blacks or whites with contempt only to have the favor returned. The party with the greater power to act on its impulses may vary by situation.

African American clergy such as the Reverend Al Sharpton led the 1990 boycotts of Asian-owned stores as he tried to shut down the Red Apple store in New York City following a dubious claim that the owners had assaulted a customer. African American activists called for Asian immigrants to surrender their stores to African Americans. Rappers such as Ice Cube sang of brutalizing Asian entrepreneurs with lyrics such as, "Pay respect to the black fist, or we'll burn your store right down to a crisp," on his *Death Certificate* album, number 2 on the Billboard charts the week after release, and Chubb Rock led a concert crowd in chanting, "Fuck you, eggroll."

The claim that Asian Americans enjoy advantages over African Americans, however, has some truth to it, albeit less truth than is supposed. Asian Americans, for example, may have access to resources not available to African Americans.[53] Even if Asian Americans were denied conventional bank loans for high-risk enterprises, just as African Americans would be, they were able to rely on private rotating credit arrangements based on ethnicity to bankroll their ventures. The observation that Asian Americans did not reside in the neighborhoods where they did business was largely true, and Asian Americans seem no more enthusiastic than whites to hire African Americans who have scant skills. Meanwhile, whites siding with Asian Americans and crowing that African Americans had shown that they were racists did not help Asian Americans or the situation. The competing claims of African Americans and Asian Americans in the inner city, all of whom were aggrieved from occupying the economic margins, require mediation

In 1992, nine Asian American small business owners were shot to death in Washington, D.C.; in 1993 fifteen were killed in Los Angeles, many by African Americans (although whether there were racial motivations in the cases is unclear). Conversely, in a highly publicized 1992 Los Angeles case, a white judge gave probation to a Korean American shopkeeper for shooting to death a fifteen-year-old African American girl, Latasha Harlins, in a squabble over a bottle of orange juice. In San Francisco public housing, racial violence among people of color has become endemic. African American children pick on Asian American children, just as whites have done. But Asian Americans who can fight back do so without remorse. Whether African American on Asian American violence and Asian American on African American violence can be appropriately juxtaposed, and if the effect is productive, requires meditation.

It was an Asian American, Desmond Nakano, who wrote and directed *White Man's Burden,* the independent movie made in 1995 with John Travolta and Harry Belafonte, depicting a world where whites are oppressed and blacks are powerful. Travolta is the white factory worker who barely scrapes by; Belafonte the black industrialist who leads a luxurious life. After Travolta is unfairly fired from his job, he kidnaps Belafonte in a reckless ploy. Everything about their society is flipped around from ours: It is whites who are stereotyped as shiftless, blacks who control media images, and white children prefer to play with black dolls. Nakano said his role reversal concept was born of his own experiences as an Asian American. (He also is credited with the script for *American Me,* the Edward James Olmos drama about Hispanic gangs in prison.) Although any individual could have conceived of the black-dominated society, Asian Americans almost always must locate an elusive place between black and white.[54]

So Asian Americans have intervened in the midst of an American tragedy, but we cannot pretend to be neutral as some observers envisaged Los Angeles Superior Court Judge Lance Ito could be in presiding over the racialized O. J. Simpson murder trial in 1995.[55] Even if some saw Ito as neutral, others made fun of him in racial terms. Most prominently, Senator Alfonse D'Amato impersonated him on the radio using a stereotypical Asian accent, even though Ito speaks with no stronger an accent than D'Amato himself.[56] Grievances can be translated, but all translations are problematic. Race can be transfigured by Asian Americans, but not by us alone.

New Models for Civil Rights

The country needs new models for civil rights, which must offer both universal principles and specific applications, with the recognition that even universal goals may be best pursued through specific strategies. The transition will not be easy, but it is already underway.

It is already possible to identify the end of one era and the beginning of another. In a commencement address given at the University of California at San Diego on June 14, 1997, President William Jefferson Clinton asked his listeners, "Can we become one America?" At any other period in our national memory, the question would have been rhetorical and could have produced only a self-congratulatory answer. To our post-modern culture, it sounds like a plea rather than an inquiry. Delivering his speech in a city that stands at an artificial physical boundary, President Clinton set forth a grand plan to make history by "lead[ing]the American people in a great and unprecedented conversation about race." He spoke of several goals: "[F]irst, we must continue to expand opportunity," including through the use of race-conscious affirmative action; second, "we must demand responsibility from every American;" and "third . . . perhaps the most difficult of all . . . [we] must build one American community based on respect for one another and our shared values."[57]

When President Clinton established the race relations commission that would advise him in these daunting tasks, the eminent members of the panel immediately fell to arguing among themselves about whether their subject was a matter of stark black and white or whether other hues were caught up in it as well. Their characteristic misunderstanding must be addressed to ensure that we can strive for social justice in a diverse democracy.

On one side was the chair of the group, esteemed professor John Hope Franklin. His *From Slavery to Freedom: A History of African Americans*[58] has become a classic. An African American who had been on the faculties of the top universities of the North and the South, the octogenarian Franklin had been prevailed upon by President Clinton personally to come out of his retirement tending orchids to serve a one-year term with the race commission.

Franklin originally stood steadfast in his commitment to confronting "the American dilemma." Swedish sociologist Gunnar Myrdal gave that title more than half a century ago to his books, the result of a massive undertaking that brought race relations to the attention of the general population as worthy of scholarship and requiring public policy.[59] Ever since Myrdal set the standard for continued inquiry and activity, his turn of phrase has referred specifically to the circumstances of blacks in this country, although Franklin probably would take issue with the spirit of Myrdal on his prescriptions to alleviate racism.

Representing the other side of the group was attorney Angela Oh. She had emerged as a reluctant spokesperson for Asian Americans—specifically, Korean Americans—after the April 29, 1992, Los Angeles conflagration triggered by the acquittal verdict in the trial of white police officers who were captured on videotape viciously beating black motorist Rodney King. She was praised publicly for her eloquent defense of a community that was talked about but not listened to, even as she was criticized privately by Korean American elders for lacking fluency in the Korean language. A third-generation Californian who could recollect when her family was the only Oh listing in the phone book, whereas now there are endless pages of Ohs, she advocated jettisoning "the black-white paradigm."

Appealing to MIT philosopher Thomas Kuhn's idea of a "paradigm shift," a fundamental revolution in our world view, Oh wanted a methodology that considers black and white as well as red, brown, and yellow. In a short entry published as part of an encyclopedia of the sciences, *The Structure of Scientific Revolutions*,[60] Kuhn details the series of intellectual innovations that have altered the very means for defining the physical universe. Kuhn himself worked a transformation in our intellectual life by bringing to the forefront an awareness of the human factors of even objective endeavors: we all have a stake in our own paradigms, right or wrong.

The exact exchange between Franklin and Oh, interspersed throughout their first official meeting, went as follows:[61]

OH: The old terms are going to be tossed. We're going to be hearing some new language, because it is time for some new language to be introduced, and we're going to help find that new language.

. . .

I do not think the concept of race is useful. It serves no useful purpose. . . . And as we move through this process of dialogue I just want to make sure that we go beyond the black-white paradigm. We need to go beyond that because the world is about much more than that, and this is sort of the next horizon. For us as a nation we need to go beyond that.

FRANKLIN: Now, some people have raised the question . . . of black/white relations in the context of the larger problem of race and ethnicity in this country. I've registered in my formal statement, I mentioned the fact that we've been anti-Semitic, we've been anti-Native American, we've been anti-Hispanic, we've been anti-Asian. . . . What I think we ought to bear in mind is that this began at a certain time and in a certain place, and that—I use a term my mother used to use, she'd say if somebody got started in a certain way, she said they cut their eye teeth on . . . . This country cut its eye teeth on racism in the black/white sphere. They didn't do it with Native Americans, they did it on black/white relations . . . . And I think that gives us the kind of perspective we need.

Franklin specified the date and the place when race relations became established in the land, long before there was a United States: 1619 in the Jamestown colony, when white traders offered a lot of black slaves for sale.

Both Franklin and Oh were right, but each saw only half the picture. They have since affirmed that their dispute was exaggerated in the press. Their words revealed differences more subtle than significant, but they were not the only ones who disagreed. They set off a debate in every forum where race was a topic of consideration.

Writing in *Emerge* magazine, a now-defunct African American news magazine, Mary Frances Berry, the influential chair of the United States Civil Rights Commission, stated that the country consists of "three nations, one Black, one White, and one in which people strive to be something other than Black to avoid the sting of White supremacy." The outspoken official concluded, "The task for us remains clear: the improvement of the life chances of African Americans."[62]

On the op-ed page of the *Los Angeles Times*, University of North Carolina professor Gerald Horne argued that geography had determined history.

He observed that a North–South divide brought about the black–white divide, but an East–West divide that is surfacing forms a "more complex" dynamic.[63]

Taking issue with both sides in the *New York Times*, Harvard professor Orlando Patterson, among others, posited that increasing economic disparities overshadowed decreasing racial discrimination.[64] Socioeconomic disadvantage was the concern that demanded our energies.

Clinton's "One America" presidential initiative was much maligned. It had few if any defenders and ended with no fanfare. Still, Franklin and Oh can be commended for their own involvement. Their capacity for working through their quarrel, respecting each other and coming to an accord, represented evolution for its substance as well as the process. Their work was one of the "promising practices" they were assigned to discover.

Franklin commands the authority of his discipline of history. The utmost split of our society has been a color line between black and white, or, more precisely, between black and everything else. In the past, whether by slavery or through Jim Crow, white supremacy—and that term is apt in this context—concentrated itself on blacks. Even today, African Americans bear the greatest burdens of racial discrimination in concrete cases where prejudice can be practiced. Asian Americans, Latinos, and others cannot as racial groups make the same claims to the same degree. Franklin is right that the events of April 29, 1992, in Los Angeles, whether they are called a riot or an uprising, cannot be comprehended without reference to the history of African Americans.

Then again, Oh is correct as an empirical matter. People who are neither black nor white have always belonged here, whether Native Americans, Latinos, Asian immigrants, or mixed-race individuals. According to the 2000 Census, people in the Hispanic category (who technically can be of any racial background) are about as numerous as people in the African American category. On college campuses, Asian Americans are the most numerous of the non-white groups. Many racial minorities who fall into the category of "other" have suffered in their own way, ranging from annexation of their territory and destruction of their culture to outright exclusion from citizenship and widespread discrimination throughout society. Their maltreatment is of a kind, if not to the same degree. The practices inflicted on African Americans and those that affected other people of color are related and mutually reinforcing. Oh is right that the events of April 29, 1992, in Los Angeles, whether they are called a riot or an uprising, cannot be comprehended without reference to the arrival of Asian Americans.

Instead of making an impossible choice between Franklin and Oh, allow me to make a modest suggestion: Whatever any of us concludes about race relations, we should start by including all of us. Whether we strive for moral principles or practical compromises, our vision must encompass everyone. Our leaders should speak to all individuals, about every group, and for the country as a whole. A unified theory of race, race relations, and racial tensions must have whites, African Americans, Latinos, Asian Americans, Native Americans, and all the rest, and even within groups must include Arab Americans, Jewish Americans, white ethnicities, and so forth. Our theory is an inadequate account otherwise.

It may be useful, however, to emphasize some aspects of the many racial issues that dominate our lives. It would be improper to treat every racial matter as identical with the next.

The Clinton administration may have come to a close without completing the mission of "One America," but it managed to issue the charge. The very goal of "one America" is contested. Whose America and what America? If "one America," which America? And if that America, how is it to be realized?

Within the foreseeable future in the United States we will make an inevitable transition that has never before been made anywhere on the globe peacefully, much less productively. In the twenty-first century, our nation will cease to have a single identifiable racial majority. Whites may be alarmed by that prospect, but they will be in a situation similar to everyone else, in numerical terms if nothing else. Asian Americans and other people of color may be less alarmed, but we are hardly better prepared than whites for the speed and the extent of the changes. We stand on the threshold and the eve. We have before us an opportunity and a challenge. Only together can we make the most of the opportunity and rise to the challenge. Ours is an as yet undiscovered country.

The Professional

I have become a professional Asian American. Much like someone who becomes famous for being famous, I am making a career out of my race. I make no apologies for this curious turn of events.[65] I would like to submit an explanation of its causes, however.

Over the past few years, I have been honored to be invited as a panelist at conferences, a speaker on radio interview shows, or a guest on television talk programs. I am flattered to be quoted now and then in various newspapers or paid to write an occasional column for op-ed pages. Over the past few years, I have delivered several dozen speeches to gatherings large and small, Asian American and integrated, and penned more than a hundred articles and essays for publications both obscure and popular. My repertoire of subjects, repeated with enough variation to hold my own interest as much as that of listeners, includes affirmative action, immigration, the English-only movement, hate crimes, diversity, and multiculturalism.

The common theme among these timely topics, and the expertise I am expected to bring to bear upon them, is an Asian American perspective. In other words, I supply the outlook of a person who is, in one of my favorite phrases, which I have learned goes over well as a sound-bite, "neither black nor white."

I am grateful for the job, but I realize that I am unqualified. I am grateful because for too long "the Oriental" on any scene bowed silently in the background. If Asian Americans spoke, it was with an accent to announce an ancient aphorism; if we were not ignored, we were isolated. East and West were not hail fellows well met.

But I am a fraud. I am unqualified, because I cannot speak for all Asian Americans. I doubt that any impostor could do any better or would desire to try that impossible task. I suspect, however, that at every appearance after I give my usual disclaimer, my audience continues to see and hear me as a spokesperson on behalf of Asian Americans. I only hope that my cousins appreciate that there is somebody who looks like them speaking out, even if they disagree with the message on occasion.

Truth be told, I know well my competition on the lecture circuit and the op-ed page: Asian Americans who will stand up to make known loudly and proudly that they are individuals and have nothing but disgust for those who would allow themselves to be characterized by a racial label.[66] They may be authentically Asian, unwilling to be "Asian American" because of its implications. Or they may even be free-riders, who profit from the civil rights movement but do not exert themselves for its causes. Maybe I am being unkind to someone who is my twin, without whom I could not survive, and for whom I am equally essential. Yin and yang, we are intertwined, in the debate over what is now called "the politics of identity" but previously was neither more nor less than life on the other side of the color line.

Ironically, the very status of people as members of a racial minority is what gives them special credibility in the argument for a theoretical color blindness, and approving of racial insensitivity allows them to leverage their claims of individuality into the illusion of representing a race. Race gives power to their statements that we should abolish affirmative action, close the borders, stop protesting, speak English, improve ourselves, assimilate, and live happily ever after. Coming from them, the claim that racial ills are contrived by people of color themselves is as harmful as it is convincing. I credit their good faith and I will address their claims on the merits, but they must also know that it seems as if they can become the darlings of whites by disparaging other people of color. When they state that they have not felt racism, I wonder if they mean to deny that I have felt it and that others endure it. I am baffled when I meet someone who is white, who tells me that he has been told by another Asian American that it is okay to use the word "chink." I would like to ask that white person if he feels he can speak for all white people, and I'd like to find that Asian American to ask how dare she give permission to others to abuse me.

Even though on some issues I, too, may have much the same opinion as my colleagues who are white or black, I believe that I can add substance. The messenger is the message. I try to demonstrate that, unlike the popular perception of politically apathetic Asian Americans, someone with an Asian face cares about the crises of the day and might even be able to respond fluently to them. Asian Americans can show their solidarity with other people of color, even if we only restate what African American leaders proclaimed previously. I also can reveal an aspect of the issues that involves Asian Americans but that affects others as well. Asian American examples are distinctive but familiar.

Over time, I'd like to show that I know about more than Asian Americans and care about more than Asian Americans. The problem is that a spokesperson becomes the stereotype. I have been cast in my role: an Asian American placed in a vacuum. Nobody wants to hear me or any other Asian American talk about welfare reform, unless the topic is turned into "welfare reform and Asian Americans." As a law professor, I can discuss the devilish details of civil lawsuits, among other subjects, by and large without the appended, "and Asian Americans." White pundits on talk shows seem to talk about everything without the same limitations. The criticism that Asian Americans seem to care only about Asian American issues, and other people of color only about what relates to them most directly, is partly caused by producers and editors who call on Asian Americans and others in a selective manner.

As much as I would like to be more than an Asian American in my public persona, I am committed to a responsibility. We cannot be reticent about race or shy about civil rights. Each of us who has the opportunity to make an appearance at the podium or to see a byline in print should remember that if we do not speak for ourselves, someone else will speak for us—or, worse, we will be ignored. We must give voice to our many views.

The Model Minority

*Asian American "Success" as
a Race Relations Failure*

Student: "Asians are threatening our economic future.
. . . We can see it right here in our own school. Who are
getting into the best colleges, in disproportionate numbers?
Asian kids! It's not fair."
Teacher: "Uh . . . That certainly was an unusual essay.
. . . Unfortunately, it's racist."
Student: "Um . . . are you sure? My parents helped me."

—Garry Trudeau
Recycled Doonesbury: Second Thoughts on a Gilded Age

Revenge of the Nerds

I am not the model minority. Before I can talk about Asian American experiences at all, I have to kill off the model minority myth because the stereotype obscures many realities. I am an Asian American, but I am not good with
computers. I cannot balance my checkbook, much less perform calculus in
my head. I would like to fail in school, for no reason other than to cast off
my freakish alter ego of geek and nerd. I am tempted to be very rude, just to

demonstrate once and for all that I will not be excessively polite, bowing, smiling, and deferring. I am lazy and a loner, who would rather reform the law than obey it and who has no business skills. I yearn to be an artist, an athlete, a rebel, and, above all, an ordinary person.

I am fascinated by the imperviousness of the model minority myth against all efforts at debunking it. I am often told by nice people who are bewildered by the fuss, "You Asians are all doing well. What could you have to complain about anyway? Why would you object to a positive image?" To my frustration, many people who say with the utmost conviction that they would like to be color blind revert to being color conscious as soon as they look at Asian Americans, but then shrug off the contradiction. They are nonchalant about the racial generalization, "You Asians are all doing well," dismissive in asking "What could you have to complain about anyway?," and indifferent to the negative consequences of "a positive image."

Even people who are sympathetic to civil rights in general, including other people of color, sometimes resist mentioning civil rights and Asian Americans together in the same sentence. It is as if Asian American civil rights concerns can be ruled out categorically without the need for serious consideration of the facts, because everyone knows that Asian Americans are prospering.

Consider the term "overachiever." I am reluctant to accept the title for myself, and not out of Asian modesty. To be called an "overachiever" begs the question: What, exactly, is it that individuals have achieved over—what others expected of them or what they deserve?

In either case, overachievers have surprised observers by surpassing the benchmark, and their exploits are not quite right. They will get their comeuppance sooner or later. Applied to an entire racial group, as "overachiever" is to Asian Americans, the implications are troubling. Asian Americans, often thought of as intellectuals, will be consigned to the same fate as intellectuals. As Columbia University historian Richard Hofstadter stated in the opening pages of his *Anti-Intellectualism in American Life*, "The resentment from which the intellectual has suffered in our time is a manifestation not of a decline in his position but of his increasing prominence."[1]

And so it is with Asian Americans. "You Asians are all doing well anyway" summarizes the model minority myth. This is the dominant image of Asians in the United States. Ever since immigration reforms in 1965 led to a great influx of Asian peoples, we have enjoyed an excellent reputation. As a group, we are said to be intelligent, gifted in math and science, polite, hard working, family oriented, law abiding, and successfully entrepreneurial. We revere our elders and show fidelity to tradition. The nation has become familiar with the turn-of-the-century Horatio Alger tales of "pulling yourself up by your own bootstraps" updated for the new millennium with an "Oriental" face and imbued with Asian values.

This miracle is the standard depiction of Asian Americans in fact and fiction, from the news media to scholarly books to Hollywood movies. From the 1960s to the 1990s, profiles of whiz kid Asian Americans became so common as to be cliches. In 1971, *Newsweek* magazine observed that we were "outwhiting the whites."[2] *People* magazine one year made celebrities of the five Asian American teenagers who swept the highest prizes in the annual Westinghouse science talent search in an article headlined "Brain Drain Boon for the U.S.," and it followed up the next year by profiling an entire family of Asian American winners.[3] Brown University history professor Stephen Graubard wrote an op-ed for *The New York Times* asking "Why Do Asian Pupils Win Those Prizes?"[4] The Asian refugee who was a finalist in a spelling bee, but who lost on the word "enchilada," has become legendary.[5] *Time, Newsweek, Sixty Minutes,* and other media outlets have awarded Asian Americans the title "model minority."[6] *Fortune* magazine dubbed us the "superminority."[7] The *New Republic* heralded, "the triumph of Asian Americans" as "America's greatest success story" and *Commentary* magazine referred to Asian Americans as "a trophy population."[8] The *New York Times* announced that we are "going to the head of the class."[9] The *Washington Post* said in a headline, "Asian Americans Outperform Others at School and Work."[10] Smith College sociologist Peter Rose has described Asian Americans as making a transition "from pariahs to paragons."[11] Memoirist Richard Rodriguez and Washington Post columnist William Raspberry have wondered whether Hispanics and blacks, respectively, might be able to emulate Asian immigrants.[12] A minority group could become the equivalent of a white real estate developer: *Advertising Age* quoted a consultant who opined that Asian Americans were "the Donald Trumps of the 1990s."[13]

Conservative politicians especially like to celebrate Asian Americans. President Ronald Reagan called Asian Americans "our exemplars of hope."[14] President George Bush, California Governor Pete Wilson, House Speaker Newt Gingrich—all have been unduly awed by the model minority myth. In a brief for the *Heritage Foundation Policy Review,* California politician Ron Unz said that Asian Americans come from an "anti-liberal Confucian tradition" that "leaves them a natural constituency for conservatives."[15] In the *National Review,* author William McGurn made the model minority myth a partisan parable: "Precisely because Asian Americans are making it in their adoptive land, they hold the potential not only to add to Republican rolls but to define a bona-fide American language of civil rights."[16]

According to the model minority myth, Asian immigrants have followed the beacon of economic opportunity from their homes in China, Japan, Korea, the Philippines, India, Vietnam, and all the other countries on the Asian continent and within the Pacific Rim. They might be fleeing despotism or Communism, backwardness or the deprivations or war and famine, but whatever the conditions of their past they know that the legend of Golden Mountain, to use the Cantonese phrase, guides their future.

They arrive in America virtually penniless. They bring barely more than the clothes on their backs. Their meager physical possessions are less important than their mental capacity and work ethic. Thanks to their selfless dedication to a small business or an advanced degree in electrical engineering—or both—they are soon achieving the American Dream.

They run a corner grocery in Manhattan, offering the freshest fruits and vegetables and serving up a take-out luncheon buffet priced by the pound. They buy a dry cleaning establishment in Los Angeles, featuring one-hour turnaround times and giving discounts to police officers. They start a motel franchise, which spreads throughout the Midwest, boasting such low rates with amenities like free cable television that other proprietors have no choice but to post signs identifying their accommodations inaccurately as "Native American Owned." They begin a computer chip manufacturing plant in the Silicon Valley, inventing the hottest miniaturized gadgets before selling their shareholdings and retiring at thirty-five. Or they open a boutique in Washington, D.C., with a display case of real-hair wigs on the wall above a bevy of manicurists chatting among themselves in another language while painting their customers' nails.

They were doctors, nurses, engineers, scientists, professors, and librarians, but they have problems pursuing their professions because the requisite license is denied to them owing to their foreign education, or they are discriminated against because they have a heavy accent. Even if they are reduced to the drudgery of jobs for which they are overqualified, they are earning what they could never have in conditions of a developing country. Although they may be sweating as a janitor despite holding a doctorate, the toil is only temporary, until they can secure the patent for their discovery. In the interim, they can save enough to send remittances home to kinfolk who want very much to come here, too.

Whatever endeavor they pursue, Asian Americans are astonishing for their gung-ho enthusiasm. They remain busy with the chores called for by their enterprise twenty-four hours a day, seven days a week, through the holidays. After they sweep out their storefront entryway, they wash down the public sidewalk.

They come to dominate their trades after less than a decade, reducing their competition to the verge of bankruptcy and then buying up their warehouse stocks. Their associations become monopolies, lending money cooperatively among their own members to preserve their collective advantage. In some cities, they hold more than half the commercial licenses and operate a majority of the downtown "mom and pop" retail outlets. Hospitals and universities have departments wholly staffed by Asian immigrants. Private industries ranging from automobile manufacturers to software developers to government agencies, such as the Defense Department, depend on them for research and development.

In turn, their American-born progeny continue the tradition with their staggering academic prowess. They start off speaking pidgin, some of them even being held back a grade to adjust. They are willing to do as they are told, changing their given names to Anglicized Christian names chosen with the help of their teachers and their friends and told matter of factly to their parents. Above all, they study, study, study.

They are brought up under the strict tutelage of parents who have sacrificed everything in the hopes that their children will garner more than what they themselves have lost. The parents defer everything for themselves and invest it in their young, giving them the mission of redeeming the family. They maintain that anything less than a straight-A report card will shame the ancestors, and they beat their children for receiving a single B-plus. The elders have faith in the school system. They instill respect for educators. They take their children to weekend language lessons instead of allowing them to watch Saturday morning cartoons on television.

The no-nonsense regimen works wonders. A parade of prodigies named Chang, Nguyen, and Patel takes the prizes at piano recitals and proceeds to graduate from high school with honors as valedictorian, salutatorian, and the rest of the top ten of the class, receiving full scholarships to the Ivy League colleges en route to graduate school and advanced professional training.

In any course on campus, Asian Americans are the best (or worst) classmates. In a physics class, they wreck the grade curve, idly twirling their pens back and forth with thumb and forefinger during lectures, solving problem sets late into the night with their peers, breaking for fried rice seasoned with pungent fish sauce and accompanied by smelly kim chee. In the laboratory, they are polishing up projects begun when they were adolescents, making breakthroughs in biology and chemistry, and publishing papers that make the faculty envious as they strive toward a Nobel prize. If they engage in frivolous activities after hours, as they rarely do, they are betrayed by their telltale red faces, which they develop after drinking just half a glass of beer.

Eventually, they land a job at a high-tech company or they start their own. Making millions, they buy big houses in the suburbs or build monstrosities right up to the property line on vacant lots. They bring their relatives over, starting the cycle over again.

In the view of other Americans, Asian Americans vindicate the American Dream. A publicity campaign designed to secure the acceptance of Asian Americans could hardly improve perceptions. They have done better here than they ever could have dreamed of doing in their homelands. They are living proof of the power of the free market and the absence of racial discrimination. Their good fortune flows from individual self-reliance and community self-sufficiency, not civil rights activism or government welfare benefits. They believe that merit and effort pay off handsomely and justly, and so they do. Asian Americans do not whine about racial discrimination; they only try harder. If they are told that they have a weakness that prevents their social acceptance, they quickly agree and earnestly attempt to cure it. If they are subjected to mistreatment by their employer, they quit and found their own company rather than protesting or suing.

This caricature is the portrait of the model minority. It is a parody of itself.

In *The Abilities and Achievements of Orientals in North America*,[17] University of Calgary psychologist Philip E. Vernon perfectly captures the prevailing opinions about Asian Americans. Vernon describes Chinese and Japanese immigrants to the United States and Canada:

> The experiences of oriental immigrants in the United States and Canada— Chinese and Japanese—provide a remarkable example of adverse environment *not* affecting the development of intelligence. There is no doubt that, in the past, they were subjected to great hardships, hostility, and discrimination. They were regarded as a kind of inferior species, who could be used for unskilled labor and menial jobs, but could never be accepted as equals into the white community. And yet Orientals survived and eventually flourished until they came to be regarded as even higher achievers, educationally and vocationally, than the white majority.[18]

Vernon's research is typical of the tradition of the model minority myth. He contrasts past discrimination against Asian Americans with the present success of Asian Americans. He reviews copious quantities of seemingly objective data from the United States and elsewhere. He emphasizes intelligence tests suggesting that Asians outperform Caucasians both in the United States and overseas. He falls back on stereotypes about Asian behavior. Vernon explains, "Chinese people still appear to whites as being exaggeratedly humble and deferential, and as oblique or devious in their business and other communications and interactions." He notes that "because they have different ways of expressing emotions from whites, they still seem to us inscrutable and reserved."[19]

Avoiding the debate over whether nature or nurture is more important to human development by assuming that race and culture more or less correlate, Vernon writes that "any genetically different groups always differ too in their cultures."[20] In later work, Vernon published findings that Asians have larger heads than Caucasians and Africans and suggested that larger head size correlates to higher intelligence.[21] Whatever the root causes for individual achievement, Vernon links the status of Asian Americans to their identity as Asian Americans. By his account, Asian Americans flourish because they are Asian Americans, and they continue to thrive only to the extent that they behave as archetypal Asian Americans. Vernon summarizes the major factor in their "educational and occupational success" as "family upbringing" that stresses seven elements:

1. Adherence to accepted conventions of social behavior.
2. Cohesion not only within a family but also with kin and the family ancestors.
3. Discouragement of egocentricity and recognition of obligations to others.
4. Loyalty and obedience to the authorities, employers, and the state.
5. Motivation for educational achievement from first entering school until maturity.
6. Firm control, not permissiveness, from about three years up.
7. The need for hard work to gain success and honor the family.[22]

By Vernon's reckoning, these seven elements are distinctly Asian. "In spite of the important differences between Japanese and Chinese cultures . . . child upbringing is similar . . . in most respects . . . and both differ greatly from Western models," he writes. "There are also resemblances to the Puritan work ethic . . . but Orientals would probably not accept the Calvinistic view that man is responsible for the effects of his own actions, or that he is fundamentally evil, but can overcome this and achieve both grace and economic success," he adds. To make the point as adamantly as possible, he warns, "When the tradition has yielded to modern American fashions, it does appear that educational achievement is lowered, and that there is more delinquency, though still much below the white norm."[23]

With his twenty-three-page bibliography of sources spanning the twentieth century and the globe, covering the whole history of intelligence testing, Vernon looks reputable. He cannot be dismissed as a crackpot, and his work becomes troubling only upon a thorough reading. He was funded by the Pioneer Fund, which has promoted eugenics and racial separatism.[24] He worked with the notorious Arthur Jensen, the University of California at Berkeley physicist who claims that African Americans are genetically inferior.

However, if the message were true it would remain true regardless of the messenger, and *ad hominem* attacks would be inappropriate. Likewise, if the assertions are incorrect they remain incorrect even if espoused by other messengers, lacking the same ideological connections. Indeed, many researchers share Vernon's convictions about Asian American behavior as well as its causes. Furthermore, they have impeccable credentials and cannot be impugned as biased. Their work, however, should not be regarded as persuasive merely because it lacks an overt racial agenda. It may be imperfect because of its racial assumptions. The flaw is embedded as an integral part of the research methodology and the worldview it represents.

Julian C. Stanley, a researcher at Johns Hopkins specializing in the academically gifted, has written a single-page article posing the title question, "Do Asian Americans Tend to Reason Better Mathematically Than White Americans?" His answer is emphatic in the opening line: "The answer . . . is a resounding 'yes,' or even 'of course.'"[25] Stanley operates a center for mathematically precocious youth, which carries out annual nationwide searches for subjects who at the age of thirteen score 700 or higher on the math portion of the SAT. For decades, he has been finding children who, before they have entered high school, have abilities equal to the top 5 percent of seniors about to graduate from high school. His samples have been as high as one-quarter Asian American.

The same tendencies have been documented among other Asian ethnicities; it is not only Chinese and Japanese immigrants who have shown spectacular skills. A group of scholars, for example, found above-average academic achievement among Southeast Asian refugee children. Their subjects were by and large not as well-to-do as either Japanese Americans or Chinese Americans in other studies. But even among this ethnic group, the "parents had served their stewardship well" and "for the most part, the perspectives and values embedded in the cultural heritage of the Indochinese had been carried with them to the U.S." and "played an important role in the educational achievement of the children."[26]

The Asian values that form the core of the model minority are inculcated early. In a report comparing Anglo-American and Korean-American preschool-aged students, the authors observed marked qualitative differences.[27] The Anglo-American play activities stressed "independent thinking," "imaginative problem solving," "emphasis on ability," "independence," "self-confidence, "individuality," "self-expression," an "individualistic orientation," and "relatively symmetrical egalitarian" relationships among children and adults. The Korean-American play activities stressed "memorization," "task persistence," "emphasis on effort," "interdependence," "traditional values," "group harmony," "self control, modesty, obedience, "collectivist orientation," and a "vertical hierarchy of status difference."

If the list sounds familiar, it is because the positive representation of Asian Americans has become so well known that it can be readily recognized even if the racial references are deleted. The model minority myth singles out Asian Americans and could not refer to any other group in contemporary American culture. If you had to picture a twelve-year-old entering Harvard, you would conjure up an Asian face.

To the extent that Asian Americans are compared with anyone else at all, it is with American Jews of an earlier era. Asian immigrants are sometimes called the New Jews. (This is a reversal of the claim that Jews are Orientals.[28]) Asian Americans have superseded American Jews in the imagination of ethnicity. An anecdote about a striving youth from the city that would have featured a Goldberg fifty years ago stars a Park today. *New Republic* publisher Martin Peretz remembered arriving at Harvard as an instructor when "it was a white shoe town" and he taught sections full of "freshmen who had 'prepped' at Exeter and Andover" who were "made up largely of George Bush look-alikes." Back in Cambridge years later, he and his friends stood near the Yard and "played a game . . . how many minutes before 100 Asians pass before our eyes?" In less then eleven minutes, they met their goal. Like the Jews of the post-Sputnik era, Peretz contends, the Asian Americans who have made "the sudden appearance at Stanford and Yale, UCLA and Michigan" should be an "exhilarating" sight to "all Americans."[29]

Cartoonist Garry Trudeau satirized the model minority myth while recognizing its continuity with the earlier treatment of Jewish immigrants. In an installment of his "Doonesbury" comic strips devoted to the subject, another excerpt from which serves as the epigraph to this chapter,[30] he portrays the following exchange between a white boy and an Asian American girl:

> "Hey, good goin' on the National Merit Scholarship, Kim! Fairly awesome."
> "Thanks, Sean."
> "Must be easier to be a grind if you grow up in an Asian family, huh?"
> "I wouldn't know."
> "Huh?"
> "I'm adopted. My parents are Jewish."
> "Jewish? Yo! Say no more!"
> "I wasn't planning to."

Non–Asian American college students have been similarly sarcastic about the model minority myth. On campuses at the end of the twentieth century, non-Asian American students joke that "MIT" stands for "Made In Taiwan" rather than "Massachusetts Institute of Technology"; "UCLA" (pronounced "UCRA" to mock the reputed Asian inability to enunciate a proper "R") means "United Caucasians Lost Among Asians"; and the initials of University of California at Irvine, "UCI," mean "University of Chinese Immigrants." The University of California-Berkeley Engineering school has been spray-painted with graffiti calling on school authorities to "Stop the Asian Hordes."

The model minority myth is daunting. The white president of Stanford University related an apocryphal story about a professor who asked a white student about a poor exam answer in an engineering course, only to receive the comeback, "What do you think I am, Chinese?" The student body president of Berkeley has said, "Some students say that if they see too many Asians in a class, they are not going to take it because the curve will be too high." A Yale student has said, "If you are weak in math or science and find yourself assigned to a class with a majority of Asian kids, the only thing to do is transfer to a different section."[31]

The model minority myth appears to have the twin virtues of being true and being benevolent. It seems to be more benefit than burden for its subjects. It is unlike theories that array human beings in racial hierarchies. On its face, it is neither outlandish nor objectionable. It does not depend on allegations that Asian blood is better or even different than European blood. It relies more on acquired behavior than on inborn biology. It is not presented as some sort of tortured justification for outright oppression, such as incredible stories about African Americans told to legitimize the "peculiar institution" of chattel slavery.

The model minority myth also looks modern. It seems to be the product of scientific research rather than reflexive superstition. It cancels out prejudices of only a generation ago. It is ostensibly founded on empirical findings of social science, primarily Census tabulations. Since the 1980s, the figures have suggested that some Asian ethnic groups, notably Japanese Americans, have attained household incomes equal to or greater than those of white Americans. The numbers are averages, but they seem about as adequate a foundation as could be found for a racial proposition.

For all these reasons, it is a considerable challenge to explain how an apparent tribute can be a dangerous stereotype and why it presents a problem to be overcome. A person who demurs to praise seems to be "politically correct." Yet declining the laudatory title of model minority is fundamental to gaining Asian American autonomy. The model minority myth deserves a thoughtful critique. It would be foolish to condemn it as wrong or racist, without discussion. It is too complex, as well as too common.

Regrettably, the model minority myth embraced by the pundits and the public alike is neither true nor truly flattering. Instead, it is a stock character that plays multiple roles in our racial drama. Like any other myth forming our collective narrative of race, it is ultimately more revealing than reassuring. Complimentary on its face, the model minority myth is disingenuous at its heart.

As well-meaning as it may be, the model minority myth ought to be rejected for three reasons. First, the myth is a gross simplification that is not accurate enough to be seriously used for understanding 10 million people. Second, it conceals within it an invidious statement about African Americans along the lines of the inflammatory taunt: "They made it; why can't you?" Third, the myth is abused both to deny that Asian Americans experience racial discrimination and to turn Asian Americans into a racial threat.

Germs of Truth Within the Myth

Like many racial stereotypes, the model minority myth has a germ of truth. The problem, however, is that the germ becomes exaggerated and distorted. On its own terms, the myth is not even persuasive as a description of the status of Asian Americans. In earning power, for example, the evidence points toward a disparity between what individual white Americans and what individual Asian Americans are paid—and not for lack of trying on the part of Asian Americans.

To figure out the facts, University of Hawaii sociology professor Herbert Barringer led a team that conducted the most comprehensive review of the research literature ever done. Barringer concludes that with respect to income, "in almost every category . . . whites showed advantages over most Asian Americans."[32]

Barringer proceeds cautiously because he is contesting the model minority myth. Even controlling for nativity—that is, native-born versus foreign-born—Barringer finds that Asian Americans who are native-born earn less money than white Americans who are native-born and possibly even than white Americans who are foreign-born. That means that Asians without cultural and language difficulties may earn less than white Americans who may have such difficulties. Barringer observes that "there seems to be no compelling reason to argue for parity" between Asian Americans and white Americans, but he does agree that Asian Americans "have certainly done much better with incomes than have blacks and Hispanics." He states that Asian Americans, including such ethnic groups as Vietnamese immigrants, might show "decided improvements" over time. He prefers "the most favorable interpretation," that "most Asian Americans are overeducated compared to whites for the incomes they earn."[33]

That interpretation, however, is most favorable to white Americans and not Asian Americans. Translated into practical terms, it means that white Americans are paid more than Asian Americans who are equally qualified. Either Asian Americans are not hired for the higher-paying jobs, or they are hired but are still paid less.

According to the 1995 U.S. Glass Ceiling Commission, a blue-ribbon corporate panel chosen by Congress and chaired by Cabinet Secretary Elizabeth Dole, individual Asian Americans make less money than individual white Americans do in many occupational categories: 10 percent to 17 percent less for Asian American men and as much as 40 percent less for Asian American women. This lack of parity appears even between Asian Americans and white Americans who have the same qualifications. Controlling for other factors, the sole explanation for the inequalities is race.

The fact that Asian Americans are better educated than white Americans on average undermines rather than supports the model minority myth. The gap between Asian Americans and white Americans that appears with income reverses itself with education. It was consistent throughout the 1980s and 1990s. In 1980, approximately 36 percent of foreign-born Asian Americans had finished college compared with 16 percent of native-born citizens. In 1990, about 42 percent of Asian Americans had finished college compared with 25 percent of the general population. Every Asian American ethnic group, except Filipinos, attends college at higher rates than do white Americans. Chinese Americans, Indian Americans, and Korean Americans attend college at about twice the rate of white Americans. The entering classes of Ivy League schools are now as high as 20 percent Asian American, California schools such as University of California-Berkeley and UCLA as much as twice that percentage as Asian Americans become a plurality on campuses with no majority. Considering all educational institutions, Asian American overrepresentation is much lower but still significant: As of 1993, Asian Americans made up 5.3 percent of the college student body but approximately 2.9 percent of the general population. Their desire for education is increasing even as that of other groups is decreasing. Between 1979 and 1989, Asian Americans increased their numbers of Ph.D. recipients by 46 percent while whites and blacks decreased their numbers by 6 and 23 percent, respectively. By 1997, Asian Americans were receiving 12 percent of the doctorates conferred by U.S. universities, and they received more than one-quarter of the doctorates in engineering disciplines.

Although the average educational levels of Asian Americans might be taken as substantiating the model minority myth, the more plausible reading is that Asian Americans have had to overcompensate. Asian Americans receive a lower return on their investment in education. They gain less money than white Americans on average for each additional degree. They are underrepresented in management, and those who are managers earn less than white Americans in comparable positions. The excuse most often voiced for the situation emanates from the stereotype itself, namely that Asian Americans would rather make less money in research and development than be promoted to management positions. The only research on the subject refutes this pretext, showing that Asian Americans are no different than whites in desiring career advancement.[34] Even though Asian Americans are associated with education, they remain underrepresented even in higher education at all levels beyond students and entry-level teaching positions in a few departments. Asian American women are granted academic tenure at rates lower than any other demographic group. Asian Americans generally are severely underrepresented throughout administrative ranks, from department chairs and deans to provosts and presidents.

The educational levels of Asian Americans verify the importance of cultural capital. Other than luck and individual attributes that cannot be generalized meaningfully, one of the most salient determinants of likely educational accomplishment of any individual is the highest degree held by her parents.[35] Having a grandfather who was a lawyer, a father who is an engineer, and a mother who is a doctor constitutes inherited assets. Researcher Stanley found in another study of his group of high-achieving Asian Americans that within the group 85 percent of the children had fathers who had earned graduate degrees, 71 percent of them doctorates; 21 percent of the mothers also held doctorates.[36] This increases the chances that a person will obtain an undergraduate degree and acquire post-graduate education. The educational success of Asian Americans is the educational success of any set of people who have well-educated parents.

Moreover, Asian immigrants start off relatively privileged. This admission must be made gingerly, so that it will not be taken as corroboration of the model minority myth. In actuality, it undercuts the myth. Most Asian Americans are not rich. But some Asian immigrants are relatively fortunate compared to the many Asians who reside in Asia, and some of them are relatively fortunate compared to native-born Americans (including, incidentally, native-born Asian Americans), even though they have not had an easy time of it in coming to the United States and even though they experience prejudice. A major study of diversity in the power elite found that almost none of the Chinese Americans who served on the boards of directors for Fortune 1000 companies were "authentic bootstrappers."[37] Almost all of them had come from well-to-do families in China, Taiwan, and Hong Kong.

University of California at Santa Cruz sociologist Deborah Woo examined more closely the media coverage of "a Korean-born immigrant who once worked the night shift at 7-Eleven to put himself through school" and who sold his company for $1 billion, as well as another Korean-born immigrant, a Silicon Valley entrepreneur who lived on ramen noodles and had to pawn his belongings to pay his phone bill, but gave $15 million to the San Francisco Asian Art Museum, "mak[ing] Horatio Alger look like a slacker."[38] Woo delved into the backgrounds of these examples of the model minority myth. In the former instance, the individual was able to start his company because he had received a government contract through a minority set-aside program. In the latter, the man was descended from the royal family that ruled Korea until the Japanese takeover of 1905, and he had been a university professor and an executive in the family business in Korea before emigrating. They are still impressive people, but they have not come from the ghetto. The sheen comes off the model minority myth once the real stories are revealed.

Asian immigrants personify "brain drain": the selective nature of immigration. More than half of the professional immigrants to the United States are Asian; Asian men are well over a majority of the professional immigrants in technical occupations. Indian doctors are the single largest ethnic group in the medical profession in this country, at about 4 percent of the total number of physicians; 11 percent of Indian men in the United States and 7 percent of Indian women hold medical degrees. Filipina women are over half the total number of registered nurses who were trained abroad; thousands more come every year. In 1990, 20 percent of all Filipino Americans listed their area of employment as health care. For many Asian ethnicities in the United States, such as Indians, the earliest cohort of immigrants following immigration policy reforms are the most qualified, and the continuing stream is less elite. Among some Asian ethnicities, such as Filipinos, the foreign-born generally make more money than the native-born. Under restrictive immigration policies, individuals who have skills that are in high demand in the United States have greater opportunities to acquire a green card. In their homelands, doctors and nurses are not nearly as common. One of nine Indian men in India is not a doctor, and Filipinas are not half the nurses worldwide. In Asia, there are millions of urban and rural poor who do not have the means to travel out of the city or the village, much less to the United States.

The gathering of Asian Americans in particular occupations is the product of circumstances beyond their control as much as of racial purposefulness. Asian immigrants often have had no choice about their field of work because of discrimination, and they are encouraged to take up jobs in industries where they have family and friends. Chinese men in China are not laundrymen, but washing clothes—a chore that in China, as in the United States, was thought to be "women's work"—was open to them in the nineteenth century when they were not permitted to compete in pursuits that were both lucrative and masculine. Southeast Asians are not donut shop proprietors by instinct, but once there are a few Southeast Asians in the business it becomes easier for others to join them, until the ethnic group becomes identified with it.

Other factors affecting Asian American income also inflate it. It is convenient to look at household income rather than individual income, but calibrating individual income causes the Asian American edge to vanish. In 1997, the latest year for which figures are available, Asian Americans made $18,569 per person; white Americans, $20,093. Like other people of color, Asian Americans on average live in larger households than do white Americans. They may have two spouses, children, grandchildren, and even cousins living under a single roof and sharing their earnings. In 1997, the average Asian American household had 3.17 people, the average white household 2.58. In 1990, among all American households, 4.9 percent had members aged fifteen or older who were related but not spouses, children, parents, or in-laws; among Asian Americans, more than twice as many—11.8 percent— had such arrangements. A slightly higher proportion of Asian American women work compared with white American women. It is not an apt comparison to match an Asian American family that earns $50,000 per year by pooling the wages of a husband, a wife, a grandparent, a child, and a cousin with a white family that earns the same amount through the salary of a single breadwinner.

Asian Americans are more likely than white Americans to be self-employed. Self-employed individuals with the same income as corporate employees tend to put in longer hours, with fewer benefits and increased risks of bankruptcy and other setbacks. The average employee of an Asian-owned enterprise is paid less than $10,000 per year.

Asian Americans also are geographically concentrated in states such as Hawaii, California and New York, all of which have incomes that on average are higher than the national average, with costs of living also higher than the national average. In 1990, 60 percent of Asian Americans resided in those three states (since then, Asian Americans have started to disperse). Furthermore, Asian Americans are much more urbanized than any other racial group, including white Americans. In 1990, 94 percent of Asian Americans lived within metropolitan areas. Asian American income is distributed unevenly. There are large numbers of Asian Americans at the top and at the bottom, rather than in the middle. Asian Americans have poverty rates higher than white Americans, 13 percent compared to 9 percent.

The model minority myth also masks great disparities among Asian ethnic groups. Japanese Americans and Chinese Americans are closest to equality with whites, but Vietnamese Americans and other Southeast Asian refugees languish at the bottom of the economic pyramid, along with blacks. In the 1980 Census, for example, Vietnamese Americans were below African Americans on average. According to the 1990 Census, 25 percent of Vietnamese Americans and 45 percent of other Southeast Asians lived in poverty. Those poverty rates were higher than the rates for Africans (21 percent) and Hispanics (23 percent).

Finally, the figures for Asian Americans are rendered unreliable by the careless inclusion of Asians who reside in the United States but who are not Asian Americans at all.[39] Hundreds of business executives with Japanese-based multinational companies spend stints of up to a few years here. Their upper-management salaries add to the average Asian American income, but they are no more representative of either Asians overseas or Asian immigrants than a white American vice-president of a Fortune 500 company who was an expatriate manager in Europe would be either average of Americans or of Europeans themselves. They are part of a transnational overclass.

To be scrupulous, the latest research must be mentioned. Arthur Sakamoto, a sociologist at the University of Texas, has done important statistical work on the wages of Asian Americans. He has revisited the leading studies by Barringer and others. Looking at data as recent as 1998 and controlling for a greater range of factors other than race than had been the case in other research (but considering only native-born persons), Sakamoto and a colleague, Satomi Furuichi, find no statistically significant support for the contention that Asian Americans "are underpaid relative to whites who are comparable in terms of gender, experience, education, and place of residence."[40]

According to Sakamoto and Furuichi, the only exceptions are for men with advanced degrees, who represent a fraction of the workforce. Among men with a master's degree, who are only about 7 percent of male workers, Asian Americans appear to be paid more than white Americans by about 20 percent. Among men with a doctorate, who are only about 1 percent of male workers, Asian Americans appear to be paid less than white Americans by about 18 percent. One-fifth of one's salary is not a small sum, and Asian American men are heavily overrepresented among recipients of doctoral degrees, but Sakamoto and Furuichi note that the racial discrepancies between Asian American and white income are smaller than class differences, characterized as the net effect of having finished high school versus having dropped out.

Assuming that Sakamoto and Furuichi are right and that native-born Asian Americans need not worry too much about racial discrimination, except at the top echelons of the labor market, they have identified a reason for all of us to rejoice about racial progress. Sakamoto and Furuichi "do not contest the view that many people may have an exaggerated image of the socioeconomic attainments of Asian Americans, nor that this image may serve to legitimate inequality in some people's eyes," but the model minority myth would have us do considerably more than believe that Asian Americans have attained income parity with white Americans. It asks us to believe that Asian Americans make more money than white Americans because of unique racial factors. It also asks us to believe that what is said of Asian Americans can be applied to other people of color without regard for racial discrimination.

Upon anything more than cursory reflection, the model minority myth becomes mystifying. The model minority myth is misleading not only because it takes for granted that racial groups rather than individual persons are the best basis for thinking about human lives, but also because it equates status and conduct. These most pernicious qualities of the myth are hidden in the open. Whatever else might be said about the myth, it cannot be disputed that it is a racial generalization. As such, it contains the premise that people can be arranged by racial group, and, furthermore, that the differences between racial groups are more significant than either the similarities between racial groups or the differences within them. It makes race the main feature of an individual as well as the leading division among people.

People who realized their stated ideal of color blindness would not be aware—and would not want others to be aware—of Asian Americans as Asian Americans, as a distinct racial group. They could not differentiate Asian Americans from whites or blacks, using racial classifications that refer to status. They could notice, for example, people who did their homework and people who did not do their homework, using nonracial categories that referred to conduct. For this reason alone, the myth is an aberration.

Ironically, the less race matters for Asian Americans, the less—not more—the model minority myth holds true. As Asian Americans approach whites, the less special we are. An Asian American is successful for the reasons any person is successful, such as doing one's homework, rather than successful because of race. The model minority myth gives the opposite impression. It turns some activities into Asian activities. It gives them racial connotations. At an extreme, to study is no longer to study but to be Asian American. Study makes a person Asian American; Asian Americans as a group are defined by study. Making study the racial activity of Asian Americans does not serve to encourage it among others. If anything, it is likely to be counterproductive.

Numerous observers have written that many African Americans already shun interest in school as "acting white," to their own detriment, without noting the origins of the attitude. There is a difference between the comments made by University of Texas law professor Lino Graglia in 1997 that blacks and Hispanics could not compete with whites academically because "these cultures are not conducive to high academic standards" and "failure is not looked upon with disgrace," and the research of University of California at Berkeley anthropologist John Ogbu on immigrants compared with involuntary minorities. Whereas Graglia attributes anti-academic attitudes to African Americans themselves, Ogbu suggests that the attitudes developed as a response to white oppression.[41] The Asian American example should make us realize that it comes from stereotypes about African Americans rather than among African Americans. As the idea becomes established that it is Asian

American to attend class and do your homework, whites too may start to shirk it because of its racial overtones. It would be uncool to become too Asian.

Researchers have tried to discern the relationship between studying and being Asian American. They have used sophisticated statistical analysis of the many factors that come together in the model minority myth in an attempt to figure out how Asian Americans have done as well as we have. Technically, the empirical work confirms only faint correlations between race itself and academic success. The Asian-ness of Asian Americans offers only sketchy explanations of the data. Its influence is scarcely more than the effects of random chance.

Asian Americans would be racially striking if and only if we engaged in the same activities as whites (or others) and somehow produced divergent results. Otherwise, what Asian Americans do is generic rather than genetic. Picture two groups of students, one Asian American and one white. They are identical except for race, the children being raised by two parents who are college graduates with modest incomes in communities that supported scholarship and have teachers who esteem them as good pupils, with role models, a support network, and positive feedback.

If both did their homework, but Asian Americans scored high on exams while whites did not, then we would have a real model minority. Or if Asian Americans did no homework while whites did, but the Asian Americans outpaced the whites on exams, again we would have a real model minority. Such a scenario being nonexistent, what we find is not inimitable: Children who are raised by two parents who are college graduates do better, independent of race. The children could be Asian American, white American, or African American, but what is important are other, nonracial criteria.

The hands-on work of mathematics professor Uri Treisman indicates that anybody who sets her mind to it and finds friends to help can do what Asian Americans do.[42] Formerly at the University of California–Berkeley and now at the University of Texas, Treisman has spent years working with Asian American, African American, and Hispanic undergraduates in intensive programs at both schools. Before teaching them, Treisman studied them. He lived with them in dormitories for months at a time to see life from their perspectives. Treisman came to realize that Asian American students who were high performers in his courses belonged to peer groups that reinforced their classwork by collaborating on their homework. When he transferred the pedagogical technique to African American and Hispanic students, including those whose performance would have been predicted to be deficient, they were able to equal the Asian American students in every respect. The experience of seeing Asian American students struggle and African American and Hispanic students succeed also benefited all groups by giving the lie to stereotypes.

The model minority myth persists, despite violating our societal norms against racial stereotyping and even though it is not accurate. Dozens of amply documented and heavily annotated government studies and scholarly papers, along with a handful of better magazine and newspaper articles supplemented by television segments and public speeches, all intended to destroy the myth, have had negligible effect on popular culture. In the latest college textbook on Asian Americans, professors Lucie Cheng and Philip Q. Yang comment, "despite an unending barrage of attacks, the model minority image has persisted into the 1990s, quite alive if not entirely unscathed."[43]

The myth has not succumbed to individualism or facts because it serves a purpose in reinforcing racial hierarchies. Asian Americans are as much a "middleman minority" as we are a model minority. We are placed in the awkward position of buffer or intermediary, elevated as the preferred racial minority at the expense of denigrating African Americans. Asian American writers and scholars have not hesitated to call the phenomenon what it is. Novelist Frank Chin has described it as "racist love," contrasting it with "racist hate" of other people of color. DePaul University law professor Sumi Cho has explained that Asian Americans are turned into "racial mascots," giving right-wing causes a novel messenger, camouflaging arguments that would look unconscionably self-interested if made by whites about themselves. University of California at Irvine political scientist Claire Kim has argued that Asian Americans are positioned through "racial triangulation," much as a Machiavellian would engage in political triangulation for maximum advantage. Law professor Mari Matsuda famously declared, "we will not be used" in repudiating the model minority myth.[44]

Whatever the effects are called, Asian Americans become pawns. We are not recognized in our own right but advanced for ulterior motives. Michael S. Greve, a leading advocate against racial remedies, said that the controversy over anti-Asian discrimination could be used to attack affirmative action: It presented "an opportunity to call, on behalf of a racial minority (i.e., the Asian applicants), for an end to discrimination. It was an appeal that, when made on behalf of whites, is politically hopeless and, perhaps, no longer entirely respectable."[45]

The model minority myth is resilient because it is a "meme." Scientist Richard Dawkins's concept of a "meme"—a piece of cultural material that can be passed on from person to person, society to society, and generation to generation—advises us that any information and any image can survive and evolve.[46] Dawkins posits that memes are to culture what genes are to biology, replicating themselves in an evolutionary process that selects the bits most likely to survive. Whether they are information or rumor, stereotypes take on their own social life. The longevity and propagation of information depends on its usefulness, not necessarily its truth. The myth is useful, even if it is not true. Its content assuages the conscience and assigns blame, a function that is psychologically needed and socially desired. It tells a comforting narrative of America as having progressed to become a place where race does not matter anymore, and it offers a cautionary parable about the good minority and the bad minority. Author Michael Lind has written that "in addition to fulfilling their immediate functions—selling egg rolls, measuring blood sugar— Vietnamese vendors and Filipino lab technicians serve an additional function for the white overclass: they relieve it of guilt about the squalor of millions of native-born Americans, not only ghetto blacks and poor Hispanics but poor whites."[47] To condemn the myth is not the same as to condemn the individual who has lived it or repeated it. We all like fables with happy endings, especially when we are the actors in the story.

Messages of the Myth

The very phrase "model minority" suggests the problems with the concept. The term begs the questions "Model of what" and "Model for whom?" "Model minority" could have either one of two meanings, both of them condescending toward racial minorities. It could imply that Asian Americans are remarkable, given that we are a racial minority group. We are "model" at least for people of color, our performance satisfying a lesser standard. Or it could mean that Asian Americans are exemplary, serving as an ideal of some sort. We are a credit as a race as some people of color are called a credit to their race, and African Americans should mimic our behavior. When Senator Daniel Inouye, a Japanese American from Hawaii, won election to the most exclusive club in the world, he was greeted by a white legislator from the South who congratulated him and asked him why the "niggers" could not be more like the Asians.[48]

The model minority myth has a long lineage, however, with roots dating back to the nineteenth century. The new myth and its precursors bear more than a family resemblance. Well before modern reactions to civil rights advances, the earliest Asian arrivals had been lauded in comparative terms that could not help but provoke racial antipathy. Even progressives, having decided that Asian immigrants endangered white workers, stopped being friendly toward them. Horace Greeley, editor of the *New York Tribune* and once a presidential candidate, remembered for purportedly having said, "Go West, young man," argued that only "Christian races" or "white races" should be allowed to settle that land.[49]

After the Civil War, southern plantation owners devised fantastic schemes to import millions of Chinese laborers to avoid hiring recently freed black slaves. Several thousand "Coolies" were brought over. As the Reconstruction governor of Arkansas conceded, "Undoubtedly the underlying motive for this effort . . . was to punish the Negro for having abandoned control of his old master, and to regulate the conditions of his employment and the scale of wages to be paid him." A Kentucky newspaperman opined more bluntly that with the coming of the Chinese, "the tune . . . will not be 'forty acres and a mule,' but . . . 'work nigger or starve.'"[50]

The brokers of Chinese immigrants argued that their laborers were more advanced than the African Americans they would replace. A Baton Rouge newspaper stated that the Chinese "are more obedient and industrious than the negro, work as well without an overseer, and at the same time are more cleanly in their habits and persons than the freedmen." It added, "The same reports come from all the sugar estates where they have been introduced, and all accounts given of them by planters in Arkansas, Alabama, and other States where they are employed in the culture of cotton."[51]

Meanwhile, in the Northern states when the labor movement was beginning to organize unions, industrialists experimented with deploying Chinese as strikebreakers.[52] In the most widely cited instance, a factory owner brought in seventy-five Chinese workers in response to a strike called by what was then the largest union in the country. He relied on the Chinese to increase his profits $840 per week. Other capitalists instituted wage reductions soon thereafter.

The Chinese laborers who built the transcontinental railroad were arranged in crews that competed against their Irish equivalents. The robber barons for whom they worked were eager to wager with each other over whether the Chinese or the Irish would be able to lay more track on any given day. The more than 10,000 Chinese were paid less and worked under more hazardous conditions. Their contributions notwithstanding, they were not invited to the Golden Spike ceremony when the distinct lines were joined together in 1869 at Promontory Point, Utah.

Just as Chinese were compared favorably with blacks in the South, they were compared favorably with Irish in the North and West. As reported by

San Francisco State University historian Stuart Miller, the *New York Times* argued that "'John Chinaman' was a better addition to [American] society than was 'Paddy.'" It "complained" that Chinese men did not drink whiskey, stab one another, or beat their wives.[53] As Miller noted, numerous "defensive articles on behalf of the Chinese were thinly disguised attacks on the Irish," and "needless to say, such sarcasm was not lost on the Irish."[54]

The rallying cry "The Chinese Must Go!" was a reaction to the same stereotypes that had previously passed as positive. Racial rivalries exacerbated economic uncertainties. Denis Kearney, the charismatic leader of the Workingman's Party, was able to leverage anti-Chinese emotions both to unite Irish immigrants and to intensify their affinity with whiteness. He managed to escalate a California concern into a national movement by maintaining that the multitude of Asian immigrants would engulf white immigrants. Even African American labor unions took the same stance. They were no more eager than white Americans to see Asians competing against them.

All along the West Coast, Chinese immigrants suffered from racial attacks. Most Chinese immigrants entered the United States at the port of San Francisco and fanned out from there. They fared no better than freed blacks at the hands of white mobs. In 1871, a lynch gang killed 19 of 172 Chinese living in the "Negro Alley" section of Los Angeles. In 1877, the Order of Caucasians tried to burn down the Chinatown of San Francisco but succeeded only in killing four Chinese farmhands on a ranch in nearby Chico. The Rock Springs, Wyoming, massacre of 1885 was the worst of the confrontations, with 29 deaths. Two hundred armed white mineworkers drove out all 600 Chinese mineworkers to take over a precious "room" the Chinese had found, torching their homes. Federal troops were called out to stop the carnage, but all of the whites were acquitted in subsequent trials because no individuals could be held responsible for the wholesale slaughter.

Japanese immigrants had to fight the same battles. Like Chinese immigrants, Japanese immigrants were prevented from naturalization by a racial bar. Much as the Chinese had been model workers, the Japanese offspring were called "model citizens." The status of Japanese Americans also depended on events overseas. They gained respect from the Japanese victory over the Russians in the 1905 war between those two nations. The catastrophe, unprecedented in the modern period, upset the world because an Eastern upstart had vanquished a Western power.

As soon as Japanese Americans began to flourish in agriculture, tilling acreage that had lain fallow, they began to experience the same animosity that had beset Chinese Americans. Between the world wars, state after state passed alien land laws intended to take away the source of their income. Although the bills were neutral in their language, making no references to race, the legislative intent was clear. The statutes prohibited aliens "ineligible for citizenship"—a category that specified Asian immigrants and nobody else—from holding title to real property.

The modern model minority myth was born during the civil rights revolution, shortly after comprehensive federal laws were passed against racial discrimination. Six months after the Watts riots, on January 6, 1966, the *New York Times Sunday Magazine* printed a profile by University of California at Berkeley sociologist William Petersen entitled, "Success Story, Japanese American Style." One scholar has called it "the most influential single article ever written about an Asian-American group."[55]

In the article, later expanded into a book, Petersen presented a magnanimous account of Japanese Americans. In the full-length version of his accidental masterpiece,[56] he expresses his surprise that the single article in the popular press outside his areas of expertise had become the most renowned work he had ever produced. In fact, his arguments were directed toward the ongoing debates over the rights of African Americans.

Petersen was evenhanded in relating the historical discrimination imposed on Japanese Americans, so much so that he might reasonably be interpreted as arguing that their oppression contributed to their integration. He begins by denouncing the wartime internment when it was still considered to be justified and before Japanese Americans had begun to demand reparations. After invoking Horatio Alger as a "patron saint," he argues credibly that Japanese Americans were "a minority that has risen above even prejudiced criticism." He claims provocatively that "by any criterion of good citizenship that we choose, the Japanese-Americans are better than any group in our society, including native-born whites."[57]

Petersen is open about his agenda: "[G]enerally, this kind of treatment,"—meaning historical racial discrimination—"as we all know these days, creates what might be termed 'problem minorities.'" The venture of studying Japanese Americans is worthwhile because the Japanese American experience was "of general interest precisely because it constitutes the outstanding exception." Their behavior "challenges every such generalization about ethnic minorities."[58]

Petersen did not have to be coy, giving a nod and a wink to his audience to gesture at whom he had in mind as "problem minorities." Each commendation of Asian Americans is paired off against a reprimand of African Americans. A novel about the internment by a Japanese American author had "the hero struggl[ing] to find his way to the America that had rejected him and that he had rejected," but the works of James Baldwin could not meet that test. Japanese American adolescents were well-behaved, except for the juvenile delinquents who had fallen in with gangs comprising "Negroes or Mexicans," especially followers of Islam. As Petersen presents it, Asian Americans also are essentially Asian and not American. Japanese Americans "could climb over the highest barriers our racists were able to fashion in part because of their meaningful links to an alien culture." The "American Negro," in contrast, was "as thoroughly American as any Daughter of the American Revolution."

At the end of the same year Petersen's article was published, 1966, following another summer of urban unrest, *U.S. News & World Report* bestowed the same accolades on Chinese Americans and made the same insinuations: "At a time when it is being proposed that hundreds of billions be spent to uplift Negroes and other minorities, the nation's 300,000 Chinese Americans are moving ahead on their own, with no help from anyone else."[59]

The Petersen article and its historical antecedents culminated in the late Richard Herrnstein and Charles Murray's *The Bell Curve: Intelligence and Class Structure in American Life.*[60] Social scientists Herrnstein and Murray attempt in their massive book to re-establish specious claims of mental deficiencies on the part of blacks, which biologists, psychologists, psychiatrists, sociologists, and educators had disproved long before. They argue that socioeconomic status is determined by general intelligence, general intelligence is inherited, and African Americans are genetically weak in this respect. Hence blacks are properly consigned to their inferior place in modern society and might even be properly sent off to "reservations" like those of Native Americans.[61] Nothing is incontrovertible, but by portraying old stereotypes as dissenting viewpoints, Herrnstein and Murray have had their racial propositions accepted without skepticism. Although Herrnstein and Murray's social science has been thoroughly debunked for overstating the strength of the correlation among variables and assuming the existence of general intelligence, the reviews of their work attracted only a fraction of the attention given to their initial invective. Their book is a testament to the unshakable grip of outrageous claims of black inferiority.

In the rancor of the ensuing debate, newspaper columnist William Safire invoked the model minority myth and called on people to look to the apex of the structure set forth by Herrnstein and Murray: "Instead of denouncing this study as roiling up feelings of black inferiority, it might be helpful to look in the other direction—toward the group that scores highest, the Asians."[62]

The use of the model minority myth becomes self-contradictory in its vacillation between color blindness and color consciousness. In 1988 at Vanderbilt University, for example, a white student disc jockey was censured for interviewing a Ku Klux Klan member on his radio show.[63] In his defense, the neophyte broadcaster argued that African Americans complained too much about discrimination and abused their racial status. He said they should imitate Asian Americans, because "Asians have a subtle approach. They go out into the community and prove themselves as individuals." His reasoning is at odds with itself. He extols Asian Americans on a group basis but also insists that he admires them for their individual behavior. By recognizing Asian Americans as a group and comparing them to African Americans, he thwarts their very attempt to distinguish themselves as individuals.

Even if the praise of the model minority myth were genuine and not feigned in a particular instance, it cannot help but send a message about African Americans. African Americans know full well what the model minority myth is all about. In Spike Lee's movie *Do The Right Thing,* a chorus of elderly African American men sitting in lawn chairs both respect and envy the Asian American shopkeeper across the street. The corner men, Sweet Dick Willie, Coconut Sid, and ML, "have no steady employment, nothing they can speak of" except that "they do, however, have the gift of gab" and with the aid of a bottle "they get philosophical." Watching the Asian American toil in his business, ML frets, "Either dem Koreans are geniuses or we Blacks are dumb."[64]

Were we to accept the usefulness of assessing racial groups against each other and forgo qualms about the morality of such an exercise, the model minority myth evaluation of Asian Americans vis-à-vis African Americans has been executed so poorly as to be worthless. Asian Americans and African Americans should not be compared in racial terms, but the model minority myth forces the task.

Acknowledging that African Americans in general have endured worse discrimination does not diminish the serious racial discrimination that Asian Americans as a group have faced. The adulation of Asian Americans considers only Asian Americans. Asian Americans are not as inspiring if the unique history and distinctive present circumstances of African Americans are fairly weighed—without supposing that African Americans have been so traumatized that they are damaged beyond redemption.[65]

We make what social psychologists call the "fundamental attribution error." We believe that other people behave as they do because of their personalities (of course, we recognize that our own failings are influenced by factors beyond our control). We discount the importance of their role, the context, and external constraints. In a racial context, we believe that if Asian Americans receive good grades, it is because they are disposed to be studious; that if African Americans receive bad grades, it is because they prefer to be ignorant; and so forth. Yet in the educational context, studies consistently show how powerful self-fulfilling prophecies can be. For example, telling teachers that some students—who have been randomly selected— will make dramatic improvements in their IQ actually tends to produce those effects. We also do not recognize the effect of an observer. Children do not behave in the same manner when parents are present as when they are absent, nor do parents behave in the same manner when children are present as when they are absent. We do not even realize that, even with the few proven correlations between behaviors and traits, they are extraordinarily weak connections.[66]

The racial discrimination, institutional and individual, historical and contemporary, that has assailed African Americans is egregious and incommensurate. It has been different in kind and in degree from anything else found in our shared past. African Americans were reduced to property through the establishment of chattel slavery, which was not the same as classic forms of servitude that were neither racial in their organization nor absolute in their terms. African American families were broken up for sale, African American children were forbidden from learning to read, African American adults were whipped, African American women were systematically raped, and African culture was purged. After slavery was banned, African Americans were then subjugated under the Jim Crow system of "separate but equal," which was as separate as it was unequal. Before the civil rights movement, even the most privileged African Americans were not in as good a situation as a majority of whites. Even if they were members of the tiny elite, they had nothing even akin to equality; in the phrase of the day, they had "no rights a white man had to respect." They faced physical segregation connoting their lowliness and outright exclusion from educational and professional opportunities, violence in the form of lynching, no protection by and even outright hostility from the law and government, and a dearth of political power that could be exercised to alter matters. The 1921 Tulsa riot, in which a white mob killed several hundred blacks and thereby eradicated a community, may not be representative, but it is symbolic.

Asian Americans also are not like Latinos. Many Chicanos are not immigrants but individuals whose forebears were on the land before it became America. Although there are many highly educated Hispanic immigrants, the proximity of Latin America also makes it much easier for unskilled laborers to come here. Asian Americans may be displaced from their homes due to U.S. actions abroad, but they have no sense of conquest and loss of the land where they reside. The distances from Asia that destitute individuals would have to travel reduce the flow of undocumented persons drastically, although not entirely.

Asian Americans are for the most part voluntary immigrants (although Filipinos are like Latinos in their former colonial status, and many Southeast Asians are refugees). Most of us had the luck to enter the country during an economic boom period. Many Asian Americans are well-educated, have resources, or both. We have not been held in bondage. Even the stereotypes are different. The model minority myth is generous by comparison. Asian Americans are depicted as honors students with pocket protectors who program laptop computers; African Americans are depicted as street thugs with concealed weapons who peddle coke bags. If the model minority myth is bad, it is modest next to the street thug image. If the former demoralizes, the latter must devastate. Even the Asian American gangster is a model minority of wrongdoing; as glamorized in movies such as Michael Cimino's *Year of the Dragon* or Michael Crichton's *Rising Sun*, he is more coolly efficient in operating a criminal enterprise as if it were any other business.

Asian Americans also may benefit just by not being black. The decreasing significance of race for some Asian American ethnic groups does not mechanically correspond to the decreasing relevance of race for African Americans. It may be that the ability of Asian Americans to pass into whiteness depends on their ability to distance themselves from blackness. None of the facile examples of the model minority myth addresses the major dissimilarities in racial patterns that have produced the caste-like status of African Americans. (Although black immigrants have been praised of late as a model minority as well, their children find themselves no less black than African Americans.[67])

The perception that African American public figures condone unproductive behavior patterns among African Americans—ranging from children having children, teenagers glamorizing crime, and college students overspending on credit cards to misogyny, homophobia, and even bigotry—is a misconception.[68] There is a strong conservative streak within African American communities that would do any critic of theirs proud. Many responsible community leaders have not hesitated to decry the misbehavior of African Americans, as Martin Luther King Jr. did in his sermon against the "drum major instinct." They have done so with the best intentions, as King did in criticizing the materialistic tendencies of African Americans, which are no different than those of whites except that African Americans lack the same financial means. But they have incorporated the disapproval within their attacks on racial discrimination and without suggesting that the traits are intrinsic to African Americans.

Added to that, telling African Americans they ought to be like Asian Americans does a favor for neither group. On the contrary, it only aggravates racial tensions among African Americans and Asian Americans. It is a paternalistic suggestion, as if whites were the elders telling the older siblings, African Americans, that they should be more like the younger ones, Asian Americans.

If I were African American, I would be enraged at the treatment of Asian Americans, all the more so if whites claimed, as they occasionally do, that they aren't prejudiced because they have accepted Asian Americans. The following exchange is a non sequitur: "You're discriminating against African Americans at your company." "No, we're not; look at all the Asian Americans here."[69] Whites and Asian Americans can like one another but dislike African Americans. There is some research that seems to show that where there are some people of color of one background, there tend to be more people of color of other backgrounds; the presence of each minority group makes it easier for the rest of them. But if the integration of Asian Americans is not to further the segregation of African Americans, our abundance cannot be used to excuse their absence.

The model minority myth becomes bittersweet through humor. Richard Pryor, one of the most successful African American comedians, joked that the first word an Asian immigrant learned was the n-word. Journalist Karl Zinsmeister reported the following comic story. A Laotian immigrant is repairing his car on the street. An African American approaches the "foreigner" and insultingly demands to know how long he has been in America, that he has a car. The immigrant answers, "Three years," and returns the question. The African American proudly answers, "All my life." The retort: "Well, then, why don't *you* have a car?"[70]

Backlash from the Myth

The model minority myth hurts Asian Americans themselves. It is two-faced. Every attractive trait matches up neatly to its repulsive complement, and the aspects are conducive to reversal. If we acquiesced to the myth in its favorable guise, we would be precluded from rejecting its unfavorable interpretations. We would already have accepted the characteristics at issue as inherent.

The turnaround is inevitable during a military crisis or economic down-turn. To be intelligent is to be calculating and too clever; to be gifted in math and science is to be mechanical and not creative, lacking interpersonal skills and leadership potential. To be polite is to be inscrutable and submissive. To be hard working is to be an unfair competitor for regular human beings and not a well-rounded, likable individual. To be family oriented is to be clannish and too ethnic. To be law abiding is to be self-righteous and rigidly rule-bound. To be successfully entrepreneurial is to be deviously aggressive and economically intimidating. To revere elders is to be an ancestor-worshipping pagan, and fidelity to tradition is reactionary ignorance.

Asian Americans cannot win by winning. We are familiar with Asian American sensations at the piano or the violin. They exhibit superlative technical prowess on the keyboard or with the bow, but nonetheless are criticized for being without passion, even bereft of a human soul. We know the notes and follow the score, but we have become too precise to be artists. We are automatons, frightening in our correctness.

A concrete example of such a spin on the model minority myth is offered by economist James Treires, who published a guest column in *Newsweek* magazine a generation after Petersen wrote his memorable essay lauding Asian Americans.[71] Treires's version of the model minority was an inversion of Petersen's original. Asian Americans were described with the same characteristics by Treires and Petersen, but Treires hates what Petersen had liked.

Calling the model minority myth "the dark side of the dream," Treires explains that everyone had heard "stories . . . of multitalented immigrants' children, usually Asian, who are valedictorians and superachievers in the arts and sciences," but he warns that "the downside of these upward-mobility chronicles is never discussed."[72]

Treires starts with doubts reminiscent of Asian Americans' own misgivings. He notes that the model minority myth was sending "the message that native-born American workers are lazy and stupid, and that black families, in particular . . . are perhaps not as American as the newcomers." He changes his tone, though, with an outlook that recalls the exclusion movement of a century earlier. He accuses Asian American parents of "using child labor in the family business" and Asian Americans as a group of "being willing to accept poor working conditions and substandard pay." He predicts that the side-effect of an Asian incursion could be to reduce "the once powerful labor movement to impotence and irrelevance." He then jumps to the conclusion that "working Americans who may want to limit immigration . . . are motivated not by xenophobia or racism but by clear evidence that the new immigrants' gains are being made at their expense."[73]

Although Treires's thesis that the model minority myth has a "downside" could have subverted the myth, he is content to repeat the hackneyed argument that Asian immigrants impose costs on the rest of society. His "downside" is not the myth, but Asian Americans themselves. By accepting the truth of the myth, he turns it on its head. Instead of realizing that many Asian Americans agree with him that the myth sends the message "that native-born American workers are lazy and stupid," he attributes to Asian Americans a message that they would renounce. With an "us" versus "them" dichotomy, by definition Asian Americans cannot be "working Americans." Instead, we become a menace to "working Americans" and African Americans.

Upside down or right side up, the model minority myth whitewashes racial discrimination. "People don't believe it," as one Asian American leader told the *L.A. Times* in 1991,[74] in discussing the prevalence of anti-Asian bias. An Asian American student leader said that, like whites, other people of color doubt claims about attacks: "Some simply didn't see us as minorities. . . . They think if you're Asian you're automatically interning at Merrill Lynch and that you're never touched by racism."[75] The myth implies that bigotry has been brought on by the victims, who must defeat it, rather than that it is the responsibility of the perpetrators, who could be compelled to eliminate it. Senator Alan Simpson, an opponent of immigration, coined the term "compassion fatigue" to describe his sense that Americans were tired of hearing about other peoples' problems (as if those other people weren't tired of their problems). Under Simpson's concept, even if Asian Americans press complaints about bias for which they have evidence, the incidents should be treated as inconsequential or written off as the cost of being a newcomer. The reasoning seems to be that because Asian Americans have theoretically surmounted the deleterious effects of racial discrimination, we cannot be actually aggrieved even if real wrongs are done to us. Certainly Treires has hinted that he would be categorically skeptical of Asian American grievances, itself a form of selective prejudice.

When the U.S. Civil Rights Commission Report released a report on civil rights issues facing Asian Americans in 1992, *Fortune* magazine scorned the findings in an article entitled, "Up from Inscrutable." Aside from playing on a stereotype, the author asks, "What's the problem?" He concludes that the government study, which detailed offenses such as hate crimes, was "easily the strangest document produced by the U.S. Commission on Civil Rights in recent years" because "the predicament, if that is the word, which we doubt" of Asian Americans could not include civil rights violations.[76] If he had read thoroughly, he may have noticed that the report that he maligned mentioned that the myth was causing government agencies with a duty to serve all citizens to fail in meeting their obligations with respect to Asian Americans. Officials simply assumed that Asian Americans as a group did not qualify for anti-poverty programs, even if they were tax-paying citizens and even if many of them as individuals met the eligibility guidelines.

The model minority myth does more than cover up racial discrimination; it instigates racial discrimination as retribution. The hyperbole about Asian American affluence can lead to jealousy on the part of non-Asian Americans, who may suspect that Asian Americans are too comfortable or who are convinced by Treires and others telling them Asian American gains are their losses. Through the justification of the myth, the humiliation of Asian Americans or even physical attacks directed against Asian Americans become compensation or retaliation.

Such an attack occurred in Detroit during the recession of 1982, becoming a defining moment for Asian Americans. Two white autoworkers used a baseball bat to beat to death Vincent Chin, a twenty-seven-year-old Chinese American engineer celebrating his upcoming wedding. The father and stepson blamed Chin for their being out of work. Using racial epithets and obscenities such as "chink" and "nip" and "fucker" in exchanging words with him at a strip joint where all of them had been hanging out, they hunted him down after they'd left the bar. When they caught him, one held Chin down and the other swung a Louisville Slugger at his head repeatedly. The clubbing broke his skull and left him mortally wounded. As punishment for their crime, the two received probation and were fined $3,780 apiece. As the Emmy-winning documentary, *Who Killed Vincent Chin?* recounted, Asian Americans in the heartland were shocked at the attack and the mild sentence. Even middle-class Asian American professionals who had a steadfast belief in conformity were shaken up.

The tensions of that time in the Motor City are hard to recall, but the context made race central to everything about the Chin case. Congressman John Dingell—whose father, also a member of the House of Representatives, had called for the internment of Japanese Americans during World War II—gave an angry speech in Congress blaming "little yellow men" for the economic woes of American automakers, whose products were facing unprecedented competition from efficient and economical Japanese imports.[77] Driving such an imported car meant taking a chance. Local car dealers held raffles for the honor of taking a baseball bat to a Toyota to bash it to pieces. Owners of Hondas reported to unsympathetic police departments that their vehicles had been "keyed" in parking lots: Vandals would take a key and run it along the length of the fender, gouging the steel so that costly refinishing would be required. People who supported the "Buy America" campaign wore T-shirts with an atomic bomb mushroom cloud over the slogan, "Made with Pride in America—Tested in Japan."

"Little yellow men" is clear enough. Chin was singled out because of his race; his only connection to Japan was racial, and it was tenuous at that. His white friends were not similarly targeted, nor were his white killers penalized severely. African Americans who have committed such transgressions have received the death penalty at disproportionate rates. The judge believed that the sentence matched the people, not their actions. Although Asian Americans over time made Chin a martyr, we, too, were initially disinclined to broach the issue of race. White observers tended to disbelieve that his murder had been a hate crime; this was before the concept of a "hate crime" had become recognized. Helen Zia, an activist who later wrote *Asian American Dreams: The Emergence of an American People*,[78] recalls that a union official even informed her that if Chin had been Japanese in ancestry, the brutal killing would have been comprehensible. Thus, to some non-Asian observers, the Chin case was appalling only to the extent that it involved mistaken targeting. Like Michigan residents of all racial backgrounds many Asian Americans were employed by and depended on the "Big Four": Ford, General Motors, Chrysler, and AMC. Unlike foreign Asians, the Asian Americans in the Detroit area helped domestic automakers, and, like other Americans, they were harmed by foreign competition. The earliest community meetings among Asian Americans in response to the Chin case were held at Ford world headquarters.

In Stockton, California, in 1989, Patrick Purdy dressed in military fatigues, took a semiautomatic rifle, went to the elementary school he had once attended, and opened fire on the playground, spraying bullets that hit three dozen victims. Five of the students were fatally wounded. Although he had purposefully aimed at a crowd of predominantly Southeast Asian refugee children, local authorities and national media dismissed immediately any racial factor even though Purdy had expressed both his animus toward Asians and his fear that the country would be taken over by immigrants.

On the widest scale, the events of April 29, 1992, in Los Angeles were another defining moment for Asian Americans.[79] The acquittal by a suburban Simi Valley jury of white police officers accused of beating African American motorist Rodney King triggered an eruption of violence, demonstrations, arson, looting, and anarchy, in which fifty-eight people died and an estimated $1 billion in property damage was caused in a place W. E. B. Du Bois had called "wonderful" for African Americans because "nowhere in the United States is the Negro so well and beautifully housed. . . . [T]here would seem to be no limit to your opportunities."[80]

The immigrant families, predominantly Asian American and specifically Korean American, whose lives were consumed by their small businesses, many barely profitable and uninsured, saw everything of theirs literally broken in a moment: a brick through a window, trespassers tearing apart the inventory before torching what they could not take, the lawbreakers joyous as they ran amok, perhaps crying out a farewell that said the Asian immigrants had finally been shown their place. The popular images of Asian Americans showed them distraught, but also armed: One image captured by the *Los Angeles Times* depicted two young Asian American men defending their property, crouched behind construction equipment, ready with handguns.[81]

A self-published analysis of the "rebellion" by thirteen black authors opens with praise for the sleeping giant of "black, unheeded masses . . . awaken[ing] with a vengeance" and praises "a thoroughly mixed population" "chanting the war cry 'No Justice, No Peace.'"[82] None of the contributions even recognizes that Asian American communities were ruined, much less expresses empathy.

It was white police officers who had flagrantly violated the civil rights of King, but it was Asian Americans who paid the price. It was not exclusively African American and Latino young men who made up the roving mobs that went on a criminal rampage, but it was Asian Americans who were besieged. More Latinos than African Americans were arrested for riot-related charges in every category except firearms possession, but there were more African American older men than Latino older men who took part in the disorder. Asian immigrants may have felt powerless in predominantly African American and Latino neighborhoods, with what they perceived as a looming threat of armed violence, given their own difficulties with language and lack of familiarity with culture and without firsthand knowledge of either Asian American history or the African American civil rights struggle. Small family-owned businesses hired few employees, and even hiring an African American security officer, who worked as a subordinate protecting the boss's business, could have the effect of highlighting the racial dynamics. African Americans also felt disempowered in their own neighborhoods; they neither owned the retail stores that looked like the means of economic advancement nor were even asked to work there. Neighborhood word-of-mouth held that Asian immigrants received special government benefits for which African Americans were racially disqualified. The rumor that Asian immigrants were given government money, although false, was widely believed.

Surveying Angelenos immediately afterward, Harvard sociologist Lawrence Bobo captured the importance of racial perspective.[83] Asked if the disturbances were mainly protest, mainly looting and street crime, or half and half, 42.9 percent of Asian Americans said it was protest and 50.5 said it was looting and street crime; among African Americans, the numbers were 67.5 and 22.8; among Hispanics, 38.7 and 51.9; among whites, 37.4 and 55.8. Bobo suggests that Asian American–Latino tensions also were running high in Los Angeles prior to the events. Korean sociologist In-Jin Yoon surveyed Korean immigrant business owners there and found that 80 percent preferred Latino employees to African American ones.[84] Sociologist Claire Kim, studying the East Coast, argues in *Bitter Fruit: The Politics of Black-Korean Conflict in New York City* that Asian American–African American conflict reproduces the model minority myth.[85] African Americans may be right to be angry that Asian Americans are seen as the model minority, but recurring African American anger only fortifies the saintly aura of Asian Americans as that model minority.

In 1987, in New Jersey groups of white and Latino young men began a series of assaults and batteries directed toward Indian immigrants. Calling themselves the "dot-busters" in an allusion to the *bindi* (the cosmetic mark on the forehead of Hindu women), the gangs beat up dozens. Even after they killed Navroze Mody and permanently maimed Kaushal Sharan, local police refused to characterize the attacks as race related.

In 1981, Vietnamese fishermen along the Texas Gulf coast took the Ku Klux Klan to court. Although the entire shrimp industry was suffering, the Klan made the competition racial, between native-born white Americans and Asian refugees. In one of the earliest cases won by Morris Dees and the Southern Poverty Law Center against a hate group, the Klan was forbidden to continue its violent attacks.

In 1996, outside San Diego, two white youths stabbed to death Thienh Minh Ly, a recent graduate of a biophysics master's degree program who had been out roller-blading. One of them recorded in his journal that "I killed a jap a while ago I stabbed him to Death" and recorded the details of his surprise attack on the Vietnamese Americans, stabbed forty times, throat slashed, face kicked in. As elsewhere, it was difficult to persuade authorities that the incident was racial.

The National Asian Pacific American Legal Consortium, a Washington, D.C.-based nonprofit group, compiles an annual report listing hundreds of cases of racial violence affecting Asian Americans. It may be impossible to trace each hate crime or racial incident to a specific stereotype such as the model minority myth, but the number of race-related assaults belies the smiling image of the myth. An incident involving two sisters, Shirley Gee and Patricia Seto, and their four children, is typical. On a one-hour plane ride back home from Disneyland in 1994, the family underwent nonstop racial harassment. Twenty drunken white passengers, returning from a wedding, surrounded them. They became belligerent toward the family. Calling them "gooks" and "whores," they pretended to shoot guns in their faces. They were gleeful and relentless. The flight crew did nothing to alleviate the problem. They told Gee and Seto that they should try to get along with their tormentors. Two of Gee's children suffered asthma attacks during the crisis. The airline and its white passengers did not apologize; Gee was unable to pursue a lawsuit because of restrictive rules protecting the companies. Others can belittle the episode as frivolous or diminish it as anomalous, but neither reaction is appropriate and neither offers comfort to Asian Americans who have had such firsthand experience with casual hatred.

The critique of the model minority myth can be informed by and also inform our understanding of other racial images. The myth does not stand in isolation; it has its counterparts. "Jews are so good at making money" and "Blacks are innate athletes" can be said with good faith, but at best they reflect superficial approval and it is necessary to listen to the words that follow.

The statement "Jews are so good at making money" is properly regarded as suspect. The debatable sincerity with which it might be uttered does not make it wholly innocent, because vicious libels against usurious Jews are as ancient as they remain evocative. In Shakespeare's day, his play *The Merchant of Venice* (also known as *The Jew of Venice* to compete with Marlowe's *The Jew of Malta*) was thought to have an uplifting ending. The merchant, Antonio, was the star of the comedy; Shylock, the Jew, was a despised moneylender. The outcome was all the more satisfying for its means. Portia, the royal beauty whom Antonio's friend Bassanio loves, is still the symbol for female lawyers. Beginning "the quality of mercy is not strained/it droppeth as the gentle rain from heaven," Portia issues the judicial pronouncement allowing Shylock to take his "pound of flesh" from Antonio as surety for the debt that is due. But Portia decrees that Shylock cannot do so without the loss of at least a drop of blood—he had contracted for only the flesh and not any blood—and, therefore he is guilty of attempted murder, and therefore forfeits his wealth and will be banished. It is only in modern times that audiences have seen Shylock as the primary character and the finale as tragic. The wretched hero, played by a star such as Dustin Hoffman on Broadway, gives a plaintive cry: "If you prick us, do we not bleed?" The abiding willingness of all too many people to become anti-Semites by accepting the hoax of *The Protocols of the Elders of Zion* should give us pause, for it reminds us that any comments on Jewish financial acumen are unsettling. The lingering echoes about a global conspiracy of bankers resonate too loudly.

To say that "Blacks are innate athletes" is to demean their individual talent. It reduces them to brute animals. As University of Texas history professor John Hoberman dissects in *Darwin's Athletes: How Sport Has Damaged Black America and Preserved the Myth of Race*,[86] the racial theories that present blacks' instincts as enhanced and their hand-eye coordination as exceptional hark back to the supposition that slaveowners bred them for strength. The corollary is that they are dim-witted. African Americans become icons of brawn, bereft of brain, fostering a fetish for their physique. They are constrained by roles even within the sports arena. They can be the journeyman linebacker on a football team, but only recently have they become the starting quarterbacks because that leadership position is more cerebral. They can entertain the fans with their game, but rarely are they allowed to become the managers or the owners who develop the strategies or control the business. If an individual African American is deficient in the athletic skills of dunking or dribbling, or if he cannot at least sing, dance, or preach, that individual ceases to be authentically "black" and loses any substantial occupation in society. Such individuals disappoint expectations that are so powerful as to have become internalized.

Stereotypes that are not racial have the same effects. The celebration of the role of women within the family serves as disapproval of their role outside the home. The approbation of the deaf as pure of heart implies that they are simple of mind.

The perverse nature of racial discourse, however, has made it difficult to critique the model minority myth. The critics of the myth, most of them Asian American, come under criticism for inexplicably refusing a compliment. Tufts University historian Reed Ueda has called their critiques a form of "false modesty." He argues that they "say more about the exigencies of the American ethnic ideology than about the state of the Asian-American community" because it is "liberal and radical Asians" who have "hastened to defy the image . . . and expose it as just another means of majority oppression."[87] Apologists for the model minority myth, like Ueda, presume it is a favor to

Asian Americans. Ueda believes that the critique of the myth is political, but does consider that the myth itself is racial. Every stereotype deserves scrutiny, and, as far as impartiality is concerned, the analysis of the myth is more objective than the myth itself.

In any event, the individuals and families whose lives have tracked the model minority myth deserve kudos. Nothing should be taken away from them because the stereotype is discredited, and they need not downplay what they have done. Their strategies for coping may well deserve copying, but they will be easier to copy if they are not regarded as racial. The assault on a stereotype should not be confused with an assault on them, but it is understandable that the generalization of the model minority myth makes it impossible to separate the individual from the group.

It would be bad enough if the model minority myth were true. Everyone else would resent Asian Americans for what Asian Americans possess. It is worse that the model minority myth is false. Everyone else resents Asian Americans for what they believe Asian Americans possess. Other Americans say that their resentment is about riches and not race, but they assume that Asian Americans are rich on the basis of race; there is no escaping that the resentment is racial. Above all, the model minority myth is a case study in the risks of racial stereotypes of any kind. It is the stereotyping itself, not the positive or negative valence it assumes temporarily, that is dangerous. A stereotype confines its subjects. The myth was neither created by nor is it controlled by Asian Americans. It is applied to but not by Asian Americans.

The model minority myth tells us that the only good Asian American is a genius workaholic, not an average or normal man or woman. The expectations of being a supergeek can be debilitating. Asian American children are not allowed to be like other children. They must be superstudents, because their parents, their teachers, and society overall expect nothing less.[88] They become misfits to their classmates. Their rarified upbringing is like that of John Stuart Mill, the great utilitarian philosopher whose father was determined to produce a polymath of the first order. Mill's homeschooling routine, sitting at a desk opposite his father for the entirety of the day except during walks when he would recite his lessons, worked brilliantly, producing a formidable scholar who was publishing learned papers as an adolescent but who also underwent a grave emotional breakdown at an early age. Other than through the model minority myth, few Americans today wish to force their children to endure the box of psychologist B. F. Skinner, with its positive and negative reinforcements to condition behavior as if we were rats to be rewarded for running a maze. Asian American adults are directed into specific occupations. Yet Asian Americans cannot sustain communities in which we all are engineers, no matter how good a profession it is. If we are not to be stunted as communities, we must have artists, journalists, lawyers, craftspeople, police officers, firefighters, social workers, and the myriad others with contributions to make to our civic culture. We should have communities that contain the spectrum of human pursuits, or we will live down to our stereotype.

Perhaps the easiest means of pointing out what is corrupting about the model minority myth would be to imagine Asian Americans exalting in it. Some Asian Americans already are either optimistic or naïve in believing parts of it. The U.S. Glass Ceiling Commission found Asian Americans oblivious to the glass ceiling it had documented. Its report notes, "None of the Asian and Pacific Islander men who participated in the focus groups identified themselves as 'minority'. . . . They perceive themselves as smarter and harder working than their white counterparts and are confident that they outperform their white colleagues."[89]

The more convinced Asian Americans become about the message of the model minority myth as a whole, the more African Americans and whites alike will be incredulous. Foreign Asians have occasionally been chastised for articulating such offensive convictions. Prime Minister Yasuhiro Nakasone of Japan in 1986 was pressured to retract his pronouncement that America was hampered in the global economy by the low intelligence of blacks and Hispanics. If all Asian Americans suddenly followed Nakasone and applauded themselves loudly and at length for being better than African Americans and whites, it would be downright embarrassing.

Asian Americans could brag about our numerous extraordinary deeds with suitable embellishments. We would sound like Asian supremacists of some sort, if we arrogantly told ourselves and everyone else about our brain power, our cultural superiority, our bank accounts, our prospects, and our likely global ascendancy. Our conceit would be terrible, even if we redacted the expressly racial terms so we weren't explicitly insisting that it was our Asian-ness that made us so good. If Asian Americans reveled in the model minority myth we would be insufferable, but the myth would still be false.

The model minority has a twin, the perpetual foreigner. Like the model minority myth, the perpetual foreigner syndrome haunts Asian Americans. In the next chapter, I fight it.

The Perpetual Foreigner

Yellow Peril in the Pacific Century

The idea is if we don't look out the white race will be—
will be utterly submerged. . . . Well, these books are all
scientific. . . . This fellow has worked out the whole thing.
It's up to us, who are the dominant race, to watch out or
those other races will have control of things.

—Tom Buchanan, in F. Scott Fitzgerald's *The Great Gatsby*

Where We're Coming From

"Where are you from?" is a question I like answering. "Where are you *really*
from?" is a question I *really* hate answering.

"Where are you from" is a question we all routinely ask one another upon
meeting a new person. "Where are you *really* from?" is a question some of us
tend to ask others of us very selectively.

For Asian Americans, the questions frequently come paired like that.
Among ourselves, we can even joke nervously about how they just about
define the Asian American experience. More than anything else that unites
us, everyone with an Asian face who lives in America is afflicted by the perpetual foreigner syndrome. We are figuratively and even literally returned to
Asia and ejected from America.

Often the inquisitor reacts as if I am being silly if I reply, "I was born in Cleveland, and I grew up in Detroit," or even if I give a detailed chronology of my many moves around the country: "I went to college in Baltimore; I practiced law in San Francisco; and now I live in Washington, D.C." Sometimes the person reacts as if I'm impertinent if I return the question, "And where are *you* really from?" People whose own American identity is assured are perplexed when they are snubbed in this manner, and my white friends of whom I have asked the question are amused at best and befuddled at worst even if one of their parents is an immigrant or all of their grandparents were. They deserve to know why "Where are you *really* from?" is so upsetting to Asian Americans even if it carries no offensive connotations to them.

Like many other people of color (or a few whites who have marked accents) who share memories of such encounters, I know what the question "Where are you *really* from?" means, even if the person asking it is oblivious and regardless of whether the person is aggressive about it. Once again, I have been mistaken for a foreigner or told I cannot be a real American.

The other questions that follow in the sequence make the subtext less subtle. Assuming that I must be "*really* from" someplace else and not here, even pausing for the preliminary "Where are you *really* from?" some people proceed to ask me: "How long have you been in our country?" "Do you like it in our country?" "When are you going back?" and "Do you have the chance to go home often?" I am asked these questions with decreasing frequency over time but still too often, and I am surprised at the contexts in which they continue to pop up.

When I give a speech, every now and then a nice person will wait to chat with me and with utter sincerity and no hint of irony, start off by saying, "My, you speak English so well." I am tempted to reply, "Why, thank you; so do you." I don't suppose, however, that such a response would make my point to anybody but myself. I am disappointed by these tiresome episodes because strangers have zeroed in on my race and seem to be aware of nothing else. Taken together, their questions are nothing more than a roundabout means of asking what they know could not be directly said, "What race are you?" Their comments imply that I am not one of "us" but one of "them." I do not belong as an equal. My heart must be somewhere else rather than here. I am a visitor at best, an intruder at worst. I must know my place, and it is not here. But I cannot even protest, because my complaint exposes me as an ingrate. I don't appreciate the opportunities I have been given. People who know nothing about me have an expectation of ethnicity as if I will give up my life story as an example of exotica.

A few people, I suspect, ask where we are from out of naiveté blended with malice. If pressed about my origins, I answer that my parents came from China, lived in Taiwan, and then came here as graduate students in the 1950s. My interlocutors sometimes say, "Oh, I thought so," and end the exchange. They have placed me in their geography of race and somehow they know all they need to know. They must feel that they have gleaned an insight into me by knowing where I am *"really"* from. They can fit me into their world order.

What makes the incidents comical is that the person waiting in line, the clerk behind the counter, the stranger on the street, and whoever else turns around, leans over, or pulls me aside to ask "Where are you *really* from?" does so as if asking me something I have not been asked before. People do not know that they are reenacting a stale scenario.

Other people, I suppose, ask Asian Americans where they are really from because they sincerely would like to know about China or Asia, or they would like to show off what they already know. They are compelled to tell me that they went to China for a vacation last year and saw the Great Wall or they ate at a Chinese restaurant where they especially liked the food. They may want to ask if it is really true, what they say about Asians, or there may be a phrase they'd like translated.

Asians and Asian Americans occasionally ask me the same question, but possibly with different meaning. Some of them are the same as anyone else; they may want to confirm a conjecture of some sort, or they wish to confide that they detest another group, say, Koreans or Vietnamese. A few would like to establish rapport with someone else who happens to be a minority and an outsider. They might need help because of their poor English or finding their way in an unfamiliar country, and they guess that I will be sympathetic toward them if not similar to them.

What makes these incidents disquieting is that the passenger at the airport, the waiter at the restaurant, the doctor, any Asian individuals who turn around, lean over, or pull me aside to ask "Where are your people from?" "Where are your parents from?" or "What province is your family from?" do so as if they are asking me what has not been asked them before. They do not care that they are reinforcing prejudices that affect them.

At an academic conference attended mainly by Asian American professors in Los Angeles a few years ago, I met a visiting scholar from mainland China who introduced himself to everyone with the greeting, "Are you Chinese?" I overheard him accosting people over and over, sometimes forgetting he'd already asked a person, "Are you Chinese?" He sounded like the lost young-ster in the children's story who asks everyone, "Are you my mother?"

A few years later, when Harry Wu, the Chinese dissident, toured U.S. universities, he was sometimes received with hostility from Chinese students studying here who balked at his assessment of their mutual country of origin. Out of a sense that he was bringing shame upon them by exposing the problems of China to the West, they shouted at him in an angry chant, "Are you Chinese? Are you Chinese? Are you Chinese?"[1]

Just as the Chinese language depends for its meaning on the inflection of a word, the different tone of the professor's words and the student's identical words gave the question dissimilar meanings in the two contexts. But the professor and the students share a worldview. Although I am embarrassed for the professor and the students—as I have no right to be—I know that they are unschooled in or unpersuaded by the American urge to avoid stereotyping. They, and not I, probably represent the majority of the world. To them, just as to nosy non-Asian Americans, it is important where somebody is from. The professor is confident that it is possible to infer meaningful information from a person's ancestral birthplace, whether that individual agrees with the proposition or not. He may as well believe in astrology. The students are convinced that a true patriot would not speak his mind honestly to outsiders. They wish to censor critics out of racial pride. (All of this explains in part why Asians often do not comprehend what bothers Asian Americans about the "Where are you *really* from?" question. Asians are not vulnerable in the same manner as Asian Americans. They fit the stereotype and they have their own stereotypes of whites. Asians are from somewhere else, they are returning there, and they are in the mainstream back home.)

As it happens, many Asians overseas—Asian Americans sometimes call them "Asian Asians"—ask one another questions that many Americans—including Asian Americans—would regard as inconsiderate. They are willing to ask immediately of a new acquaintance, "How old are you?" "Are you married?" and "Do you have children?" If you are over thirty and single, you will be asked, "Why aren't you married?" And if you are over thirty, married but childless, you will be asked, "Why no children?"

Although I don't wish to make allowances for these intrusive inquiries into personal matters, they are arguably different than "Where are you *really* from?" They are different because they are asked of virtually everyone, not just some people. In addition, they are different because they are consistent with values held by the individual doing the asking. The person who asks "Why aren't you married?" or "Why no children?" is openly signaling disapproval of being a bachelor or being childless, and that person means to do so. The person who asks "Where are you *really* from" also is signaling an effort to separate individuals within society on the basis of race but may deny doing so.

In a similar vein, I am not reassured when Asians or Asian Americans tell me that they don't have to ask where somebody is really from, because they can guess about an Asian person's specific ethnicity. By looking at the flatness of the face, the slope of the head, the peak of the nose, the distance between the eyes, or based on some other vague combination of arcane factors, they claim to be able to gauge whether an Asian person is Chinese, Japanese, Korean, or Vietnamese. They are only too happy to share their secret knowledge with their non-Asian friends, who then repeat it and apply it because the source makes it authoritative; they have prompted some of their non-Asian friends to apologize, saying, "I'm not very good at telling different Asians apart; where are you *really* from?" None of them realize that a playful system of assessing racial identity from physical features shares a family resemblance with much more sinister measurements. Phrenologists of only a century ago had elaborate charts to diagnose character by feeling bumps on the head. The Nazis had pictorial tables that relied on facial appearance to sort out European stocks. A famous magazine article of the World War II era informed Americans "how to tell our friends [the Chinese] from the Japs." Among the hints were some about face and body; others about dress and behavior: "some aristocratic Japanese have thin, aquiline noses, narrow faces and, except for their eyes, look like Caucasians," "most Chinese avoid horn-rimmed spectacles," and the Japanese are "positive, dogmatic, arrogant" while the Chinese are "more placid, kindly, open."[2]

In today's United States, we have decided that we will not be bound by our collective past. Yet we remain acutely aware of race—which is not to say that we are racists. We want to know about race, but for many different reasons.

The question "Where are you *really* from" shows that we interact with others around us with a sense of race even if we are not aware of it. Being asked "Where are you *really* from?" likely will not result in my being denied an apartment or a job, except in isolated instances. I wonder what people are thinking, though; when I was interviewing for a position as a law professor only seven years ago, I was told by a senior faculty member at one school (in California no less), "How appropriate that we have the Asian candidate today"—he was referring to December 7, Pearl Harbor Day. I believe the questions and statements are signals, along a spectrum of invidious color consciousness that starts with speculation but leads to worse. To be met with it so quickly and so often reminds me, over and over, that I am being treated differently than I would be if I were white.

Yet some people who want to talk to me about where I am from want to share with me where they are from literally or where they are coming from, so to speak. For that rare individual, asking "Where are you *really* from?" is intended as an invitation to a dialogue about what it means that each of us has come here from elsewhere and where we can go together. The great philosopher of pluralism Isaiah Berlin once wrote, "Only barbarians are not curious about where they come from." But he included that subject of self-inquiry in a lengthy list of topics in "the pursuit of the ideal." He thought that the civilized person ought to care about, just as important, "how they came to be where they are, where they appear to be going, whether they wish to go there, and if so, why, and if not, why not."[3]

Whether "Where are you *really* from?" begins or ends the conversation is crucial, then. The answer depends on why the question is asked.

Unfortunately, there is worse. Whenever I have had the privilege of appearing in a public forum discussing a controversial topic—and any issue worth discussing in a public forum is likely to a controversial topic—I receive letters, phone calls, and e-mails from people who disagree vehemently with my perspective. I enjoy the fifteen minutes of fame, but I am taken aback by a few of the messages. They run along the lines of, "Yeah, and what do they do in China?" I have been told, for example, that because it would not be easy for a white person to become a Chinese citizen, it is obvious that all countries value their sovereignty. Thus, according to this reasoning, the United States is no different in making it hard for a Chinese person to become an American citizen.[4]

When I argued for affirmative action against conservative author Dinesh D'Souza on the C-SPAN program *American Perspectives,* I had the greatest exposure and the worst reaction. Because the two-hour show taped from Brown University in late 1997 was aired on New Year's Day and rerun repeatedly, viewers channel-surfing cable stations between football games saw the two of us discussing the most racially divisive of current political issues. D'Souza, who jokes that "there aren't any Asian American civil rights activists—and it's a good thing, too," remarked to me before the cameras started rolling that it isn't often that an Asian American is invited to comment on civil rights, much less two Asian Americans. As much as I disagree with his opinions, I agree with him that more Asian Americans should be offering theirs. I am dismayed that some reviews of his work open with the observation that he is from Bombay, or that he is Catholic, or that he is an immigrant; a few critiques don't progress much beyond that. What happens to me extends to him as well. Ironically, as diametrically opposed as our opinions might be, for some observers we are identical for racial reasons. The difference is not our arguments, but our identities: I'm the Chinese guy; he's the Indian guy. I am chagrined when I am told, "Hey, that was a good debate you had with that Indian guy."

I must have impressed a few in the audience, and not favorably. The correspondence I received was about two to one in my support, but in the negative mail were some warnings. One writer advised, "You'll learn." He sent materials purporting to show that African Americans were apes. He enclosed printouts of material from white supremacist Internet websites as his authoritative sources. Another writer asked whether they have affirmative action in Japan. I am tempted to retort, "How would I know?" Or with too much cleverness for my own good, I could come back with, "What does that have to do with the price of tea in China?"

The put down of opinions held by Asian Americans through an allusion to their presumed homeland is an *ad hominem* attack in its classic form. It has nothing to do with the substance of an argument and everything to do with the identity of the person advancing it. The writer who asked me about Japan had it wrong, doubly. I am Chinese American, not Japanese American. But even though my parents came from China, I have never even set foot on the Asian continent.

I have heard the point as a direct taunt. It comes as the heckler's jeer, "If you don't like it here, then go back where you came from." Or it comes as the snubbed host's uncomprehending whine: "Don't you like everything this country has given you?"

When I send my mother a videotape of a television program on which I have appeared, she usually calls me up. After she advises me I need a better haircut, she tells me not to be too controversial. She says, "It will be bad for your career." I don't have the heart to tell her I've made a career out of being controversial. But as mothers usually do, mine has a point. To be a critic requires being accepted as a citizen. The effective commentator on American affairs must have standing as a fellow American. That status eludes Asian Americans.

Since I have been giving speeches for over half my life, taking up forensics in high school to overcome a stutter, I don't mind too much the insinuation that I am not supposed to have a seat at the table. I worry, however, that many Asian Americans are silenced through racial intimidation—along with Latinos, recent immigrants, and all the others who are made to feel that they don't belong. They grasp that they are expected to remain polite, even silent, as the condition of their very presence in the United States. So they keep their mouths shut, even though all citizens have a right as well as a responsibility to take part in our political process. Stereotypes become self-fulfilling. Asian Americans act according to script: submissive, passive, agreeable, docile, deferential, and polite. We are disqualified from being opinion makers.

Although Asian Americans are often stereotyped as intellectuals, we are not expected to be public intellectuals. In an influential article in the March 1995 *Atlantic Monthly*, New York University journalism professor Robert S. Boynton praises the rebirth of the public intellectual.[5] Boynton argues that the public intellectual has a new guise. He identifies African American public intellectuals as the most prominent of this breed, celebrity thinkers such as the triumvirate of Harvard professors, Henry Louis Gates Jr., Cornel West, and William Julius Wilson. Asian Americans are conspicuously absent from the television talk shows and the op-ed pages; we have no Jesse Jackson or Al Sharpton, much less a Gates, West, or Wilson. Whatever we may think of their strategies for activism or the substance of their commentary, we know their names, we expect them to have something to say, they are given a forum, and they are influential. We are even missing from the conversation when the subject is Asia. We are simultaneously expected to have something to say about Asia and precluded from speaking as authorities about Asia. Our comments have the presumed credibility of an Asian face and the negative caveat that we cannot be objective.

It seems as if Asian Americans must denounce Asia before we can talk about civil rights in the United States. Although I believe Asian racism is as deplorable as American racism (and, to me, Asian American racism is the worst of all), Asian Americans should not have to criticize Asia as a racial prerequisite to offering any criticism of our own country, the United States.[6] We live in the United States, not in Asia. Our primary concern is and properly should be the treatment of all peoples in the United States, and the practices of other countries are simply irrelevant. White Americans are not asked to deprecate European countries before they are allowed to talk about the United States, although they may be eager to denigrate Asian countries for human rights abuses. When people (including a few Asian immigrants) say that Asian Americans should be more concerned with Asian governments, because it is they, not the U.S. government, that are oppressing Asians, they make their concern racial.

To the extent that the Chinese, Japanese, Indians, Koreans, or Filipinos may conceive of citizenship as racial, that is unfortunate though similar to the attitudes of the British, French, Germans, Italians, or Russians; they are the Old World (although even the Old World has always been much more polyglot than its inhabitants care to admit).[7] The United States has a different conception of citizenship; it is the New World. We are not like Great Britain after the sun has set on its empire. There MP Enoch Powell delivered his infamous 1968 speech while Asian immigrants from Africa were arriving in large numbers, decrying the admittance of non-Anglos as "mad, literally mad" and likely to lead to a "river of blood," and MP Norman Tebbitt gave an interview in 1990 introducing his "cricket test" of loyalty, based on whether Asian immigrants cheered for teams from their lands of origin. Our equivalents of Australian politicians who are anti-Asian, despite their presence in the Pacific and dependence on the Asian economy, are neither as audacious nor as successful. We have not seen the likes of Charles Perkins, the top-ranked aborigine in the government who in the late 1980s argued that Australia should not allow more Asian immigrants because it already had enough home-grown criminals and who likened Asians to a contagious disease, or Pauline Hanson, who led her "One Nation" party to its spectacular rise and fall in the 1990s. In this respect, the United States is better, not worse, than other countries. Our high ideals, however, exaggerate our shortcomings.

Ours is citizenship based on consent, not descent. We Americans, who presume that we can claim the entire continent for ourselves through our name, should not allow our self-importance to get the better of us. Canadians, who are often held up as a negative example due to the separatism of the Quebecois, should be considered a positive example for numerous reasons. Their history is different, of course, but they accept more immigrants as a share of their population than the United States does; they have done more to acknowledge the rights of native peoples; and the most insightful writers on contemporary multiculturalism have come from the north, chief among them political philosophers Will Kymlicka and Charles Taylor.

The perpetual foreigner syndrome can be expressed as empathy. Now and again, people introduce themselves to me by speaking pidgin Chinese, or they make an elaborate show of bowing that is so inept that it might as well be a parody. They don't realize that I speak English perfectly well and am accustomed to shaking hands.

I have listened to people explain to me, trying their patience as much as mine, that they appreciate how I as an Asian American may face discrimination here, because when they as Americans were traveling as tourists in China or Japan they, too, felt prejudice. As much as I value efforts at mutual understanding, even these kindly people are offering up an analogy that is frustratingly inappropriate. It shows both what is wrong with the way Asian Americans are characterized and the nuance of the error.

As a law professor, I help train people to argue from analogy and to distinguish among different cases. Some analogies are persuasive; other analogies
are inapt. The proper comparison to the treatment of white Americans overseas—where they are in fact "foreigners"—is the treatment of non-white
Americans overseas—where they are in fact "foreigners." If the idea is to
match up the situations, then the appropriate counterpart to the treatment of
a white American in Asia is the treatment of an Asian American in Europe.
Otherwise, the necessary implication is that America is a white nation. Incidentally, a non-white U.S. citizen visiting "the Continent" is likely to be
regarded as a *bona fide* Yankee. I am as able as my neighbor to be an ugly
American: a loud, rude, English-speaking tourist expecting to be catered to.
When I am outside the United States, it is readily apparent to the rest of the
civilized world where I come from as soon as I open my mouth.

"Chinese Are Not Nice People" and "Japanese Are a Very Cruel Race"

Most people don't see the slippery slope leading from governments and companies to nations and peoples and then to races and cultures; it is a swift slide
from an overseas group to an American individual by way of the catch-all
phrase "you people," as in, "if you people hadn't bombed Pearl Harbor . . . ."
The distinction of U.S. citizenship, seemingly all-important, is blurred away. It
is as easy now as it was a century ago to find diatribes about the Chinese government or Japanese companies that speak in terms of China or Japan as
monoliths or that conclude "the Chinese are a military threat" or "the Japanese are an economic threat." The further proclamations that "the Chinese are
belligerent" or "the Japanese are devious" don't have a clear stopping point.

During the spy plane crisis with China, a respected journalist such as
David Broder could say on national television in April 2001, "Chinese are
not nice people" in a matter-of-fact manner without repercussions. In the
hit movie *Bridget Jones' Diary*, released in 2001, one of the heroine's suitors
has an ex-wife who is Japanese. She apparently is assigned that racial identity, which otherwise is not important to the plot, so that the other characters can remark that the Japanese are "a very cruel race."[8] Imagine if Broder
had said, "Africans are not nice people" or characters in a hit movie said
"Jews are a very cruel race." At the peak of Japanese economic gains, when
in 1989 the Mitsubishi conglomerate bought Rockefeller Center, politicians
and pundits took it as a dire sign that the soul of America was for sale. In
1989, television curmudgeon Andy Rooney wrote about the sale of "Lock-

afella Centa," the mispronunciation being, in his sarcastic words, "a sick, racist joke, of course," which he repeated "merely to illustrate what bad taste some people have" before going on to tell his own gags about the Japanese buying the "Gland Canyon" and "Mount Lushmore." His serious point was that "there should be some things in America the Japanese can't buy for money." He preempted critics who might accuse him of being anti-Japanese as follows:

> Well, yes. A little. Maybe I am. I admire the Japanese. I admire how much better they're making things than we are, but sure, I have some negative feelings. I'm vaguely anti-Japanese. Don't ask me why. Just prejudice, I guess. I'm very comfortable with some of my prejudices and have no thought of changing them now.[9]

In 1992, opponents almost blocked the sale of the Seattle Mariners baseball team to the founder of Japanese game-maker Nintendo, who wanted to save the franchise for the city and forestall its move to a larger market. In contrast to the fallout from Japan-bashing, there were no such concerns about the British and Dutch companies that owned more U.S. properties than the Japanese even during the latter's buying frenzy, nor in 1998 when the German Daimler conglomerate, makers of Mercedes-Benz, merged with Chrysler, effectively taking it over. (Showing the pointlessness of asking about the nationality of international conglomerates, Daimler and Chrysler both owned part of Mitsubishi.[10]) A shelf's worth of books promote their claims about Chinese and Japanese influence as emphatically as their titles would suggest, including Steven W. Mosher's *Hegemon: China's Plan to Dominate Asia and the World*, Bill Gertz's *The China Threat: How the People's Republic Targets America*, Pat Choate's *Agents of Influence: How Japan's Lobbyists Manipulate America's Political and Economic System*, and Clyde Prestowitz's *Trading Places: How We Are Giving Our Future to Japan and How to Reclaim It*[11] and thrillers about a coming war with Asia.

There is a difference between the "America First" doctrine and "Buy America" campaign on the one hand, and a "White First" doctrine or "Buy White" campaign on the other hand; or, rather, there should be. Whether "America First" and "Buy American" are advisable policies can and be must be mulled over, but they cannot be dismissed out of hand as illegitimate. In the history of each movement, however, they have taken on racial overtones all too often. When people refer to Wang Computer, which during its heyday was one of the largest high-tech companies under its immigrant founder, or the boutique of Vera Wang, the upscale bridal gown designer, as foreign ventures, then it becomes apparent that "America First" and "Buy America" serve as a cover for something worse. Asian Americans cannot be—and apparently would not be invited to be—part of this mutation of "America First" and "Buy America."[12]

The original points that critics make about the handful of totalitarian leaders of the Chinese Communist Party or a few top business executives in a Japanese industry may be well founded and even persuasive, but they are generalized beyond all reason. Whether by intention or through carelessness, an anti-Asian outlook appears to encompass Asian immigrants and even Asian Americans. Those who exclaim, "but we don't mean Chinese Americans or Japanese Americans," should realize that others do, and it is as difficult for people to distinguish between the two positions as it is easy to clarify what is meant. Such precision would weaken the rhetoric; it is more emphatic to exclaim "the Chinese" and "the Japanese" than to talk about Chinese government or Japanese companies, but it also is dangerous and wrong. After Congressman John Dingell made his remark about "little yellow men," mentioned in Chapter 2, he later told his colleague, Congressman Norman Mineta, that he didn't mean to include Mineta. Mineta, who, as a Japanese American, was interned during World War II, told a reporter, "Who did he think he was talking about?" Mineta said that his office was receiving calls with inquiries such as, "Who do you represent, us or them?"[13]

There is, of course, a connection between Asians and Asian Americans. Asians only become Asian Americans through immigration. The perpetual foreigner syndrome supports the movement to close the borders, and vice versa. Anti-immigrant forces have struck back with a vengeance. Just as was true a century ago, the United States is experiencing a massive wave of immigration. Unlike earlier waves, the majority of today's newcomers are non-white. It is no coincidence that some of the calls for a moratorium on immigration have come exactly when the influx has changed color.

In his polemic against immigration, *Alien Nation*,[14] British immigrant Peter Brimelow articulates a thesis that probably is frightening to most racial minorities as well as many white Americans: "The American nation has always had a specific ethnic core. And that core is white." In the most influential book on immigration published in the past generation, Brimelow is not faint-hearted in his endorsement of the permanence of such an ethnic core. He quotes President Calvin Coolidge to the effect that "America must be kept American." He adds, "Everyone knew what he meant."[15]

Brimelow writes fondly of the 1950s, because, "as late as 1950, somewhere up to nine out of ten Americans looked like me . . . and in those days, they had another name for this thing dismissed so contemptuously as 'the racial hegemony of white Americans.' They called it 'America.'"[16] He believes "race and ethnicity are destiny in American politics," because the concept of a nation "intrinsically implies a link by blood" and it is "in a real sense an extended family" that is bound together by biology.[17] He argues "the role of ethnicity and race has proved to be elemental—absolute—fundamental" and he pessimistically concludes that multiracial societies are prone to civil war.[18] He preempts any charge that he is a "racist," with the witticism, "I usually shrug such smears off by pointing to its new definition: anyone who is winning an argument with a liberal."[19] Although he makes economic and political points, even they are based on racial and cultural premises.

Brimelow can count on our confusing types of discrimination. We have, as we should, a penchant for discriminating among types of discrimination. Other than among a few idealists, as a nation we accept discrimination on the basis of citizenship as necessary. But except among a few extremists, as a society we reject discrimination on the basis of race as immoral. As a consequence, wherever our laws draw lines among people the type of line determines whether it is acceptable. Lines that distinguish between citizens and aliens are acceptable; lines that distinguish between whites and people of color are not. With Asian Americans, it is clear that lines that appear to be based on citizenship can cover up lines that are based on race. Once citizenship is defined by race, it becomes convenient to refer to the innocuous lines based on citizenship in lieu of the odious lines based on race. Non-Asian Americans can discriminate against Asian Americans by turning us into noncitizens, either officially by prohibiting even legal long-term residents from naturalizing or informally by casting doubt on our status. Our objection to such discrimination is obviated before it is even made, because the discrimination looks legitimate as having been founded on citizenship rather than race. The alien land laws, passed to drive Japanese immigrants out of farming, are the prime example. They mentioned only "aliens ineligible to citizenship," but everybody knew they were intended to target Japanese immigrants, and they did just that quite effectively because there were no persons but Asians who fit the description.

Federal immigration policies had their beginnings in racial prejudice. The model minority myth portrayed the earliest Asian immigrants as racial competition that had to be stopped. It dovetailed neatly with the perpetual foreigner syndrome, which depicts Asian immigrants as inassimilable. In 1882, Congress passed the Chinese Exclusion Act. Over time, the legislation was extended to create an Asiatic barred zone. The Supreme Court's approval of the Chinese Exclusion Act in 1889 created its "plenary power doctrine," which continues to this day to be its guiding principle for evaluating immigration policies. The justices characterized Chinese immigration as "aggression and encroachment" equivalent to actual warfare, because any Chinese individuals were "foreigners of a different race" and "their exclusion is not to be stayed because at the time there are no actual hostilities with the nation of which the foreigners are subjects."[20] In a later case concerning not exclusion but expulsion of those Chinese immigrants who were already in the country, the justice who was the most favorably inclined of the jurists toward Chinese immigrants, was moved not by a desire to protect the people from prejudice but rather by a fear of the precedent and its reach: "It is true that this statute is directed only against the obnoxious Chinese; but if the power exists, who shall say it will not be exercised tomorrow against other classes and other people?"[21]

Consequently, Asian immigrants were not allowed, with only a few exceptions. Many came illegally, masquerading as the "paper sons" of individuals who were already legally present; they were "sons" only on paper and not in reality. University of Akron law professor Brant Lee, telling his own family's story, wondered whether people would condemn his grandfather, who had been such a "paper son," technically an "illegal immigrant." Lee asked whether Asian individuals who used trickery would be compared with the corresponding European individuals: "My Irish father-in-law is always telling stories about smooth characters who sweet-talk their way into and out of trouble."[22] University of California at Davis law professor Bill Ong Hing has said of these immigration policies: "It's no accident that the Statue of Liberty faces Europe and has her back to Asia and Latin America."[23]

Such sentiments were not limited to Asians, and they were undeniably racial, ethnic, and religious in all their manifestations. The signs of the birth of a nation being conceived of racially—as the D. W. Griffiths movie of that title portrayed it—can be cataloged from a multitude of sources, even though large numbers of Native Americans, African Americans, and non-British colonists were obvious at the founding. Before the United States had declared independence, Benjamin Franklin was already imagining "increasing the lovely White" on the continent by excluding "all Blacks and Tawnys" from Africa and Asia. Even among the white, the enlightened Franklin worried that Pennsylvania would "become a colony of *aliens*, who will shortly be so numerous as to Germanize us instead of [our] Anglifying" them.[24] The nativist movement sought to restrict the number of Europeans who were Southern and Eastern, Catholic and Jewish. They brazenly wished to preserve the white Anglo-Saxon Protestant dominance of the country, setting their quotas for visas based on the percentages of each group's representation in the country at the turn of the century.

The federal government opposed citizenship even for native-born individuals of Asian ancestry. In a test case in 1895, the solicitor general—the government's lawyer to the Supreme Court—opposed the application of Wong Kim Ark for citizenship. Wong had been born in San Francisco to parents who were Chinese. His hopes sprang from the Fourteenth Amendment to the Constitution, which overturned the *Dred Scott* decision depriving African Americans of citizenship, and which continues to guarantee everyone "equal protection" under the law. The Fourteenth Amendment opens, "all persons born . . . in the United States, and subject to the jurisdiction thereof, are citizens of the United States."

In his brief to the Supreme Court, the solicitor general presented the official view of the government by reviewing the precedent that appeared to support Wong before invoking the sacredness of citizenship. He states, "For the most persuasive reasons we have refused citizenship to Chinese subjects . . . and yet, as to their offspring, who are just as obnoxious, and to whom the same reasons for exclusion apply for equal force, we are told that we must accept them as fellow-citizens, and that, too, because of the mere accident of birth." He asks whether "Chinese children born in this country" should "share with the descendants of the patriots of the American Revolution the exalted qualification of being eligible to the Presidency of the nation." His answer: "If so, then verily there has been a most degenerate departure from the patriotic ideals of our forefathers; and surely in that case American citizenship is not worth having." Nonetheless, the Supreme Court ruled in favor of Wong by a divided vote. It wrote that the citizenship conferred by the measure was "general, not to say universal, restricted only by place and jurisdiction, and not by color or race."

The Supreme Court was not always as willing to allow Asian immigrants to naturalize. From the inception of federal regulation over immigration, Congress had maintained the rule that only "free white persons" could naturalize. In 1870, it amended the statute to allow "persons of African nativity, or African descent" to naturalize as well. Thus, Asian immigrants had to plead either that they were "free white persons" or "persons of African nativity, or African descent." In dozens of cases, they lost repeatedly.

Takao Ozawa, a Japanese immigrant, and Bhagat Singh Thind, an Indian immigrant, both had their cases heard by the Supreme Court; both of them lost within three months of each other in 1922–1923. As University of California at Berkeley law professor Ian F. Haney Lopez detailed in an excellent study, *White By Law: The Legal Construction of Race*,[25] Ozawa wrote an autobiographical brief before retaining a former U.S. Attorney General to argue his case.[26] Ozawa attests to his assimilation: "In name, General Benedict Arnold was an American, but at heart he was a traitor. In name, I am not an American, but at heart I am an American." Called a paragon of assimilation by later scholars, Ozawa reviews his own life: his flouting of Japanese laws requiring that he report himself, his marriage, and his children's birth to its government; his lack of affiliation with Japanese organizations; his children attending an American church and an American school; his use of English, and his children's lack of knowledge of Japanese; his education at American schools; his continuous residence for twenty-eight years; his preference for an American-educated wife; and his readiness to "return the kindness which our Uncle Sam has extended me." Moreover, Ozawa argued he was literally white, even more so than "the average Italian, Spaniard or Portuguese." The Supreme Court rejected his claims without much difficulty. It reasoned that "white" and "Caucasian" were synonymous. Japanese were not white, because they were not Caucasian. Their skin color was inconsequential, because skin color was not the only test of racial identity.

Thind tried a different tactic, to no avail.[27] Exactly as the precedent set by *Ozawa* suggested would be appropriate, he referred to the many taxonomies of race that had been devised by social scientists. Within the leading schemes, Asian Indians were not only Caucasian but also Aryan. The Supreme Court should have been caught by its own equation of "white" and "Caucasian," but it disposed of Thind's petition with the same alacrity it had shown Ozawa. It backed away from the scientific test, reasoning "the words 'free white person' are words of common speech, to be interpreted in accordance with the understanding of the common man." By that standard, "the physical group characteristics of the Hindus renders them readily distinguishable from the various groups of persons commonly recognized as white."

The law has changed, but the popular culture has not. When twenty-one-year-old Yale student Maya Lin won the competition for the Vietnam War Memorial commission, her profound design, with its black granite displaying a stark list of all the 58,000 Americans who died in the conflict and set into a gash in the earth, was controversial for more than its aesthetics. The selection process was anonymous, and the Ohio-born Lin was identified by only a number until her sketches were selected. Once her face was attached to her art, there were murmurings that she was the wrong choice because she was a "gook." For example, businessman Ross Perot, a major promoter of the project, frequently called Lin "eggroll" and, according to press accounts, "he hated that she was Asian."[28] Although her monument has become the most popular tourist attraction in the nation's capital, bringing together veterans, protesters, and families, who make crayon rubbings of their loved ones' names, the reticent sculptor still expresses shock at the attempts to discredit her because of race even though, in her own words, she "grew up almost completely oblivious to [her] Asian heritage."[29]

Against this background, in the remainder of this chapter I discuss how the perpetual foreigner syndrome works to deprive Asian Americans of civil rights and transform us into a racial threat. Two episodes in Asian American history—the internment of Japanese Americans during World War II and the 1996 campaign finance scandal—and recurring anxieties about Asian dominance of America, exemplify the syndrome. The Yellow Peril images of Asians are being transformed through transnationalism, but the developments may be hazardous for Asian Americans because of the emphasis on racial bonds to Asian homelands.

"A Jap's a Jap and That's All There Is to It"

More than any other episode, the internment of Japanese Americans during World War II confirmed that Asian Americans are not accepted.[30] Even before December 7, 1941—"the day that will live in infamy" in President Franklin Delano Roosevelt's famous war declaration—when the Japanese Empire bombed Pearl Harbor, Japanese Americans were widely disliked. When James D. Phelan ran for reelection to the Senate in 1920, for example, his posters showed a white hand in a shirt sleeve with the stars and stripes, restraining a brown-yellow hand with claws. The text read, "Let him finish the work he now has underway to stop the Silent Invasion."[31] Although Issei, first-generation Japanese immigrants, were barred from becoming citizens due to the racial prerequisite for naturalization, Nisei, the second-generation children, acquired citizenship through the birthright doctrine of the *Wong Kim Ark* case. Two-thirds of the Japanese population of 120,000 on the West Coast were Nisei. The Japanese citizenship of the Issei made them technically enemy aliens, but they had no choice. They could not have avoided that status, no matter how long they had lived in the United States or how assimilated they were. The U.S. citizenship of the Nisei hardly mattered, because they were treated identically with their parents. For Issei and Nisei alike, it was race that determined how their government would treat them. The Nisei were not even designated as citizens, but instead as "non-aliens."

As the United States entered the war, investigations that sought to attribute blame for the sneak attack on Pearl Harbor and collective wrath at Japanese treachery combined to make the tiny population—1.6 percent of the California population in 1940—of Japanese Americans a scapegoat. Edward R. Murrow, the famous wartime newscaster, was just beginning to establish himself as the definitive voice of the radio medium. He warned that if his native Seattle were ever bombed, "you will be able to look up and see some University of Washington sweaters on the boys doing the bombing."[32] Similar claims, all of them unfounded, were made about Japanese pilots who flew in the Pearl Harbor raid.

Military leaders viewed the conflict as a racial war.[33] Lieutenant General John L. DeWitt, who was in charge of the Western Defense, declared, "A Jap's a Jap, and that's all there is to it." DeWitt stated, "I am speaking now of the native-born Japanese. . . . In the war in which we are now engaged racial affinities are not severed by migration. . . . The Japanese race is the enemy race and while many second and third generation Japanese born on United States soil, possessed of United States citizenship, have become 'Americanized,' the racial strains are undiluted. . . . It, therefore, follows that along the vital Pacific Coast over 112,000 potential enemies of Japanese extraction are at large today." He also said, "American citizenship does not necessarily determine loyalty."[34] DeWitt claimed that there had been extensive "fifth column" activity on the part of Japanese Americans, including signaling to the Japanese fleet. Not a single such instance was documented at the time; none has been since.

Others agreed with the permanence of racial loyalties. The *Los Angeles Times* editorialized in favor of the internment. It rejected any distinction between the Issei and the Nisei: "A viper is nonetheless a viper wherever the egg is hatched—so a Japanese American, born of Japanese parents—grows up to be a Japanese, not an American."[35] Those who had qualms about the internment acquiesced to it, because they conceded that it would be too difficult to sort out the loyal Japanese Americans from the disloyal ones. They argued that the Oriental mind was too deceptive.

Every aspect of the Japanese American experience was used against them. Their success was especially unpopular. A white farmer told the *Saturday Evening Post*, "We're charged with wanting to get rid of the Japs for selfish reasons. We might as well be honest. We do." He said, "It's a question of whether the white man lives on the Pacific Coast or the brown man. They came into this valley to work, and they stayed to take over ." The farmer wanted to appropriate Japanese American property on a permanent basis: "If all the Japs were removed tomorrow, we'd never miss them in two weeks, because the white farmers can take over and produce everything the Jap grows. And we don't want them back when the war ends, either."[36] The Native Sons of the Golden West had long been working to rid the West Coast of any people of color. They pronounced California "the White Man's Paradise." Their Grand President, William P. Canbu, wrote, "California was given by God to a white people, and with God's strength we want to keep it as He gave it to us."[37] The group even filed suit to have all Japanese Americans stricken from the voter rolls.[38]

The mayor of Los Angeles asserted that Japanese American assimilation was a charade. "Of course they would try to fool us," he said, because "they did in Honolulu and in Manila, and we may expect it in California." He argued that past discrimination against Japanese Americans justified further discrimination against them. The earlier discrimination was likely to have made them angry, and that resentment made them untrustworthy.[39] Before Pearl Harbor, Congressman John Dingell had already written to the White House to urge the Roosevelt Administration to establish "a concentration camp of ten thousand alien Japanese in Hawaii" as a "reprisal reserve."[40] After Pearl Harbor, journalist Westbrook Pegler was more explicit in proposing that internment camps be set up to provide a stock of Japanese Americans who could be killed as retribution for Japanese war atrocities.[41]

Liberals such as California Attorney General Earl Warren and newspaper columnist Walter Lippmann supported the internment as well. Later, as Chief Justice of the Supreme Court during an era renowned for its progressive decisions advancing civil rights, Warren was able to advance his career through the prominence he achieved as a backer of the internment. A celebrated intellectual, Lippmann offered the circular reasoning that would be repeated by everyone else: Even though Japanese Americans had not done anything wrong, their very innocence "is a sign that the blow is well-organized and that it is held back until it can be struck with maximum effect."[42] Lippmann's biographer noted the "deft bit of sophistry" by which he had reasoned that there was no assault on civil liberties, because "all persons are, in principle, treated alike." As the biographer said, "he neglected to point out that the only citizens who had to justify their presence on the West coast 'battlefield' were those of Japanese ancestry."[43]

Out of guilt by association, then, Japanese Americans were deprived of liberty, livelihoods, and property in what was euphemistically termed evacuation. Under President Franklin Delano Roosevelt's Executive Order 9066, they were sent to ten internment camps in deserts and swamps, where they lived in makeshift barracks hastily erected by the Army, behind barbed wire, in the shadow of gun towers and under armed guard. They were treated as a group. Individuals were interned without regard for due process. Only a few of them received hearings, and, except for those who brought test cases challenging the constitutionality of the measures, none was convicted of criminal acts.

In San Francisco's neighborhood the Western Addition, a young Maya Angelou, later to be poet laureate of the United States, recalled that "as the Japanese disappeared, soundlessly and without protest, the Negroes entered with their loud jukeboxes, their just-released animosities, and the relief of escape from Southern bonds." As Angelou tells it, "no member of my family and none of the family friends ever mentioned the absent Japanese. It was as if they had never owned or lived in the houses we inhabited." She reasoned that "the sensations of common relationship were missing" because the Japanese Americans "were not whitefolks" and the African Americans were thrilled to be "a Boss, a Spender" and dazzled by "the chance to live in two- or three-story apartment buildings (which became instant slums.)"[44] Chinese Americans wore buttons that said they were Chinese; Korean Americans wore ones that said, "I Hate the Japs More Than You Do."

Once the internment was underway, even the American Civil Liberties Union (ACLU), which was sympathetic to the Roosevelt administration, declined to assist the Japanese Americans who wished to sue the government.[45] Its California chapters had to break off from the national organization to lend their support to Fred Korematsu, Gordon Hirabayashi, Min Yasui, and Mitsuye Endo in litigation that culminated in landmark cases heard by the Supreme Court, which gave its imprimatur to their imprisonment.

The Supreme Court's majority opinion in the *Korematsu* case[46] was disingenuous. Although it has since become enshrined in constitutional law as the source of controlling doctrine on racial classifications and has never been overruled, the poor quality of its legal reasoning was recognized immediately. Justice Hugo Black wrote that Korematsu, who had had crude plastic surgery in an attempt to pass as Hispanic and stay with his white girlfriend instead of reporting to an internment camp, "was not excluded from the Military Area because of hostility to him or his race." Instead, Black expounds, "he was excluded because we are at war with the Japanese Empire" and because there is "evidence of disloyalty on the part of some." Justice Black notwithstanding, the crux of the matter must have been race. For aside from being of Japanese ancestry, Korematsu was simply another citizen. Apart from his ancestry, he had nothing to do with either the Japanese Empire or other Japanese Americans.

The racial difference becomes apparent from the treatment of German Americans and Italian Americans. If the problem were enemy aliens, there were thousands of German nationals and Italian nationals who had the same status as the Issei. The German American Bund and Italian American fascists were active organizations, holding rallies that attracted thousands, and urging the United States to remain neutral or to support the Axis powers. Although a few hundred German Americans and Italian Americans were investigated and interned, they were a fraction of the total populations of the respective ethnic groups. They also were given individualized hearings. German U-boat patrols menaced the Atlantic shoreline, but German Americans as a whole were too large a population to abuse. They had faced severe prejudice during World War I, but any wholesale suspicions of them had subsided. Nor were Italian Americans persecuted. Baseball star Joe DiMaggio's parents were held up as an example of the people who would be affected if Italian Americans in general were rounded up. President Roosevelt himself joked that Italian Americans were "a bunch of opera singers" and not potential saboteurs and spies. DeWitt said, "You needn't worry about the Italians at all except in certain cases. Also, the same for the Germans except for individual cases. But we must worry about the Japanese all the time until he is wiped off the map."[47]

The weakness of the arguments for the internment also is shown by the treatment of Japanese Americans in Hawaii: They were not interned. If the military necessity argument were well-founded, it would have been most persuasive as to the Japanese Americans in Hawaii—the territory was the home of the Pacific fleet and was within the theater of operations. But the internment of such a substantial portion, over one-third, of the population would have been impractical and would have brought the economy of the islands to a standstill.

Apologists for the internment suggested that Japanese Americans should submit to the internment to prove their allegiance to the United States. They compared the treatment of Japanese Americans to the treatment of American prisoners of war held by Japan. They ignored the fact that Japanese Americans were being held by their own government, not by a hostile government, and once again equated Japanese Americans with Japan. They likened the internment to protective custody, keeping Japanese Americans free from vigilante violence. They ignored the fact that government leaders themselves were at the forefront in agitating against Japanese Americans, and that there were no Japanese Americans requesting such protective custody. They even said that Japanese Americans were being offered special treatment: They would be allowed to wait out the war, with its attendant privations on the home front, under better conditions than other Americans faced. They ignored the ascetic conditions of the camps—single-room accommodations for families; communal latrines; inadequate heat; only as many personal belongings as individuals were able to carry with them—alleviated only by efforts to plant gardens, organize social activities, and create some semblance of ordinary life, on the part of Japanese Americans themselves. Once the military decided that it would allow Japanese Americans to serve as troops in the European theater and interpreters and intelligence officers in the Pacific theater, Japanese American families suffered the same wartime casualties as other families, but in their case compounded by the shame of their own captivity. Inernment defenders discounted the huge financial costs incurred when businesses and homes and property were confiscated or had to be abandoned, not to mention the personal loss of liberty. Yet government officials also must have been uneasy about aspects of the internment camps: Ansel Adams was allowed to shoot an historic series of photographs at the Manzanar site in northern California, but he was not allowed to take any pictures of barbed wire, gun towers, or armed guards. Adams worked in subtle signs of the guard towers, the guards, and the barbed wire: He took photos from atop towers, shot a "Stop—military police" sign, and included the hazy line of barbed wire running in front of a pastoral scene.[48]

The internment itself was disliked only to the extent that Japanese Americans were despised. Wyoming governor Nels Smith told Milton Eisenhower, the original administrator of the camps, that he would refuse to accept Japanese Americans. Transcripts indicate that Governor Smith said, "If you bring the Japanese into my state, I promise you they will be hanging from every tree." Eisenhower, the general's brother, later resigned and predicted that the internment camps would be regretted.[49]

The top officials who ordered the internment, however, were aware that Japanese Americans posed no serious military threat. FBI Director J. Edgar Hoover had already conducted an initial round up of Japanese Americans, German Americans, and Italian Americans whom he believed were especially dangerous; he came to oppose the internment as unnecessary. A naval counterintelligence operation led by Lieutenant Commander Kenneth Ringle had apprehended the only Japanese operatives in California, a group led by Itaru Tachibana, a Japanese naval officer posing as a language student. Writing anonymously, Ringle published an article in *Harper's Magazine*, in which he summed up: "The entire Japanese problem has been magnified all out of its true proportion, largely because of the physical characteristics of the people. It should be handled on the basis of the individual, regardless of citizenship, and not on a racial basis." He did distinguish the "kibei," those Japanese Americans who had been born in the United States and sent to Japan for their childhood education as the "most potentially dangerous element of all."[50] A Chicago businessman named Curtis Munson, working as a freelance operative for the White House, submitted a confidential report to President Roosevelt exactly one month prior to Pearl Harbor. Asking "What will these people do in case of a war between the United States and Japan?," Munson answers that there might be "the odd case of fanatical sabotage by some Japanese 'crackpot,'" but "for the most part the local Japanese are loyal to the United States, or, at worst, hope that by remaining quiet they can avoid concentration camps or irresponsible mobs." He reports, "we do not believe they would be any more disloyal than any other group in the United States with whom we went to war. Those being here are on a spot and they know it."[51]

As University of California at San Diego legal historian Peter Irons documented in *Justice at War: The Story of the Japanese American Internment Cases*,[52] government lawyers had serious reservations about the claims of military necessity as they argued in favor of the internment camps. Based on additional investigations they requested from the FBI and the FCC, the authors of the government briefs had concluded that the claims were dubious and that any military necessity that may have existed had subsided by the time the cases were heard. They wrote an internal memorandum excoriating the report filed by General DeWitt. They had found that Japanese Americans had not, contrary to DeWitt, been "engaged in extensive radio signaling and in shore-to-ship signaling" prior to Pearl Harbor. They wrote, "The general tenor of the [DeWitt] report is not only to the effect that there was a reason to be apprehensive, but also to the effect that overt acts of treason were being committed. Since this is not so, it is highly unfair to this racial minority that these lies, put out in an official publication, go uncorrected."[53] Accordingly, they had drafted the government briefs to avoid relying on what they were convinced were falsehoods, even alerting the justices to the evidentiary problems in the record. However, after the government briefs had been finalized and sent to the printers, their supervisor intervened and had the presses stopped. As a result, the justices issued three major decisions approving the internment, based on erroneous information about everything from Japanese American housing patterns to language education.

Long after the Allied victory and the release of Japanese Americans, some officials continued to insist that the internment had been reasonable. In an interview given on the condition that it be published posthumously, for example, Justice Black told the *New York Times* that the internment was right:

> We had a situation where we were at war. People were rightly fearful of the Japanese in Los Angeles, many loyal to the United States, many undoubtedly not, having dual citizenship—lots of them. They all look alike to a person not a Jap. Had they attacked our shores you'd have a large number fighting with the Japanese troops. And a lot of innocent Japanese Americans would have been shot in the panic. Under these circumstances I saw nothing wrong with moving them away from the danger area.[54]

Twenty-five years after Pearl Harbor, Justice Black still spoke in racial terms. His "people" who were "rightly fearful" are clearly white people (or non-Asian people). He regards Japanese Americans as an indistinguishable mass, with the claim that Asians all look alike. He repeats the canard that Japanese Americans would have joined a Japanese invasion force, and even treats the internment as if it were for the benefit of Japanese Americans.

Chief Justice William Rehnquist later published a book, *All The Laws But One,* contending that the internment was proper at least insofar as the Issei were concerned, because they technically remained foreign nationals. He overlooks the fact that they could not possibly become U.S. citizens due to the racial bar on naturalization.

Eventually, federal courts vacated the convictions of Korematsu, Hirabayashi, and Yasui. Korematsu later received the Medal of Freedom, the nation's highest civilian honor. President Gerald Ford apologized to all Japanese Americans who had been interned. In 1980, Congress impaneled a national commission to study the internment. In its two-volume report, *Personal Justice Denied*, it concluded that the internment was motivated more by racial prejudice than by military necessity. In a point-by-point review of the evidence, the commission concluded, "the record does not permit the conclusion that military necessity warranted the exclusion of ethnic Japanese from the West Coast."[55] In 1988, Congress responded to the report by approving legislation for reparations. Individual internees who were still alive received $20,000 each.

The internment lingers in national memory, and Japanese Americans have continued to be linked with Japan. Emotional responses today produce the same logical errors that were made during wartime. Discussions about the internment trigger rebuttals about Japanese war atrocities. When the Smithsonian Institution opened its internment exhibit, "A More Perfect Union" in 1987, its director received death threats and veterans groups protested. During the debate over reparations, Senator Jesse Helms insisted that the United States should not compensate Japanese Americans until Japan paid the families of those killed at Pearl Harbor. It was a Japanese American Representative, Mike Honda, however, who introduced legislation in 2001 allowing U.S. servicemen to sue Japanese companies for being treated as wartime POW slaves.

Asian Americans in military uniform still face suspicion. During the Vietnam War, Asian American servicemen were pointed out by drill instructors, who told their fellow soldiers, "this is what the enemy looks like."[56] In 1994, after a lengthy legal struggle, Bruce Yamashita finally won his commission in the Marines. The third-generation American from Honolulu had been told by his superior officers at his Quantico base, "We don't want your kind here; go back to your country" and "during World War II, we whipped your Japanese ass." They consistently used racial slurs and called him "Kawasaki," "Yamaha," and "kamikaze." The student body president and football team captain in high school, and a Georgetown Law School graduate, he was dropped out of his officer's training program two days before graduation for his leadership failure (four of the five individuals who were dismissed were people of color). The military eventually offered him an apology, and he was made a captain; the military also initiated a review of possible racial discrimination in its officer training.

Not all Asian Americans were satisfied: A Vietnamese refugee who became a Marine Corps captain, serving in Desert Storm, defended such harassment, pointing out that he had been subjected to the same treatment based on his heritage. He called Yamashita a "disgrace" for protesting, and recalled the gunnery sergeant who had called him "Chong, Fang, Fond, or whatever your [expletive deleted] name is . . . are you a Viet Cong spy?" then "pour[ing] it on" by saying, "That's it. Go ahead and cry. We don't want babies around here."[57] In 1999, explaining his incredulity in a newspaper op-ed, Ted Lieu told the following story: "'Are you in the Chinese Air Force?' the elegantly dressed lady sitting next to me asked." He was dressed in his U.S. Air Force uniform, "complete with captain's bars, military insignia and medals" and attending an awards dinner.[58]

"Wouldn't You Like to Have Someone Out There Named O'Reilly?"

In late 1996 Asian Americans reached a turning point in their political empowerment.[59] We were transformed from invisible to infamous. A parade of Asian faces showed up on the television news and a lengthy list of Asian names appeared in the newspaper headlines, as the "Asian Connection" raised claims of foreign influence arising from their campaign contributions to the Democratic National Committee (DNC). Whatever the merits of allegations about individual wrongdoing or Chinese government intentions, the "Asian Connection" affair incorporated racial stereotyping. The allegations, the investigation, and the treatment of Asian American complaints all raise troubling implications about the acceptance of Asian immigrants as U.S. citizens and their ability to participate as equal stakeholders in shaping public policy. Although some of the individuals implicated in the fiasco were guilty of wrongdoing, all Asian Americans who were active in politics also were unfairly affected by racial stereotyping.

The affair called the "Asian Connection"—given that name by *New York Times* columnist William Safire—introduced the general public to Asian Americans as political actors. The extraordinary attention paid to Asian Americans ended only as independent counsel Kenneth Starr shifted the Whitewater investigation toward the relationship of President Bill Clinton and White House intern Monica Lewinsky. Until then, Asian Americans were at the center of arguments over the corruption of government institutions. The change in perceptions of Asian Americans was as sudden as it was negative.

Before 1996 Asian Americans had been widely regarded as politically "apathetic." Despite their relatively low voter turnout, Asian Americans have always contributed money to political candidates. Well before the fund-raising matter developed, empirical evidence and anecdotal reports suggested that Asian Americans were financially involved in electoral politics. Their generosity, coupled with their growing presence and prominence, made Asian Americans an attractive voting bloc to win over. Both major political parties had begun to pursue Asian Americans as a racial group as early as the 1988 presidential campaign.

The context for the fund-raising scandal involved more than Asian Americans. The disputed donations were minor elements of a larger nationwide trend toward campaign expenditures of incredible proportions. In the 1996 election cycle the Democratic Party raised $123.9 million in soft money and $221.6 million in hard money. The Republican Party raised $138.2 million and $416.5 million, respectively, in the same categories. Each party's soft money expenditures in 1996 were more than 200 percent higher than in the previous election cycle.

This combination—Asian Americans as an emerging voting bloc and the need for soft money—created the circumstances that led to the "Asian Connection." Asian Americans sought not only to follow the rules of the game, which they understood to require giving money, but also to gain credit for their donations through centralized record-keeping. Asian American Democrats believed that after Clinton's reelection they would be recognized with political appointments commensurate with their contributions.

At the center of the allegations was DNC fund-raiser John Huang. But to describe Huang as being the center of the events, as distinct from the allegations, may be misleading. Because the investigations originated from Huang's work and his DNC files, he appeared to be the focal point of any developments. This was especially true because of the administrative protocol that credited Huang with donations even if, in fact, he had nothing to do with them.

After arriving in the United States from Taiwan as a graduate student, Huang pursued a banking career. At one time, he headed the banking operations of the Lippo Group, an Indonesia-based business conglomerate owned by the Riady family, who were ethnic Chinese. Based in Los Angeles, Huang became involved in partisan politics. His objectives appear to have been mixed. They ranged from protecting immigration rights to possibly lobbying the federal government on behalf of Lippo for permission to bypass federal regulations on lending to racial minorities.

Although Huang had donated money to candidates of both political parties, he ultimately secured a mid-level appointment in the U.S. Commerce Department during the first term of the Clinton administration. Before the 1996 election Huang joined the DNC fund-raising staff, filling the newly created position of "vice-chair" of finance. There, he was assigned the task of raising money for the DNC from Asian Americans—or, as political operatives have described it, "dialing for dollars."

As the "Asian Connection" unfolded, Asian Americans were accused of wrongdoing ranging from common but unseemly campaign finance practices to serious conspiracies verging on treason. Many allegations were credible, and some resulted in admissions of guilt. But the allegations also were accompanied by racial stereotyping, as politicians and pundits charged essentially that Asian Americans were by their very nature likely to engage in bribery, or that their behavior implied that all individuals with Asian-sounding surnames should be suspected of illegal conduct. Many statements issued employed overt racial references; a few resulted in public apologies.

The initial assertions concerning improper fund-raising were directed against an Indonesian couple, the Wiriadinatas, business associates of the Riady family, lawful permanent residents of the United States, who gave $450,000 to the DNC. Lawful permanent residents, although technically foreign nationals, are allowed to donate to U.S. political parties under a post-Watergate amendment to the campaign finance statutes. Foreign nationals who are not lawful permanent residents are barred from such donations. The rationale for allowing lawful permanent residents to make donations is that they, as immigrants and taxpayers, are "citizens in waiting" who may (but are not required to) naturalize after five years. This exception to the rule barring donations by foreign nationals was sponsored by Democratic Senator Lloyd Bentsen of Texas, and it passed Congress by wide margins. The potential problem developed because lawful permanent residents are not allowed any more than anyone else to give money on behalf of another individual, operating as a "conduit" or "front."

Accordingly, if the Wiriadinatas had given their own money, their activities would have been well within the applicable law. Similarly large donations from others had met with minimal objections from the press or the public. But if the Wiriadinatas had given money on behalf of the Lippo Group or the Riady family, they would have violated the applicable law, even if they had been naturalized citizens. It would have been improper because they would have acted as a "conduit" or "front." Safire and others suggested such a scenario: The Wiriadinatas had served as a means for the Lippo Group to give money to the DNC that the Lippo Group could not have conveyed directly.

In the fall of 1996, which saw the Clinton-Gore ticket reelected, numerous Asian Americans—most of them Chinese Americans and affiliated with the Democratic Party—were accused of unethical conduct associated with their behind-the-scenes political activities. In addition to Huang, there was Yah Lin "Charlie" Trie, a Little Rock restaurateur who had raised more than a half million dollars for the Whitewater legal defense fund, an unregulated private entity that contributed to those Clinton legal costs not covered by public expenditures. Johnny Chung, a California entrepreneur who had raised hundreds of thousands of dollars for the DNC, was another. He had been given access to the White House for informal tours, on which he was accompanied by Chinese government officials with alleged military agendas. Maria Hsia was a California consultant who organized a visit by Vice President Al Gore to the Hsi Lai Buddhist Temple in suburban Los Angeles, where political donations may have been made on religious property. And then there were Nora and Gene Lum, a Hawaiian couple who had donated money to both political parties and who were business associates of Clinton Commerce Secretary Ron Brown, who was killed in an airplane crash in 1996 while on a diplomatic mission. There were others who were implicated, who were not Chinese American or not Democratic: Pauline Kanchanalak, a Thai businesswoman; Yogesh Ghandi, a distant relative of Mohandas Ghandi; and Jay Kim, the first Korean American elected to Congress, a conservative Republican.

The allegations led to numerous official investigations. The DNC itself initiated a voluntary audit after the 1996 elections, resulting in the return of more than $3 million in donations. The Federal Election Commission also conducted an investigation, and the Justice Department set up a task force that at one point employed 120 attorneys and investigators. Both the Senate and the House held public hearings beginning in summer 1997. Criminal prosecutions were initiated against Tric, Chung, Hsia, and the Lums, resulting in plea bargains from all but Hsia, who was ultimately convicted by a jury.

The most extensive of the responses was the hearings held by the Senate Committee on Governmental Affairs Committee and chaired by Republican Senator Fred Thompson of Tennessee, rumored at the outset of the proceedings to be considering a 2000 presidential campaign. The hearings opened with Thompson's spectacular claims of "hard evidence" of a Chinese scheme to influence the presidential elections. After thirty-three days of hearings, with more than 70 witnesses, over 200 interviews, approximately 200 formal depositions, and some 400 subpoenas issued, the committee came to a much more modest conclusion. The majority report cited the year-end deadline and the need to protect confidential intelligence data as justification for the investigation not procuring enough information to substantiate the initial claims.

Meanwhile, the House Committee on Government Reform Oversight held hearings chaired by Republican Dan Burton of Indiana, but in summer 2000 it postponed the matter indefinitely. The investigations were set back by staff resignations, partisan disagreements, and the chairman's reputation for polemical attacks. While it was in session, the committee issued more than 570 subpoenas, requesting information from a list of individuals with heavy Asian and Asian American representation.

As the scandal simultaneously became racial, a pattern of investigatory techniques and public perception overtook events. Asian Americans were treated as a single group, presumed guilty by association, by members of both political parties and independent candidate Ross Perot, as well as by leading journalists and news organizations, which were then much less likely to point out the problems they had helped to generate.

The DNC and the popular media engaged in similar strategies for their investigations. Using donor lists compiled by the DNC or appended to filings with the Federal Elections Commission, they contacted individuals in racially determined categories or who had Asian-sounding surnames. The DNC audit exemplified the racial stereotyping of the ensuing investigations. According to the DNC memorandum on its "in-depth contribution review," a leading accounting firm and law firm were retained shortly after the elections to survey 1,200 contributions in seven major categories: (1) any contribution from an individual who gave more than $10,000 in any of the years 1994, 1995, or 1996; (2) contributions in 1996 for which the DNC headquarters in Washington, D.C., was listed as the donor's address; (3) contributions solicited by John Huang, where the donor gave more then $2,500 and "was not well known to the DNC"; (4) contributions made in connection with the April 29, 1996, event at the Hsi Lai Buddhist Temple in southern California; (5) contributions made or solicited by Charlie Trie, his wife, or his company; (6) contributions by Johnny Chung or his company; and, most important, (7) "contributions made in connection with any DNC fund-raising event targeting the Asian Pacific American community."[60]

In announcing the audit results, the DNC revealed how its interviewers proceeded. On the script for calls to contributors, question 13 dealt with citizenship status, with follow-up questions about how long a person had been a citizen and whether he or she held a Social Security card. Other questions were: "What is your annual earned income?," "Who is your employer/supervisor?," and "Would you authorize us to obtain a credit report to verify the information you have given us?"

The instructions for the calls to donors were detailed. They advised, for example, that "when possible, the interviewer should be female. Female callers are less threatening and often more successful at getting respondents to cooperate." Interviewers were told to "anticipate that the person answering may not speak English." Fluent Mandarin and Cantonese speakers were employed to conduct interviews, with translation capabilities for other Asian languages available as well.

Interviewers also were told to "avoid revealing the organization or the purpose of the call until the interviewer is talking to the person he/she is seeking" and not to leave telephone messages or their own phone numbers.

But if they had no choice, they were to "obtain the name of the person taking the message and make the message compelling." The suggested message was, "Please call the Democratic National Committee to confirm your contribution." Audit targets were asked to send written confirmation of their phone interviews. Persons who refused to cooperate were threatened: They were informed that their names would be released as individuals suspected of having violated campaign finance laws.

Based on the audit, the Democrats decided to return $1,492,051 in donations (124 contributions) from 77 individuals and corporations. (The DNC had made a series of refunds earlier and would continue with refunds later; the audit produced the largest single set of refunds.) DNC officials confirmed that some of the donations were illegal, but others were deemed inappropriate even if they were permitted by statute.

The Democrats provided a table detailing Huang's accomplishments. He was credited with 424 contributions, of which 88 were refunded. Thus, 336 or approximately 80 percent of the contributions raised by Huang were legitimate and appropriate. Because some contributors donated more than once, and in differing quantities, the 88 contributions raised by Huang and returned accounted for 21.8 percent of the contributions, or 54.8 percent of the dollars returned and 47.4 percent of all dollars raised by Huang. All of the money associated with Trie and Chung also was returned. Eighteen of forty-six contributions "connected" with the Hsi Lai Buddhist Temple event were returned as well. The DNC emphasized that all the contributions returned represented one-one-thousandth of a percent of the total number of contributions, or slightly more than 1 percent of the total dollars received by the DNC between 1994 and 1996.

The DNC later performed an additional audit of Asian American supporters who had given less than $5,000. At the February 28, 1997, press conference at DNC headquarters announcing the results of the initial audit, the DNC's outside legal counsel stated that another audit either had been conducted or would be undertaken. He said, "In addition, you ought to be aware that there are a number of contributions solicited by Mr. John Huang, each under $2,500 in amount, which still have to be reviewed by the DNC. These amount to 171 contributions, and they total $104,000. The results of this review, I am advised, will be made publicly available to you as well." Thus the average donation in the later audit was about $608.

Notwithstanding the wording of category 7 and other indications that the audit was focused on Asian Americans, some might argue that the later audit was appropriate because it was nominally directed at solicitations made by

Huang. This argument is belied by the DNC's own accounting practices. It is conceivable that non-Asian Americans contributed through events "targeting" the Asian American community, but the DNC identified no such individuals.

As the DNC's outside legal counsel himself conceded, "The more I got into this, the more I looked at the documents at the committee, it's clear that some or all of the attribution of contributors to a specific individual such as Mr. Huang or Mr. Trie or staff of the DNC is sometimes exaggerated and inaccurate. And so there is no precise mathematical way of saying that in the case of any return contributor that this was precisely something solicited by Mr. Huang." The DNC's general counsel made the same admission. He said, "I think, as [outside legal counsel], and particularly when it comes to DNC staff who have solicited contributions, a lot of the attribution is bookkeeping and is not an accurate indication of who solicited the contribution."[61]

Even though the later audit ostensibly was limited to donations "solicited" by Huang, it affected a much larger category of donors. These donors were attributed to Huang by the DNC, even though they may not have had any relationship with him. Most strikingly, for Asian Americans all contributions (above and below the initial $2,500 threshold) were included in the audit; for others, only contributions over $10,000. At an average donation level of $608, Asian Americans were audited even though they gave far less than the $10,000 minimum that triggered suspicion of others.

It is reasonable to conclude, then, that the DNC applied different standards to Asian American and non-Asian American supporters. Whereas Asian American donors were audited because of the identity ascribed to them through the crediting to Huang, other donors were audited because of their individual conduct and only if they had contributed large sums. Ironically, the DNC audit was conducted by the beneficiary of the "Asian Connection" and directed at its own supporters. The majority of the individuals who were targeted in an invasive manner turned out to have been exercising their constitutional rights. The DNC, including its co-chairs Roy Romer and Steve Grossman, later apologized for insensitivity in conducting the audit. They personally visited Asian American political leaders throughout the country in an effort to renew these leaders' ties with the party.

Similarly, the public discourse on the fund-raising controversy included repeated allusions to the race, ethnicity, and national origin of the individuals implicated. The very definition of the scandal as the "Asian Connection" highlighted its racial element. Much of the description of the matter consisted of expressly racial language, along with racial images. Just as problematic as the derogatory content of the statements was their general nature, encompassing more than the specific persons who were involved in the controversy and extending to all people of Asian descent.

Reform Party presidential candidate Ross Perot, for example, gave two major speeches on the "Asian Connection." The speeches were so well received that some observers speculated they might have an effect on the electoral college results. In one speech, delivered at the University of Pennsylvania the week before election day, Perot stated, "Now then, Mr. Huang is still out there hard at work for the Democrats. Wouldn't you like to have someone out there named O'Reilly? Out there hard at work. You know, so far we haven't found an American name." Later, after individuals named Middleton and Wood (who were white) were implicated, Perot stated that those were "surnames to which Americans can relate," adding rhetorically, "I wonder if anyone in this country's giving money?"

During the later investigations, Senator Sam Brownback joked using broken English "no raise money, no get bonus," to explain Huang's conduct. The singsong is an allusion to the stereotype of Chinese laundrymen, who used to be characterized as chiding customers "no tickee, no washee." Brownback later apologized. White House spokesperson Michael McCurry joked "two Huangs don't make a right." The pun is an allusion to the joke about miscegenation: "A Chinaman is told by his doctor that his wife has cheated on him, when she gives birth to a Caucasian baby. The doctor tells him: two Wongs don't make a white."

Other government officials made remarks such as, "in my opinion, Mr. [Charlie] Trie's activities are classic activities on the part of an Asian who comes out of that culture and who embarks on an activity related to intelligence gathering"; "Illegal donations are apparently only the tip of the eggroll"; and "if you have a friend by the name of Arief and Soraya, and I cannot even pronounce the last name, Wiriadinata or something like that, who donated . . . and was friends with a guy named Johnny Huang . . . then there's a high probability that it's money from foreign nationals, . . . I could go on with John Lee and Cheon Am, Yogesh Ghandi, Ng Lap Seng, Supreme Master Suma China Hai, and George Psaltis."[62]

The media engaged in the same tactics as the government, calling numerous donors with Asian surnames and demanding to know about their citizenship, occupation, income, and other personal facts, on the assumption that any donor with an Asian surname was linked to the scandal. The editor of the right-wing *American Spectator* referred to the matter as "the Chop Suey connection." The conservative *National Review* published a cover story "The

Manchurian Candidates," with an illustration of President Clinton, First Lady Hillary Clinton, and Vice President Al Gore caricatured as Asians, including buck teeth and slant eyes, in stereotypical Chinese garments. The inclusion of Jay Kim, a Republican, in stories about John Huang, a Democrat, when the two had nothing to do with one another and were involved in scandals that were unrelated, only underscores the racial perceptions that linked them. All they had in common was their race. Doing stories about both of them (but not others) would be no different than doing stories about two individuals accused of crime who were both African American or both Jewish, but otherwise different, implying that their race explained their behavior. Indeed, there was hardly any mention of Thomas Kramer, a foreign national who was not Asian, who was fined $323,000 for making improper contributions through conduits; or Empire Sanitary Landfill, a Pennsylvania company not owned by Asian Americans or Asians, that was fined $8 million for its donations.

Worse than the casual and repeated references to race were the indifferent responses to Asian American protests. In October 1996 in Washington, D.C., Los Angeles, and Chicago, Asian Americans affiliated with both political parties participated in a coordinated series of press conferences criticizing the portrayal of Asian Americans as a racial group. In September 1997 a coalition of more than a dozen Asian American community organizations filed a complaint with the U.S. Civil Rights Commission, requesting that it consider the racial aspects of the ongoing investigations and media coverage.

Between those two events, on March 20, 1997, Senator Daniel Akaka, a Hawaiian Democrat of Asian heritage and a member of the Senate panel investigating the matter, delivered a lengthy floor speech. Akaka recounted at length the history of Asian Americans and he noted their contemporary accomplishments. His central themes were paired: "I think I speak for the entire Asian American community in expressing the hope that we can get to the bottom of this whole controversy, wherever the cards may fall." But "let us avoid focusing on such irrelevancies as the ethnicity of the participants in the affair [and] let us cease characterizing individuals by meretricious stereotypes; conversely, let us avoid judging an entire community by the actions of a few individuals." Akaka added that "those responsible for violations of laws or improper conduct should be identified and appropriately dealt with by the relevant authorities." And he implored, "let us keep our attention on matters of substance—the laws that were possibly broken, the processes and procedures that were bent, the individuals who circumvented or corrupted the system, and most of all what we can do to prevent abuses in the future."[63]

On all three occasions, and in written materials the activists prepared, Asian American political leaders took pains to point out that they supported appropriate investigation and that they had asked for Asian Americans to be held accountable under the same standard as any other individuals. They further agreed that it was possible and even plausible that Huang and others were guilty, but they argued that the majority of persons of Asian heritage were innocent of corruption.

Yet because Asian Americans raised these objections, their concerns were dismissed as "playing the race card." Despite their insistence on universal standards and their willingness to entertain credible claims against Asian Americans as individuals, they were charged with presenting self-interested and partisan defenses or offering some sort of special pleading. For example, Senator Akaka's office immediately received a series of faxes, e-mails, and phone calls admonishing him for "playing the race card."

In an editorial on the Whitewater investigation, the *Washington Post* wrote about the "Asian :" "The president suggested one day that some of the questioning verged on Asian-bashing. . . . But what a disingenuous defense that is." The *Post* later devoted an entire editorial to refuting an "Asian-bashing defense" that it imputed to defenders of Huang, who, at least among Asian Americans speaking publicly, were nonexistent.[64] Critics failed to realize that there could be two scandals playing themselves out simultaneously, one involving alleged transgressions by individuals and the other involving racial stereotyping of a minority group.

Yet Asian Americans do have a connection to Asia, through the dynamics of immigration. Influenced by both foreign policy and domestic politics, immigration is a complex issue. Immediately before the 1996 elections Asian Americans' political activities were heavily devoted to immigration issues. In the DNC memo setting a $7 million fund-raising goal for donations from Asian Americans, immigration led the list of issues important to Asian Americans. History, the factual circumstances surrounding immigration today, and the political possibilities explain this emphasis.

Asian Americans were especially interested in persuading the Clinton administration to support the fourth preference family-based visa category. It allows sponsors to bring over their brothers and sisters and is both heavily used by Asian families and under attack as a means of facilitating "chain migration" of extended families. Working in coalitions with Latino groups, Jewish groups, and immigrant groups, Asian Americans also were joined by agricultural and business lobbies interested in the ability to hire foreign workers; antigovernment groups concerned about the proposals for a national identification system; and the Christian Coalition, which supported family-based immigration policies. The Clinton administration eventually endorsed a "split the bill" strategy. It argued that illegal and legal immigration should be split and considered in separate pieces of legislation. That procedural maneuver, common in Congress, ensured that the fourth preference would be saved temporarily.

Although "illegal immigrants" were most often stereotyped as Latino and specifically Chicano, Asian immigrants in some areas were regarded as "illegal immigrants" trying to sneak in and gain access to welfare benefits. On the east coast, the crash of the ship Golden Venture, with its cargo of smuggled human beings, in 1993 near New York City was a contributing spark in the debate over immigration. In California, Minnesota, and Wisconsin, where there were large local settlements of Southeast Asian refugees, longtime residents quickly blamed them for being a burden on municipal budgets. While running for governor of Massachusetts in 1990, Boston University President John Silber asked, "why should Lowell [Massachusetts] be the Cambodian capital of America?" and suggested "there has got to be a welfare magnet going on here." (Studies showed that in Lowell, as elsewhere, most welfare recipients are white.)[65] Although some Asian immigrants tried to separate themselves from Latino immigrants, the proposals against immigration, if passed, would have affected them equally.

After their legislative defeat, the sponsors of bills that would have cut back legal immigration, Representative Lamar Smith and Senator Alan Simpson, hypothesized that national interests in reducing immigration had been sacrificed because of foreign influence. They identified a fund-raiser organized by John Huang as the crux of the shift. In two articles the *Boston Globe* reported that Smith and Simpson "said they believe Clinton's fundraising prompted the policy reversal. . . . Smith said he believes Clinton switched course 'because he was more interested in political contributions. It now fits the pattern.'" Simpson was quoted as agreeing, and adding, "I never in my 18 years in Congress saw an issue that shifted so fast and so hard."[66]

Immediately after the *Boston Globe* stories appeared, the Federation for American Immigration Reform (FAIR) issued a press statement demanding that the fourth preference be revisited. Its director, Dan Stein, stated, "It is clear to everybody that the White House caved in to special interest pressure on the immigration bill. . . . Beyond serving the narrow interests of people who want to import relatives they chose to leave behind, there is no public policy justification for the fourth preference category."[67]

Representative Smith's and Senator Simpson's assertions that foreigners should not influence immigration policies perhaps should be conceded. It is an odd assertion, however, given the history of immigration control and the global nature of the phenomenon. Before the U.S. Congress adopted the Chinese Exclusion Act, the executive branch negotiated directly with the Chinese government on the subject and entered into the Burlingame Treaty. Now the White House is conducting bilateral talks with the Mexican government about all aspects of labor migration, including possibly reinstating a guest worker program that would allow Mexican migrant workers to come north on a legal basis.

Nevertheless, even if Asians are excluded from any role in discussions about immigration, Asian Americans can and should have a part to play. Like much of the discourse surrounding the "Asian Connection," the remarks by Smith and Simpson are ambiguous, appearing to cover not only Asians but also Asian Americans. The *Boston Globe* reporting in particular was based on DNC memos discussing Asian American political interests in immigration levels; those memos mention nowhere Asian interests, either on the part of individual foreigners or the Chinese government. Furthermore, the newspapers juxtaposed Smith's and Simpson's comments with an analysis that consistently referred to Asian Americans trying to influence immigration policies. The inaccurate reporting in the popular media has been accepted as the standard account of the legislative consideration of the fourth preference.

But even if Simpson's and Smith's speculations were assumed to be true, their argument suffers. If the fund-raising by Huang caused the Clinton administration to alter its policies, that may well be distressing—but because of the influence of money, not the influence of Asian Americans. To dismiss Asian American efforts to seek increased immigration (or merely to maintain current levels) would be to disenfranchise individuals selectively because of their racial background. To impugn Asian American participation in the immigration debate, but to condone anti-Asian sentiments to influence the same process, would be even worse. Latinos encountered the same resistance to their efforts to affect immigration policy: Marchers in Los Angeles who carried the Mexican flag to oppose California Proposition 187, an anti-immigrant ballot initiative passed in 1994, were blamed for the success of the measure.

American Jews face similar accusations of "dual loyalty," but they have not been deterred from lobbying activities related to the Middle East. Many American Jews, like the United States itself, have been active in not only promoting support for Israel but also advancing the peace process. Many African Americans have long been concerned about the fate of Africans and Africa.

Randall Robinson, the founder of Transafrica, was a key player in putting pressure on U.S. companies and the U.S. government to cease its support for the apartheid regime in South Africa. Many Cuban Americans in Miami have been among the most active participants in the politics of U.S.-Cuban relationships. In each of these instances, the American citizens who take an interest in "homeland politics" can aid understanding in both directions. It is likely that, simply due to their experience of having lived within the democracy of the United States, they will bring to bear the influence of the culture of the United States. It is possible that some individuals who care about "homeland politics" are driven by ulterior motives, ranging from racial sympathies to self-interest. In that respect, however, they are no different than anyone else: businesspeople, whether white Americans or Asian Americans, who seek to make a profit by opening the China market, exporting to Japan, normalizing relations with Vietnam, and so forth, are susceptible to the same charges of valuing their own gains over patriotic priorities.[68]

Even Asian Americans with impeccable conservative credentials are not immune from political attacks that are injected with racial elements. When Matt Fong, an Air Force academy graduate and former officer, received the 1998 Republican nomination to be U.S. Senator from California, journalists for a major magazine asked him, if war came with China, which side would he fight on.[69] Elaine Chao, who served in the administrations of both the elder and junior Bush presidents, was accused of being at the center of a conspiracy, "the buying of [her husband, Senator] Mitch McConnell and the Heritage Foundation by the People's Republic of China."[70] Wendy Gramm, the Korean American wife of Senator Phil Gramm, was the subject of campaign flyers that urged voters to avoid Gramm when he ran for president in 1996 because, as the anonymous propaganda said, he had divorced his white wife to marry an Asiatic.[71]

Otherwise, if Asian Americans cannot affect immigration policies, we remain in a vicious circle. Immigration policies, with their racial effects, prompt Asian Americans to organize as a group, which in turn leads others to treat Asian Americans negatively as an organized group. Among the adverse consequences are restrictive immigration policies, with additional racial effects, which only give Asian Americans even greater impetus to behave as a group. The fears of Asian invasion through Asian immigration are not new.

Back to the Future

Futurists forecast that the twenty-first century will be the Pacific Century. Despite the punning title ("pacific" also means peaceful), some racial doomsayers dread the apocalyptic prospect of an America that faces Asia rather than Europe. They have revived the paranoia about an Asian horde that will over-whelm the white people of the world. The role of Asian Americans in such a scheme is ambiguous, but we seem to be the literal embodiment of the simultaneous decline of the West and the rise of the East. Neither trend is welcome. Asian Americans are the first group that seems to jeopardize the dominance of white Americans, so that the racial segregation of "separate but equal" ceases to be beneficial to the majority.

Camp versions of the Asian take-over theme can be found in pulp fiction and comic book characters such as Sax Rohmer's Fu Manchu. Science fic-tion novelist Robert Heinlein, who became famous when the countercul-ture took to his neologism "grok" (Martian for an holistic understanding) from his 1961 Hugo-winner *Stranger in a Strange Land* , wrote about Asian American traitors in one of his earliest works, a World War II-era novella entitled *The Sixth Column*. Updated variations are still a staple of science fic-tion. Cyberpunk author William Gibson, who predicted the advent of the Internet (the "cyberpunk" moniker refers to his coining of the term "cyber-space" and the punk sensibilities of his work), also reinvented the ascendan-cy of Asia. He was not averse to it, but depicted it as inevitable. In his 1984 debut novel, *Count Zero*, the first book to ever win the Hugo, the Nebula, and the Philip K. Dick awards, and in his 1986 bestseller *Neuromancer*, he anticipated that Asian corporate conglomerates and yakuzu criminal syndi-cates would rule the economy and thus the culture. In his short story "John-ny Mnemonic" (later made into a movie starring Keanu Reeves), a courier rents space in his memory, and Shanghai is one of the new post-industrial economic capitals.

In numerous other cinematic versions, the Asianization of the universe has won large audiences. The cult classic film *Bladerunner*, directed by Ridley Scott, uses sleek cinematography to show a terrestrial dystopia where Asian culture has taken over a perpetually raining Los Angeles. Everyone who has the means to do so has escaped "off-world." The colonization of off world is advertised with the jingoistic slogan, "So come on America, let's put our team up there. This announcement is brought to you by the Shimato-Dominguez Corporation—helping America into the New World." Played by Harrison Ford, Deckard is a "bladerunner" who hunts down fugitive "replicants" to "retire" them. Trained in detecting them using the Voight-Kampff machine, he does not realize that he is an android like them with an implanted iden-tity. The argot spoken by street denizens is a composite lingua franca, but when it is first heard on-screen it can be briefly recognized as derived from a language Deckard never mentions in his list of its sources, namely Korean. The major Asian character, Chew, is a biotechnology engineer; he makes eyes.

One of the screenwriters of *Bladerunner* later wrote the script for *Soldier*, a movie that was not well-received because of its amoral violence; the lead characters are virtually mute, except for replying, "Yes, sir" and "No, sir" as they shoot their way through the plot. Kurt Russell is the title superfighter, raised from childhood as a mercenary to be sent into battle and expended if need be. He is superseded by an improved Asian model, genetically engineered to be smarter, faster, stronger, and with greater endurance. The two fight, and the Asian combatant promptly dispatches three lesser foes in a ritualized orgy of carnage; the victor suffers only the loss of an eye, which has been gouged out. Presumed dead, Russell is dropped onto a planet that serves as a giant garbage dump. Later, his Asian successor—who is no more than an obedient lackey for the martinet who is in charge—leads a crew that lands on the same planet for a training exercise in which they are to destroy any life residing there. In the final showdown, Russell is able to command a forgotten community of almost all white space settlers in vanquishing the Asian enemy who has encroached on their home.

The symbol of a bleak future for white America is the Asian boss. In the popular *Back to the Future* movie trilogy, Michael J. Fox travels through time to a world in which he must kowtow to an Asian supervisor who appears on his home television-phone to give him orders. In the blockbuster *Alien* cinematic quartet, Sigourney Weaver fights the salivating head-within-a-head monster designed by H. R. Giger as well as the Company, which wishes to capture it to reproduce for sale as a biological product to be added to weapons arsenals. The Company has a stereotypically Jewish middle manager played by Paul Reiser, who betrays the Marines in the second installment, but it is revealed to be a greedy Asian firm that uses a Caucasian android as its front man in the third installment.

The anxieties about Asian conquest of the planet are not limited to the pages of fiction and movie screens. Like the multitudinous adversaries of the prototypical video game, Asian Americans are "space invaders" in reality. The story was played out in Monterey Park, California, a middle-class bedroom community outside of Los Angeles. During the 1980s, it became a suburban Chinatown. White residents gossiped that an elderly Asian gentleman was riding his bicycle through the streets, stopping to visit white homeowners, and offering to pay cash, in full and on the spot, to buy their properties. The elderly Asian gentleman appears to be apocryphal. But the white residents put up homemade posters in their windows expressing their racial resignation. Their signs read, "Will the last American left please turn out all the lights?"

Writers and academics have lent credence to the speculations. They give it a certain respectability. A prime example comes from the pen of Renaissance man Gore Vidal. In 1986, toward the end of the Cold War, he wrote a set of essays for the *Nation* magazine that have since become ill-famed because he was accused of anti-Semitism. Although Vidal attracted enough attention that *National Review* editor William F. Buckley Jr. was prompted to edit an anthology asking whether he and others were culpable of blood libel, the anti-Asian facets of his pieces were ignored.[72]

In the first essay, Vidal announces that the American Empire is coming to its degenerate end. He pleads for "the alliance of the two great powers of the Northern Hemisphere" which would be necessary "to survive, economically, in a highly centralized Asiatic world."[73] Vidal writes that, "Now the long-feared Asiatic colossus takes its turn as world leader, and we—the white race—have become the yellow man's burden. Let us hope that he will treat us more kindly than we treated him."[74]

In a follow-up essay, entitled "The Empire Lovers Strike Back," Vidal elaborated in an aside. He is mainly occupied with chastising the husband and wife team of Norman Podhoretz and Midge Decter. Vidal takes them to task because they urge military support for Israel. Vidal says that Podhoretz's "first loyalty would always be to Israel," although "he and Midge stay on among us, in order to make propaganda and raise money for Israel—a country they don't seem eager to live in."[75] Vidal also postulates:

> For America to survive economically in the coming Sino-Japanese world, an alliance with the Soviet Union is necessary. After all, the white race is a minority race with many well-deserved enemies, and if the two great powers of the Northern Hemisphere don't band together, we are going to end up as farmers —or, worse, mere entertainment—for the more than one billion grimly efficient Asiatics.[76]

Although he cultivated controversy with respect to American Jews, Vidal later chided critics for not recognizing that his mention of Asians was comic. A fair reading of the pair of essays, however, shows them to be perhaps hyperbolic and pedantically witty, but with nothing in them to suggest that Vidal meant to induce laugher with such lines as "if the foreseeable future is not nuclear, it will be Asiatic," "now the sun has set in our West and risen once more in the East," and "the Sino-Japanese axis . . . will dominate the future just as Japan dominates world trade today."[77]

Vidal appends a footnote to the version of the early essay collected for posterity in his massive *Essential Gore Vidal* reader, exclaiming that his "plain observation was interpreted as a racist invocation of 'the Yellow Peril'!" His gripe is curious, for it is he who explicitly refers to his themes in the terms of "the white race" and "the yellow man"; his critics have only quoted his words verbatim and in context. Vidal was not only wrong about Japan maintaining its position in world trade, as its "bubble economy" burst shortly after he wrote, but his racially defined nationalistic competition cannot help but give Asian Americans the same untrustworthy role that he assigns to American Jews.

After the Cold War, Harvard professor Samuel Huntington published an article entitled "The Clash of Civilizations?"[78] that prophesies an ultimate war among Westerners, Muslims, and Chinese. The distinguished defense analyst expanded his ideas into a book that offered a straightforward argument about immigration. Vidal may have been joking, but Huntington is serious. He presents immigration as an "invasion" and a "problem" that may wreck Western values.

Vidal and Huntington are erudite, but not original. Madison Grant and Lothrop Stoddard had expressed the same apprehensions in their bestsellers, *The Passing of a Great Race* and *The Rising Tide of Color.*[79] In both, the two now-forgotten social Darwinists posited an imminent racial conflict arraying black, brown, and yellow against the superior white. More extreme than Oswald Spengler, the historian who devised the idea of the decline of the West, Grant and Stoddard were especially worried about "race suicide" by the internal weakening of the stock of the Nordic or the Anglo-Saxon.

As chair of the New York Zoological Society, Grant argued on a biological basis for global segregation of barbaric from civilized races. With his interest in museums and environmentalism—he formed a society to save the redwood forests—Grant represented the blend of privilege and prejudice, with culture and science, that shaped public policy.

Although he had a moneyed pedigree that dated back to the colonial age, Grant was a self-proclaimed democrat. He averred that wealthy classes had introduced both black slaves and Asian immigrants, to the detriment of common people. But like others who have borrowed haphazardly from Marx, he did not indict the wealthy for seeking their own advantage, instead expressing hostility toward the people who were exploited. "If there had been an aristocratic form of governmental control in California," he said, "Chinese coolies and Japanese laborers would now form the controlling element, so far as numbers are concerned, on the Pacific coast."[80] In other words, it was the Asian workers who were the enemy.

A magazine editor and radio broadcaster who authored more than a dozen books, including a history of children, Stoddard was a disciple of Grant's. Several of his works advocated nativism and eugenics. Before World War II, he reported from Germany as an enthusiast of Hitler's regime. He posited an "iron law of inequality." Stoddard stated that the "obviously dangerous Oriental" was someone "against whose standards of living the white man cannot compete."[81] He viewed "the brown and yellow worlds of Asia" as "the effective centres of colored unrest." He worried that Asians would endanger whites because they had their own "admirable cultures rooted in remote antiquity and worthy of all respect" but they also "are to-day once more displaying their innate capacity by not merely adopting, but adapting, white ideas and methods." He disclaimed any "disparagement of the Asiatic."[82] Stoddard argued that both Asians and whites were justified in winning opportunities in new lands, but "the hard facts are that there is not enough for both" and the Asian "automatically crushes the white man out."[83]

Grant and Stoddard were influential before their ideas of white superiority were repudiated in the aftershock of the horrors of Nazi death camps. Their ideas should not be brought back, as if they can be rehabilitated without the taint of blatant racism. Grant and Stoddard are even memorialized in the American literary canon. Stoddard is fictionalized as "Goddard" in F. Scott Fitzgerald's *Great Gatsby*, an excerpt from which is given as the epigraph to this chapter.[84] The charming Jay Gatsby of the eponymous tale is fabulously wealthy, throwing the best parties in New York City. He courts Daisy, the woman who once spurned him. Daisy's husband Tom Buchanan, a dull bully, declares that he has been reading books of tremendous magnitude, those of Goddard/Stoddard. He is incapable of seeing that the tranquillity of his life is jeopardized by Gatsby and not "those other races" whom he fears so much. All of them, except the narrator Nick Carraway, are finally done in by their own privileged status.

Yet there are Chinese and other Asians who speak of Chinese Americans as "Chinese overseas" who may return to lead the Chinese mainland and so forth. They are only likely to be taken by Vidal and Huntington as proof positive of the conspiracies of which they speak. For example, in a monumental reference work, *The Encyclopedia of the Chinese Overseas*,[85] editor Lynn Pan assembled a collection of essays not likely to be rivaled. She considers Chinese overseas, everywhere throughout Asia to Africa, Europe, and North America. She presents a diagram representing the varieties of Chinese, in which the center consists of China, surrounded by a ring representing aspiring migrants, students, Taiwan, and Hong Kong, in turn placed inside a larger concentric circle of overseas Chinese, all within the broadest circle of the assimilated Chinese (although even that outermost portion is represented as belonging to the diagram).[86] It would be wrong to chastise Pan for being Sinocentric. After all, China and the Chinese are the subject of the study. But her depiction of the Chinese is chauvinistic, as in accounts of relationships between overseas Chinese and "non-Chinese," or in the dismissive treatment of intermarriage. Chinese American activists are taken to task for an "entirely positive view of the ideals of North American culture," a "seemingly alienated stance in relation to Chinese culture."[87] The grandiose visions of a "Greater China" are likely to be alarming, and understandably so, to people who are outside its aegis.

Toward Transnationalism

In an essay calling for cosmopolitanism, published with responses as *For Love of Country: Debating the Limits of Patriotism*,[88] University of Chicago philosophy professor Martha Nussbaum asks a provocative question: "Why should we think of people from China as fellows the minute they dwell in a certain place, namely the United States, but not when they dwell in a certain other place, namely China?"[89] Nussbaum means the question rhetorically, because she believes we should extend the sense of fellowship beyond the borders. But others could regard it rhetorically in a contrary sense, to suggest that we not accept as fellows even those "people from China" who do dwell in the United States. In any event, the actual answer is that we—many of us anyway—do not think of people from China as anything other than "people from China" and do not accept them as hail fellows well met. Nussbaum envisions a world in which "people from China" are fellows wherever they happen to be, following the lead of Diogenes the Cynic, who declared himself to be "a citizen of the world."[90]

The world may not be ready for cosmopolitanism, but it is already becoming transnational. Well before the technological boost of the Internet, ideas migrated freely and could not be contained. Civil disobedience was a peculiarly American idea as proposed by Henry David Thoreau to protest the Mexican War and carried out by him alone in his prison cell to the embarrassment of family and friends. It became a mass movement only once adopted by Mohandas Ghandi as he became the Mahatma, responding to the Amritzar massacre and conducting his Calcutta fast, throwing off British rule and gaining independence for hundreds of millions. It returned to the United States and was modified into nonviolent resistance, taken up by a young Martin Luther King Jr. as he became involved in the Montgomery bus boycott, with interpretive assistance from a reclusive white librarian in the city, Juliette Morgan, who wrote letters to the local newspaper comparing Ghandi and King and predicting, "history is being made." The Chinese students butchered on Tiananmen Square raised a facsimile of the Statute of Liberty, holding its torch high. The protest of Japanese war crimes, ranging from the Rape of Nanking to the use of "comfort women" for forced sex with soldiers, has been given sustenance and its greatest successes due to American involvement and leadership.

Yet the relationship of white Americans to Europe is treated differently than the relationship of Asian Americans to Asia. The existence of Europeans does not undermine the claim of the descendants of European immigrants to be Americans, but the very existence of Asians by some means imperils the claim of the descendants of Asian immigrants to be Americans. Nor do the campaigns on the part of some European governments—in Ireland and in the new market economies—to encourage white Americans with ancestral ties to return there weaken the patriotism of the other white Americans whom they are abandoning. Former Chrysler chairman Lee Iacocca, a businessman-celebrity who was proud of his Italian ancestry, was never called upon to apologize for the fascism of Benito Mussolini or the failing of Fiat. He toyed with naming a Masarati-designed luxury model after himself as "the Lido."

Historically, Chinese immigrants and Irish immigrants arrived at about the same time and competed against one another in the same endeavors and geographic areas. But Chinese Americans have not been accepted in the same manner as Irish Americans. By way of explanation that glosses over race, Asian Americans have been told that we are treated like perpetual foreigners because so many of us are sojourners.[91] The claim treats Asian Americans as a monolithic bloc, under the assumption that what is true of some most be true of all. In addition, the claim is not true. The tendency of young men to journey here seeking adventure or trying to make a fortune was the same across racial lines, but the treatment of the travelers was different. Historical figures for Asian return migration are scarce. University of California at Berkeley professor Ronald Takaki, the leading historian of Asian Americans, cites a figure of 55 percent for Japanese immigrants between 1886 and 1924 as typical.[92] The only comprehensive study of the same phenomenon among

European immigrants provides government figures ranging from a high of 89 percent for Bulgarians, Serbians, and Montenegrins to figures above the 55 percent of Japanese immigrants for southern Italians, Magyars, Romanians, and Slovaks, during the overlapping time period 1908 to 1923.[93] It provides further estimates such as the British government's combined rate of 55 percent remigration for the English and Welsh and independent estimates such as 48 percent for the French and 46 percent for Scots. Nobody supposes that these high rates of emigration render people of Bulgarian descent who have stayed here any less loyal. If there were any disparity between the departure rates for Asian and European immigrants, it would hardly be surprising given that the former were prohibited from naturalizing while the latter could attain citizenship.

The emigration of white Americans is not taken as a sign of perfidy. British Prime Minister Winston Churchill had a mother who was a white American, but nobody would cast aspersions on all white Americans because his mother happened to move to England. White Americans living abroad are fashionable. Ernest Hemingway, Gertude Stein, and the "lost generation" of 1920s Paris were living it up and creating art on an extended grand tour of the Continent. Ireland today even recruits Irish Americans to return there. But whites who move to Asia permanently are eccentric. J. B. S. Haldane, the famous biologist, was born a British subject and became an Indian citizen in 1960; he died at home in Calcutta just four years later. He is singular in his reversal of the flow of migration.

Patriotism may be the last refuge of the scoundrel, but nationalism is the first refuge of the liberal. Liberals who oppose immigration are especially appalling because of their hypocrisy. They argue that every country has a right, if it is to be sovereign, to protect its borders. But they assume that establishing the right forecloses discussion on exercising the right, as if it follows from the right itself that it must be used restrictively. At least Brimelow and his ilk are forthrightly racial in their advocacy. They have the virtue of consistency, if nothing else, to recommend their opinions. They are principled, even if they are wrong. Liberals aren't aware of the sense of possessiveness that pervades the discussion; Brimelow asserts it shamelessly. The claim is often put as a rhetorical question: "You can't be asking Americans to give up the feeling that we're at home in our own country, can you?" The rhetorical question begs the real question: "Who are the 'Americans' who own the country?"

For some liberals, their most fervently held progressive ideals seem to stop at the border. They would be disgusted if a well-to-do and predominantly white suburb located next to an impoverished minority neighborhood decided to close its parks to outsiders, or if a state declared that it would eliminate welfare benefits for anybody who had moved there from another part of the country. Yet many of them turn out to be indifferent toward plans to build a wall along the southern border and some are even enthusiastic about harsh legal procedures intended to deter immigrants. Although in the former cases these liberals may ask whether racial motivations were at work, in the latter cases they scoff at the possibility. They would reject an argument based on states' rights, but they accept its exact analogue based on national sovereignty.

The proposals to restrict migration at the local, national and international levels are the same, albeit on different scales, as University of Toronto political philosopher Joseph Carens argued in his "case for open borders."[94] In symbolic terms, they all reinforce the boundaries between the inside and the outside. In practical terms, they also are related because immigration correlates to internal migration. Non-white immigrants are flocking to a handful of states and cities. White residents are fleeing those places, following the same pattern as the "white flight" that occurred in Northern cities as Southern blacks moved in. California and New York City are only the most prominent examples of the phenomenon, which is creating regional disparities within our increasing diversity.

Other than the strictly utilitarian, virtually all arguments about immigration are arguments over race. In its most basic sense, the leading popular and philosophical justification for immigration control is racial. It is racial, however, not in the straightforward sense that some people continue to believe that only ethnic Germans can be true Germans or ethnic Japanese true Japanese, and so forth. It is racial, rather, in the more tortuous sense that all the justifications for immigration control ultimately are based on racial conceptions of membership in the community. Glenn Spencer, an organizer of the "Save Our State" campaign to support California's Proposition 187, attacks only Latino immigration, which he portrays as a reconquest of the lost territories of Aztlan. He and his supporters speak of wishing for a state like the one they remember growing up in. They describe immigrants, even legal immigrants, as remaining loyal to Mexico City.[95] Other leaders such as Barbara Coe, who also worked on the Proposition 187 campaign, describe immigrants, focusing on Latinos but without distinction between legal and illegal, as criminals, bandits, savages, and worse. There are vigilante groups that have started to patrol the Southern border, armed, stopping Latino-looking persons and asking them to prove their right to be in the country. (One of the few forms of pure xenophobia, unadulterated by racial concerns, is hostility of African Americans toward black immigrants. It is all the more regrettable, not commendable, that among people of color distinctions would be made based on the arbitrary categories of citizens and aliens with as much force as they are made based on race in other contexts.)

Determining who must justify immigration policies—the would-be restrictionists who occupy the land or the would-be immigrants who wish to settle there—determines the course of the argument. Immigration policies are matters of first principles, so that whoever bears the burden of persuasion is virtually certain to fail in making a case. The prerogative of controlling immigration is assumed, not argued. As Carens points out, when asked why a particular group should have the absolute power to decide whether other groups of people can settle on the land, the answer from immigration restrictionists is, in its popular rendition, "we were here first," and in its philosophical version, "priority in time." This concept, articulated by Immanuel Kant among others, has almost never met with objections.

Among the peculiar ideas of Thomas Jefferson, perhaps derived from his admiration of the French Revolution, was his answer to the question "whether one generation of men has a right to bind another." The Jeffersonian penchant for revolution, refreshing the tree of liberty from time to time with the blood of patriots and tyrants, was expressed in his view, "which I suppose to be self-evident, that the earth belongs in usufruct to the living." He believed that all laws and contracts should expire with each generation, or about every nineteen years.[96] By that view, immigration control could not rest on "priority in time." As each generation expired, so would its control over the borders. Each successive generation would have to reestablish its authority. There are few principles other than power that would suffice. But Jefferson's generational sovereignty, running through time rather than over place, seems as fantastic now as it did then. None propose following it. Thus, the reason other groups of people who are already present in the country—never mind the would-be immigrants, who have no recognizable right to enter—lack the same privilege in that "they haven't paid their dues yet." The Pilgrims were the founders; others were not.

The line of reasoning that follows from these premises is racial, even if it is not explicitly so. Leaving aside factual problems, such as European immigrants reneging on treaties with Native Americans and the role of African slaves in building the country, the claim depends wholly on heritage and group identity; it turns on the status of the people making the claim, not on the merits of the claim. Hence a century ago, anti-immigrant advocates spoke of "hereditary Americans" as the only true Americans.

The claim is absurd without its basis in ancestry. The "we" who "were here first" are not the individuals who make the statement, but their forebears. Otherwise, the claim would be, "I was here first;" in other words, "I am older." Yet nobody starts an argument about immigration by saying "I was here first," and "I am older," therefore I can decide who else can come here. Indeed, sometimes the claim is, "I've been here for seven generations." That declaration is inherently false and even nonsensical in its confusion of individuals with their lineage, but the pride with which it is usually advanced reveals the problem. Even if the justification for immigration control is reinterpreted as not relying on race, it cannot be gainsaid that it relies on inherited privilege.

Michael Walzer, the Princeton political philosopher, provides the most liberal version of these arguments. In his highly regarded *Spheres of Justice: A Defense of Pluralism and Equality*, he is very much concerned with distributive justice within a community. He insists that everyone within a community must be equal. There cannot be any doubt that he would abhor racial restrictions on entry into a community. Yet he accepts the political nature of decisions about membership in a community, and he is solicitous of the right and need of any community to be able to define itself. In comparing the nation to neighborhoods, clubs, and families, he concludes that whichever the appropriate analogue, membership decisions are "a matter of political decision" and nothing more. The people to make the decisions are "the men and women who are already there." (He does grant that we are bound to offer a place to refugees, especially those whom we have forced into such status.)[97] His position is unfortunately vulnerable to being overtaken by the most restrictive rules on immigration, including those that rely on race. If those happen to be the membership decisions made as a matter of political decision by the men and women who are already there, his view has nothing much to offer in opposition if they vote thus. He recognizes as much, writing that "states are simply free to take in strangers (or not)—much as they are free, leaving aside the claims of the needy, to share their wealth with foreign friends, to honor the achievements of foreign artists, scholars, and scientists, to choose their trading partners, and to enter into collective security arrangements with foreign states."[98] Furthermore, as a descriptive matter, he is convinced that "historically, neighborhoods have turned into closed or parochial communities . . . whenever the state was open," so that openness at the local level requires closure at the national level. Walzer does not consider the possibility that his prerequisite of equal membership will not be satisfied even for those already within the community, if those whom they resemble are not allowed into the community. Asian Americans, who as a minority often have their views dismissed as a special interest that runs against the national interest, cannot help but be lowered in status if Asians are excluded.[99]

Contrary to Walzer, Yale law professor Bruce Ackerman has demonstrated that a liberal polity has great difficulty justifying any type of immigration restriction without resorting to race or inherited privilege, both illiberal foundations. If it is not to be hypocritical, a liberal polity must abide by certain principles, unless it departs from its liberalism and simply asserts that it is a community defined in racial terms or equally simply declares that it need not provide any rationalization of its decisions other than that it has made them. In his *Social Justice in the Liberal State,* Ackerman suggests that among the core principles of liberalism is that when an individual with power is questioned about the legitimacy of her power, "the power holder must respond not by suppressing the questioner but by giving a reason that explains why he is more entitled to the resource than the questioner is."[100] He then brilliantly imagines a dialogue between two groups who are governed by this principle as they compete over the same resource, namely space. One has arrived before the other (there is no problem of generations in this hypothetical case; it is a contest between the first two arrivals, not their descendants), and the former cannot defeat the latter without appealing to distinctly antiliberal arguments such as raw power.[101] Even the thinkers most inclined toward open borders, such as Ackerman, who stop short of calling for them as does Carens, create loopholes that can be exploited. Ackerman concludes that "the *only* reason for restricting immigration is to protect the ongoing process of liberal conversation itself."[102] Ackerman does not anticipate the possibility, but Asians have long been accused of being exactly the type of corrupting presence that will ruin democratic processes. We are accustomed to Oriental despotism, the liberal argument runs, and we yearn to spread its rule.

Other arguments about immigration contain a racial component. People sometimes propose, for example, that immigration should be prevented for the benefit of the source country rather than for the benefit of the destination country. Their idea is that Indians have a responsibility to help advance India instead of forming the "brain drain" leaving it, and so forth. Leaving aside doubts about the sincerity of their advice for Indians, and even disregarding the benefits India receives from diaspora sending back remittances and shuttling back and forth with knowledge, the crux of their suggestion is that Indians have a racial bond with India, and its special duty is so strong that even non-Indians have standing to invoke it. In contrast, non-Indians are not regarded as owing the same obligation toward India, and they are not advised to emigrate there.

Within these dynamics, Asian Americans have stressed their citizenship rather than their race, because they have sought protection for their rights on the basis of citizenship against the deprivations that would be worked on the basis of race. Asian Americans make the only choice they can between citizenship and race, preferring the former over the latter. But perhaps we, all Americans and all people, would be better off if the choice were recast as one between rights that extend to all people or rights that are offered only to citizens, allowing us to prefer the former over the latter.

In the next chapter, I enter the affirmative action debate. Instead of engaging in angry confrontation, I look at meritocracy and color blindness as means of defining membership in the community. With Asian Americans as active participants in the dialogue, the affirmative action debate can be transformed into a productive discussion.

Neither Black Nor White

Affirmative Action and Asian Americans

The confrontation route was the only road. So the Chinese, the Japanese, the Chicanos, the Indians picked up on mau-mauing from the bloods. Not only that, they would try to do it exactly *like* the bloods. They'd talk like the bloods, dress like the bloods, wear naturals like the bloods, even if their hair was too straight to do it. There were Spanish and Oriental dudes who washed their hair every day with Borax to make it fluff up and sit out. When anybody other than black people went in for mau-mauing, however, they ran into problems, because the white man had a different set of fear reflexes for each race he was dealing with.

Whites didn't have too much fear of the Mexican-American, the Chicano. The notion was that he was small, placid, slow, no particular physical threat—until he grew his hair Afro-style, talked like a blood or otherwise managed to seem "black" enough to raise hell. Then it was a different story.

The whites' physical fear of the Chinese was nearly zero. The white man pictured the Chinese as small, quiet, restrained little fellows. He had a certain deep-down voodoo fear of their powers of Evil in the dark . . . the Hatchet Men . . . the Fangs of the Tong . . . but it wasn't a live fear. For that matter, the young Chinese themselves weren't ready for the age of mau-mauing. It wasn't that they feared the white man, the way black people had. It was more that they didn't fear or resent white people enough. They looked down on whites as childish and uncultivated. They also found it shameful to present themselves as poor and oppressed, on the same level with Negros and Mexican-Americans.

—TOM WOLFE, *Radical Chic and Mau-Mauing the Flak Catchers*,
REPORTING AS THE ORIGINAL "NEW JOURNALIST" ON SAN FRANCISCO
BUREAUCRATS ADMINISTERING AN ANTI-POVERTY PROGRAM

Racial Rhetoric

As a strong supporter of affirmative action, I am often asked to debate it. But whether the forum is a television show or a college campus, I always try to decline. Another divisive debate is not what our society needs, and a debate over affirmative action by itself is the wrong place to start attacking racial discrimination. The debate over affirmative action threatens to overwhelm the civil rights movement, without advancing us meaningfully toward racial justice.

A debate is a spectacle, with its angry slogans and rhetorical tricks. Even in the most thoughtful settings, for example, at an Ivy League school among bright and interested students, the sophistry of a debate limits the exchange and simplifies the opinions that are aired. A debate channels participants into its format of diametrically opposed pro and con viewpoints. Mutual concessions and reconciliation would represent a defeat for each and be a disappointment to the audience. Spectators at a debate root for their chosen cause or assume a passive role. They come out to watch the contestants fight it out as entertainment more than education. Rather than staging debates, we should encourage dialogue, which could generate consensus, and sooner rather than later produce cooperative and constructive action. We ought to stop debating, and start doing.

In addition, instead of focusing obsessively on affirmative action programs, we should concentrate on the realities of racial disparities. Taking up "reverse discrimination" and not regular discrimination shifts our attention toward the remedies prematurely, inducing us to find faults with potential solutions while ignoring the original problems of racial bias.

Those of us who believe in systematic efforts to attain racial justice should reform the terms of the public discourse. We make a strategic mistake by continuing to debate affirmative action on terms set by the other side, of quotas and preferences, innocent white victims and unqualified, undeserving people of color. As every debater of any skill grasps, the ability to define the question effectively determines the answer. The question should not be whether we will abolish this program or amend that plan. The question should be, "What will we do to address continuing racial disparities?" Changing the initial question revises every other question that follows. The perennial question asked of affirmative action should be turned toward racial discrimination: "When will it end?"

Allow me to lay out an alternative approach for the conversation about affirmative action. In doing so, I should admit that I have become convinced of the importance of affirmative action by study and experience, but I was not always persuaded of the justice of affirmative action. At various times, as an Asian American, I have been included in the programs, excluded from them, assumed to be included when I was excluded, informed erroneously that an affirmative action plan meant my application had to be rejected, and told brusquely that decision makers did not have to answer my questions about the process. Nevertheless, I have learned how affirmative action can work for society as a whole while recognizing that ambivalence about it can keep us honest. In the conversation I propose, let me show how Asian Americans can add innovations to the case for affirmative action and strengthen it. Our perspective can only help the process of considering these contentious issues, because whether or not we admit it, each of us—white, black, brown, or yellow—shares in the outcome. A forthright and productive conversation about affirmative action proceeds through three phases: a statement of the racial problems, a determination of principles, and a dedication to pragmatism.

Racial Problems

We must begin where it is proper to begin. Opponents of affirmative action, white and non-white, use the misnomers "racial preference" or "reverse discrimination." They rely on a crucial tactic, namely making race abstract. Once race refers to any race as if discrimination struck uniformly, opponents are able to say with some credence that whether we have regular discrimination or affirmative action depends only on power and whim. Whites prefer whites, blacks prefer blacks, and so forth. If race is removed from history and context, as if whites and blacks in America were already equal, slavery and affirmative action are turned into equivalent forms of racial tyranny. Of course, proponents of affirmative action appear to be driven by raw self-interest and favoritism. Restored to reality, racial discrimination and its remedies are nothing like each other. Whether we can and should come up with programs and plans that neutralize racial discrimination and its effects become pressing inquiries. But the prerequisite for any consideration of the topics is acknowledging racial discrimination and racial disparities.

All sides in the affirmative action debate pay lip service to the notion of racial discrimination, but they neglect all but the worst types. The problem, however, is racial disparities in all their many forms. To be sure, America has made racial progress within the past generation. Our evolution should be neither denied nor overstated. It has been only through bitterly contested lawsuits and against state-led "massive resistance," in nervous fear of demonstrations and riots, that we have broken the institutions of state-sanctioned racial segregation. The Jim Crow system of "separate but equal" was more separate than equal, but it has been destroyed. The better public schools are supposed to be open to all. The "whites only" signs at apartment rental offices, "no blacks or Filipinos need apply" restrictions in classified job ads, and "colored at the back of the bus" instructions are fading memories that many are indisposed to believe. Lynching is no longer common enough to be a real terror. Almost all Americans subscribe to a basic understanding that bigotry is wrong. A majority of us declare that we support actual equality of opportunity. Each of these changes has transpired within the lifetime of today's adults.

Yet racial discrimination persists. These wrongs are concrete and contemporary, and they cannot be dismissed as theoretical or historical. Social science indicators and real-life daily experiences tell us that people of color, especially African Americans, continue to enjoy dissimilar life prospects compared to whites who are identical other than for their skin color. The advantages are to whites, the disadvantages to people of color, primarily African Americans, in almost all aspects of life. Whether we look at infant mortality, life expectancy, housing segregation, educational outcomes, employment opportunities, or the glass ceiling, copious objective data and persuasive personal narratives indicate that there remain differences that correlate with race to a greater or lesser extent.

Sociologist Andrew Hacker reports in his best-selling *Two Nations: Black, White, Separate, Hostile, Unequal,*[1] a comprehensive compilation of data on race, that, in the most acute instances, in cities such as Washington, D.C., more than 95 percent of African American students attend segregated schools, and in states such as Louisiana, five times as many white teachers as black teachers have passed competency exams. Given the environment,

Hacker writes that academic achievement does not result in the same payoff for blacks and whites: "Among men with bachelor's degrees, blacks earn only $764 for each $1,000 going to whites at that level. Even worse, the racial ratio for black men is actually lower than that for black men who finished only high school."[2] He notes, "Hence the advice so often offered to blacks, that they should stay in school, seems valid insofar as . . . that with additional education they will move ahead of others of their own race" but it does not "improve their positions in relation to whites."[3] Hacker is not surprised that more than four times as many black families as white families live in poverty.

Black and white immigrants, even if they are more or less identical except for skin color, undergo the inexorable process of racialization. The *New York Times* published a lengthy series of articles in 2000[4] on "how race is lived in America," later collected into a book, containing profiles of two Cuban immigrants to the United States, one white, one black. Both Cuban in every sense before they arrived, they assimilated into two different Americas once here.

As the newspaper correspondent reports, "Pretty much anywhere else in America, Valdes," the white Cuban, "would fit nicely into the niche reserved for Hispanic immigrants. . . . Here he is not a member of any minority group. He is Cuban and he is white. This, after all, is a city run by Cubans, white Cubans." In contrast, "Miami is deeply segregated, and when Ruiz," the black Cuban, "arrived, he settled into one of the black urban sections" because he had family there. "The first thing Ruiz noticed about his new world was the absence of whites. . . . This was Miami, and in Miami . . . skin color trumps nationality."[5]

Admittedly, some of the differences among the haves and have-nots can be traced to socioeconomic class or common hardships. Poor white Americans may suffer as much as poor African Americans because their impoverishment causes deprivation, or individual cases of misfortune may lead to misery. But for African Americans their adversities, even their triumphs, are compounded by racial effects. The declining significance of race is not the same as the utter insignificance of race. Few whites would be willing to be black.

As sociologists Melvin L. Oliver and Thomas M. Shapiro have shown, black Americans and white Americans who earn the same incomes are likely to possess different levels of wealth. In their book, *Black Wealth, White Wealth*,[6] Oliver and Shapiro argue that income, the amount of money a person is paid in any given year, does not reflect socioeconomic status as fully as wealth, the property that a person owns on a permanent basis, such as a house, a car, and investments. Even African Americans who make middle-class incomes do not enjoy the same secure socioeconomic status as white Americans who make as much money but also have accumulated wealth. Such wealth is not just acquired but inherited. As slaves, African Americans were property, and few had anything they could bequeath to the next generation. Even as late as 1948, they had difficulty buying homes—the single largest asset owned by most families—because of the open enforcement of racial covenants on real estate, coupled with the refusal of banks to give mortgages to blacks and the government to insure loans to them. With continuing discrimination and the lower appreciation on their houses in black neighborhoods, Oliver and Shapiro document that African American families who are in "upper white collar" occupations still have an average net worth of $21,430, compared to whites with $47,854; after subtracting their debts, African Americans are left with only $230 compared to whites with $9,000.

Racial discrimination can manifest itself in many forms. There are the ruthless crimes and the egregious conduct, but there also are the subtle patterns and the pervasive folklore. All require responses. It is painless enough to condemn the shocking incidents and severe situations, but the ease with which we can denounce the former should not lull us into condoning the latter. Almost all of us are horrified by the hate crimes targeting certain people for violence, even death, on the basis of their racial, ethnic, or religious background. The last years of the twentieth century produced a gruesome series of such hate crimes.

In 1998 in Jaspars, Texas, three white men, two of them avowed white supremacists who had met during an earlier stint in prison, tied James Byrd, a disabled African American man, to the rear of their pickup truck and drove along back roads until his head and limbs were torn from his body. The two who were white supremacists were sentenced to death by lethal injection, becoming the first whites to receive capital punishment in the state for killing a black since 1854.

In April 2000 in Pittsburgh, Richard Scott Baumhammers, a white man who resented racial minorities and had paranoid delusions of being under government surveillance, allegedly shot his Jewish neighbor, four Asian Americans, and an African American, killing all but one of his victims. He awaits trial.

Over the Fourth of July weekend in 1999 in suburban Chicago, Benjamin Nathaniel Smith, a follower of white supremacist preacher Matt Hale who had written in his college newspaper that "it is pretty clear that our government has turned against white people," went on a shooting spree, killing two and wounding seven: an African American man jogging with his children, six Orthodox Jews leaving their synagogue, and an Asian American couple leaving church (he also shot at but missed an Asian American couple driving on the road). He killed himself while a massive manhunt was underway.

In April 1999 near Los Angeles, Buford O. Furrow, a white man who wanted to send "a wake-up call for Americans to kill Jews," shot five children at a Jewish day care center before shooting to death a Filipino American postal carrier because he was a racial minority who worked for the federal government. Furrow pled guilty to sixteen felonies in a plea bargain that carried a sentence of five life terms in prison without the possibility of parole, averting a trial that could have led to imposition of the death penalty.

Almost all of us are dismayed when we learn that a company has had a policy of hiring or promoting only whites in violation of moral norms and anti-discrimination laws. Texaco, Denny's, and the U.S. Agriculture Department, along with hotel chains, insurance companies, and funeral homes, all have paid millions of dollars in the past several years—in some instances, more than $100 million—to resolve civil litigation over claims of racial discrimination filed by job applicants, employees, and even consumers. By the terms of the settlements, although they have not admitted guilt, they have been willing to start remedial measures. The huge sums of money concerned and the large numbers of consumers, job applicants, and employees who are involved show that these are not frivolous complaints. The cases remind us that, civil rights advances notwithstanding, individuals and institutions among us still practice their prejudices.

Yet we may not comprehend the prevalence of another type of racial bias. It consists of everything else racial: the present effects of past discrimination, the stereotypes that the mass media propagate interminably, and unconscious decisions with unconscionable consequences. The facts and figures of Hacker and Oliver and Shapiro substantiate the racial patterns. The lack of racist intentions behind these racial patterns is no defense, for it may indicate a mindset no better than apathy toward their racial effects. In some sense, this furtive racial bias is more profound than the overt kind, exactly because we are tempted to put it out of our minds. In isolation each action may seem minor and not even racial, but taken together they generate a cumulative impact that is major and markedly racial.

Such decisions are made, for example, by white home buyers who choose to live where they know the neighbors, the streets are safe, the schools are good, the parks are nice, there is convenient shopping, the restaurants are trendy, and property values are rising.[7] They are just more comfortable there, and they don't expect to be scolded for it. Even though not more than one in a hundred of the residents on that side of town will say that he also likes the mostly white character of the neighborhood, the area ends up mostly white. The effect is unmistakable, and blocks become color-coded. Such decisions are made by a law firm that does not have any explicitly discriminatory policies, but does not have any non-white attorneys either. Such decisions are made by each of us who would rather spend time with people who look like us, despite our best intentions of being color blind.

This systematic structure of racial discrimination is easy to underestimate, because it forms part of our common culture. The eagerness with which we denounce extremists who are racists by their own admission may make us reluctant to concede the banality of evil, loath to become acquainted with the full spectrum along which racial transgressions may be arrayed, with everyday lapses at one end. But it does not take a hard-core unreconstructed bigot sitting behind a big desk in a fancy office at the country club writing memos stating "No Latinos here" to convey that some people will be welcomed as if they are old friends, whereas others will be unwelcome as dangerous strangers. Even if a specific perpetrator cannot be identified, an injustice may be done—and it may be done every bit as harmfully as if it were maliciously intended. Even if we were to investigate thoroughly and identify all racist individuals, removing them from all positions of authority and power, we would still have lingering problems of race.

Perhaps the most vexing problem that must be overcome to even confront racial discrimination is denial.[8] As the reactions to the O.J. Simpson trial showed, it would be an understatement to say that white Americans and African Americans by and large perceive the status quo differently.[9] In particular, they tend to give definitions of racism that are at odds with each other. Many white Americans seem to dodge evidence of racial discrimination: changing the subject to racial progress, arguing that statistics can be manipulated and are not as persuasive as individual cases, but then arguing that anecdotes are subjective and are not as reliable as hard numbers, and, finally, setting aside the irrefutable examples as extreme.

Many white Americans regard racism as the calculated oppression of a racial group. Under their standard, slavery qualifies as racism. But to them, a panicked reaction to a black man walking behind them late at night does not rise to anywhere near the same level. In crossing the street, they are only concerned with their own security and not trying to subjugate anyone. They have "the gift of fear" that protects them from crime.[10]

Many African Americans describe racism as any attitudes and all practices that result in disadvantages to a racial minority group. By their description, slavery is the worst form of racism. But for them, much of modern society is also racist even though "the Man" who perpetrates and perpetuates the wrong attitudes and actions is an icon rather than an individual. In enduring a subordinate status, they can find little solace in knowing that whites may take pity on their depressing condition and are not inclined to dominate them. They remain the "faces at the bottom of the well" of a bountiful society, in the words of New York University law professor Derrick Bell.[11]

Martin Luther King Jr. was able to speak across this divide. In his *Letter from a Birmingham Jail*, written in April 1963 when he was serving his sentence for leading protests, he replied candidly to white moderates, fellow clergymen, who had published an open letter calling on him to stop his crusade of nonviolent resistance and wait for time to bring about racial amends. King recognized the importance of explaining to decent people how in standing by they may do more harm than wrongdoers, because there were so many whites who were complicit in this manner. He saw that even though they were aloof from his struggle, they could be made to care by shame if nothing else. His widely reprinted pamphlet had its intended effect of winning over the unsure, testing whether they would live up to their professed ideals. He wrote, "Shallow understanding from people of good will is more frustrating than absolute misunderstanding from people of ill will. Lukewarm acceptance is much more bewildering than outright rejection."[12]

An advantage of introducing Asian Americans into the dialogue about civil rights is that, for white Americans and African Americans, it becomes easier to discuss the merits of racial possibilities. If we add Asian Americans to the dialogue, we can see how people of all backgrounds operate through sets of racial assumptions. The issues become less personally sensitive, to white Americans and African Americans anyway. By including Asian Americans, blacks and whites alike can see how multiple interpretations can be given to a single occurrence. A casual instance of no moment for one party can continue a trend of lasting significance for another party. The statement, "You Asians are all doing well," and the question, "Where are you really from?" exemplify this type of racial happening. The model minority myth and the perpetual foreigner syndrome are apt examples, as discussed in Chapters 2 and 3. Each shows how race can work its effects without racism coming into play. Leaving out Asian Americans from consideration of affirmative action and relegating us to the role of bystanders suggests that we are neither American nor minorities. We can no longer be portrayed as the original "New Journalist" Tom Wolfe does in *Radical Chic and Mau-Mauing the Flak Catchers* (1970), his report of San Francisco bureaucrats administering an anti-poverty program, an excerpt from which is the epigraph to this chapter.[13]

Regrettably, Asian Americans have been inserted cynically into the affirmative action debate. Critics have tried to hold affirmative action responsible for ceilings on Asian Americans in college admissions. Sociologist Hacker, for example, wrote about the complexities of affirmative action in 1989, that "[s]plintering the discussion even further is whether ceilings for Asians result from the expansion of Black and Hispanic admissions, and thus are the result of affirmative action."[14] Their argument in the affirmative runs as follows: If there are minimum quotas for one racial group, it follows that there are maximum quotas for another racial group—respectively, African Americans and Asian Americans. Their argument is illogical and counterfactual, but it sounds plausible and thus is important to rebut thoroughly. This argument caused a commotion among Asian Americans during the 1980s and 1990s (much as a similar argument had perturbed American Jews a generation earlier). The ensuing college admissions dispute was for many Asian Americans their initiation into civil rights. As a preliminary matter, it is important to dispense with two distracting premises.

First, affirmative action has costs. Affirmative action proponents would be foolish to maintain that it has none whatsoever. But every public policy, including the lack of public policy, has drawbacks. A sensible decision maker asks of any proposal, "Do the benefits outweigh the costs?" and not "Are there any costs?"

Second, any system other than open admissions to educational institutions with unlimited class sizes would have a disproportionate effect on Asian Americans. This is so because Asian Americans are disproportionately interested in pursuing education. Anything that brings down admissions rates, even if it were not anti-Asian or were practical, such as a system that rejected people at random or that set an overall enrollment total at a campus, would affect a higher percentage of Asian Americans than of other racial groups (including whites) because there is a higher percentage of Asian Americans than other racial groups in the applicant pool relative to their respective proportions of the general population. A just decision maker asks, "Are Asian Americans somehow singled out to bear the entire burden of affirmative action?" not "Do Asian Americans, like others, bear some burden from affirmative action?"

Logically, affirmative action could have a concentrated effect on Asian Americans only if it were designed as a blatantly illegal tit-for-tat quota whereby an Asian American was rejected for every African American who was accepted. Under those unfair circumstances, Asian Americans would be subjected to "negative action," in UCLA law professor Jerry Kang's words.[15]

Yet Asian Americans would be making way for whites, not for African Americans, under such a regime. A system in which an Asian American was rejected for every African American who was accepted would be affirmative action as much for whites as for anyone else. In such a system, whites would be guaranteed a definite number of slots. In effect, whites could safeguard their seats at a college by capping the maximum number of people of color. Any effort to stabilize the representation of whites must come at the expense of non-whites who are non-beneficiaries of affirmative action. The only group qualifying for the unenviable honor is Asian Americans. With white numbers constant, people of color would compete against only one another. Asian Americans would be forced out, under the guise of making room for African Americans but in actuality making room for whites. (Furthermore, the largest groups that are competitive with one another in college admissions at elite institutions under traditional criteria are whites and Asian Americans.)[16]

Factually, this seems to have been the case. None of the cases that were investigated in the 1980s and 1990s showed that affirmative action for African Americans produced enrollment limits on Asian Americans. The U.S. Education Department found discrimination unrelated to affirmative action in an investigation of UCLA, and it found disparities between white and Asian American admissions rates that it attributed to other factors, such as alumni and athletic preferences, at Harvard.[17]

The lawsuit filed in 1995 by Chinese Americans who challenged the desegregation of San Francisco public schools is the best example of "negative action." Chinese Americans sued because they had to achieve higher scores than anyone else—including whites—to gain admission to Lowell High School, indisputably the finest in the district. The Lowell litigation was all the more bitter because of its unique history. Ever since non-Native Americans settled there, San Francisco has had a sizable Asian American population. But until recently, San Francisco mistreated its Asian American residents. At the turn of the twentieth century, the city tried to set up segregated schools for Japanese students, precipitating a diplomatic row between the White House and the Japanese Empire. In 1973, Chinese Americans had to fight up to the Supreme Court to gain bilingual education (later, African

Americans grumbled that they, not whites, were placed in classrooms with immigrants). The police department, fire department, and local government contract programs included few if any Asian Americans until affirmative action was adopted for all people of color. The Lowell suit, however, pitted Asian Americans—specifically, Chinese Americans—against African Americans, because the NAACP had won the school desegregation suit that necessitated a 40 percent limit on enrollment of any single ethnic group at Lowell. Neither side noticed the affirmative action for whites. As the largest group competing with Chinese Americans, whites benefited the most from the limit on Chinese Americans. The multiple sides were able to devise a settlement just as the trial was scheduled to start. With court approval, they agreed that Lowell could "consider many factors, including the desire to promote residential, geographic, economic, racial and ethnic diversity in all . . . schools" but "race and ethnicity may not be the primary or predominant consideration" and no student can be assigned to "a particular school . . . on the basis of . . . race or ethnicity."[18]

Although anti-Asian American bias can exist anywhere regardless of affirmative action, there is a risk that Asian Americans will be sacrificed to preserve white privileges even without alumni preferences. Sociologist Hacker predicts that whites will not "cavil" when better-prepared Asian Americans are admitted ahead of whites to prestigious universities, but he is too optimistic.[19]

As early as 1977, a white ethnic author argued in a *New York Times* op-ed that white ethnics should be included in affirmative action in college admissions because "we are certainly much worse off than Orientals."[20] Shortly before he declared his candidacy for the Presidency again, syndicated columnist Pat Buchnan wrote a remarkable column in November 1998 demanding a quota favoring white Christians at elite universities. He called them "the real victims of ethnic bigotry in America," and cited the overrepresentation of Jews and Asian Americans as an example of "a liberal elite salving its social conscience by robbing America's white middle class of its birthright, and handing it over to minorities, who just happen to vote Democratic." As he finally began to come under serious criticism for appearing to be an unabashed apologist for Nazism in his latest book, Buchanan said on talk shows that he had been joking when he'd written, "If Harvard balks, denounce it as bigoted and demand a cut-off of federal funds. If proportional representation is the name of the game, Christian and European-Americans should get into the game, and demand their fair share of every pie: 75 percent, and no less."[21] Whether Buchanan wished to retract his suggestion as a jest, others have sproadically made the same argument and stood by it. They are not kidding about re-instating white preferences.[22]

During the 1980s, one University of California official told a reporter that "if we keep getting extremely well-prepared Asians, and we are, we may get to the point when whites will become an affirmative action group," and another wrote in an internal memo that the UCLA campus "will endeavor to curb the decline of Caucasian students," which may cause "concern from Asian students and Asians in general as the number and proportion of Asians students entering at the freshmen level declines—however small the decline may be."[23] A Stanford professor argued in 1994 that Asian Americans and Jews are "way overrepresented" and "white Christian students" correspondingly underrepresented.[24]

The move from affirmative action for blacks to affirmative action for whites was facilitated by using Asian Americans as an example. Assistant Attorney General for Civil Rights William Bradford Reynolds testified before Congress in 1988 that "where admissions policies are skewed by a mandate to achieve some sort of proportional representation by race . . . then, inevitably, there will be pressure to squeeze out Asian Americans to make room for other minorities (or for whites)."[25] The parenthetical comment at the end of Reynolds's remarks is anything but trivial. It shows that the linkage of limits on Asian Americans to affirmative action for African Americans is more rhetorical than real.

The proponents of affirmative action for whites cannot find support in any rationale for affirmative action other than a racial spoils system that no affirmative action plan has ever embodied. This is not to suggest that white males are to be categorically excluded from even consideration for affirmative action because of race and gender. Rather, it is to suggest that there are few if any cases in which white men are underrepresented because of discrimination, whether past or present. Even where white men are a numerical minority group, which they are in many contexts, they usually are a dominant minority group. In Hawaii, for example, it is only recently that white men ceased to own most of the businesses and land as well as operating the government and the cultural institutions. The sense that white men will be displaced because of remedial programs arises only because they have been able to take advantage of opportunities denied to others. The objection that, as the Federal Glass Ceiling Commission found in 1995, almost all Fortune 500 senior management and board positions are held by white men is not to suggest that those individuals are not deserving. It is, rather, to suggest that they are not the only individuals who are deserving.

If in Hawaiian universities whites became underrepresented because of discrimination, then they would have a credible claim to affirmative action. In cases where Asian Americans are overrepresented, it is not due to discrimination by Asian Americans on behalf of Asian Americans. We have become overrepresented at institutions where Asian Americans were few and far between until only a generation ago. Asian Americans are still rare among the decision makers: department chairs, senior administrators, provosts, presidents, and trustees. We can even be simultaneously overrepresented and still subjected to racial discrimination.

The displacement of Asian Americans should be troubling, and not only to Asian Americans. It shows that for some foes of affirmative action, the apprehensions are all about whose ox is being gored. They'd rather it was the black ox than the white ox—or, if the black ox is shown special solicitude, the yellow ox should fall before the white ox. We can do better than that.

Racial Principles

We should challenge ourselves to be principled. Affirmative action debaters often resort to charging their adversaries with being unprincipled or proceeding in bad faith. But although we can agree to proceed on the basis of principle and trust that everyone else will do likewise, that is not the same as agreeing on a specific principle. There are principled arguments for most opinions, and we must elect among them. We can consider many different ideals: Do we value rights or responsibilities, do we care about intentions or consequences, and are we worried about individual cases or societal patterns? Those who highlight rights, intentions, and individual cases have a worldview that allows them to disavow culpability for and even concern about responsibilities, consequences, and societal patterns. They may be principled, but they have the wrong principles. Yet rights, intentions, and individual cases ought not to be debased in the zeal to take up responsibilities, consequences, and societal patterns. There are principled compromises as well.

Affirmative action represents equality and integration, just as opposition to it represents color blindness and meritocracy. Many of us have the same aspiration of all Americans to become stakeholders in an open society. Both Presidents Bill Clinton and George W. Bush bragged about diversity. Democrat Clinton said his high-level advisors would "look like America." Late in his second term, Asian Americans were pleased that he tapped Norman Mineta, a Japanese American who had been mayor of San Jose and a long-time member of Congress, to become the first-ever Cabinet appointee of Asian descent. In the first six months of his administration, Republican Bush touted his range of top nominees who were not white men. Among them, joining Mineta (retained as a Democrat for viewpoint diversity) was Elaine Chao, a Chinese American who had been a senior fellow at the Heritage Foundation thinktank, as the labor secretary.

Most of us envision all of us belonging to all our institutions, elite and public, making them legitimate and relevant: a nation where African Americans, whites, Asian Americans, Latinos, and Native Americans all appear in the halls of Congress, boardrooms of companies, and behind the podiums in university lecture halls, instead of one where some groups are found in prisons and on reservations. We do not expect exact proportions of each group in all walks of life, but neither are we satisfied with token numbers at the top. We are dispirited, however, that we have never fulfilled our pledges of equality and integration, which were made by America to itself, not by whites to blacks. Sociologist Gunnar Myrdal gave the title "the American dilemma" to his work to refer to the gap between what our culture proclaims our ideals to be and what we really do to meet such goals; it does not refer to African Americans.

Affirmative action is the applied component of this commitment to work toward achieving a society that not only happens to be racially diverse but also strives to be egalitarian and inclusive. Affirmative action is about membership in our community. It tries to transform the nature of our community and the terms of membership. Responsible corporate leaders have practiced affirmative action. Microsoft and General Motors have opposed lawsuits that would end it. In the jargon of the business world, affirmative action "implements" and "operationalizes" our dreams and objectives.

Color blindness and meritocracy are ideals, but they are illusory ideals. When we think critically about the goals of color blindness and meritocracy, it turns out that they, too, are about community and membership, but they support different conceptions of the community and criteria for membership. If the consequences of color blindness and meritocracy are set forth, the community they would constitute and the membership they would delineate become much less appealing. The means do not justify the ends.

Color blindness is not what it seems, either historically or today. The concept comes from the dissenting opinion written by Supreme Court Justice John Marshall Harlan in the 1896 case of *Plessy v. Ferguson*[26]. Harlan opposed the "separate but equal" doctrine that a majority of the high court upheld. In one of the most famous passages in the annals of jurisprudence, Harlan wrote: "In view of the constitution, in the eye of the law, there is in this country no superior, dominant ruling class of citizens. There is no caste here.

Our constitution is color-blind, and neither knows nor tolerates classes among citizens." Announcing an argument that was remarkable for his time and remains so in ours, Harlan continued, "In respect of civil rights, all citizens are equal before the law." Although Harlan was unable to win over even one of his colleagues to his proclamation of color blindness, he has been applauded ever since for saying that "the destinies of the two races, in this country, are indissolubly linked together."

From its inception, however, color blindness has been duplicitous. Celebrated as he has become, Harlan was a hypocrite. As University of Cincinnati law professor Gabriel Chin has argued, his reputation as "the great dissenter" is undeserved.[27] Harlan believed only that African Americans were equal in a formal and technical sense—as laypeople sometimes contemptuously regard the law, as only a game of semantics. Harlan did not flinch from declaring that African Americans are inferior in every other respect. Even as he invented color blindness, he wrote that "the white race deems itself to be the dominant race in this country. And so it is, in prestige, in achievements, in education, in wealth and in power." He was shrewd about it: "So, I doubt not, it will continue to be for all time, if it remains true to its great heritage, and holds fast to the principles of constitutional liberty." In this fashion, Harlan expected that by acceding to color blindness in law "the white race" will protect its role as "the dominant race in this country."

Moreover, from its inception color blindness has been partial. Reneging on his own color blindness, Harlan was consistently anti-Asian. Chin reviews Harlan's career, showing that time and again Harlan was conspicuously color conscious toward Asian immigrants. He authored another dissent, whose burial only burnishes his reputation, in which he argued that the native-born children of Chinese immigrants cannot be U.S. citizens because of their race. He would have eviscerated the literal language of the Fourteenth Amendment, which he is renowned for upholding through color blindness, by giving it a racial interpretation to prevent Asians from even becoming citizens who could assert rights. He added in *Plessy*, as a caveat on color blindness, that "there is a race so different from our own that we do not permit those belonging to it to become citizens of the United States. Persons belonging to it are, with exceptions, absolutely excluded from our country. I allude to the Chinese race." Furthermore, Harlan dissented from "separate but equal" in part for the very reason that it treats Asian immigrants as equal to white Americans: "by the statute in question, a Chinaman can ride in the same passenger coach [of a train] with white citizens of the United States, while citizens of the black race cannot." To Harlan, color blindness was for whites and blacks, but not Asian immigrants.

These aspects of Harlan's dissent, integral to his reasoning, have been excised from the euphemistic version of color blindness. In his book *Ending Affirmative Action: The Case for Colorblind Justice*,[28] for example, Reagan administration official Terry Eastland follows the customary course of citing Harlan and providing a few inspirational excerpts out of context. Many of our cherished ideas have dubious origins, but we owe it to our intellectual integrity to become familiar with their provenance and to consider whether theories can be rehabilitated if they are suspect at the outset. Certainly Asian Americans may pause before reciting Justice Harlan's *Plessy* dissent as their creed once they have perused it in its entirety.

The rubric of color blindness takes in two distinct meanings. It can be a legal doctrine, or it can be a moral imperative. In either case, color blindness as a hope should not be confused with color blindness as a reality. Otherwise, we become blind not to race but to racism. We act with color consciousness but refuse to admit it, and in turn accuse an observer who points out our own color consciousness of "playing the race card" as if such a trump existed.

Some anti-affirmative action propagandists endorse color blindness as a legal doctrine, but only as a legal doctrine and nothing more. Many of them contend that we should repeal not only affirmative action but also all civil rights laws. University of Chicago law professor Richard Epstein and Washington activist Clint Bolick would prevent the government from recognizing race as it attempts to eliminate racism. They also defend the right of individuals to be racist in their decisions about whom to hire, buy from, sell to, serve, or rent to, because they would protect freedom of association and the right to contract. The decisions lie beyond government purview. To Epstein and Bolick, liberty and equality are incompatible, and they choose liberty over equality. Epstein claims that, "An antidiscrimination law is the antithesis of freedom of contract, a principal that allows all persons to do business with whomever they please for good reason, bad reason, or no reason at all."[29] Bolick adds that "using the coercive power of the government to regulate private attitudes and actions . . . constituted a major departure from the [civil rights] movement's traditional objectives."[30]

Epstein and Bolick expect that everything will work out because, by the tenets of the free market, the African American who cannot rent an apartment from a white bigot who doesn't take black tenants can walk down the street and rent from a black bigot who refuses to accommodate whites. If any bigoted landlords are behaving irrationally, they will be disciplined by the loss of rents. They will either self-correct for the sake of their pocketbooks, or they will be driven out of business by the lost revenue. Epstein and Bolick are recommending the worst of all conceivable combinations, prohibiting public responses to race but permitting private practices of racism. They are respectable advocates for an unconditional libertarianism and ought not to be maligned as racists, but they are willing to disregard the realities of white political, economic, and cultural advantages, not to mention the numerical advantage of majority status. (They also cannot oppose affirmative action if it is practiced by private parties rather than by the government.)

Even worse, they are supported by a resurgence in pseudo-scientific social Darwinism. The writers who follow this tradition repeat the worst racial stereotypes, arguing that they are true and therefore form a proper basis for judgment. Accepting their writings at face value without imputing to them any ulterior motives, they must at least agree that they do not champion color blindness as it is commonly understood. They are unabashedly color conscious, insisting that their color consciousness is factually based. An egregious example is Richard Herrnstein and Charles Murray's *The Bell Curve* (discussed in Chapter 2). Another incendiary example is author Dinesh D'Souza's tract *The End of Racism: Principles for a Multiracial Society*.[31] D'Souza ostensibly refuted Herrnstein and Murray's claim of biological determinism with his own pronouncement that African Americans are culturally pathological. By his fantastical history, it is not racism that has produced African American behaviors but African American behaviors that have produced racism. African Americans have only themselves to blame for their lot in life. D'Souza distinguishes himself from Murray and Herrnstein, arguing that his is an attack on African American culture, which may be amenable to change, but theirs is an attack on African American nature, which cannot be as readily changed. D'Souza's distinction is too fine to make any difference, because he still stereotypes by judging the content of character on a group basis. He tends to turn every variety of counterproductive or antisocial conduct into specifically African American conduct, displaying selective sensitivity about whom he criticizes, much as white observers have long looked at white neighbors hanging out on the front stoop of their city rowhouse as socializing and black friends standing on the corner by the store as loitering.

From the earliest writers to the most recent writers, race and culture have been correlated so strongly as to be rendered equivalent. Count Arthur de Gobineau, the nineteenth-century race theorist, believed that race was the genesis of culture. Michael Levin, a philosophy professor at City College in

New York, is as candid as Gobineau. Writing a scholarly monograph for a major publisher in 1997, Levin cites Murray and Herrnstein, D'Souza, Epstein, and Bolick, but wishes they would be more frank. He writes that they "defend a similar position," but, speaking for himself: "I add specifically that, by ordinary standards, the desire of whites to refuse voluntary association with whites is often reasonable." He wonders whether under "ordinary standards of prudence" it is "wise to offer blacks the same 'safety net' that whites offer each other." University of Western Ontario psychologist J. Phillipe Rushton is similarly adamant about black intellectual inadequacy.[32] One cannot be both a believer in color blindness and these works. Yet one also cannot be merely a believer in color blindness and thereby countermand the effects of these works.

Other anti-affirmative action propagandists promote color blindness as a moral imperative, without considering its paradoxical nature. The typical white wedding illustrates the phenomenon. The average couple invites all their family and friends to the wedding, and it turns out that everyone on the guest list is white, except possibly a few Asian Americans from college and maybe a lone African American couple. Their wedding may not be color conscious in the sense that they sat down and jotted down a list that included whites and excluded blacks, but it is color conscious in the sense that the acquaintances they made during childhood and under their parent's upbringing, throughout school and on into the workplace and their adult social life, are all white, or almost all white and Asian American. Without their having made a single intentional decision to practice racial segregation, but not by accident either, the story of their lives bears out the breadth and depth of the racial abyss. Doubtless they are not even aware of how the guests seated at the tables match, not unlike so many place settings of fancy china selected with care. But the black or Latino staff serving the food at the reception will notice.

To observe that the guests at the party are all white (or mostly white with a few Asian Americans, scarcely a major upgrade in the status of African Americans) is only to observe the obvious. It cannot be that the bride and the groom who have created the absence of African Americans, along with the cousin who is tactless enough to notice it, are identically color conscious. In the unlikely event that the newlyweds were embarrassed by the deficiencies in diversity among their social circle, when they returned from their honeymoon they could not do anything about it without taking into account race to neutralize the racial tendencies that otherwise would determine their actions.

The paradox is this: Color blindness requires color-consciousness, or it becomes impossible to discern itself. In the white wedding case, when the guest list is color conscious—all white or all white with a few Asian Americans is about as color conscious as it could be—we cannot know it by being color blind. In the contrary case, if the guest list were color blind—that is, it had people of all racial backgrounds—we would know it only by being color conscious. We cannot disabuse ourselves of race without using race.

Indeed, people who truly would like to be color blind must be willful to the point of perversity. Imagine what their lives would be like if they censored race fastidiously. They must assume that it is equally likely that a white, black, and Asian person whom they encounter is foreign-born, speaks Chinese, or is named "Wu." They could only deduce, without directly asking, that it was the Asian person who was foreign-born, spoke Chinese, and was named "Wu" if they impermissibly relied on race. They could not decide that the Chinese restaurant with many Asian diners is "authentic." They would have to refrain from telling two friends who were meeting one another for the first time beneath the clock tower at Grand Central Station that one should look for a white woman and the other should look for a black woman. They could not study the test gap—differences in average scores of whites and blacks on the SAT, wide enough that even lower-class whites outscore middle-class blacks on average—because they could discern high scores and low scores but could not differentiate between white and black test-takers. They could devote themselves to increasing the scholastic accomplishments of all American youngsters, but not specifically African American kids, for the same reason of their invisibility. In each of these situations, they could not use race to draw inferences about individuals, to give complete identifications of them, or to do academic research.

If they balk at any of these limitations, it can only be because they would like to make an exception to their rule where it is customary to be color conscious or when it would be a bizarre affectation to be color blind. They may conclude that they cannot bring themselves to say "Wu" and look expectantly at the white person while turning away from the Asian person, or to say, "oh, this Chinese restaurant must be authentic" if the patrons are all black, or to omit race in describing their friends to one another and expect them to find each other. They may want to alleviate the test gap. They do not, then, treat skin color as the equivalent of eye color, as color blindness is sometimes defined. They take skin color to be meaningful for various reasons that the color of eyes is not. We may agree with them, and in doing so we replace color blindness with common sense. As University of California at

Santa Cruz philosophy professor Richard Wasserstrom has written, "Eye color is an irrelevant category; nobody cares what color people's eyes are; it is not an important cultural fact; nothing turns on what eye color you have." He argues, "it is essential to see that race is not like that at all."[33]

Perhaps what we need is a color conscience, a meta-color consciousness, not color blindness.[34] The prefix "meta" refers to a logical level above that under consideration. Despite its mystical sound, it is not mystifying. For example, we engage in meta-conversation quite often: conversation that is about conversation, as when we talk about how rudely so-and-so speaks to her spouse. Meta-color consciousness just means consciousness of our color consciousness. We would strive to be aware of our prejudices, eliminating them if possible but not suppressing them.

Meritocracy is not all that it seems either. Meritocracy is a considerable improvement over a good-old-boy network in which connections determine opportunities or an ad hoc system of variable criteria that can be abused for discriminatory reasons. Most of us agree with the gist of meritocracy, that people should set high standards and work hard. We like the underlying assumptions that the good things in life are distributed equitably. We have confidence that people receive what they deserve, and vice versa. Merit does deserve praise. It has no opponents, and affirmative action supporters who argue against it are sure to be trounced.

Yet the opposite of meritocracy is not mediocrity. Affirmative action principles compel us to realize that merit comes in many forms, and the distribution of rewards can be made more just. In most selection processes, decision makers must pick among many competitors who meet the threshold qualifications, not between a single person who is patently more qualified in every respect and everyone else. In the University of California system, for example, admissions officers are forming an entering class from among thousands of students who are "U.C. qualified."

As we make these decisions, we should keep in mind that paper credentials and real-world performance may not be the same. Paper credentials are just predictors of merit, not merit itself. We use them in a gatekeeping function. They have no intrinsic meaning but are an administrative device that allows us to sort out up front, conveniently and efficiently, the people likely to do well from those not likely to do well.

The best means of guessing individuals' future success and their likely socioeconomic status is to look at their childhood and their parents' socioeconomic status. If our society were placing bets on people, which in crass terms is exactly what we are doing when we admit them to an elite institution, we could do much worse than to bank on the individuals who are already rich, powerful, or both. Few of us would be rewarded if we substituted paper credentials with the better gauge of inherited privilege. Although paper credentials may be better than inherited privilege, they are only slightly better. In a diverse democracy, individual opportunity should not be circumscribed by either paper credentials or inherited privilege.

The most significant paper credentials that people acquire nowadays are their scores on standardized tests such as the SAT. Our culture has become enamored of tests and has given them a role out of all proportion to their degree of accuracy. The makers of standardized tests, however, will admit that their products give rough forecasts, no more; they are not numbers pulled out of a hat, but they are certainly not measures of our worth as human beings. Each test predicts performance at the next level, and not beyond: The SAT predicts college grades, the LSAT predicts law school grades, and so forth. The tests predict only within a margin of error. All lawyers know the joke about "A" students becoming professors, "B" students becoming judges, and "C" students making a lot of money, which suggests that grades are associated inversely with material success. The joke is not off the mark. A 2001 study of University of Michigan law school, a highly selective institution, and its graduates showed that an admissions index using grades and LSAT did not predict salary, job satisfaction, or civic contributions.[35]

Paper credentials also have racial problems. Standardized tests may not be as valid for people of color, particularly African Americans, for complex psychological reasons that can be proven even if they are not fully understood. The rudimentary attacks on test bias concern questions that incorporate crude racial stereotypes or that require knowledge of middle-class white culture. The most recent studies of the test gap reveal a much more significant set of problems not amenable to the cure of thorough editing. In the 2001 University of Michigan law school affirmative action trial, students who had intervened to support affirmative action called expert witnesses (I appeared as an expert witness on Asian Americans) who testified on these insidious forms of test bias.

Jay Rosner, director of the Princeton Review Foundation, and David White, director of Testing for the Public,[36] explained in their expert reports and trial testimony how test scores, despite their seeming objectivity, may not be as reliable for African Americans. Standardized tests are "normed" to ensure their validity. If people who do well on the test tend to do poorly on a specific question, while people who do poorly on the test do well on the same question, then the question is deemed unreliable. The refinement of the test skews it toward the racial majority. There are many questions, which have no noticeable racial or cultural connotations, on which whites tend to do better than African Americans, and a few on which African Americans tend to do better than whites. The former are preferred, because questions on which a minority outperforms the majority may produce anomalous results. The following SAT question, for example, was eliminated because African Americans were able to do better than whites:

The actor's bearing on stage seemed _____; her movements were natural and her technique _____.

    a. unremitting . . . blasé
    b. fluid . . . tentative
    c. unstudied . . . uncontrived
    d. eclectic . . . uniform
    e. grandiose . . . controlled

(The correct answer is c.)

Two studies, conducted twenty years apart, by Joseph Gannon and William Kidder,[37] respectively, also show that African American students and white students who have done as well in school still perform differently on standardized tests. Gannon and Kidder each found that by looking at students accepted to law school and matching up black and white students with the same grades (to within .1 on a 4.0 scale), in the same majors, at the same institutions, the black students had done less well on the LSAT. These studies suggest that there are more significant problems that arise from standardized tests.

The racial disparities may be explained by racial discrimination. Stanford psychologist Claude Steele[38] has performed experiments using African Americans (and, in parallel experiments on gender, using women) that point toward the existence of what he calls "stereotype threat." He finds that African Americans who have done well in the past on standardized tests continue to do well on the tests, if they are told beforehand that African Americans and whites have performed comparably. However, if they are told nothing or if they are asked merely to identify themselves by race prior to starting the test, their scores are lowered. They need not be told blacks do less well than whites, and nobody need intimate to them that they are under scrutiny. They already know full well that there is a racial gap that makes others suppose they are stupid, and that more rides on their performance than on that of whites or Asian Americans. Steele hypothesizes that African Americans, especially those who value academic achievement, are plagued by "stereotype threat," a fear, brought on by racial stereotypes, that they risk confirming images of black intellectual inferiority. He provides the following metaphor: "Blacks in America are like people on thin ice. Any little crack means a lot."[39] The test may be the same, but its context varies by race.

As Nicholas Lehman, author of *The Big Test: The Secret History of the American Meritocracy*,[40] has argued, because of its dependence on standardized tests, meritocracy may be a poor model for higher education in a democratic society. By a meritocratic conception, higher education becomes a reward for the past rather than an opportunity for the future. Because of the importance of higher education to socioeconomic success, people's lot in life should not be largely determined by standardized testing. Lehman's exposé has been provocative. In February 2001, Richard Atkinson, a psychologist who is president of the University of California system, proposed to other university presidents that their schools make the SAT optional; the University of California system is at the forefront of considering college applicants' entire portfolio. In spring 2001, the National Urban League began to mobilize corporate leaders to back its call for replacing the SAT with consideration of creativity, motivation, and other tests that measure learning more comprehensively.

Merit is also an artificial construct that is not neutral. We make it up to suit ourselves in many situations. Choosing the definition of merit chooses the identity of the people who possess it. In the process of bidding for federal government contracts, such effects are apparent, and even a fair system can easily be rigged. The simplest criterion for evaluating the sealed bids submitted by competing firms is cost: The low bid is the winning one. However, virtually all projects can be described differently, varying merit wildly. If the work to be done is put out to competitive bidding in small lots, as when a county administrator responsible for the upkeep of public buildings looks for private firms to take care of the painting, plumbing, electrical, masonry, roofing, and janitorial services, respectively, then small businesses can participate. The family-owned painting firm can compete effectively. But all it takes is a decision by the county administrator to "bundle" the work, so that the contract is for painting, plumbing, electrical, masonry, roofing, and janitorial services together, and suddenly only big businesses can participate. No matter how good the family-owned painting firm might be, its limited merit is extraneous. Affirmative action moderates this effect.

Merit is subject to other influences as well. In the process of bidding for federal government contracts, most of us would consider more than just cost. We desire other features, derived from societal ambitions that may be subjective or hard to quantify and that have nothing to do with the particular project that we put out to bid. As we should, we incorporate ethical judgments into our meritocratic calculations. However, each such ethical judgment detracts from the pure meritocracy that finds the low bid. We require the bidders to be licensed and unionized, to pay minimum wage and to buy American; we enforce occupational health and safety rules and collect contributions to workers' compensation funds; and we prohibit them from hiring children or undocumented immigrants. We are not impressed by a firm that advises the county administrator that if it is allowed to circumvent these rules it could deliver the same services—even better services—for a lower price. A requirement that a contractor have a workforce that is integrated rather than segregated is no different than the requirements that its employees be old enough to work and not underage or that they be citizens and legal immigrants and not unauthorized workers.

As it is, all of us have skills and talents that cannot be calculated or readily compared. Athletic ability, musical aptitude, leadership talent, language proficiency, and numerous other characteristics are laudable. Major universities regularly recruit African American athletes who would not be admitted if they could not bring glory to the school wearing its colors in the stadium, showing a willingness to define merit for their own use. Most of us would agree that an individual who is willing to move or return to an impoverished neighborhood that would lack a doctor without her is demonstrating a trait that is commendable and should be counted. But these factors cannot be easily and routinely assessed without a formula for weighing each. The formula, and the merit it measures, is meaningless without value judgments.

We can see this at any university. The higher education setting is where affirmative action has been most significant and most contentious. At any school, even with its general mission of spreading knowledge, merit is exhibited in several ways and should be evaluated accordingly. The faculty are a good example. Among the faculty, there are always a few whom the students hate and avoid as boring, confusing, or pompous, or all three at once. The students may not know that the same professor won a MacArthur Award or a Pulitzer Prize or has received major grants to conduct much-needed scientific research. He brings distinction to the school, which attracts the students. He has merit as a scholar but not as a teacher.

There also are some faculty whom the students love because they turn dull academic specialties into scintillating subjects and mentor their pupils to pursue a new major and even a career of which they weren't aware before. This teacher's academic colleagues may think poorly of her, if they consider her work at all, because she may be unknown, having published nothing. She serves the pedagogical purpose of the school, for which the students and their parents have paid a ransom in tuition. She has merit as a teacher but not as a scholar.

Then there are people who serve as excellent administrators, seeing to it that the faculty are paid, the students receive financial aid, funds are raised for new libraries, and everything operates efficiently. They also perform a function that is vital but underappreciated. Their colleagues who are able scholars and fine teachers may be unable to manage their own offices, much less lead the school.

All of these professionals have merit. None is likely to excel in each and every dimension of merit. It may even be that some of the forms of merit are demerits by another measure. The professor who writes well and publishes too many articles for a lay audience may be teaching, but each additional op-ed piece in a newspaper counts against that teacher in a peer review of specialized scholarship. Applying a one-dimensional definition of merit would lead to overemphasis on one factor at the expense of others. No top-flight university could exist with only scholars, only teachers, or only administrators. Diversity is as advisable for a school as it is for a stock portfolio.

Meritocracy also must be moderated if it is not to be detrimental to democracy.[41] A voter for meritocracy is a voter with hubris. He thinks that he lives in radio commentator Garrison Keillor's fictional Lake Woebegone, where all the children are above average. In reality, few of us would prosper in a harsh system in which societal entitlements were distributed on the basis of standardized test scores from high school. It should not need to be said, but half of us will always end up in the bottom half of the class. Shakespeare's Hamlet had it right when he recoiled at everyone receiving his just deserts, for none of us would escape a whipping.

Perfecting meritocracy would not improve it. A genuine meritocracy would be an elitist brave new world. The better the meritocracy, the worse the social stratification. In a meritocracy, people at the bottom deserve to be at the bottom. We would be sorted out by our respective statuses, without the corruption of biased decisions or the luck of random chance. The scheme would foster a mandarin class that had mastered only exam-taking, as in the courts of ancient China, or it would call for intense competition, as in modern Japanese schools.

Beyond the problems with color blindness and meritocracy, opponents of affirmative action may not favor either in their pure forms. Juxtaposing the backlash against affirmative action with the campaign to close the borders shows how some people are capricious in their use of color blindness and restrictive in their definition of meritocracy. They may start with the conviction that we should not see race in attacking affirmative action, but they revert to looking straight at race when they attack immigration policies. If affirmative action is an argument against immigration and vice versa, the risk is that both will be lost.

In *Alien Nation*,[42] Peter Brimelow declares in an aside that he dislikes affirmative action because it is unfair to judge people based on skin color. Like any parent, Brimelow is concerned about the fate of his "blonde-haired blue-eyed" son. Recognizing that his protective comments about his "blonde-haired blue-eyed" son have been widely quoted, he defended himself at a symposium at Rutgers University in 1998. He said that he was speaking of the interaction between immigration and affirmative action: "It absolutely matters to those of us who have white children. We have to ask ourselves what kind of country this is going to be. We have to ask ourselves why our children should be disadvantaged by the inflow of people who have no historical relationship with the country."[43] As more than one observer has noted, it is not altogether clear what historical relationship Brimelow himself—as a British immigrant—can claim to the United States, unless he can take advantage of a tacit racial tie between his homeland and his adopted country. If such a racial tie can form the basis of a historical relationship, then Africans can make the same claim through their ancestors who were slaves, Latinos through their ancestors whose territory was conquered, and even Asians through those who were sojourners and early settlers. By his own admission throughout his book, however, Brimelow's anxieties extend beyond affirmative action. Even without affirmative action, he is still against immigration for a host of specious reasons. Despite his appreciation of color blind meritocratic competition, in the immigration context he quite quickly becomes nationalistic and protectionist. He uses race to demarcate citizenship, then uses citizenship to limit the scope of competition.

Wholly aside from affirmative action, we have adopted the opposite of color blind meritocracy with respect to Asian immigrants. In most instances, for would-be immigrants who seek to come to the United States for employment to obtain visas, the company trying to hire them must demonstrate that there are no "able, willing, and qualified" native workers.[44] The federal government, through the Labor Department, must certify that the test has been passed. The phrasing of the requirement is important: The immigrant is held to a higher standard than the citizen, not the same standard. Even if the immigrant is exceptionally capable and the citizen only marginally competent, the immigrant must give way to the citizen.

On university campuses, there is even a trend directed more away from color blind meritocracy, coincidentally as Asian students have become ubiquitous.[45] Many public universities are facing political demands from state legislatures to cut back the number of international students they accept. Some schools have Ph.D. programs in technical fields with enrollments that consist entirely of overseas visitors. These Asians—along with some Africans, Europeans, and Latin Americans—who are temporary residents during their education are perceived as a menace. Either they will stay here to practice their profession, taking jobs away from real Americans, or they will return home to become adversaries, stealing trade secrets.

As many administrators of research universities will volunteer, however, international students are a positive asset. They fill low-paid teaching slots that Americans aren't interested in. Our Gen-X-ers with bachelor's degrees in electrical engineering rush to join a high-tech start-up company and start making more money than their professors immediately, instead of wasting years in a graduate program. The latest statistics from the National Science Foundation show that after five consecutive years of declining enrollment in graduate programs for technical disciplines, in 1999 there was a slight rise, due entirely to the foreign student contingent rising to 110,000 (against a total in citizen students of 300,000). Plus, the foreigners pay full tuition for their degrees and are not allowed to access many scholarships.

The movement against immigrant workers and international students reveals a discrepancy. If we were committed to hiring and enrolling the best-qualified individuals in a color blind meritocracy, we would embrace the best applicants wherever they come from. By color blind meritocratic measures, we should treat foreigners the same as we do citizens, even or especially if they are rivals whose competition is intimidating. Instead, our competition is bounded and citizens are favored.

There are other preferences in higher education that constitute affirmative action but that are not controversial. At elite private universities, alumni children—referred to as "legacies"—are sought after and admitted under special standards. Century Foundation fellow Richard D. Kahlenberg reported in *The Remedy: Class, Race, and Affirmative Action*,[46] his brief for class-based affirmative action, that Harvard College enrolled more such alumni children in its 1988 entering class than African Americans, Mexican Americans, and Native Americans combined. At numerous schools, admissions rates for legacies are more than twice as high as within the general applicant pool even though the legacies who are admitted have lower test scores: Harvard admitted alumni children at the rate of 40 percent for its 1995 class, compared to 14 percent for the general applicant pool (although Harvard used to admit alumni children at the rate of more than 90 percent); at University of Pennsylvania, the legacy admittance rate was 66 percent in 1995; at Duke, 50 percent in 2000. A few less well-known private schools are even offering $20,000 scholarships to legacies.

An alumni preference policy gives special treatment mainly to whites, and not only just any whites but well-to-do whites. They are fortunate enough to be born with fathers and grandfathers who attended the schools when they were virtually all-white and absolutely all-male. As recently as fifty years ago, these schools discriminated among even white men, taking few white ethnics and poor students; they had a "gentlemen's agreement" on the number of Jews. In admitting alumni children, their identity rather than their academic qualifications takes precedence. Individuals are welcomed who, if they were not legacies, would not stand a chance.

Although many critics of affirmative action claim that it stamps some sort of stigma on its beneficiaries, the same stigma does not afflict alumni children. American University economist Barbara Bergmann, in her book *In Defense of Affirmative Action,*[47] observes that people who take advantage of nepotism tend to pride themselves on being, like their forebears, where they feel at home. They are able to join the same dining clubs at the alma mater as their parents belonged to and attend classes in buildings named after relatives.

In response to this comparison, some opponents of affirmative action declare that they are not fond of alumni preferences either. They can write off alumni preferences as a debater's point, but they do not bother with a full-scale attack against alumni preferences, by arousing public furor, organizing ballot initiatives, filing lawsuits, and the like. University administrators rationalize enrolling legacies as the ordinary course of business, nurturing ties between a family and the institution and bringing in donations.

The best public universities have their own preference programs with their own message about who belongs. Every state with a higher education system that is selective (California, New York, Michigan, Texas, Virginia) favors residents and discriminates against non-residents. Resident students and out-of-state students typically have different credentials. More accurately, state residents are less academically qualified on average than out-of-state students as measured by test scores. Just as galling to the out-of-state residents, they must take out much higher loans to receive exactly the same education, because they pay twice the tuition as resident students sitting next to them in the same classes. The University of California system even has a special "VIP" admissions program for the select few who can obtain a recommendation from a regent. There has never been a victorious legal challenge to state resident preferences in college admissions, and the University of California has retained its "VIP" program throughout its deliberations over affirmative action.

At this point, many sensible people will object, "Come on, it's obvious why we do that, treat residents and non-residents differently." Yet it is obvious only because we all assume that some people are members of the community who understand that they own its institutions. Other people are outsiders who cannot lay claim to community institutions. The entitlements enjoyed by insiders are so obvious that they are taken for granted by those who possess them as well as those who are denied them. For whatever reason, most of us are not as livid about advantages given to native-born citizens, alumni children, state residents, or the politically connected, although some of us are resentful of relatively modest efforts to promote racial integration. Some winners (native-born citizens and alumni children at universities) are regarded as deserving even though they have not complied with the rules of color blind meritocratic competition, but other winners (Asian immigrants in graduate school and African Americans at elite colleges) are regarded as undeserving even if they have played by the rules. If state residents or VIPs are given preferences, we may understand "that's just the way things are done." In the 1996 case of Cheryl Hopwood,[48] who sued the University of Texas law school for reverse discrimination, the evidence showed that dozens of white individuals with lower composite grades and LSAT scores were admitted ahead of her, no differently than the African Americans. Her complaint did not assert that those white individuals had cheated her.

Some of the most prominent people in society would fare poorly under color blind meritocracy but have done well by other forms of preference. During the 2000 presidential elections, investigative journalists broke the news about some of the leading candidates having had abysmal SAT scores, well below the range that would be acceptable for admission to exclusive schools then or now. They were admitted regardless. Democratic contender

Bill Bradley was a basketball player who starred for the Princeton Tigers; the ultimate winner, President George W. Bush, was a "double legacy" with a father and grandfather who had been Yalies, and his family was politically connected. (Former Vice President Al Gore tested well on IQ tests and had a 1355 on the SAT, equal to a 1420 by today's scale; he would have had a 50–50 chance of acceptance to Harvard even were he not a senator's son.)

The other preferences show that the costs of affirmative action are paltry compared with either those of other preferences or with the benefits of affirmative action. The benefit of affirmative action to African Americans as communities dwarfs the costs to the majority; in college admissions, that majority consists of whites and Asian Americans together. Even if a single African American has ousted a single white or Asian American, that single African American constitutes ten times as much of the African American population as the single white or Asian American makes up of the majority. Rid of affirmative action, almost all whites and Asian Americans who were rejected (and had cursed affirmative action) would remain rejected. They would lose out, however, to other whites and Asian Americans. Some 4,000 students with straight-A averages are denied admission at University of California–Berkeley every year. That number has not been affected by the end of affirmative action.

If opponents of affirmative action lived up to their principles of color blind meritocracy, they would set their priorities straight. They would seek to put an end to the many other preferences with racial effects: better funding for suburban schools; the availability of an advanced placement curriculum that also gives a boost to grade point averages because a "B" in an AP class is counted as an "A"; and the highly effective private tutoring for standardized tests that claims to raise scores by 100 points or more on the SAT— among other programs that are directed primarily to whites and to a lesser extent to Asian Americans. (It would be ironic, though, if alumni preferences ended just as there were ample numbers of minority legacies ready to take advantage of their largesse.) They would eliminate political patronage, which places as much importance on partisan connections as it does on any form of merit, in the hiring process for government jobs.

By itself, none of these examples is an argument for affirmative action. Taken together, however, they show a certain uniformity. Our behavior is consistent, not with color blindness and meritocracy, but with our sense of community and membership. Our conceptions of community are not color blind. Membership confers merit. We accept that some people belong in certain places. They belong at certain institutions just as the institutions belong to them. The elimination of affirmative action does not magically restore neutrality; what preceded affirmative action was outright hostility toward African Americans. Where affirmative action has been eliminated, what has followed has not been a removal of stigma from the few African Americans and Latinos who have remained; it has been, instead, a worsening of their feelings of exclusion.

Affirmative action should not be regarded as nihilistic. We should not abandon all attempts to set standards, nor should we hire and promote unqualified individuals over qualified ones. But the inconsistencies cast doubt on how well opponents of affirmative action adhere to the principles of color blindness and meritocracy, hinting that the standards we choose may be arbitrary. They oblige us to ask how to offer expanded opportunities.

In its comprehensive forms, affirmative action helps whites directly. Although affirmative action is often discussed in racial terms without consideration of its gender effects, white women have been the largest beneficiary class. The more affirmative action expands, not based on assumptions that whites are disadvantaged but on undoing preferences such as alumni preferences that favor some whites over other whites, the better off whites will be. Such expansion comes about because affirmative action leads to reconsideration of exclusionary practices beyond those affecting African Americans. The plaintiff in the most famous reverse discrimination case, Allan Bakke, who sought admission to medical school, almost certainly faced discrimination unrelated to race that was widespread a generation ago; he probably would be part of any affirmative action program now. Bakke was a nontraditional student; that is, he was an older individual who wanted to become a doctor as a second career. Medical school admissions officers stereotyped on the basis of age, assuming that only youthful college graduates would be able to handle the stress. (Medical school faculties reportedly still do this informally and illegally.)

In all this, Asian Americans face a decision. The imperative to be principled is clear. Affirmative action seems to present Asian Americans with stark choices. In 1996, when considering California Proposition 209, an anti-affirmative action referendum, we could have aligned ourselves with whites or blacks. The majority of whites voted for the ballot measure; the majority of blacks, against it. Asian Americans split the difference. We voted with other people of color against the measure, but without the same decisiveness that whites and blacks displayed.

Privately, some Asian Americans consider affirmative action as if the only issue is whether their children can attend Harvard or Stanford. They forget the importance of remedial programs, which include them alongside other people of color and rightly so under the circumstances, in opening access to jobs on the San Francisco police force and its fire department or opportunities to win federal government contracts. They are elitists who do not serve well the majority of Asian Americans, whose ambitions are not to be the chief executive officers of Fortune 500 companies but to have their own small business. Their wealth makes them less sympathetic toward other racial minorities as well as less fortunate Asian Americans. (After passage of Proposition 209 in California, for example, Filipino Americans, like African Americans, were "zeroed out" at University of California at Berkeley's Boalt Hall School of Law; they suffered several years with no students of Filipino descent, despite the Bay Area having one of the largest Filipino populations in the country.)

Among Asian Americans, these speakers will tell their appreciative audiences, "we must be color-blind in college admissions, because if we are not it will hurt our children." Their color blindness is immediately belied by their concern for "our children"—meaning Asian American children alone—but it is ingrained so strongly that they do not comprehend their own reasoning. The problem is that their claim is not (and could not be), "we must be color-blind in college admissions, because if we are not it will hurt all children." If they were genuinely color blind, they would care about all children. On the contrary, their professed color blindness serves a selfish color consciousness. They are more honest when they say, "we must look at grades and test scores, because that would help our children." That is different than the claim, "we must look at grades and test scores, because that would be more objective." When the claims are made simultaneously, the former is obviously couched in terms of the latter for rhetorical purposes. It sounds more crass to "help our children" than to "be more objective." That these sentiments tend to be voiced privately makes them all the more regrettable.

Other Asian Americans oppose affirmative action in college admissions and entry-level corporate hiring because they expect they and theirs will pay the costs, but they support it in efforts to break through the glass ceiling at the corporate workplace or for government contracts because they expect to gain direct benefits. Of all the positions they could take, this is the worst. People naturally want to do well for themselves and want what is best for their children, but short-term self-interest does not even serve long-term self-interest, much less the collective good. At least opponents of affirmative action who would like to do away with it completely can claim that they are consistent. If Asian Americans cannot abide affirmative action in college admissions, then they cannot agitate for any remedy to the glass ceiling in the corporate workplace. Other than on the grounds that they personally may be helped in one instance and possibly hurt in another instance, there is no distinguishing between the remedy that considers race in college admissions and the remedy that does so for promotions at the workplace.

Even if Asian Americans thought about only the consequences for Asian Americans, we should see that if we urged support for affirmative action when we would profit but fomented opposition to it everywhere else, blacks and whites alike would become aware that we were pursuing a selfish agenda. We would find ourselves shunned by other communities, because we could not be counted on to engage in the mutual give and take of democratic politics.

Racial Pragmatism

Once we have stated the problem, racial discrimination, and affirmed our racial principles, equality and integration, we must develop policies that work. Pragmatism is an American intellectual movement. Its only axiom is abstaining from the axiomatic. From philosopher Charles Peirce, psychologist William James, and especially educator John Dewey, we have inherited a tradition of emphasizing the tangible consequences of our actions over the hypothetical implications of vague ideologies. James, for example, was a radical empiricist who tested all possibilities as he looked for the "cash value" of each theory.

Pragmatism is creative. It demands that we analyze whether we would be better or worse off with each of the many options. By its methodology, legal liability is less germane. Parties guilty of racism should accept responsibility for causing grievous injuries, but even apparent bystanders can be supportive. Individuals exonerated of racial guilt still have civic responsibilities. Although most of the general population can proclaim honestly that their ancestors were not slaveholders, even Asian immigrants who arrived after the Jim Crow era have indirectly gained advantages from their own nonblackness. Their assimilation has been eased because they can and do distinguish themselves from African Americans. As citizens, all of us can and should play a part in any remedial efforts.

In a highly competitive global economy, our nation gains nothing if a major portion of the population is excluded. In a diverse democracy, it is not acceptable to have a university, especially the flagship campus of a public system, that is all-white or all-white and Asian American. Without some sort of affirmative action, that outcome at elite institutions, especially professional schools and graduate programs, is a foregone conclusion.[49]

All but the most diehard opponents of affirmative action recognize that such a situation is untenable. Harvard sociologist Nathan Glazer and Boston University economist Glenn Loury, staunch opponents of affirmative action, have come around to subdued support.[50] Even the Center for Individual Rights, which once obstinately opposed the goal of diversity, now sometimes gives in to the goal of diversity while continuing to defy direct means of achieving it.

Coalitions in California and Texas have strained to restore a semblance of integration without affirmative action. In California, they have tried class-based affirmative action for the University of California. In Texas, they have used a 10 percent plan that admits the top graduates of every state high school to a state college. We all know that race is volatile; everybody wishes that blacks and whites had the same average standardized test scores, without the depressing effects of "stereotype threat"; and nobody wants to make decisions based on race, inciting resentment among whites or Asian Americans. Given all that, if we do not want institutions that have few if any African Americans and Latinos, we have a choice to make.

We are faced with a series of possibilities. Considering each option in turn makes the case for affirmative action. We could do nothing, for either of two reasons. On the one hand, we could deny that there is any problem. We could be indifferent to whether African Americans have acquired their share of society's bounty and unwilling to see that society has problems related to race. On the other hand, we might acknowledge that African Americans have been held back for racial reasons, but we could aver that a system of laissez faire libertarianism would be the best response. The distinction between the rationales and the possibility that someone might privately be indifferent but publicly espouse laissez faire libertarianism is not especially important, because doing nothing is irresponsible.

Whatever the motivation, inaction is a doomed course. A combination of internal and external forces, ranging from a grassroots civil rights movement and powerful Supreme Court decisions to responsible corporate leadership and a panoply of government programs, produced what racial equality we have. The dynamics of the marketplace are a terrific engine for economic growth. They have produced amazing results here and around the world, but eliminating bias does not appear to be among them anywhere unless purposeful measures are taken with that aim in mind. The market itself is invented and regulated. Market failures occur.[51] Market conventions can incorporate incentives that either promote racial progress or inhibit it. Enough people have a preference for racial discrimination that they will pay a price for it, meaning that exclusion commands a premium. Left to their own devices, even businesses whose owners are not themselves interested in discrimination find it lucrative to cater to customers who are discriminating. Properly used, affirmative action itself is a market-based solution. It alters the market to reward racial diversity.

Harvard sociologist William Julius Wilson has argued persuasively that structural problems in the workplace hamper African Americans seeking jobs.[52] Companies have moved away from major cities, especially manufacturers with high-paying, low-skill jobs in the Midwest. They have relocated in outer suburbs of edge cities, predominantly white regions, or even out of the country. African Americans tend to have social networks that are much more densely interconnected but that are not tied to employers. Because the majority of hiring is done by people who have a prior relationship of some sort with their prospective employees, African Americans are left at a loss. Unlike even whites of comparable socioeconomic backgrounds, the average African American in the slums of the inner city does not have extended family connections to a plant manager or secretarial supervisor.

We could exhort people to be color blind. Our beliefs, good or bad, are significant. Preachers from their pulpits and leaders of every type have inspired revelations and revolutions of the heart and the head. Individuals experience epiphanies, and families inculcate anti-discriminatory ethics. The determination to be color blind, however, is not sufficient by itself although it is necessary. As noble as they may be, good intentions are only good intentions; admonitions can be heeded in the breach; and rules are empty without enforcement. Other than with respect to racial problems, there are few areas of public policy where people even entertain the idea that promises to be better are adequate.

We could enact legislation forbidding racial discrimination. The many civil rights acts, with their provisions for lawsuits, have been powerful weapons in battling racial intolerance, but they are no panacea, because they offer redress only if evidence is of the "smoking gun" variety. As much as it pains lawyers to admit it, litigation should be a last resort, because it is among the least satisfactory means for resolving society's disputes. It is complex, contentious, expensive, and uncertain, as well as proceeding deliberately after the fact on a case-by-case basis.

If discrimination cannot be eradicated on its own accord, or by exhortation and legislation, we could urge African Americans toward collective self-improvement following the accommodationist route of Booker T. Washington. Like other measures, the plan is partial at best. Although all of us could better ourselves, suggesting to African Americans that they can vanquish discrimination by doing so accepts the premise of the prejudice—namely, that African Americans are not as good as other Americans and must grow. It blames the victims, as if what is wrong is African Americans themselves and not discrimination.

Collective self-improvement for African Americans also resigns us to color consciousness. If anything were to lead to balkanization, the idea that each racial group ought to tend to its own and only its own would subvert our civic culture. African Americans have pursued economic self-empowerment through a combination of entrepreneurial spirit and black nationalism. They have started small businesses and called for spending of money within their communities and among their own. Regardless of the viability of these efforts, they are in no sense color blind. The boycott of an Asian-owned grocery store and a fight to replace it with a black-owned counterpart employs race as a basis for organizing people and as a decisive factor for directing behavior. The impetus is toward self-segregation, not integration.

As the culmination of a sequence of unsatisfactory options, then, affirmative action becomes more attractive. In the most expansive sense, affirmative action means measures that refer to race to address problems related to race. The crux of affirmative action is the use of race to respond to racial disparities. Affirmative action was initially the moderate or even conservative option to liberal direct aid. It was proposed by President Lyndon Johnson in a commencement speech at Howard University in 1965, using the metaphor of a footrace in which one runner is shackled as the others make their way around the track; freeing the shackled runner and shouting "compete" is unfair.[53] But it was carried out most extensively by President Richard Nixon, who plotted to use it for driving a wedge between traditional liberal constituencies of labor unions and African Americans.[54] It worked as he had foreseen.

Whatever the political impetus, recent studies have confirmed that racially conscious remedial programs can be successful. They also have documented that without the use of race the same outcomes could not have been obtained.

Charles Moskos and John Sibley Butler, two sociologists, one white and one black, have tracked the salutary effects of affirmative action in the U.S. Army. In the preface to their acclaimed study, *All That We Can Be: Black Leadership and Racial Integration the Army Way*,[55] they explain that as military veterans who had become academic researchers, they were drawn to their subject. They remark wittily that the Army intrigued them because it was the only place in American society where whites were routinely bossed around by blacks. They explain that the military branch flourished in spite of the transition from a segregated force formed through conscription to an integrated fighting force made up of volunteers. It now boasts African Americans throughout the ranks, making up 27 percent of the total Army, far exceeding their proportions in the overall population, from the lowliest levels of enlisted personnel to flag officers and the Joint Chiefs of Staff; they are not cannon fodder.

The Army managed to arrive at this extraordinary result only through aggressive use of affirmative action, setting goals and revising timetables. It finds its pool of racial minorities, retains them, and trains them—with programs for African Americans that are available to everyone—to make certain that it always has enough people who are qualified to promote to the next level. If it falls short, it redoubles its efforts. With a culture that is new and demeaning to both blacks and whites, the military also instills "unit cohesion," an esprit de corps bonding among soldiers that transcends any form of divisions, turning individuals who have nothing in common into comrades willing to die for one another.

Moskos and Butler say that a level playing field is not enough, but they are not doctrinaire. They argue that it is more important to give blacks opportunities than to eliminate racism, without recognizing that the former lacks a rationale without the latter. The military has a command hierarchy, zero tolerance policies, and other characteristics that civilian society cannot or would not wish to emulate, but its outstanding use of affirmative action is a counterpoint to those who write off the programs as liberal.

William Bowen and Derek Bok, the former presidents of Princeton and Harvard, respectively, examined college admissions since before the advent of affirmative action. Their exhaustive survey, *The Shape of the River: Long-Term Consequences of Considering Race in College and University Admissions*,[56] covers some 80,000 students and selection processes for the entering classes at twenty-eight of the most selective institutions of higher education from 1951 to 1989. Among the schools in the top tier, Bryn Mawr, Duke, Princeton, Rice, Stanford, Swarthmore, Williams, and Yale are included. Major public universities were also included Miami of Ohio, Michigan, North Carolina, and Penn State. Between 1960 and 1995, African Americans increased their college graduation rates from 5.4 to 15.4 percent. Between 1951 and 1989, they increased their enrollment at highly selective colleges from less than 1 percent to 7 percent. Their representation at law schools between 1960 and 1995 rose from 1 percent to 7.5 percent; at medical schools between 1964 and 1995, from 2.2 percent to 8.1 percent. The African American students in the study are phenomenal: In 1989, 90 percent scored higher on the SAT than all other black test-takers, and 75 percent scored higher than the white average. They scored higher than the 1951 average for students enrolled at the same schools. Only at SAT scores of over 1500 are African Americans certain to gain admission (with the same scores, about two-thirds of white students are accepted).

Bowen and Bok found that even though African American students matriculated through affirmative action had somewhat weaker records by conventional criteria such as test scores, they graduated at only slightly lower rates. The graduation figure is more heavily influenced by socioeconomic status than by grades, and African American students came from backgrounds that are less privileged on average. They went on to further study at the same rates, before continuing on to lead lives that are comparable to their white peers in every respect. In 1976, for example, approximately 700 students at elite schools had been admitted through affirmative action. Of these, 225 attended graduate or professional schools, 130 became lawyers or doctors, and 125 became business executives. Although African Americans made less money than whites, especially among men, that itself is likely a sign of further racial discrimination even among African Americans with resumes above reproach, because much of the disparity cannot be explained no matter how many other variables are introduced. African Americans surpassed whites in civic involvement, especially in taking leadership positions. In life satisfaction, the African American graduates and the white graduates were similar. Bowen and Bok also disproved many of the oft-made claims about affirmative action. Its beneficiaries do not feel stigma, they do not take less rigorous majors, and they would not have done better at less selective institutions. The white students at these schools had been exposed to African Americans they would not likely have met as equals elsewhere, and their own educational experiences had been substantially enriched.

Moskos and Butler, Bowen and Bok, and many others have made plain that whatever arguments are raised against affirmative action, its effectiveness is established. People who are direct beneficiaries have shown that the content of their character, not the color of their skin, is what counts. They have been able to do so only with an opportunity that would not have been available but for affirmative action. They also have given back to society.

Nor can class-based affirmative action do what race-based affirmative action does. Proponents of class-based affirmative action in lieu of race-based affirmative action already accept the propriety of collective action and distributive justice as well as the goal of racial diversity, so it is unclear why they would prefer an indirect remedy to a direct one. Opponents of race-based affirmative action who are ideological oppose the ends as well as the means; they are as much against class-based affirmative action designed to promote racial diversity as they are against other approaches to the same goal. Although class-based affirmative action may be worthwhile for its own sake, it cannot substitute for race-based affirmative action. Even though race and class are related, they are different. Blacks are disproportionately poor, but whites make up the majority of the poor. As sociologist Wilson says, class-based affirmative action would be unfortunate in college admissions: Middle-class African Americans best able to use the opportunities would not be allowed to have them, and the truly disadvantaged African Americans who would be given the opportunities would be woefully ill-prepared for them.[57]

Supporters of affirmative action are not so short-sighted as to believe that it can do everything. Not every problem in society is caused by race, and affirmative action is not the solution to every problem of race. We should consider all strategies that are proven effective in addressing racial discrimination, without supposing that they are mutually exclusive. Many of those strategies would complement affirmative action and be enhanced by racial sensitivity. Improving prenatal and postnatal care for high-risk mothers and their babies probably would do more at the beginning of life or in its early years than affirmative action would years later. Upgrading public education and equalizing race-related disparities among school districts likewise would produce benefits that would ameliorate the need for affirmative action. These other techniques for dealing with racial disparities, starting with newborns and children, which do nothing for adolescents and adults, cannot be traded for affirmative action, because they would require that another generation of African Americans be sacrificed and racial progress be deferred once again.

Analogies may augment the arguments for affirmative action. Affirmative action may be likened to inoculation against contagious disease. We vaccinate ourselves by accepting tiny dosages of the very causes of illness. The shot alerts our bodies to the problems and stimulates us to build up antibodies as a preventative measure. Similarly, affirmative action relies on race, which is admittedly hazardous. However, it does so with a prescribed amount of the toxin. Thus, it prepares our society for racism and helps us to develop interracial relationships as a protective measure. It is well established that contact among people of different racial backgrounds on equal terms, as with students in a classroom, is the single best means of eliminating racial prejudice.[58] Affirmative action also can be compared to disaster relief. As a society, we offer disaster relief following a hurricane or an earthquake, even though no one caused the problem. Blame is not pertinent. With affirmative action, the case for offering relief for adversity is even stronger, because at least some people are answerable for racial discrimination. Disaster relief for catastrophic cases is warranted, even if other programs exist for systematic concerns. We offer local disaster relief, even though we engage in general efforts of infrastructure development, and we do not forgo immediate disaster relief because we have planned long-term infrastructure development. Similarly, affirmative action is appropriate as a particular remedy, even though we may be trying to overhaul primary education as a universal remedy.

By supporting affirmative action even if we are not directly included in the specific program, Asian Americans strengthen the argument for affirmative action as a matter of principle. We do so because we support it for reasons that cannot be called selfish. It is not unheard of for Asian Americans to be affected by racial discrimination but excluded from racial remedies. The 1991 Civil Rights Act was prompted by a Supreme Court decision raising the bar for individuals complaining of discrimination. But the legislation exempted the parties in that case, Asian Americans and Native Americans who had been paid less and subjected to worse working conditions in Alaskan fishing canneries.[59] Asian Americans also disprove the claim that it is affirmative action, rather than racial discrimination, that makes whites resentful of people of color. Asian Americans are not included in affirmative action in college admissions, and that fact is widely known, but some whites are less than elated to find themselves surrounded by Asian Americans in classrooms. But if Asian Americans, like whites, are non-beneficiaries of affirmative action, whites cannot claim that the plans impose a burden on them alone. The costs of the program are borne by the majority, or, more precisely, by the segments of society that are not included in affirmative action for the particular institution because they are not underrepresented there due to racial discrimination. So if Asian Americans accept the same duty as whites vis-à-vis affirmative action, without begrudging the gains of other people of color, whites hardly have any cause for complaint. After all, Asian Americans would then be under the onus of regular racial discrimination without the remedy of affirmative action. Whites by and large cannot claim the former is true, only the latter. Asian Americans can set an example—not one that defeats affirmative action, one that rescues it.

Like many other public policies, affirmative action is not optimal but is necessary. It is only a means to an end and not an end in itself. In the perpetual conversation about race, Asian Americans can open up new possibilities.

In the next chapter, I consider a new form of racial discrimination. Proponents of rational discrimination argue that they are not racists but rather reasonable people who make considered judgments based on the facts. They may be right in their claim that their form of discrimination is different than prejudice, but it is even more perilous.

True But Wrong

New Arguments Against New Discrimination

We've got to remember the Chinese are everywhere, as far as our weapon systems, not only in our labs that make our nuclear weapons and development, but also in the technology to deliver them. They're real. They're here. And probably in some ways, very crafty people.

—SENATOR RICHARD SHELBY,
DURING THE INVESTIGATION OF THE NUCLEAR WEAPONS SPY CHARGES,
ON NBC-TV's *Meet the Press*, MARCH 1999

The Suspect Traveler

When I was growing up, I enjoyed visiting Windsor, Ontario, in Canada, for Chinese food. Chinese American families and many Detroit area residents of various races and ethnicities would regularly journey across the Ambassador Bridge and through the tunnel for dim sum or bargain shopping on weekends and holidays. The hour drive from the suburbs and wait in the smog of stop-and-go traffic was well worth it, because the food was superior and the prices lower.

As we entered the territory of our northern neighbor, Canadian border guards typically carried out a perfunctory inquiry: "What country is your citizenship? Where are you going? How long will you be there? Why are you coming? Okay." They would wave us through with a smile, sometimes even recommending their favorite restaurant. They appeared to be comfortable with a car full of Asian people who flashed U.S. passports.

Returning to my homeland could lead to a somewhat different encounter. When I was a law student at the University of Michigan in Ann Arbor just over a decade ago, I organized a trip to Windsor. On our way back, we were stopped by our own Customs Service. I was in a car with two other Asian Americans. We also were with another friend of mine, a woman whom I was dating at the time, who was white.

Recalling fondly the trips I had taken in the past, I had suggested that we take time from our studies and make an excursion for dumplings and tea. After having chosen plenty of dishes from the procession of carts that had come around, returning home on a full stomach, carrying leftovers in a big bag already showing grease soaking through the paper, we were told that we would have to answer a few extra questions by the uniformed sentries who stood on duty.

Parking our car by the vehicles that were being inspected, their trunks open and their contents laid out on the ground, we went inside the office and waited with about ten other people. Only two of them looked to be non-Hispanic whites, and they had foreign accents.

The agents asked each of us where we had been born and what we did for a living. For some reason, the agents decided to inquire further of my white friend and myself. They wanted to know, for example, how we had met, how long we had known one another, and what the nature of our relationship was. Interviewing us separately, they wanted to make sure that our answers were consistent.

Eventually they were satisfied by our responses and released us. The entire episode lasted a quarter of an hour. It was not anything terrible. Afterward, though, I wondered what the agents had thought we were doing. So I wrote to the Customs Service.

A month later, I received a reply from my government. The official correspondence was worse than the initial incident. It states, "Contrary to belief, law enforcement officials, including Customs and Immigration inspectors, cannot distinguish between honorable, law-abiding citizens and violators on the basis of their physical appearance alone." Of course, they are right. Indeed, that is just the point. That is why you should not guess, especially when you might be focusing on race, either consciously or unconsciously. Other than race, I cannot identify any difference between my white friend and myself that would have triggered the suspicions of anyone who saw us, together or apart. We had similar social, economic, and educational backgrounds. We spoke the same language. We were even dressed alike. (She later became a law professor as well!)

The letter continued to explain why agents doubted the "authenticity" of the relationship between my white friend and myself: "Many attempts at alien smuggling are made by people posing to be friends to a 'non-suspect' traveler. . . . Even though the questions may seem irrelevant or out of place to you, there is a purpose for asking them." Although the letter refrained from referring to race, it did not enlighten me about what factors were used to distinguish between the suspect friend and the non-suspect traveler. Nothing explained why I was suspect and my friend was not. The reasoning it implicitly used to sort us out works only if the reader accepts assumptions about individuals that are rooted in race but not articulated explicitly.

From my glimpse into the machinery of bureaucracy, I have come to believe that I saw a small part of a larger pattern. I know many people who have crossed the border at that same place throughout the years, and most of the people of color have similar stories about the startling hostility of public servants. Upon reflection, although I would concede that the Customs Service has it right at a trivial level, I am convinced it has it wrong in a profound sense. We will be much more able to talk about race and racial discrimination if we consider how the Customs Service, practicing what has come to be called "racial profiling," could be both right about a stereotype and wrong about civil rights.

When I tell my anecdote, some people wonder why I would have supposed the Customs Service to be anything but selective in its interrogations. About half of my friends say earnestly that the agents were only displaying common sense, and the other half of my friends say cynically that the agents were exhibiting racial prejudice. What nobody considers is the more challenging possibility that such common sense and racial prejudice can be one and the same.

In this chapter, I use the spectacularly failed criminal prosecution of Los Alamos physicist Wen Ho Lee, accused of being "the Chinese spy," as a case study in racial profiling, a particular type of what has been called "rational discrimination." I explain why most observers, whether they supported the prosecution or the defense, were unable to understand one another. In discussions of the *Lee* case and racial profiling in general, the two sides usually talked past each other. Before explaining how they could communicate and without presupposing that racial profiling is either right or wrong, it is important to explain the facts of the *Lee* case. It is then possible to critique not only racial profiling but also other forms of rational discrimination. I explain how racial profiling works as a form of rational discrimination.

I then present three arguments against racial profiling as rational discrimination: First, we are not good at calculating probabilities, and thus we use erroneous premises; second, it creates a self-fulfilling prophecy by altering statistics and by creating antisocial incentives; and third, it reduces our interactions to a utilitarian cost-benefit analysis. I do not argue either that racial profiling is always irrational, because it is sometimes rational, or that it is racist, because it is sometimes not racist.

The Chinese Spy Who Wasn't

Wen Ho Lee is a naturalized citizen of the United States. The sixty-year-old Ph.D. scientist was an immigrant from Taiwan. He came to the United States in 1964 as a student, earning his doctorate from Texas A & M University in 1970, and along the way meeting his wife at the Rose Bowl. He gardens, cooks Chinese food with a Southwestern flavor, plays bridge, listens to classical music, and reads Western literature; Charles Dickens and Victor Hugo are his favorite authors.

Lee was a career employee of Division X at the Los Alamos national laboratories near Albuquerque, New Mexico. He is an expert in the arcane field of hydrodynamics, how solids behave as they turn into liquids under pressure, and he had the duty of archiving sensitive computer data. The Los Alamos lab has been responsible for the top-secret technology of the nation's nuclear arsenal ever since the Manhattan Project set up shop there during World War II to construct the Little Man and Fat Boy hydrogen bombs. The Los Alamos facilities, along with Lawrence Livermore in California and Oak Ridge in Tennessee, all operated by the Department of Energy, are where the research and development is done on the most destructive weapons in the world.

Lee reminded many Asian Americans of themselves or their relatives, especially Chinese Americans who, like Lee, had come from Taiwan for technical training or those whose parents had done so. Like most of the hundreds of Asian Americans who are integral to the military-industrial complex, he was an unassuming researcher who tried to stay out of politics and avoid conflict. To many Asian Americans who read the news reports that portrayed him as devious if not sinister, his conduct seemed common or even customary. He was devoted to his work, which he took with utmost seriousness. He was friendly toward Chinese foreigners, even hosting them politely when they visited. But twenty years into his career and despite being appreciated for his intellect, Lee had not progressed up the workplace hierarchy and was well aware that he was vulnerable to being laid off.

While Lee was preoccupied with his mathematical equations, mainland China had become the new archenemy of the United States, following the demise of the Soviet Union. Intelligence agencies speculated that its Communist government might have acquired the plans for the most advanced U.S. warhead, the miniaturized W–88. They were alarmed when in 1995 a Chinese official walked in and voluntarily provided the CIA with documents that hinted China had become capable of manufacturing a knock-off of the W–88. (Some experts would later conclude that the Chinese official was a double agent and the document was not what it purported to be.)

Based on such fears, the U.S. government launched a massive counter-espionage operation the following year, christened "Kindred Spirit." From literally hundreds of leads, the spy hunters focused on a single suspect, Lee, because—as the name of their investigation insinuated—they surmised that if the Chinese military had sought an inside source, they would have found an ethnic Chinese. By their racial reasoning, Lee was a natural suspect.

The ongoing investigations were further fueled by partisan politics. Following the 1996 campaign finance imbroglio (reviewed in Chapter 3), the U.S. stance toward China has become a major issue. As congressional committees probed whether the White House had been soft on China, some of President Bill Clinton's critics even accused him of having sold out national security in a treasonous fashion. The view of the chair of the Senate Select Committee on Intelligence, Richard Shelby, on the threat posed by the pervasive Chinese is expressed by the epigraph to this chapter. Shelby had ample company in his racial paranoia.

In May 1999, the House Select Committee on U.S. National Security and Military/Commercial Concerns with the People's Republic of China released its three-volume Cox report, named after its chair. The late journalist Lars-Erik Nelson wrote, "Most irresponsibly, the Cox report suggests that every Chinese visitor to this country, every Chinese scholar, every Chinese student, every Chinese permanent resident, and even every Chinese-American citizen is a spy, potential spy, or 'sleeper agent,' merely waiting for the signal to rise up and perform some unimaginable act of treachery."[1] Five experts from Stanford University presented a critique of the Cox report, which concluded: "Important and relevant facts are wrong and a number of conclusions are, in our view, unwarranted."[2]

It was not Republicans alone who had singled out Lee. *Los Angeles Times* columnist Robert Scheer, the most vocal critic of the government's conduct in the *Lee* case, as well as the press coverage of it, argued afterward that the Democratic Clinton administration "wanted to prove to its critics that it was tough on Chinese spying, whether or not that spying existed and whether or not it had anything to do with Wen Ho Lee."[3]

At the time the Cox report came out, Lee had been absolved of any wrongdoing related to the W–88. Despite its scale, the investigation of Lee had not turned up sufficient evidence to make it worthwhile to press charges against him. By the time it was all over, in pursuit of Lee alone the government had conducted 1,000 interviews around the world; the FBI had undertaken its largest ever computer forensic examination, its agents had visited every private storage facility in New Mexico, they had traced years of Lee's phone calls, subjected Lee to around-the-clock "bumper-lock" surveillance conducted by multiple officers, executed simultaneous searches on the homes of all Lee's immediate family members and relatives in the United States, formally interrogated Lee more than twenty times, and unearthed everything in the county garbage dump.

In August 1998, secret agents also had run a sting operation. An agent posing as a Chinese military official asked Lee to meet. Lee said he could speak about his work on the phone, because what he could say he could say openly. He later refused to meet, but agreed to take the agent/official's beeper number. Ironically, Lee's own wife had worked for both the FBI and CIA as an informant.

By early 1999, Robert Vrooman, the ex-CIA career officer who served as the counterintelligence chief at Los Alamos, had concluded that Lee was undoubtedly innocent of espionage, although he may have been guilty of naiveté. After watching a final interrogation, "Everyone was convinced he was not a spy. We all concluded there was no evidence. We figured we'd put this puppy to bed."[4]

Lee may have had a respite in the interim before the Cox report came out, but the report gave the sensational media coverage further momentum. Well before any official action was decided on, improper leaks to the press had virtually convicted Lee in the court of public opinion. The *New York Times* broke the news that a mole inside the defense establishment had given away the "crown jewels" of the nuclear arsenal to America's foe. In a series of articles that looked like they could become Pulitzer prize contenders, based on unnamed sources, the *Times* identified Lee as the suspect. Other papers soon followed its lead as the newspaper of record. Over time, the breach of national security was being depicted in ominous terms as the worst since the case of Ethel and Julius Rosenberg, who were executed for treason in 1953. The headlines asked not whether the accusations against Lee were true but rather who was to blame for not catching him sooner. While still a free man, Lee found himself transformed into "the Chinese spy."

In December 1999, Lee became the only government scientist in the fifty years since passage of the obscure federal statutes on nuclear data confidentiality to be subject to criminal prosecution for violating the protocols. The allegations were staggering. Lee and his family were said to have in their possession the means of altering the military and political balance of the world forever. Lee could signal a family member with a seemingly innocuous message such as, "Uncle Wen says hello," and that would be the prearranged tip-off about what to do with the nuclear secrets that had been hidden away. A prosecution witness told the judge that how he ruled on bail for Lee would be "a you-bet-your-country decision."

The fifty-nine counts filed against Lee charged him with nothing more than carelessly mishandling data, although if he had been convicted he would have faced the possibility of life imprisonment. What he was charged with was not as important as what he was not charged with. The government omitted any intimation that Lee had given anything to anybody, much less that he had intentionally given warhead plans to the Chinese government. The government in due course admitted that he was being prosecuted for matters unrelated to the W–88 warhead, which they had happened to come across while pursuing him. In other words, the claims bought against Lee had nothing to do with the initial scrutiny of him.

As the case continued, it turned out that Lee in fact had engaged in some suspect activities. The circumstantial evidence was accumulating, to his detriment. He had downloaded files against regulations, massive quantities of data containing formulas generated in his work. (He later said, and there is no contradictory evidence, that he had saved the data as a backup but decided to destroy the tapes.) He had accessed his computer improperly and tried to do so while overseas. He also entered the lab after he had been terminated. He had given his computer password to his children so they could play games while they were away at college.

As the U.S. attorney who brought the case against Lee resigned to run for Congress, the prosecution's theory about Lee's illicit motive also changed. Prosecutors toyed with the possibility that Lee was trying to help Taiwan, not China. Lee had many contacts in Taiwan, China's nemesis and America's ally. Prosecutors hypothesized that he might have been worried that he would be downsized out of a job. He may have wanted to be able to use his files to impress a prospective employer. They presented a list of countries Lee may have wanted to work for: He had drafted letters—although they later admitted there is no evidence that he ever sent them—to contacts in Australia, France, Germany, Hong Kong, Singapore, Switzerland, and Taiwan. Although he had not written anything to anyone in China, prosecutors added China to the list of potential bosses. The U.S. district judge presiding over the case, James A. Parker, noted that although enhancing one's resume in this fashion may not be commendable, it is also not the same as giving nuclear weapons design data to a Communist enemy.

Other than that, the mistrust of Lee was not based on much. Journalist Scheer said that "the main [piece of evidence] is that a Chinese nuclear scientist whom Lee had met during a lab-approved visit to China publicly embraced and thanked Lee when the Chinese scientist later visited the Los Alamos lab. If Lee were a spy for China, why would that Chinese scientist so dramatically blow Lee's cover by publicly embracing him?"[5]

After he was denied bail, Lee was kept in solitary confinement for all but one hour of the day, his arms and legs shackled, a light bulb kept burning at all times to facilitate observation. He was permitted to see his family one hour per week.

As the case proceeded, the charges against Lee became increasingly suspect. As he whiled away the time writing a textbook, his lawyers—among them the prosecutor of Heidi Fleiss, the "Hollywood Madam," and a defender of Marine Lieutenant Colonel Oliver North—ascertained that most of the data downloaded by Lee were publicly available and some were classified only retroactively. John Richter, one of the designers of the W–88, said that he had come to believe that the prosecution's claims were based on hyperbole and that Lee had suffered enough. He said that 99 percent of the information was publicly available, although he later modified the statement to indicate that he was referring to the basics. His sentiment was that "keeping him locked up the way he is much more injurious to the reputation of the United States."[6]

The material that was classified could have come from many sources. The Presidential Foreign Intelligence Advisory Board, specially impaneled to conduct an independent examination and chaired by former Republican Senator Warren Rudman, stated, "This information had been widely available within the U.S. nuclear weapons community, including the weapons labs, other parts of D.O.E. [the Department of Energy], the Department of Defense, and private contractors, for more than a decade. For example, key technical information concerning the W–88 warhead had been available to numerous U.S. government and military entities since at least 1983 and could well have come from many organizations other than the weapons labs."[7] All told, there were at least 548 other sites to which the W–88 design data had been disseminated.

Bit by bit, Lee's lawyers started to prove him innocent. Their biggest break came when the prosecution's lead witness acknowledged that he had been dishonest in court about Lee's possible motivation, and the transcript of the final FBI interrogation became public. The lead FBI agent on the *Lee* case, Robert Messemer, recanted his claim that Lee had lied to a colleague of his and borrowed a computer to download nuclear secrets while saying he needed access to his resume. Messemer said that he had made "an honest error" and did not wish "to mislead you or anyone in this court or any court."[8]

Opposing Lee's release, Messemer later would caution that because of the prosecution, Lee had developed a reason to turn over his information to a foreign power: "to take revenge against the United States for removing his liberty." He also conjectured that Lee could still pass along secrets through code: "for example, what if he were to say to someone, his brother in California, 'the fish are not biting today?'"[9]

Even worse was the transcript of the interrogation. According to the transcript, two FBI agents, one of them trained in hostile interrogation techniques the day before, told Lee he had failed a lie detector test that he had actually passed. They then asked him if he had heard of the Rosenbergs: "The Rosenbergs are the only people that never cooperated with the federal government in an espionage case. . . . You know what happened to them? They electrocuted them, Wen Ho."[10] Contrary to the FBI statements to Lee, CBS News reported, "The polygraph results were so convincing and unequivocal, that sources say the deputy director of the Los Alamos lab issued an apology to Lee, and work began to get him reinstated in the X Division."[11]

Lee was unfazed, but the FBI agents did not relent in their bullying. They presented Lee with a confession they had prepared for his use. It contained an admission of espionage, a capital offense. His lawyers were not present, but he had sense enough not to sign it. The *L.A. Times* has quoted an official who has reviewed the confession as saying, "Poor bastard, he didn't understand. . . . He kept crossing things out and trying to correct it. He was trying to help them. He still didn't get what was happening."[12]

Meanwhile, security chief Vrooman had come forward and admitted that his colleagues had targeted Lee because of his ethnicity. He said in public speeches, "This case was screwed up because there was nothing there—it was built on thin air." He testified through a sworn affidavit filed with the court, "Based on my experience and observations, I concluded that racial profiling of Asian Americans as a result of the investigation indeed took place." He said that thirteen whites who had engaged in the same activities as Lee—visiting the same institute in China and meeting the same people—were never investigated.[13]

Vrooman himself had been no fan of Dr. Lee's, expressing his concern "that Dr. Lee did not understand the ruthlessness of intelligence agencies in trying to collect information being vital to national survival." Vrooman's critics said that he had turned on the investigation because he had been reprimanded for his leadership of it.

Others also came forward voluntarily from inside the lab. Michael Soukup, another Los Alamos physicist who specialized in studying China's nuclear capability, agreed that Lee was targeted because he was Chinese American. Soukup explained that the "suspicion matrix" used to identify suspects was "a sham." He said, "I fit their matrix perfectly, and I was never interviewed and questioned."[14]

Not only Asian Americans but also the scientific community were aghast at the cavalier ignorance about scientific methods and the treatment accorded Lee. In December 1999, just after Lee was arrested, Los Alamos astrophysicist Stirling Colgate, part of the Manhattan Project team, called the case "a real American tragedy" and said that Lee's conduct was not "secret, clandestine, and nefarious" as it had been described. Of the investigation, he added that "they could have done it right and they didn't."[15]

In September 2000, just before the dénouement of the *Lee* case, the leading scientific organizations in the nation—the National Academy of Science, the National Academy of Engineering, and the National Institute of Medicine—expressed their concern about the incarceration of Lee in an open letter to Attorney General Janet Reno. Although the three institutions have protested the detention of scientists in China and elsewhere, they had never before intervened on behalf of an American scientist. They said that Lee "appears to be the victim of unjust treatment" and his prosecution "reflects poorly on the U.S. justice system."[16]

The lead investigator on the *Lee* case, Notra Trulock, was soon being simultaneously praised as an honest whistleblower and vilified as a self-aggrandizing bigot. A Soviet expert trained by the National Security Agency, Trulock was said by colleagues to have commented that "'ethnic Chinese' should not be allowed to work on classified projects, including nuclear weapons" and "just the fact that there are five Chinese restaurants here [in

Los Alamos] meant that the Chinese government had an interest" in conducting espionage. Trulock denies having made either remark.[17]

A former investigative colleague of Trulock's, Charles Washington, submitted a sworn affidavit in Lee's case stating that Trulock "acts vindictively and opportunistically," "improperly uses security issues to punish and discredit others," and "has racist views toward minority groups." Washington, who is African American, says Trulock spat on him during a disagreement. Washington settled a discrimination case he brought against the Energy Department. Three other such complaints also were filed against Trulock.[18]

Even those who did not charge Trulock with racial prejudice were not confident of his judgment. Former Senator Warren Rudman, in the course of his work, wrote to Trulock that he had made "wildly inaccurate assertions and reckless accusations."[19] While the *Lee* case was underway, Trulock himself was investigated by the FBI for allegedly trying to sell an account of the Lee case that contained classified information. After the *Lee* case ended, Trulock filed a defamation lawsuit against Lee claiming that he had been labeled a racist by Lee's supporters.

The *Lee* case also compared unfavorably to similar cases. Coincidentally, even as the *Lee* case was disintegrating, another investigation had exposed that John Deutch, the retired CIA director, had committed similar transgressions by downloading data onto a personal computer and bringing the material home. Deutch, like Lee, was foreign-born. He was the first intelligence director to be foreign-born; he had emigrated from Belgium. His subordinates were even caught and disciplined for engaging in a cover-up to protect him. Deutch received only the sanction of losing his security clearance, preventing him from carrying on lucrative consulting work. The disks on which he downloaded data were never recovered. Even as some observers wondered whether Deutch was being overly punished to mollify critics of the Lee investigation, he was given a presidential pardon the day before he was scheduled to finalize a plea bargain.

Shortly after the *Lee* case concluded, one of the worst espionage cases in modern history came to light. Unlike Lee, Robert Hanssen was actually guilty of all the charges leveled against him, and those charges represented the worst breaches of national security. Unlike Lee, Hanssen is white. Even though Hanssen, a top FBI counterintelligence operative, was a genuine mole who had passed numerous secrets over the course of many years to the Soviet Union, the public reaction to his case was quite different. As he accepted a life sentence (that averted the possibility of the death sentence), observers applauded prosecutors for allowing his wife—who, with their children, had been portrayed as having endured an ordeal—to receive a portion of his government pension. He had been a member of Opus Dei, an international Catholic organization, but there was no widespread scrutiny directed toward it. Investigators assumed that his conduct was antithetical to, not representative of, the secret order's tenets.

A series of further mishaps at the Energy Department, such as the sudden disappearance and reappearance of computer hard drives with classified files, confirmed that security breaches were rampant. Another case also was revealed, code-named "Buffalo Slaughter," in which an Energy Department employee—not an Asian American—passed classified secrets to a foreign government but was given full immunity in return for agreeing to a debriefing on the incident.

The conclusion of the case was as shocking as its outset. Many Asian Americans had regarded the likely outcome as a foregone conclusion: Lee would be punished severely, and there was no helping him. But suddenly, the government case imploded. After the court issued an order granting the defense lawyers access to materials to be used to corroborate the claim that selective prosecution was taking place, the government agreed to a plea bargain. Also, the court appeared ready to allow Lee's lawyers to introduce evidence into the open record concerning the secrets he had allegedly downloaded, to support his defense that the material was already public. In exchange for cooperating with the prosecution and submitting to a lie-detector test (under penalty of facing renewed prosecution if he failed), Lee pled guilty to a single felony count and was sentenced to time served.

On September 13, 2000, Judge Parker, a Republican appointee to the bench, freed Lee. In an extraordinary statement from the bench, Parker chastised the government while apologizing to Lee. He called the case "an embarrassment to the nation." He said that Lee had been held before trial under "demeaning, unnecessarily punitive conditions" and that he personally was "sad and troubled because I do not know the real reasons why the executive branch has done all of this." Judge Parker added:

> What I believe remains unanswered is the question, What was the government's motive in insisting on your being jailed pretrial under extraordinarily onerous conditions of confinement until today, when the executive branch agrees that you may be set free essentially unrestricted? This makes no sense to me . . . A corollary question, I guess, is, Why were you charged with the many Atomic Energy Act counts for which the penalty is life imprisonment,

all of which the executive branch has now moved to dismiss and which I just dismissed?[20]

Afterward, government officials exchanged mutual recriminations. President Bill Clinton said he was "troubled" by the case, but added that he did not believe it was wrongful racial profiling. The retired head of internal security for the Justice Department, John L. Martin, co-wrote a newspaper article characterizing the fiasco as "a case study in how an espionage case should not proceed."[21] Trulock suggested it was not he, but the energy secretary, who had identified Lee to the media.

Even the *New York Times* published an uncharacteristic analysis of its own coverage, albeit without admitting any errors. Appearing in the space used for running corrections but not headlined as a correction, the lengthy piece stated that the paper remained "proud" of its coverage but that its editors "found some things we wish we had done differently in the course of the coverage to give Dr. Lee the full benefit of the doubt." An editorial pointed out that the paper had "warned about the dangers of racial profiling" but noted that it "should have looked more searchingly at the conditions under which [Lee] was confined and the government's arguments for denial of bail."[22]

Upon leaving prison, Lee said that he would be going fishing. With legal debts of well over $1 million for just the expenses (the lawyers donated their services), he agreed to write his memoirs and cooperate on a docudrama.

The Justice Department and the FBI still appear to insist—but not as loudly as before—that relying on ancestry was appropriate because its staff believed that China tried to enlist agents from among Chinese American communities. Neil Lewis of the *New York Times* reported after the case ended:

> To be sure, some Justice Department investigators felt . . . that they were the ones who had been treated unfairly. To them, it was thoroughly legitimate to consider Mr. Lee's ethnic background, among several other factors, in forming suspicions that he might have helped Beijing. It was especially logical, they said, because the Chinese government has a well-documented history of using ethnic Chinese in other countries to help gather intelligence.[23]

The internal study by the Justice Department, conducted by former federal prosecutor Randy Bellows (and known as "the Bellows report"), was harsh in its criticism of mistakes and the failure to consider other suspects. Even Bellows, however, endorsed the idea that pursuing people of Chinese ethnicity was acceptable because the Chinese government reportedly sought them out as well. Accordingly, Bellows declined to find racial profiling at work.[24] The Bellows report, portions of which are classified, is too restrained. As Thomas Joo, a University of California at Davis law professor, argued in a newspaper op-ed, the Bellows report called the inquiry that led to Lee "so poorly written and organized that this alone made it difficult to evaluate and comprehend," and it criticized the investigators for their "inconsistent and contradictory statements as well as unsubstantiated assertions." Nevertheless, as Joo notes, if Lee is presumed innocent until proven guilty and if he is treated like any of his co-workers of a different ethnicity, the Bellows report shows that there is almost nothing that should have made him a suspect. Joo concludes that nobody has answered the question: "Why Lee?"[25] The strategy used on Lee was a failure even on its own terms. The attention directed toward Lee means that the person who should be held to account for the transfer of secrets to China, if that person exists, is still at large. In its follow-up coverage, the *New York Times* quoted an unidentified senior federal official as saying the leads were so old that capturing any spy was "an undoable problem."[26]

The case also had unanticipated costs. Because Asian immigrant and Asian American scientists left government jobs or declined to take them in the wake of Lee's travails—activists had organized a boycott of the labs—U.S. defense programs may have been imperiled. In its overreaction to the possibility of espionage, the Energy Department alienated employees with proposals such as a badge system that would require employees to identify their national origins; due to the internal reactions, it never adopted the plan. The department ended up hiring an ombudsperson, Jeremy Wu, to work with employees on their concerns about racial discrimination. Incidentally, the Energy Secretary introduced Wu at a press conference where he was asked if he'd wanted an Asian American for the job. He answered yes, but added that he was not engaging in racial profiling, only trying to respond to the employees who felt most affected by racial discrimination, who were predominantly Asian American.

Regardless of the racial aspects of the Lee case, it shows the Kafkaesque power of an unrestrained prosecution. Whatever Lee's race, it should give pause to all of us that the investigators had identified him as a suspect and then found a crime with which to charge him. Prosecution supporters reiterate that Lee admitted that he broke the law, but that by itself does not justify either the strategy of racial profiling or the punishment the government sought to mete out. The inquiry as to whether he had committed a crime on the one hand, and the inquiry as to whether he was able to preserve his civil rights and whether he was given due process on the other hand, are different inquiries, but the former must be subordinate to the latter. A reversal of priorities only ensures that we will be persuaded by a guilty judgment even if it is likely faulty. The civil rights–due process matter will be deferred and then, once a guilty verdict is in, it will be dismissed however untrustworthy the guilty verdict.

The *Lee* case suggests that Asian Americans should redouble their efforts at forming pan-Asian American and multiracial coalitions. During the *Lee* case we were moderately successful in maintaining pan-Asian American coalitions, although even in that respect Japanese Americans with memories of the internment identified with Chinese Americans much more visibly than other Asian ethnicities. We were largely unsuccessful in connecting the *Lee* case to "driving while black," and some Asian Americans may have wished to avoid the association with African Americans. Privately, Asian Americans were indignant that Lee was a Ph.D. scientist being treated worse than drug dealers. Ironically, they appeared largely unaware of the possibility that their selective sympathy would confirm the accusation that Asian Americans were acting out of ethnic solidarity.[27]

As important as the *Lee* case is to his family and to Asian Americans, ultimately what is more important are the principles involved. In thinking about the *Lee* case as the furor subsides, we ourselves should avoid the oft-asked question of whether wrongful racial profiling took place. Just as the designation of "the Chinese spy" can refer to either a spy for China regardless of race or a spy who is of Chinese extraction regardless of loyalties, the question of whether wrongful racial profiling occurred in the *Lee* case confuses two distinct sets of issues, the first having to do with discovering the facts and the second with deliberating our values. The first set of issues asks whether racial profiling occurred: Does the Chinese government seek out Chinese Americans for its ignoble purposes, playing on racial sympathies, and does the U.S. government also rely on race in its law enforcement, following racial suspicions? The second set of issues asks whether something wrongful occurred: Is racial profiling rational, and is it right?

At the heart of the controversy over racial profiling is our confusion of the factual inquiries with the value judgments. On the one hand, when the prosecution and its supporters argue that "There was no wrongful racial profiling," it is never quite clear whether they mean they did not engage in it or they were justified in doing so. On the other hand, when the defense and its supporters argue that "There was wrongful racial profiling," they not only assert that it did occur but also assume that it is inherently wrongful.

To have an intelligent discussion, we have to agree on what to discuss. There are not two but four possibilities: We could decide that racial profiling did occur and should be condemned; that it did occur but is acceptable; that it did not occur and should not be condoned; or that it did not occur but should be allowed.

The facts seem to suggest that the Chinese government might try to use Chinese Americans for espionage, but even if the Chinese government openly declared that it did so, that should be inconsequential. In no other case (other than the Japanese American internment) has the U.S. government yielded to the notion that a foreign government, by its unilateral actions, can waive a U.S. citizen's civil rights. It is only by treating Lee or an Asian American as more Asian than American can such a deprivation be countenanced. Certainly if the U.S. government told the Chinese government that it could, if it so desired, surrender a white American's civil rights, the response to both governments would be outrage.

The facts also establish about as strongly as possible that the U.S. government has responded by using race as well. It is rare that an insider such as Vrooman admits as much. The equivalent would be a police chief stepping forward to say that the department's officers do stop African Americans on the highway because they are wary of anyone "driving while black." It is also infrequent that another case unfolds simultaneously with sufficiently similar facts that parallels can be drawn, as happened with the Deutch pardon. The equivalent would be a wealthy white driver, not wearing a seatbelt and with a broken taillight, zipping by a speed trap without being pulled over, moments after a cop has finished ticketing a black driver for the same conduct. If an insider admitting to racial profiling and other cases simultaneously being handled under a double standard is not enough to show racial profiling, then nothing suffices to show racial profiling. It is well established that racial profiling occurs in other contexts, for if the patterns are not the result of racial profiling, they are altogether inexplicable.[28]

Understandably under the circumstances, supporters of Lee resorted to arguing that it was unreasonable to suppose that Lee would be a spy for China because of race, or that there was any greater likelihood that someone of Chinese descent would be a spy for China for that reason. Their approach suffered from acute flaws that mirror those of their adversaries. Either their pronouncement that Chinese Americans are the same as other Americans must be taken on faith, or the debate degenerates into an empirical free-for-all with both sides trying to prove or disprove that people's heritage influences their behavior to some degree, and how much. Theirs is a plea that the government be rational in its conduct, not a demand that the government respect civil rights. An argument for rationality is ineffective if there is fundamental disagreement over what is rational, and it commits its proponents to rationality whatever the result.

The better approach requires a concession for the sake of argument. Some are not willing to make this concession for ideological reasons. The concession is as follows: It is reasonable—or at least not absurd—to feel that an individual who has ethnic ties to a foreign country would be more likely to betray the United States to that other country than would someone else who is basically the same but has a different heritage. (It is important to emphasize that this is a concession for the sake of argument. There is no strong evidence about it one way or another, other than the allegiance of Japanese Americans to the United States during World War II, which cuts the other way.)

All of the debate notwithstanding, lingering uncertainty over what might or might not have happened in the *Lee* case should not delay the important task of considering how our society should address these racial issues. The fact inquiry may never be resolved satisfactorily (was Wen Ho Lee a spy for China?), but the value judgment still must be made (should we rely on race in our law enforcement?).

Finally, it is important to address the objection that any suspicion of Lee was not racial but ethnic. This is a distinction without a difference. Race and ethnicity are often enough used as interchangeable; until two generations ago, "Chinese" was as much a race to some as it was an ethnicity to others. Both race and ethnicity are presumed to be biological and immutable. Both are conceptualized as matters of heritage. Ethnicity only seems to be more precise and has less of a negative connotation. Ethnicity was developed as a euphemism, because race was discredited.[29] If it is wrong, however, to judge people by their heritage, it remains wrong whether it is the broader category of race or the narrow category of ethnicity that is used. Otherwise, racial profiling would be more tolerable if it were applied not to every person with the same skin color but only to those with a specific complexion within the range.

Once these preliminaries have been set forth, the genuine issues have been joined. The real debate can be conducted. That debate is whether in those rare instances where racial discrimination is in fact rational discrimination it is a course of action we as a society wish to sanction. The *Lee* case—like the internment of Japanese Americans during World War II, discussed in Chapter 3—is an ideal test of our principles, because national security and even the very existence the United States are invoked as the factor to be balanced against civil rights. National security is about the most serious countervailing factor that could possibly be set against any other factors, so it should compromise civil rights if anything ought to be accepted as doing so. But if it is not sufficiently compelling, then nothing is.

Many of my friends who share my passion for civil rights are horrified that I concede that rational discrimination can ever be what it professes to be, namely rational. I hope to demonstrate that the concession is crucial, not adverse, to our shared cause. Rational discrimination has two parts to it. I say, concede the rationality of the practice and fight the discrimination of it. Arguing with a person over what to believe is even more difficult than arguing about how to behave. Granting that rational discrimination can be sensible and not racist in the classic sense dispenses with the former issue and forces people to consider the latter issue. Believing something to be true does not determine how someone ought to behave about it.

Racial Profiles

The great journalist Walter Lippmann wrote in his 1922 book, *Public Opinion* that, "A pattern of stereotypes is not neutral." He argued, in an original text that applied psychology to politics, that our pattern of stereotypes "is not merely a way of substituting order for the great blooming, buzzing confusion of reality. It is not merely a short cut." As he stated, "it is the guarantee of our self-respect; it is the projection upon the world of our own sense of our own value, our own position and our own rights." He continued, "they are the fortress of our tradition, and behind its defense we can continue to feel ourselves safe in the position we occupy."[30]

Although Lippmann lent his considerable prestige to the demands for Japanese American internment, and, as a Jew, supported quotas on the maximum number of Jews at Ivy League schools—two episodes that show that all thinkers, however insightful, can lead themselves astray—he concluded that "any disturbance of the stereotypes seems like an attack on the foundations of the universe" and thus "an attack on the foundations of our universe," for "where big things are at stake, we do not readily admit that there is any distinction between our universe and the universe."[31] So it is, too, with racial profiling. It forms a foundation of the universe for some of us and therefore becomes part of the foundation of the universe for all of us. Its practitioners defend it as if their integrity depends on it, and perhaps they are right.

Racial profiling is "rational discrimination." Unlike classic racial discrimination, which advances beliefs that people of color are biologically inferior, the modern rational discrimination relies on statistics to suggest that, whatever the reasons, some stereotypes are more or less true. A person who practices rational discrimination—a "rational discriminator"—relies not on animus but on analysis.

Rational discriminators are increasingly common; they will say that each of us is one of them. Without mincing words, University of Southern California law professor Jody Armour has called the rational discriminator "the involuntary negrophobe" in an excellent study of the phenomenon.[32] Rational discriminators can even proclaim that they are reluctant to make a negative judgment about such-and-such group; they are uneasy about the implications for the subjects of the stereotype; sorry about the circumstances that may have affected them; interested in helping them improve themselves; and so forth, but they do what they do because they are compelled by the facts. They disregard rights, causes, contexts, and consequences, and heed only the numbers. They do not ask why more African Americans males are in prison than in college. They proclaim defensively that they cannot fairly be called racist, because they have no grand goals of racial hegemony. They treat race as a classification, a marker, a signal, not an absolute identity that determines the value of a human being. For them, race only sets defaults and probabilities, not certainties or rules. Individuals who are subjected to a stereotype can rebut the presumption, although they bear its burden unless they do so. The rational discriminators' explanations take the form of urban legends along the lines of the political joke that a conservative is a liberal who has been mugged. Their stories begin, "It's a terrible thing to say, but it really is true what they say about X group, because a friend of mine just had this experience . . . ."

There are, of course, false rational discriminators just as there are disingenuous people who abuse any idea. They follow the classic racial discrimination until they no longer can, and they are heartened by the prospect of rational discrimination allowing them a respectable return to their habits at long last. They may be bigots through and through who always have nursed the same feelings but now have a pretext to exercise them. They may be unwilling to change their attitudes, even if their generalization is proven false as to a specific person. They may use their beliefs to select statistics rather than allowing statistics to shape their beliefs.

There are enough rational discriminators in good faith, however, that even leaving aside the significant problem of the bogus rational discriminators, the genuine rational discriminators must be addressed. Rational discriminators can be of any racial background. Asian Americans have been found among their ranks. They can even be of the same racial background as the subjects of the stereotype they use. African Americans have been found among their ranks, too. Even civil rights leader Reverend Jesse Jackson, who is himself black, has spoken about his pain at his own reactions to race: Hearing somebody walking behind him at night, he is relieved to turn around and see a white person.[33]

Well before racial profiling became the latest buzzword, the sheriff of suburban New Orleans (Jefferson Parish) in 1986 announced that his officers would stop African Americans found in white neighborhoods because of a rash of armed robberies of shoppers who had just entered their homes. The affable law enforcement official, Harry Lee, is Asian American. The "Chinese Cowboy," as he calls himself, has been a folk hero since winning office in 1979. He has been popular enough that he considered running for governor in 1995, and he is still serving. He said, "We will stop everybody that we think has no business in the neighborhood. . . . If you live in a predominantly white neighborhood and two blacks are in a car behind you, there's a pretty good chance they're up to no good." He was specific, indicating that he meant blacks driving "rinky-dink cars." After protests, he backed down. When he was inducted into the state hall of fame in January 2001, he commented on controversies in which he had been embroiled over the years, "If I have a choice of lying to you or offending you, I'll offend you every time. You can forgive me for offending you. But you can't forgive me for lying to you."[34]

In the winter of 1999 in Miami, a Japanese immigrant restaurateur caused an uproar when he added the tip to the bill of African American patrons.[35] He later admitted it was his practice to do so, because he believed blacks did not tip well; never mind that the stereotype of Asian immigrants is also that they do not tip enough. The county subsequently passed an ordinance requiring that gratuities be added to the check automatically, which prevented discrimination and worked to the advantage of restaurant owners.

In 1999, Bernard Parks, chief of the Los Angeles Police Department, told the *New York Times* that in addressing violent crime against jewelers, "the predominant suspects are Colombians. We don't find Mexican-Americans, or blacks, or other immigrants. . . . It's a collection of several hundred Colombians who commit this crime. . . . [S]hould we play the percentages? It's common sense."[36] Parks himself is African American.

In 1999, *New York Times* reporter Steven A. Holmes wrote an honest account about his own days as a college student doubling as a taxicab driver in New York City. African American himself, Holmes mulls over an incident in which police officers stopped him in a predominantly white neighborhood in Washington, D.C. He wonders as he calms down, "Hadn't I done the same thing myself?" He writes that "fear chastens." He recounts that, as a hack, after having been robbed twice, "my sense of tolerance and racial solidarity was tested every time a casually dressed young black man, especially one in sneakers, tried to hail my cab." He confesses that years ago, "most times, I drove right by."[37]

In the *Wen Ho Lee* case, President Clinton was liberal, his administration had even staked out a position of opposing racial profiling, and he had appointed more Asian Americans than any of his predecessors. The secretary of energy who initially approved the choices in the *Lee* case was the highest-ranking Hispanic then in the federal government, and he had been active in Hispanic causes. The replacement U.S. attorney who oversaw the prosecution was Chinese American, like Lee himself.

Doubting the validity of the rational discriminators' excuse without doubting their sincerity is essential to persuading them that their thinking and the actions that follow from them are racially problematic. The effort requires new arguments. Almost all Americans have renounced classic racial discrimination, but many people are stymied by the modern rational discrimination. Even if we are reluctant to follow its directives, we are unsure of what is wrong with doing so. If it was a challenge to dissuade reasonable people from relying on irrational prejudices, it is even more of a test to persuade them to give up rational beliefs. Calling them "racists" may be ineffective; Reverend Jackson is not a racist.

Rational discrimination appears to have the best defense available to any belief, that it is true. Consequently, the better the traditional arguments have been against racial discrimination, the worse they seem to be against rational discrimination. Traditional arguments against racism were developed to confront racial oppression, which was crazily irrational. Those arguments, which were persuasive because they appealed to logic and reason rather than emotion or tradition, established that Jews do not have horns or tails and that blacks are qualified to vote and sit down next to whites. The conventional arguments to refute racial prejudice lose their force if the racial generalizations seem plausible, likely to be accurate. Once we have pressed for logic and reason, we seem to be more susceptible to rational discrimination, because even if its foundation is not as strong as is claimed, it has a foundation.

Rational discrimination is about our interactions with strangers. It rests on the venerable proposition that, in the words of the forgotten moral philosopher Joseph Butler, "probability is the very guide to life." It is the process of using a known characteristic such as race to guess at who someone is, how he is likely to behave, or both.

The rational discriminator assigns traits to an unfamiliar person using Bayesian reasoning, named after Sir Thomas Bayes, who invented the nonstandard form of statistical reasoning that has come into fashion among academics recently. Bayesians—as Bayes's disciples call themselves—work each additional fact they learn into their appraisal of a situation. The evidence informs them of how confident they should be of a hypothesis.

Bayesians give an easy example of the technique. A newborn who had no prior knowledge may want to know whether the sun would rise the next morning. To a strict empiricist, the sun rising one day is no guarantee it will rise the next morning. To a Bayesian, the sun rising two days in a row increases the likelihood it will rise again the third morning, and the sun rising that third day increases the likelihood it will rise again the fourth morning.

Baby Bayesians may wish to keep track of their investigation into the sunrise. They can do so using marbles. They can start by assuming that there is an equal likelihood that the sun will rise and that the sun will not rise. So they can place a white marble (signifying sunrise) and a black marble (signifying no sunrise) into a jar. At each successive dawn, they add a white marble. By the end of the year, their confidence in daily sunrises is about as high as needed for real-world purposes. They have 363 white marbles and 1 black marble, and that lone black marble is there only because they assumed a 50–50 chance of a sunrise that first night.

Bayesian statistics claim to be intuitive and practical. Fictional detective Sherlock Holmes was a Bayesian. Every time he uttered one of his famous deductions to the befuddled admiration of Dr. Watson—"You have been in Afghanistan, I perceive" is the greeting that opens one of the great fictional friendships of English literature—he was a Bayesian; often his observations were based on race or ethnicity. The Microsoft Word Office Assistant is a Bayesian avatar. The irritating paper clip pops up with its helpful hints, based on fuzzy logic programming, because it relies on its memory of a user's past actions.

Rational discriminators are flexible, unlike the classic racists who cannot mend their ways. Rational discriminators impute traits to an unfamiliar person, who then does or does not meet the expectations; in turn, rational discriminators adjust the formula. The assumption is not that all Asian Americans are foreigners but that there is a good likelihood that any random Asian American is a foreigner. Rational discriminators can couch their racial profile in caveats, but even if that changes the intention slightly it changes the effect not at all; they can insist that they are neither saying nor implying that all members of group X display trait X, but only that it is slightly more likely that members of group X compared to non-members of group Y display trait X. Whatever the nuances to their beliefs, there is no difference in their actions.

Rational discrimination is rigorous and respectable. Writers such as Nobel Laureate Gary Becker, federal judge Richard Posner, law professor Richard Epstein, and others affiliated with the Chicago school of law and economics have made powerful arguments for it. Journalist Richard Cohen introduced a popular version of the "jeweler's dilemma" in a 1986 column for the *Washington Post*. Cohen argued that we all have an unspoken understanding that we resort to rational discrimination as we go about our daily lives. Responding to the Bernard Goetz case, in which a white subway rider in New York City shot four black youths after they asked him for money—which, Cohen suggests, everyone knows is a prelude to a mugging—Cohen writes succinctly:

> In order to be admitted to certain Washington jewelry stores, customers have to ring a bell. The ring-back that opens the door is almost perfunctory. According to the owner of one store, only one type of person does not get admitted: Young black males. The owner says they are the ones who stick him up . . .
>
> Of course, all policies based on generalities have their injustices. A store-keeper might not know that the youths he has refused to admit are theology students—rich ones at that. But then insurance companies had no way of knowing I was not a typical teen-age driver. I paid through the nose anyway. . . .
>
> Let he who would open the door throw the first stone.[38]

To attend to the crux of the jeweler's dilemma, a host of distractions must be disposed of. At the outset, it should be obvious that rational discriminators must give up both any pretense of color blindness and any claim that they are not prejudiced. They must use race (or ethnicity, which is functionally the same) in the major and minor premises of their syllogism, and they do so to reach a conclusion that is a prejudgment:

Premise: A random Asian American is more likely than a random white to be foreign-born.
Premise: Fred is an Asian American.

Therefore: Fred is more likely than a random white to be foreign-born.

They also can link their syllogisms:

Premise: Fred is more likely than a random white to be foreign-born.
Premise: The foreign-born are more likely than the native-born to be disloyal.
Therefore: Fred, who is more likely than a random white to be foreign-born, is more likely than the native-born to be disloyal.

Rational discriminators also prejudge Fred. They could always try to determine directly whether Fred is foreign-born or disloyal, but the whole point of rational discrimination is its utility in situations where it is not feasible to ask Fred or when asking him is not likely to produce the truth. Rational discrimination offers efficiency, not equality.

But as important as it is to note that rational discriminators are color conscious and prejudiced, they should not be condemned outright on those bases. If we are serious about considering whether rational discrimination is right or wrong, we cannot characterize it as color conscious and prejudiced and assume that is enough to end the discussion.

Rational discriminators cannot avoid criticism by claiming that they rely on the truth, because they conflate the truth about a group with the truth about an individual. But critics of rational discrimination also cannot prevail simply by pointing out that it relies on generalizations, because they must show what is wrong with generalizations. After all, we engage in other forms of rational discrimination constantly and we rely on generalizations as well. We are required by daily life to make judgments about people with a modicum of data, very quickly, and under stress, and it would be futile to pretend otherwise. Individuals must do it; so too must groups and the government. We would be paralyzed if we had to gather every bit of data before making a decision and executing it. Our ability to generalize is a hallmark of higher intelligence as well. A failure to discriminate would not be utopian but disturbing; few of us treat our family as we do strangers, and we don't marry people chosen at random. There may be some critics with the radical worldview of post-modern epistemology who would reject rational discrimination for irrational non-discrimination. But they are, by their own admission, not amenable to reason. (Philosophers David Hume and Karl Popper, however, have mounted the case against induction, arguing that it cannot logically prove anything because it can only be an approximation.)

Insurance companies, which must make judgments about large groups of people, use actuarial tables that provide facts about aggregate groups, not actual individuals. They assemble inputs about an applicant for an insurance policy, ranging from age and family history to occupation and marital status. Most people would agree—and it doesn't especially matter whether they do, because it is true—that young people are a better risk than older people for life insurance, a person with no history of heart disease is a better risk than someone whose parents both died of heart attacks for health insurance, and so forth.

At every physician's office, we can see an example of rational discrimination hanging on the wall: a table of heights and weights. Given a person's height, we can estimate her weight with fair accuracy, because height correlates to weight. Tall people tend to weigh more; short people, less. There are variations in body shape and there are exceptions, such as tall thin people and short stout ones, but they are at the outlying ends of the normal distribution. With height and weight, we go on to be both descriptive and prescriptive: We list for every height range an ideal weight range.

Racial profiling is used for commercial purposes as well. Defenders of racial profiling often point out that companies that sell to specific demographic groups, whether by buying mailing lists with Asian surnames or using Spanish-language commercials, and tailoring their appeal to their audience, are using racial backgrounds to infer consumer preferences.[39] It is not only purveyors of overseas telephone calling plans and banks issuing "affinity" credit cards to ethnic organizations who rely on ethnic marketing. Con artists have long depended on their ability to establish rapport with their marks, and ethnic solidarity is proving an increasingly popular means of defrauding immigrants. The General Development Corporation land fraud, for example, one of the largest Florida real estate swindles ever, used targeted marketing in this manner, according to prosecutors.

If race is to be ruled out as a peculiar taboo, there must be a rationale for distinguishing it from other criteria. In the eyes of rational discriminators, race is just another variable from which inferences can be drawn. There is a good argument from history, not logic, that race is different because of slavery, Jim Crow, the legacy of discrimination, and everything we have learned about racial prejudice that makes it different in degree and kind from other generalizations when it is used to reinforce stereotypes. Yet the argument from history works only to the extent that rational discriminators suppose history to be better than logic. We use race to connect people, but not other characteristics. Because Japanese Emperor Hirohito was short, had a mustache, and a name that started with "H," Americans did not bear any animus toward other people who were short, had mustaches, or names that started with "H." Even if they shared all those traits with someone whom we hated, we did not extrapolate from such features that they would be dangerous or infer that they stood in solidarity with one another.

It also does not much matter if the racial inference is positive or negative. Rational discriminators could infer that an Asian American is a good student, a likely spy, or both. For them, the issue is whether the connections are supported, not whether the conclusion is a compliment or an insult, a minor slur or a major cruelty. In an issue of the *New Republic* magazine dedicated to the jeweler's dilemma, George Mason University economist Walter E. Williams, himself African American, argued that if a person who had to field her own basketball team "must select five out of 20 people who appear to be equal in every respect except race and sex," five each of African American women, African American men, white women, and white men, "most would confine their choice to males, and their choice would be dominated by African American males."[40] Williams argues that this is sensible, because the impromptu manager of the basketball team has obtained information through the proxies of race and sex about basketball proficiency. Williams notes that he has faced the unfavorable version of this "mistaken identity" about African American men, but it is "not the same as racism."

Even seemingly positive forms of racial profiling can become negative. It is deceptively easy to concur that testing for sickle cell anemia among blacks and not others is a sound medical protocol founded on epidemiological research indicating that sickle cell anemia is overwhelmingly a disease correlated to race. Yet people of Mediterranean, Arab, and Latin American origins can and do develop sickle cell anemia. It is true that Asian and Asian American women tend to develop cancer at lower rates than other women. It would be preventable folly to forgo screening for cancer or ignore early indicators of it among Asian American women, but that medical malpractice happens frequently.[41]

The most important objection to rational discrimination also is the least effective. The most important objection to rational discrimination is that rational discriminators have miscalculated their premises. They have overestimated the correlation of race to status, the correlation of status to conduct, or both. For example, they have overestimated the probability that an Asian American (race) will be foreign-born (status), the probability that foreign birth (status) produces treason (conduct), or both. This is an important objection to raise, because it often will be the case that rational discriminators do not start from a blank slate like the Bayesian newborn wondering if the sun will rise, but instead substitute odds that have been influenced by stereotypes.

For example, rational discriminators may estimate that the probability that an Asian American will be foreign-born is higher than that a white will be foreign-born. They would be right about that, given current demographics. But they may also estimate that the foreign birth increases the probability of treason. They cannot point to strong evidence for that ancient fear. Ideology, self-interest, bribery, blackmail, and sex all rank higher than ethnic ties as impulses for espionage. Furthermore, they may gloss over the difference between status and conduct or substitute a strong inference about status for a weak one about conduct. Studies show, for example, that people greatly overestimate the proportion of people of color within the general population.[42] Our generally poor abilities at statistical thinking should caution us against entrusting decisions to snap judgments about speculative probabilities. We forget how many events there are that make even extremely improbable occurrences, such as plane crashes, happen on a predictable basis, and how the minority status of people of color magnifies our perceptions.

This objection will resolve the cases of defective rational discrimination, but that is all. It repudiates only the specific application of rational discrimination, not the general propriety of using rational discrimination. That is, this argument does not say that rational discriminators ought to stop their practice but that they should perfect it. Rational discriminators can revise their formula.

For example, Asian Americans are not only more likely to be foreign-born than non-Hispanic whites but also more likely than not to be foreign-born, period. Well over half, approximately two-thirds, of Asian Americans are foreign-born. People, such as border guards, who had to guess at whether a person was foreign-born would be playing the odds quite well if they guessed that every Asian American was foreign-born. Just as there are tall thin people and short stout people, there are Asian Americans who are bad students and African Americans who are bad basketball players. Most of us confound the generalizations in one manner or another. Yet the Customs Service is right: I am the suspect traveler; its questions are not irrelevant.

Accordingly, although activists should continue to devote their efforts to debunking the fallacious premises that may be used by armchair rational discriminators, they should consider fallback arguments. A general refusal to accept Bayesian statistics is not worthwhile—although the scholarly debate between those who use Bayesian statistics, who are a minority, and those who use conventional statistics, who are the majority, is not yet settled—because sophisticated rational discriminators are really relying on nothing more than logic, and activists would not serve their cause by opposing logic itself. There will be cases in which discrimination is based on premises that are true. But there also are better lines of attack against rational discrimination.

Rational discrimination fails on its own terms. It should be rejected because it is not responsive to rights, causes, contexts, consequences, or any morality beyond the bottom line. Everyone generalizes. We should strive to become aware of all generalizations even as we eliminate those that are odious.

Libertarians sometimes assert that rational discrimination, like any judgments people make about others, must be protected because we have the right to set the terms of our interaction with strangers. But libertarians especially should resist rational discrimination. Heirs of Patrick Henry who prize independence should see that that very independence is infringed upon by rational discrimination, because it imposes involuntary group membership on individual subjects. Those individuals to whom a generalization is applied falsely lose their freedom of association. An Asian American who is a citizen and not a foreigner, or an African American who is a law-abiding member of the community and not a law-breaking hoodlum, may have nothing in common with the individuals about whom a racial stereotype is true. Even if either of them were a brother to the individual who fit the stereotype, they are not morally culpable for that person's status or conduct. The rational discriminator imposes the connection.

Racial Prophecies

Rational discrimination, like any prejudice, can easily become a self-fulfilling prophecy. It is exceptionally destructive, because the worse it is in reality the more it justifies itself in the abstract. It can become perfect, having no correspondence to the truth but concocting its own truth. It does so because it sets off a vicious cycle in which "you find what you look for."

A simple hypothetical case will illustrate this problem. Consider a town that hires a law-and-order police chief who is a rational discriminator. Bear in mind that this no-nonsense police chief can be of any racial background and need not be racist in a classic sense. The police chief may conjecture that African Americans are more likely than whites to be breaking the law. He may have conducted research before coming to that conclusion.

The police chief's premise is faulty. According to most studies, African Americans commit most crimes—including those involving drug usage—at approximately the same rates as whites. The apparent differences between black and white criminality—especially with respect to drug usage—arise in the punishments meted out. Societal sympathies are not the same across the color line. For example, many white drug users are diverted to rehabilitation by hopeful families who conduct interventions, whereas most of their African American counterparts are condemned to prison by sentencing guidelines that impose harsh mandatory minimums. Regrettably, African American men really do commit some crimes at higher rates than white men. As Harvard law professor Randall Kennedy has pointed out, young black men are responsible for a disproportionate amount of street crime. African Americans, at about 12 percent of the population, are arrested for about 62 percent of armed robberies.[43]

Nonetheless, based on a superficial sense that African Americans are slightly more likely to break the law, the police chief could implement a strategy of rational discrimination and order the officers to employ racial profiling to concentrate their energy, time, and resources on enforcement directed toward African Americans. The chief has common sense on his side, because the department's energy, time, and resources are admittedly limited and the officers would be best deployed to respond to the greatest needs. The chief's premises may have been wrong, and he may have made logical errors, but his program would meet with the approval of Cohen's jeweler; this is how rational discrimination operates if it is applied more systematically.

Even if the proportion of African Americans in the town who deserved suspicion was the same as or lower than the proportion of whites who were similarly situated, the policy itself will almost certainly produce a higher rate of apprehensions among African Americans. Unless improbably high numbers of whites turn themselves in for their infractions, the arrest figures it generates will feature an even higher concentration of African Americans among those arrested than previously. Hunch confirmed, the police chief can hardly be faulted for then ratcheting up the rational discrimination. The officers will direct their scrutiny even more closely toward African Americans, and the ensuing predicament of all African Americans will worsen rapidly.

If we give numbers to the scenario, the consequences become clear. Assume that the town has 10,000 residents. Say African Americans number about 1,000 or 10 percent of the total. To keep it simple, and to use the type of assumptions typical of rational discrimination analysis, let us posit that each percentage of effort expended by the police department results in a single arrest, that no individuals are subject to multiple arrests, and that everyone who is arrested has an equal chance of being found guilty of an offense.

To use likely figures, perhaps in the first year under this regime the police chief allocates a relatively modest one-quarter of police efforts to investigating African American suspects. At the end of the first year, the police chief and the officers will have on their hands 25 African Americans with arrest records and 75 non-African Americans with arrest records. Virtually all African Americans in the town—97.5 percent—are upstanding citizens who are as law abiding as anyone else. The chance that any given African American resident has an arrest record is only 2.5 percent, which is hardly an alarming figure by itself.

But African Americans are a racial minority group, constituting only 10 percent of the population in the town. That makes all the difference to the proportions and the generalizations. Even though African Americans are 10 percent of the population, they make up 25 percent of the arrestees. Although non-African Americans are 90 percent of the population, they make up only 75 percent of the arrestees. African Americans are distinctly overrepresented in the pool of arrestees. There is three times the chance that any random African American will have an arrest record compared to any random non-African American (25/1,000 or 2.5 percent, compared to 75/9,000 or .83 percent). Note that this effect is obtained no matter who is committing crime. Remember that we set as a premise that African American and white crime rates are the same.

In this town, what matters is the comparison of African Americans and non-African Americans. Based on the latest statistics, the police chief is vindicated. He may become more enthusiastic, devoting three-quarters of police efforts to African Americans to match his priorities to the problem, or more accurately, to his artificially distorted perception of the problem. If any African American is three times as likely as any non-African American to have an arrest record, the police chief can infer that any random African American is three times as likely as any random non-African American to be up to no good. This casual use of statistics may not satisfy anyone with serious training in the subject, but it passes the layperson's test of common sense. The fallacies here include the confusion of a relatively higher rate of characteristic within a group with an absolutely high rate of that characteristic within the group, the belief that the proportion of X who are Y is equal to the proportion of Y who are X, and the failure to account for the influence of the law enforcement strategies that generated the statistics in the first place.

In the second year, the police chief and the officers will arrest 75 more African Americans and 25 more non-African Americans. The overwhelming majority of African Americans—90 percent—remain upstanding citizens who are as law abiding as anyone else. The chance that any given African

American resident has an arrest record has risen to only 10 percent (the 2.5 percent from year 1 plus the 7.5 percent from year 2), which although troubling is still fairly low.

But African Americans will make up five times as much of the pool of arrestees as they do of the overall population. They constitute 1,000 out of 10,000 of the population, but 100 out of 200 of the arrestees over the two years. Whites are the other 100 arrestees in the same time period. The likelihood that a random African American has an arrest record has risen to nine times as high as the likelihood that a random white has an arrest record (100 out of 1,000 or 10 percent, compared with 100 out of 9,000 or 1.11 percent). Now the police chief decides to focus law enforcement nearly exclusively on African Americans. The result is decimation of African American communities.

Racial profiling operates inexorably toward its extreme. As the police chief directs more and more of the officers to respond exclusively to complaints against African Americans, more and more of the law-breakers they apprehend will end up being African American. But the police chief also manufactures a quandary for himself. Because he directs more and more of the officers to concentrate on African Americans, more and more of the white criminals will escape their attention and continue to ply their trade. In all likelihood, the citizens of the town will demand action in response to the crime spree. In response, the police chief will bear down even harder on African Americans. If the citizens of the town are satisfied, the same result is reached. His constituents will be happy, and the police chief will continue on his course.

Rational discrimination depends on logic, and it can be undone only by what seems like illogic. Once the police chief has started on rational discrimination, he can extricate himself only by adopting a seemingly imprudent policy. He can return to sanity only by devoting fewer resources to pursuing African Americans than it appears they warrant. Otherwise, the only question is whether he will incarcerate all the African Americans before he incarcerates all the criminals.

There are police departments that have behaved in this manner, even more clearly than recent studies have shown. The police in Oneonta, New York, acted rationally but indefensibly in 1993 after an elderly white woman was attacked by a black man who received a cut on his hand during the ensuing scuffle. The police, working with administrators at the State University of New York campus in the town, decided to question all 125 black male students enrolled there. They tried to have each of them show their hands as well.[44] In a town of 14,000 residents, with only 300 blacks, the decision to find every black male after an assailant has been identified as a black male can be given a credible rationale. Yet it violates the rights of the racial minority, both because it casts suspicion on everyone based solely on race and gender, and because a similar treatment would be unimaginable with respect to the white majority (it might be dismissed as impractical in such a case, but the meaning of the action is independent of the reasoning behind the decision). Especially if it is played out repeatedly, the scenario relegates all black men to the status of permanent suspects. (When the students sued an administrator who violated privacy regulations by releasing their personal information, they lost; the administrator's lawyer called their case "political correctness run amok.")[45]

Even African American law enforcement personnel are stereotyped. In Washington, D.C., between 1995 and 1998, three black cops were mistaken for criminals and shot by white officers, two of them fatally. These rates are higher than in other cities, and the reverse appears not to occur; that is, white cops are rarely mistaken for criminals and shot by their black fellow-officers.[46]

As if that were not enough, rational discrimination is doubly effective because of the incentives it sets up. It is done in by its own precepts. The economic analysis that is its mainspring posits that the human beings who are actors in the system are guided by rationality and not some metaphysical morality. Each and every one of them will maximize personal gain and none of them should prefer anything less. Rational discrimination turns out to be detrimental over the long run because, under its principles, the individuals subjected to its stereotypes ought to conform to the negative images. The more severe the racial profiling, the more sensible it becomes for its subjects to conform to its stereotype. If the racial profile is highly negative and widely accepted, then individuals who are affected by it should follow its model. The costs of refusing to conform to it are too great, especially given the understandable frustration of doing so. Being treated like a traitor makes being a traitor an attractive choice, being treated like a thug makes being a thug an attractive choice, and so forth.[47]

Look at it from the perspective of Asian Americans who are assumed to be disloyal. They can either be loyal or disloyal. If they are loyal but are assumed to be disloyal, they gain no benefit from disloyalty but incur the costs of disloyalty. They accrue no benefits from loyalty. If they would like to persist in their loyalty, they must repeatedly pay the cost of proving their loyalty to rebut the presumption against them. They are at a competitive disadvantage, because non-Asian Americans need not prove their loyalty. The stereotype operates at a societal level, but they can react only at an individual level. For them, disloyalty begins to look attractive. By following the market forces directing them toward disloyalty and converting to disloyalty, they realize the benefits they are not enjoying while paying no more than the costs they already pay.

To make it more concrete, the stereotype of disloyalty may be manifested in denial of a security clearance to work on military contracts. An Asian American engineer who specialized in weapons design who would like to work for the United States, but cannot do so because she cannot pass a security clearance test—say she has family in Asia, a condition that is neither unusual for Asian Americans nor especially upsetting to Asian Americans— has no choice but to quit her profession or leave the country. In outline, this is similar to the historical case of the architect of the Chinese nuclear weapons program, a promising young scientist in the United States until racial prejudice ruined his career. Qian Xuesen, a graduate of both MIT and Cal Tech, had become an Air Force colonel—a U.S. Air Force colonel— before he was hit with unfounded allegations of disloyalty.[48] Having lost his security clearances and with no prospect of continuing a life free of suspicions, he was invited by China in 1955 to return there. He accepted, becoming the inventor of the Silkworm missile that forms the basis for the Chinese retaliatory strike force aimed at the United States.

Likewise, the African American young man who is perceived by virtually everyone—including many members of his own community—to be a thug might as well actually become one. If mainstream society shuns him but street gangs welcome him, he is behaving exactly how anybody else would under the same circumstances in choosing the subculture where he is embraced and expected to excel. Along with his new peers, and exactly as anybody else would do to have a positive self-image, the new recruit is likely to valorize the traits of thuggery he has been assigned. Told he is a thug, he can revel in thugdom.

An example of this phenomenon of ennobling the ignoble occurred when Novelist Toni Morrison called Bill Clinton the nation's first black president in an essay for *New Yorker* magazine. By way of analyzing the Monica Lewinsky matter, Morrison wrote, "Clinton displays almost every trope of blackness: single-parent household, born poor, working-class, saxophone-playing, McDonald's-and-junk-food-loving boy from Arkansas" with "unpoliced sexuality" who "was metaphorically seized and body-searched" for his failure to "assimilate at once." Although ridiculed by some critics, she was brilliant in turning around the stereotypes of African Americans. To those who would judge blacks by the very behaviors she cites, she demonstrates that a powerful white man qualifies as black under those criteria. She does even better than that. She celebrates the traits they would condemn.[49]

The same phenomenon occurred when *The Simpsons* became a hit television show in 1990. Eight-year-old Bart, the delinquent hero of Matt Groening's animated series, was especially popular as an iconic figure among African American males. He was so successful in his subversiveness, which so resembled their stereotype of the knucklehead, that bootleggers peddled "black Bart" t-shirts that gave him black features.[50]

Rational discriminators cannot object to either the Asian American who becomes a weapons designer for an Asian nation or the African American male who becomes a violent robber. Rational discriminators themselves behave on the basis of probabilities and stereotypes, so they must accept others who do so as well. In relying on probabilities, they favor cost-benefit analysis and forego any other ethical code. Likewise, their victims favor the corresponding cost-benefit analysis and also eschew any other ethical code. In looking at stereotypes, rational discriminators are guided by premonitions and not realities. It does not much matter that the individual Asian American or African American may not conform to the image. Likewise, their victims are guided by premonitions and not realities. It does not much matter that opportunities in legitimate enterprises are much better than they may seem.

Because stereotypes are such poor generalizations, their benefits can be outweighed by the combined costs of false positives and false negatives. A false positive occurs when our racial stereotype is overinclusive. During World War II, thousands of Japanese Americans were assumed to be disloyal even though they were perfectly loyal. Society loses little, but each Japanese American individual and the Japanese American community is devastated by the loss of liberty, property, and income. A false negative occurs when our racial stereotype is underinclusive. During World War II, white Americans who were actually disloyal were automatically assumed to be loyal. Society may lose enormously, because a saboteur is allowed to roam free; during and after World War II, all the ten or so individuals tried as Japanese agents were non-Asian American.

The false positives are what law professor Armour has called a "black tax." Under its impositions, the anger of African Americans, even or especially if they are middle-class, becomes understandable. As professor Kennedy has said, "Even if it's the case that police officers or others are engaging in rational discrimination, a lot of black people are going to believe that they're being subjected to racist treatment. This perception has, albeit erroneous, a huge cost" in "feelings of resentment and alienation."[51]

The false negatives are what critical race theorists have called "white privilege." Through its benefits, white Americans are able to proceed through life without sharing the concerns of many people of color, without even being aware of the radically different circumstances that shape their respective lives. Most white Americans need not worry about rampant drug dealing and gun violence in their neighborhoods, false arrests, police brutality, selective prosecution, or the death penalty. Being killed by one of their peers, the leading cause of death for African American young men, is not a major fear for their white cohorts.

Rational discrimination also produces rational discrimination as a reaction. When Malcolm X was at his most nationalistic, between his assimilationist childhood and his final humanist phase, he believed every white person was a racist. Malcolm was a rational discriminator in his own way. Because he had had enough experience with white racists, he made the plausible assumption that he should treat all white people as racists. His reasoning mirrors that of those who would look at black as miscreants.

Taken together, these externalities make rational discrimination a racial tragedy of the commons. In the jargon of economics, externalities are simply the costs of an action that an actor does not bear but can instead impose on others. A tragedy of the commons occurs whenever individual short-term self-interest runs opposite to collective long-term group interest (or even individual long-term self-interest, for that matter). Rational discrimination is essentially a form of selfish behavior that drives a society into a tragedy of the commons.

The classic tragedy of the commons occurs when a shepherd looks at the large public pasture, or green, and thinks that its vastness behooves her to add one more sheep to her flock grazing there. The benefit to the shepherd is greater than any costs. The trouble arises because each shepherd follows the same principle when looking at the greens. Each is justified in coming to the same conclusion. The danger is that the community will suddenly have too many sheep consuming the limited amount of grass available. What was advantageous for each shepherd is not advantageous for all shepherds. To reach equilibrium will require that every shepherd appreciate the necessity of compromise, for the sake of her own flock as well as others' flocks. We face a racial tragedy of the commons because rational discrimination is excessive. The shepherd who adds more sheep to her flock on the public green is identical to the taxicab driver who, using rational discrimination, passes up the African American male standing on the downtown corner late at night.

In the racial tragedy of the commons, each cabbie glances at the potential fare and drives on. The problem is that the person will stand there waiting forever and be literally left behind. Even if we were to exaggerate the risk that the passenger is dangerous and make an extravagant estimate, the effect is grossly unfair. If 5 percent of African American men were armed robbers— needless to say, an absurd assumption—then 95 percent of them should be picked up by the cabbie. But that 5 percent risk is high enough that all 100 percent of African American men will be left without a ride home. What may have been tolerable in a single instance becomes unbearable in totality for African American men (not to mention the not trifling cost to cabbies of depriving themselves of this segment of possible income).

Critics of this example often say that the consequence to the cabbie and the consequence to the neglected fare are different. The cabbie may lose his life if he makes the wrong choice, but the neglected fare merely has to walk home. The cabbie does have a fear that should not be scoffed at, but the neglected fare does more than walk home. He is reminded again of everything else the speeding taxicab represents, and his despised status. Although devising the means to ensure the cabbie's safety may not be easy, the remedy requires that taxicab drivers open their doors to African American men.

Racial Rationalizations

Rational discrimination exemplifies what sociologist Max Weber called "instrumental rationality." Rational discrimination is an exercise in utilitarianism. Started by Jeremy Bentham and improved upon by John Stuart Mill, the utilitarian school of thought offered more powerful insights into human conduct than any of its philosophical predecessors. Its systematic conceptualizations were emancipatory: Mill articulated the rights of women, although he also argued that "free institutions are next to impossible in a country made up of different nationalities."[52]

Utilitarianism was revolutionary but so successful that most of us are utilitarians without even being aware of it. Utilitarianism offers its adherents a life of refined hedonism and comes to be seen wrongly as a proposition against which there are no opponents. Mill defines utilitarianism as "The creed which accepts as the foundation of morals Utility, or the Greatest Happiness Principle, holds that actions are right in proportion as they tend to promote happiness, wrong as they tend to produce the reverse of happiness."[53]

We accept the modern mode of decision making derived from calculations about benefits and costs—some crude, some complex—but methodically aimed at attaining optimal outcomes. Whether we are negotiating annual budgets for government spending, developing corporate business plans, or just considering among family members whether to buy a new house, we often list the pluses and the minuses of all the options, striking a balance for the best net results. One person, one vote; the option with the most pluses is the best.

Classical economists and evolutionary psychologists further declare that, even if we are squeamish and deny we are engaging in stark calculations, we always still manage to judge the advantages to ourselves of every set of decisions we confront. We automatically pursue our own highest self-interests, even if we compromise or do not fulfill our goals, for that is the raw egotism of human nature.

Yet it also has become clear that utilitarianism is a failure as an ethical system. Bentham insists rigidly on quantitative measurements only, but his disciple Mill recognizes flexibly that people have different values, and those values are not all on a par. Mill says, "It is better to be Socrates dissatisfied than a pig satisfied."[54]

Utilitarianism may describe how we think, but it does not prescribe how we should act. As much as we may trust it as a system for pointing toward what is economical, few of us would turn to it for guidance in determining between fundamental right and wrong. The overwhelming majority of us, whatever our views are about a subject, reject the idea that the real dilemmas with which we must cope can be resolved adequately by toting up sums. Accounting is not enough.

The most elegant example of utilitarianism is Pascal's wager. The famous gamble about divinity is a cunning but empty display. The seventeenth-century mathematician Blaise Pascal, a prodigy and contemporary of René Descartes who preceded Mill by a century and a half, is probably best known for his aphorism, "the heart has its reasons which reason does not know." He invented the barometer, the hydraulic press, and the syringe. He developed the field of probability theory before undergoing the religious revelations that caused him to enter a monastery to devote his life to writing Christian meditations.

Pascal said that believing in God was the best bet. He reasoned as follows: If he believed in God and turned out to be right, the potential gain was great with relatively little labor; if he believed in God and was wrong, he would have no eternal soul to be bothered by the mistake anyway. If he did not believe in God and he turned out to be right, he would have no soul after death to verify his atheism and therefore could take no satisfaction in his skepticism. But if he did not believe in God and was wrong, the consequences were final and huge. (Agnosticism is not an available choice. To decline to make any choice serves effectively as a denial of God's existence.)

The logic is impeccable. We could grouse about the assumptions that the existence of God is correlated to the existence of an eternal soul or that the existence of God correlates to the existence of the Christian God, but to quibble about such details would be to miss the beauty of the logic. The reasoning is compelling only as a logical matter, however. Pascal's wager has won over few converts, Pascal himself included. The argument is too clever, proving only that a person should believe in God, not that God exists. Arguably, a person who was swayed by it is not truly religious at all.

The same fault of utilitarianism is evident with all great issues. Abortion of fetuses, euthanasia of the disabled, and assisted suicide of the elderly are rarely advocated with the frightening claim that we as a society would be better off. Only sometimes are they advocated with the suspicious claim that the individuals themselves would be better off. Such assertions are so anathema that proponents of the causes probably would rather disavow any association with them. This is so even or especially if the utilitarianism might be persuasive. We avoid even thinking about it, because we will not abide by benefit-cost analysis.

Likewise, most of us would find it appalling if we observed an individual deliberating the pros and cons of marrying a potential spouse or cultivating a friendship. We would be disgusted if we discovered that our spouse has chosen us because her market value matches ours and she has figured that she can do no better in competitive bargaining, or that our friends have sought us as companions for what we can do on their behalf without too much expense to them. Such decisions are inhumane, because they reduce us to items on a list, players in strategic interactions, devoid of intimate value.

The limitation is intrinsic to utilitarianism. Utilitarianism functions only after we have already formed preferences. It does not guide us in setting priorities. It tells us we all ought to prefer what makes more of us happy, but it does not guide any of us in choosing what makes each of us happy. Mill admitted as much: "The sole evidence it is possible to produce that anything is desirable, is that people do actually desire it. If the end which the utilitarian doctrine proposes to itself were not, in theory and in practice, acknowledged to be an end, nothing could ever convince any person that it was so."[55] That task, however, of identifying goals is the heart of the examined life and civic culture. We must know what to value as individuals and as a society. Utilitarianism ends where morality begins.

Whether we value achievement of racial integration or the elimination of racial discrimination is a question about such preferences. If most of us were slightly pleased by integration, some of us very pleased by segregation, and a few of us apathetic, utilitarianism would help us develop a map for locating homes. But it could do nothing to win over more people to integration from segregation, or vice versa, much less to protect any notion of rights. Utilitarianism offers no guidance in allocating weights to the many factors in a complete formula involving the comparison of incommensurable concepts such as equality and liberty. It also cannot overcome the impossible problem of tallying up individual interests into a societal judgment.

Opponents of utilitarianism like thought experiments, but racial realities are test enough. In a typical thought experiment, a utilitarian is asked whether she would sacrifice the life of one to save the lives of ten or if she would protest slavery. Racial realities show that a majority of whites, with a minority acting directly and many others standing by, did sacrifice the equality of African Americans for the privileges of whites. Southern institutions that upheld legal segregation and their Northern counterparts that maintained social segregation produced benefits for a few at the expense of the many. University of Chicago economist Robert William Fogel argued in his book, *Time on the Cross: The Economics of American Negro Slavery*,[56] that slavery was a well-organized institution. Historians who misread him as advocating slavery missed the mark. They look at the profit sheet more than he did; they had the misapprehension, as he had not, that profits justified human bondage. Even if slavery produced more benefits than it did costs as measured by the masters, the losses of equality and liberty are enough that we must side with the slaves. As Fogel himself said in his acceptance speech for a 1993 Nobel Prize, "If you want me to say [slavery] was unprofitable and inefficient, I won't. . . . But I don't think anyone would say it was moral."[57]

The best that utilitarians can manage is exemplified by Oxford philosopher R. M. Hare's explanation of "what is wrong with slavery."[58] Hare argues in a fine essay that utilitarianism can prove that slavery is wrong, rather than merely protest that it is so. He relies, however, on people taking a stand against slavery because of rights that precede the utilitarian analysis. The hitch is that he turns to reasons that are extrinsic to utilitarianism itself. That hardly makes for a good philosophy.

Our judgments are informed by utilitarian analysis. They should not be determined by vulgar versions of it. Mill himself was concerned with using education for moral development, especially to cultivate empathy. His confidence in independent thought and the free exchange of ideas is betrayed by racial stereotyping of any form.

The rejection of utilitarianism with respect to discrimination is not unique to racial distinctions. Suppose a law firm wishes to discriminate in favor of single persons without children in hiring junior associates. The preference meets the threshold test of rationality. It is likely true on average that a single person without children will have more energy for work, greater dedication to his career, and fewer outside commitments, regardless of whether it holds true in every instance of a mother who has balanced her plans to pursue her profession outside the home (compared, say, with a bachelor who boasts a busy social life). The law firm must make hiring decisions from among many applicants; it cannot be bothered to investigate every aspect of every individual's qualifications. Thus, the generalization is important, not the exception.

Legislation for the most part protects prospective employees from this hypothetical law firm. But the law protects us because we have made ethical judgments that we value more than efficiency, not because the law firm is irrational. Even if the discrimination against married people with children were applied evenhandedly, so that fathers as well as mothers were disadvantaged and it wasn't a cover for gender discrimination, it still would be deplorable—rational, but deplorable. We have countervailing values. Those values are unrelated to whether a single person is superior to a married person for the job. Our society and indeed our species places value on having families and raising children. Rational discrimination gives way to a desire to encourage families and nurture offspring. All of us are better off with employers that care about more than output.

Rational discrimination takes an even more egregious form than racial discrimination, one that subsumes racial discrimination within it: genetic discrimination. The human genome project threatens to give us knowledge for which we are not ready. All of us have hidden weaknesses, some incurable and even fatal. We will meet in genetic testing the most aggressive form of rational discrimination, which may lead to an acknowledgment that utility is a means and not an ends. An employer or its insurer that turns down an applicant for a job or a policy based on genetic screening cannot be faulted for being irrational. Responsible geneticists admonish us that there is no single "fat" gene or "heart attack" gene, but they also advise us that there are genes that may increase our propensity for obesity or cardiac arrest.

If we prohibit an employer or its insurer from using this information, it is exactly because it is rational and not because it is irrational. The jeweler's dilemma is much worse than it seems. If the jeweler will not open the door to an African American young man, he cannot object if the insurer refuses to cover him because he is disabled, elderly, or someone who has been diagnosed with a propensity for developing a costly illness. The principle is the same in each case; the data will be even stronger in the latter.

A modified utilitarianism emerges. The utilitarianism that succeeds is tempered. Rationality is necessary, but not sufficient, for our actions and our public policies. Civil rights also must be valued and protected, above and beyond calculations of benefits and costs, in a constant balancing process. Rationality must be trumped by rights, in most instances; if rights were trumped by rationality, they would be worthless.

In a diverse culture, we evolve many mutual agreements with the minimal goal of reducing conflict and a maximal hope of increasing cooperation. These agreements, which make up our social contract, range from driving on a particular side of the road and obeying traffic signals to extending the franchise to all adults and adopting representative democracy. Disavowing "rational discrimination" should be a core component of the civic society to which we aspire. If we do not give it up, we will have a racial contract that benefits whites as the majority (or, eventually, the plurality), instead of a social contract that binds all of us.[59]

In the next chapter, I ponder the relationship of race to culture and discrimination to diversity. The case study of dog-eating introduces the choices each of us as individuals and all of us as a society face between assimilation and multiculturalism. It may be possible to transcend the dilemma they present through the great experiment of America.

The Best "Chink" Food

Dog-Eating and the Dilemma of Diversity

"People live too easy, that's the trouble with the world," he
said. He wiped the bloody knife again and again on his
apron. "They watch the stupid TV, they read the stupid
Reader's Digest and the stupid best sellers, they eat trucker
tomatoes that got no taste and no color, no value in the
world except they're easy to ship, they go to work, go home
again, just like cows to the milking—" He picked out
another knife, a long one with a blade eight inches wide,
raised it, and brought it down once very hard, WHUMP!—
and the dog's head fell off, blood splashing. . . . The dog's
head looked up at me with the tongue hanging out through
the big, still teeth, an expression of absolute disbelief.
. . . The horror was too solidly there to look away from.

— JOHN GARDNER, *The Art of Living*

Buster and Ding Ding

I love dogs. I live with two of them in a canine-centered household. Buster
is a 95-pound mutt whom I adopted after he had been abandoned at a local

pet shelter. He is named after my wife's cousin's dog, whom the cousin raised while he was director of the Peace Corps mission in Tonga years ago. Our Buster has needed extra training to overcome his many anxieties. A deep-chested shepherd mix who is golden, with white paws and a white tip on his tail and a scar on his nose from breaking through a second-story window, he is powerful but timid. He spends his days chewing on tennis balls and loung-ing on top of his crate. At the first sound of thunder, however, he runs to the basement to hide.

Ding Ding is a 25-pound stray whom I rescued when she was a puppy. She is named after the beach resort in Taiwan where I found her, wandering around alone and scavenging for insects. She was issued a doggie passport verifying that she had had all the requisite vaccinations and, at six months of age, she cuddled up in a basket I was able to tuck under the airplane seat. Looking like an elegant basenji-sight hound cross with a black and tan coat, long legs, and a doe-like face, she is spoiled and fussy. She barks at strangers and likes to sleep in guests' laps.

I subscribe to the school of thought that says, "The more I know of man, the better I like my dogs." I am appalled both by the idea that anybody would eat dogs and by the question of whether Asians eat dogs. How we as a soci-ety address the taboo on dog-eating presents an excellent case study for con-templating the meanings and limits of diversity in all its forms. Dog-eating is neither as easy to tolerate as chopsticks instead of silverware nor as easy to forbid as violence against women justified as a venerable custom.

In the first half of this chapter, I ask the question "Do Asians eat dogs?" and provide a tentative answer, "What do you think?," as a means of model-ing a dialogue on diversity. In the second half of this chapter, I look at assim-ilation and multiculturalism as competing means of attending to diversity. Considering the advantages and disadvantages of each, I suggest that a prin-cipled compromise may be best.

We only taste diversity. Our festivals of diversity tend toward the superfi-cial, as if America were a stomach-turning combination plate of grits, tacos, sushi, and hummus. We fail to consider the dilemma of diversity, where our principles conflict with our practices. Still, as philosopher Roland Barthes wrote with the French expressly in mind, "food permits a person to partake each day of the national past."[1] For most Americans, dog-eating is not even conceivable as a gustatory pleasure representative of the national past.

The most popular feature of the annual ethnic carnivals organized in city parks every summer is the long line of food booths giving off the intermin-gled aromas of their unique fare. Each of the family-owned restaurants that have rented a space competes energetically to sell a consumable introduction to the national culture its owners represent, giving the misleading impression that to eat is to understand. Nowadays, Asian flavors dominate the menus. Passersby can satisfy their appetites with Americanized versions—at once bland, cheap, and greasy—of pho soup, chicken satay, bi bim bop, samosas with chutney, shrimp and vegetable tempura, or fried dumplings with soy sauce. They can refresh themselves with iced coffee sweetened by condensed milk or a mango lassi yogurt drink. They may even be able to find sac sac grape juice, green tea ice cream, or red beans on shaved ice. .

It is unlikely, however, that any of the Asian entrepreneurs would dare to offer up a bite of dog stew even though the entrée would be authentic as well as expected, once found throughout China, Korea, Vietnam, the Philippines, and elsewhere in the Pacific Rim. It has been the subject of lurid stories from epicurean tourists ever since Captain Cook and his crew landed on what they referred to as the Sandwich Islands, which we now know as Hawaii. At the Bishop Museum in Honolulu, there are a multitude of necklaces strung together with dog teeth, still displayed in the glass cases alongside other artifacts of the former glories of the islands. Yet even the editor of a volume called the *Anthropologist's Cookbook*[2] acknowledges that "there are limits, nevertheless, in matters of taste" and "some readers may object" to the instructions for preparing roast dog in an earth oven. At a luau, the slow-moving and reputedly dim-witted poi dogs, named after the tarot root (poi) on which they were fattened up until ready to be baked at two years of age, have long since ceased to be the main dish. In St. Louis, which once had an area named Dogtown due to sensationalized legends dating back to the 1904 World's Fair, it is improbable today that dogs would be grilled for guests.

Asian cookbooks in English abound, but dog-eating is not on the menu anywhere. There is no literary champion such as M. F. K. Fisher savoring asosena ("dog meat" in the Filipino dialect of Tagalog) as the specialty of a Manila street vendor as she would a rustic repast at a Provence inn, like a good friend possessed of a palate attentive to the fine details of pâté, cheese, and a proper *digestif*, and the talent to give readers a vicarious sensation on their tongues.[3]

An exception is the late novelist John Gardner, whose short story provides the epigraph to this chapter.[4] In the title piece of his 1981 *Art of Living* collection, which exemplifies his moralistic fiction, he portrays dog-eating as a reverential ritual. A motorcycle gang steals a dog so a chef can prepare a banquet centered on Imperial Dog. The chef is paying homage to his son, who had written to him about eating dog before being killed in the Vietnam War.

The story, illustrated with woodblock prints, ends with everyone beholding a vision "in the darkness beyond where the candles reached." The lost son is surrounded by "a thousand thousand Asians bowed from the waist."

The typical reference to dog-eating is the warning given by a dying man to his dog, Mr. Bones, in inventive novelist Paul Auster's *Timbuktu*:[5] "You get yourself a new gig, or your days are numbered," man's best friend is told, because "there's a Chinese restaurant on every block, and if you think mouths don't water when you come strolling by, then you don't know squat about Oriental cuisine."[6]

Dog-eating is an international urban legend with some truth to the tale. Everybody knows that Asians eat dogs. Transcendentalist philosopher Ralph Waldo Emerson joked about it in his journals: "The Englishman in China, seeing a doubtful dish set before him, inquired, 'quack-quack?' The Chinese replied, 'bow-wow'."[7] The sheep's head hanging in the window of the Chinese shop is supposed to be a signal that they will sell dog meat to those privy to the secret. In *Strange Foods: Bush Meat, Bats, and Butterflies, An Epicurean Adventure Around the World*,[8] explorer Jerry Hopkins states that the Chinese Kuomintang political party began their meetings by eating dog. Hopkins tried dog as a staple and treat as he wandered across Asia, even seeing in Thailand "a kind of Oriental dog tartare, where raw dog meat is chopped almost to a mince, mixed with a few spices and finely chopped vegetables, and served with the dog's blood and bile" and dog "deep-fried into a sort of jerky that was very hard to chew." (In the same adventuresome spirit, he ate the placenta after the birth of his son.[9])

Even in Asia, dog-eating has become simultaneously a source of shame and pride. When the Olympic games were hosted by Seoul, Korea, in 1988, the government tried vigorously to ban dog-eating to enhance its image with the West. Since then during major sporting contests, high officials have continued to make a show of opposition to the culinary custom. Boosted by vocal support from many of the visiting athletes, their efforts have met with no more than modest success. A 1993 Korean study found that over one-third of adults in the country had sampled dog stew in the past year. Press reports in the United States on such studies usually include quotes from Koreans who are indignant about denigration of their way of life. They are not about to be lectured by foreigners with a tone of superiority.

In the United States, the response to dog-eating is more likely to be revulsion. In 1989 in Long Beach, California, Cambodian refugees bludgeoned to death a German shepherd puppy, before slashing its throat and skinning it. The judge dismissed the misdemeanor indictment against them.

He found that they had not inflicted unreasonable pain on their meal. Animal rights groups were outraged by the ruling. As one of their spokespersons stated, "I think that what these defendants did offends the sensibilities of the community."[10] To ensure that the next prosecution would be successful, the California legislature passed a statute making it a misdemeanor to eat dog or cat. They later amended it to encompass any animal ordinarily kept as a pet or companion. The only recently reported case in which a defendant was convicted for eating a dog concerned a man, apparently not Asian, who barbecued the ribs of his neighbor's dog to avenge a perceived insult. In that 1992 California case, the unrepentant defendant received a sentence of three years.[11]

Performance artist Joey Skaggs, who stages elaborate pranks, fooled activists and the media alike with a 1994 stunt in which he mailed letters to animal shelters nationwide offering to buy dogs for export as food at ten cents per pound. Masquerading as a Korean businessman, he sent letters from a nonexistent company whose name, Kea So Joo, translates as Dog Meat Soup. "Dog is good food. Dog is good medicine," his letter read. "Dog no suffer. We have quick death for dog." Callers to his answering machine, which played a bilingual greeting with dogs yapping in the background, left thousands of messages denouncing the scheme before it was revealed as a hoax. The reaction was also racial: Skaggs received messages calling him a "filthy yellow devil" and suggesting that Asians be deported or killed. The mischievous Skaggs stated that he wanted to demonstrate the vagaries of cultural chauvinism.[12]

"Do Asians Eat Dogs?"

Let us imagine the range of potential reactions to the clichéd allegation that Asians eat dogs. When comedian Joan Rivers, hosting a television program before the 2000 Academy Awards, quipped before a commercial break that viewers could take their dogs for a walk, or if they were Filipino eat them, protests by Filipino organizations goaded Rivers into subsequently delivering a halfhearted apology. (The following year, Rivers remarked, "It's wonderful to see so many Asians here. It just gives [the program] a whole international flavor.") The joke that makes the rounds nowadays has had the Hmong substituted for the other Asian ethnicities that used to be the punchline: "What's the name of the Hmong cookbook? *101 Ways to Wok Your Dog.*"[13] The Asian American child who is taunted that the fastest animal on the street is her pet Rover, who most run awfully fast to avoid ending up in the dinner pot, probably does not realize the complex implications of the various options open to her.

How Filipino American organizations, how the child, how each Asian American responds to the stereotype ends up affecting all of us. To the mocking inquiry, "Do Asians eat dogs?" no riposte however sharp can effectively convey, "I speak for myself alone." The initial assimilationist answer to the charge is face-saving defiance: "Asians don't eat dogs."

Ironically, a denial serves as an admission. Indeed, the angrier the answer the more assimilated the answerer. To refute the claim that Asians eat dogs is to grudgingly admit that it would be wicked to do so. To protest also allows people to speak of Asians as a whole, so that the protester is actually acquiescing to the general practice of stereotyping.

Novelist May Lee Chai, a resident of Laramie, Wyoming, invoked this kind of protective stereotyping in a letter to the editor of *The New York Times* in 1994. She wrote to complain about a news item telling of dog-eating in mainland China. She called it "false information" and recounted a tradition of keeping dogs as pets and revering them as symbols of fidelity in artwork. She closed with an anecdote that reversed the roles: "In my two years of working and traveling in China, the only people I saw eating dog there were a group of American students. The Americans, newly arrived in Nanjing, went about the city in search of a restaurant that served dog. They found none. Finally they persuaded a private entrepreneur to procure a dog (for a sizable fee) and found someone willing to cook it in a stew. When the time came for the 'feast,' a crowd of amazed Chinese gathered and snapped pictures as the Americans ate a German shepherd."[14]

The subtler assimilationist answer may be more truthful but no more satisfying: "Other Asians might eat dogs, but I don't; I don't even condone it." Like the previous disclaimer, this retort reflects the majority norm that devouring dogs is deviant behavior. It differs from the other approach in drawing a line between the group and the individual. In this manner, the respondent repudiates both the reputation and the culture. He suggests that Asians are not all alike, but at the cost of disavowing other Asians, even the community of which he is a part. He may be sacrificing his family to cultivate a relationship with the majority, saying in effect "Bad Asians eat dogs; I am not like them."

This is a plausible interpretation of the Korean government policy. In Jessica Hagedorn's novel, *Dogeaters*, which was nominated for a National Book Award in 1990 and adapted for Broadway a decade later, the title refers to the name the rich call the poor.[15] The high culture distances itself from the low culture. The dog-eating recidivist is the superstitious peasant, not the urbane sophisticate.

Asked "Do Asians eat dogs?," the multiculturalist accepts the description but rejects the prescription: "Asians eat dogs, and who are you to criticize them?" This aggressive argument applies to a limited extent, but it falters at an emotional level. The subject is literally too visceral. The censure is a gut feeling.

Many Asians dine on delicacies that would disgust most Anglos, but their supper becomes a spectacle as a consequence. Raw fish has become enough of an upscale fashion that sushi aficionados can find the delectable fatty tuna (toro) as easily as they can the plain tuna (maguro). Tofu is a vegan necessity with multiple brands, ranging in texture from firm to silky, stocked at every supermarket. Bee pollen, ginseng, kava, and all sorts of herbs and medicinals have become domestic harvests lining the shelves at health food stores. Edamame, young soybeans that have been boiled and salted, which are eaten while drinking, are starting to rival beer nuts. Shrimp chips can be found alongside pork rinds. Calpis and Pocari Sweat sport drinks are being imported, embarrassing names and all. However, eyes plucked out of a steamed whole fish and the head of the fish, stinky tofu, slimy sea cucumbers, seaweed salad, bear paw, warm snake bile, congealed blood, wrinkled chicken feet, slimy giant water bugs, savory baked cocoons, bitter cow dung, and fried duck embryos have attracted no more of a broad following than non-Asian ethnic dishes such as pigs' feet. They do not appear likely to follow the bagel as comfort food into the gastronomic mainstream.

It is too facile to note that most dietary restrictions, even religious proscriptions, are socially constructed and historically contingent. They have their origins in sensible precautions to stave off food poisoning and infection in times before refrigeration and the germ theory, but they have developed into an elaborate set of customs that help shape identity. Eschewing beef or pork may once have been a sanitary concern, but it has become just as much an ethical apprehension. Hindus who think of the cow as sacred or Jews who deem the pig to be filthy should be protected as a minority. But in a society where Hindus or Jews are the majority and when they are strictly observant, it would be imprudent to advocate for an increased intake of steaks and pork chops, respectively.

Nowadays, few Americans can comprehend keeping chickens in the backyard until their necks are wrung so that they can be eaten for dinner, and a thinning number still shoot game for their family's sustenance. Whether we are shoppers for bulk discounts at the supermarket warehouse or samplers of the latest organic concoction at the health food chain store, we are phony gourmands without any conception of how our food reaches the table. The staunch individualist Henry David Thoreau was a poet-scientist who fantasized about eating a woodchuck raw while he lived in his cabin by Walden Pond. There was a brief moment when African Americans and Asian Americans as well as white ethnics would shop together on weekends at downtown warehouses where "fresh" meant alive, and catfish swam in tanks next to display cases of organs and blood sausage, below a row of hooks from which hung almost every type of carcass fit for human consumption. But no more.

Another multiculturalist answer proposes a philosophical attitude: "I don't eat dog, but if I did, what would be wrong with that?" There is no great incentive for pressing this intellectual viewpoint. The individual who in fact does not eat dogs but who protects the right of others to do so in turn must persuade others to permit and respect practices they neither engage in nor approve of. But dogs are too much members of our household, especially as we Americans lavish our largesse on them, paying for cosmetic surgery to enhance their competitiveness in the show ring and hiring professional walkers to take them ten at a time for a stroll in the park, equipping them with designer trench coats and high-tech booties for their paws to protect them in snow and rain, buying them miniature sofas and cedar-chip-stuffed beds for their relaxation, giving them the same antidepressants we swallow for self-help for their personality development, and feeding them super premium kibble for healthy growth. We are no more tempted to put them in the broiler than we would our own children. Most Americans are indisposed to permit dog-eating within the Latin maxim, "de gustibus non est disputandum"—"there's no arguing about taste"—no matter that the great physician of antiquity, Hippocrates, reported that puppies could be eaten as a curative. Dog recipes were published in Paris reportedly as late as 1870 and worries about mad cow disease have rendered horse meat edible in Europe. Busy people cannot be bothered to peruse a catalog of customs as found in the trilogy of structuralist Claude Levi-Strauss, with diagrams of the triangular relationship between the raw, the cooked, and the rotten, as structures of the human psyche.[16]

Even if we are convinced, as most are, that freedom of expression is laudable, few of us espouse an unconditional moral relativism. Although we might consent to eating dogs, that does not mean we would like to broaden our open-mindedness to human cannibalism, or, for that matter, gobbling up powdered horns and preserved penises from species on the verge of extinction based on unfounded claims about aphrodisiac properties, chewing up live octopus in the macho rite of ikezukuri before its death struggle chokes the intrepid diner, or cutting open the skull of a monkey to scoop out his brains even though he shares most of his genes with us. Even "geophagy," the eating of dirt—actually, clay—which was a common practice in the South among black and white alike, is ceasing.

"Do Asians eat dogs?" The worst reply diminishes the possibility of a civic discourse to which everyone can equally contribute: "Whether or not I eat dogs, you don't have to worry because I promise I won't eat your dog." This response is flippant and does not deal with the real question, which is whether eating your own dog is wrong. There is no need to declare that it is inappropriate to eat someone else's dog; eating it would violate their property rights if nothing else. The Honolulu newspapers reported a dispute in 1950 that foreshadows later anxieties about dog eaters.[17] A man said by Margaret Acosta to have eaten her missing dog, Floppy, successfully defended himself by admitting he had eaten a dog on the night at issue. He said, however, that his meal had been a black dog and not a white dog. He was acquitted, because Floppy was white.

But the reassurance about not eating other people's dogs is the worst reply, because it forecloses discussion. It isolates each of us within a culture and makes us outsiders to all others. Each of us can watch these others and study them, but none of us can comment or interact. The animal rights groups that censured the Cambodians in Long Beach were not mollified that the perpetrators were eating only their own dog, which was certainly not a pet. And in bringing into play "the sensibilities of the community," they denied that immigrants might contribute to those sensibilities or be part of that community.

We forget that people can eat Asian foods but still have contempt for Asian peoples. They can tune in to the Japanese television show *Iron Chef*, where a challenger and a master compete to produce an entire meal from the theme ingredient—for example, turning three dozen crabs into the appetizer, entrée, soup, garnish, and dessert—in Japanese, French, Chinese, or Italian cuisine, but make fun of the antics of Asians as if a game show represented a people. They can patronize the obsequious maître d' and the subservient waiter, confusing the deferential manner of service professions with the innate behavior of racial groups. They can talk about the best "Chink" food or the best "Jap" food, even as they attempt clumsily to use their chopsticks to stab that morsel they have dropped on the table. Eating at a Chinese restaurant is not the same as "breaking bread" with Chinese people. A patron at a Japanese restaurant can ridicule racially the teppenyaki chef whom he has erroneously assumed cannot comprehend his rank prejudice. More than one Asian American customer has cringed at the spectacle of the next table, where an Asian immigrant is humiliated by the whites whom he is serving, the Asian smiling nervously in a gesture that is misconstrued by whites as assent to the abuse. The spectator may be more keenly aware than the subject but be similarly powerless because there is no means of saving face.

"What Do You Think?"

There is a better answer to the question, "Do Asians eat dogs?" It answers the question with another question: "What is the point of asking whether I eat dogs?" The accuser is cross-examined.

This rebuttal ensures that the question is not rhetorical, a set-up line rather than an invitation to talk. Joan Rivers cannot be taken seriously, but she cannot be left alone. Detractors of dog eaters, such as those infuriated by Joey Skaggs, must be dispatched because they proceed in earnest. They believe that Asian Americans are dog eaters, and they do not hesitate to reprimand them on that basis. In San Francisco in 1989, as officials sought to respond to rumors that Vietnamese immigrants were hunting dogs in Golden Gate Park, Vu-Duc Vuong, executive director of a refugee center, said, "There have been very few, if any, instances of pet eating. . . . Far more numerous are anti-Asian prejudices and violence based on no more than false or racist stereotypes of Asian-Americans."[18]

Before taking up the merits of the issue, I would like to recommend some preliminary rules. To begin with, we need to inculcate within ourselves a sense of proportion. Dog-eating becomes an excuse to make Asians the butt of jokes. Dog-eating is leveraged to disrespect complete cultures as primitive. Reducing the inhabitants of the Asian continent to dog eaters, defining them by a minor aspect of their multifaceted ways of life, becomes absurd. That characterization forms the basis for believing that Asians are inferior: The dogs are cute; the people are despicable. It is a circular trap. Only by assuming that American culture is superior can its vantage point be used to judge Asian culture in this regard. Insiders assume that their culture is superior. They find, based on their assumption, that it is so.

Likewise, the behavior of Asian Americans may be of interest to non-Asian Americans for various reasons, but asking whether they are in the habit of eating dogs should not rate high among the priorities. Asian immigrants adjust their dietary routines anyway. Studies of Asian students who have moved here show them gobbling up generous quantities of American-style junk foods.[19] Asian parents lament that their American children clamor for hamburgers and French fries, turning their noses up even at celebratory dishes served on holidays. Pacific Islanders put together ingredients of their own with those from the United States, in a homemade fusion cuisine. They have invented, for example, the inimitable snack of spam masubi: frying the processed meat product and then wrapping it in seaweed on top of vinegared rice as a gristly variation of sushi. Due to their genetic adaptation to food scarcity, imported fatty diets are causing an epidemic of morbid obesity.[20]

There are a few more rules that are conducive to discussion. Whoever attacks a cultural practice must understand it. Few of us have suffered as many Southeast Asians have, civilians on the battlegrounds of war, homes destroyed, stomachs empty—or as Koreans and Chinese have, enduring famine brought on by the authorities. Asian immigrant mothers may tell their children to finish the meat first because it has the highest nutritional value, but they probably do not tell their children to think of the starving children in Europe to cajole them into cleaning off their plates.

If we critique a cultural practice, its origins and its context are relevant. Dogs compete with humans for resources. University of Pennsylvania professor James Serpell reports in his book, *In the Company of Animals: A Study of Human-Animal Relationships*,[21] that in Chinese culture, "whereas the ruling elite took their affection for dogs or cats to bizarre and outrageous extremes, the mere idea of being fond of a dog or indeed any other kind of domestic animal was a concept alien to the mentality of the majority peasant population."[22] Eating dogs appears to be a compensatory adaptation to material deprivation and the lack of reliable sources of other meats.

If you can criticize my cultural practices, I should be able to criticize your cultural practices. The criticism must be reciprocal and between equals. If either of us calls on standards that are not generated within the culture we critique, we must do our utmost to make such standards as neutral as possible rather than just the enlargement of our preferences. It may be impossible to produce principles in a vacuum without the influence of our own backgrounds so as to bracket and set aside everything that is culturally specific, but at least we can become conscious of the constraints of either an Eastern or a Western worldview and compensate appropriately. Lest you be a hypocrite, you should be able to live up to the standards you would set.

If as a nation we settle on stopping the practice of dog-eating here and elsewhere, we likely will be more effective if our means to that end blend internal calls for reform with external demands for conformity. Otherwise,

Asian Americans who may not crave dogs may become justifiably resentful about regulations imposed on us without our input. Asian Americans who refuse to submit to any interrogation about dog-eating, frivolous or humorless, should be viewed sympathetically. No more than individuals do groups take kindly to being told what to do by the self-righteous.

These prerequisites to conversation should pertain to all communications across cultures. Without such indications of good faith, the responses—ranging from hostility to indifference—become much more appealing to Asian Americans and anyone else who has minority status. "Do Asians eat dogs?" should not make Asian Americans vulnerable.

It may be too difficult to satisfy all the conditions. We may need to proceed imperfectly, but each proviso that is not satisfied compromises the argument. For example, former starlet Brigitte Bardot's campaigns against dog-eating are a luxury for her, disguising her involvement with French right-wing groups that aim to curtail immigration for racial reasons. She connects mistreatment of animals with an influx of non-Western peoples. Her high-profile antagonism toward dog-eating is a confirmation of her privileged position and part of an extreme political agenda. It does not seem to have been produced by study. The dealings with her do not occur on fair terms.

The power to control the exchange distorts it. In Michael Moore's satirical 1989 documentary *Roger & Me*, the pundit interviews an impoverished woman who is selling rabbits by the roadside. She asks him if he wants one for a pet or for food. While the audience laughs out of squeamishness, they may be touched by her naïve honesty. She recognizes more poignantly than any wit both her own predicament of poverty and the fate of her furry animals.

This meta-discourse about dog-eating—talking about how we can talk—turns out to be imperative. Setting the terms for the discussion becomes the discussion itself. The terms of discussion are transformed. The improved case against eating dogs that ought to command respect, possibly the only case that merits notice, is the ascetic case for a vegetarian lifestyle. The prohibition against eating dogs becomes only a particular example in that line of reasoning. Many animal rights groups recognize as much.

It is at this point, but not before, that the concession can be made that killing dogs to eat them is not a commendable activity. The dogs who are eaten are beaten to death to tenderize their flesh. They are intelligent enough to know about their impending execution; they are trusting enough to allow it; and, most of all, they are feeling enough to experience pain.

Pursuant to the revised argument, the objection to eating dogs must be expanded to include other animals—for example, pigs. It should be extended to similar cases to prevent being suspect as a selective sensitivity. Pigs also can be housebroken, although they will revert to feral status in just two generations if returned to the wild. Vietnamese pot-bellied pigs even acquired momentary status as chic pets. More than dogs, pigs resemble human beings. It is for that reason that pigs are widely used in medical research on human disease, and xenotransplants of porcine hearts are a realistic possibility. The modern processing plants for pigs, which are as smart as dogs, are hardly more humane for the efficiency of their mass slaughter. Upton Sinclair's muckracking 1906 novel *The Jungle*[23] was an accurate report of the grisly methods of meat packing. If any stage of the process were photographed, the pictures of "Babe" from the movies meeting his demise would be as disturbing as that of any dog hanging by a homemade noose. Were we all still to visit the local butcher before cooking supper or if we had to raise and slaughter our own fowl for guests who came over, rather than ingesting packaged and prepared products, it might either ease our resistance to eating dogs or prompt our swearing off all meat.

After all, the guests at a down-home pig pickin' line up to help themselves to moist pork plucked by hand from the remains of a pink and smooth-skinned suckling that sports a baseball cap that has scrawled on it the name it was given the day before in homage to the guest of honor who is being feted. The swine has a tomato stuffed in its open mouth and cherries where its eyes once sat, and its ears are still pricked up as if to hear the comments about its delicious haunches. The replacement of a word or two about the dead mammal that has been tended diligently all day long as it turns on the barbecue spit or that is hidden under the lid of a fancy serving tray in the buffet line is enough to turn our impatient craving into the urge to vomit. How puzzling it is.

We need not pursue the arguments here. Dog-eating is only an example of the many issues of our increasing diversity. If we can work out how to talk about dog-eating, we can grapple with the problem of how we think about diversity.

The Dilemma of Diversity

Virtually all people proclaim that they favor diversity, but almost nobody has thought critically about it. The concept is as vague as it is in vogue. Whether the kinetic diversity of our nation will be a strength or a weakness depends on the interpretation that together we give to it. Diversity takes on its variable meanings through the concrete details of our daily lives, public as well as private, and not by proclamation in an abstract theory or simple slogan. As the eminent psychoanalyst Erik H. Erikson stated in *Childhood and Society*,[24] the single book that introduced "identity" as a topic to be discussed: "We begin to conceptualize matters of identity at the very time in history when they become a problem. For we do so in a country which attempts to make a super-identity out of all the identities imported by its constituent immigrants."[25] Such a super-identity can take two forms.

Because it can be given various meanings and has not yet become controversial, it is easy enough to substitute "diversity" for other terms; "integration" and "pluralism" are old-fashioned, "assimilation" and "multiculturalism" are too loaded. These are not synonyms, however.

We Americans have an exceptional ability to assert our belief optimistically in contradictory principles.[26] Most of us casually consider both integration and pluralism to be forms of equality, although they are mutually incompatible except in the most casual sense. They are mirror images, joined in "e pluribus unum." Integration approves the universal and the individual; pluralism, the particular and the group. Integration requires assimilation; pluralism results in multiculturalism. Assimilation gratifies the ego of the whites who are assimilated toward, multiculturalism the ego of the people of color whose multiculturalism is celebrated. Assimilationists say that newcomers must do what the multiculturalists say they cannot do.

The conflict between the forms of assimilation and multiculturalism has become worse rather than better, because of the extensive dissatisfactions of postmodern life. Either assimilation or multiculturalism can be pointed to as cause or cure for alienation, apathy, selfishness, inequality, vacuousness, viciousness, and the multitude of ills that bedevil society as we know it. The stakes are high in choosing one or the other, for the issue is whether and how a liberal democracy that is racially heterogeneous can survive and flourish.

Progressive leaders of the civil rights era heralded racial integration as their noble goal. Although they focused on African Americans, the unwillingness and subsequently the inability of white America to integrate blacks has given assimilation its lasting impetus and greatest trials. It is white ethnics—those who two generations ago would have portrayed themselves and have been perceived as less white and more ethnic—who have passed more readily into this abiding paradigm of upward mobility. The confident claim of the integrationist and the assimilationist follows these lines: "I am an individual who is like the next individual; I demand to be treated in the same way."[27]

Other utopian thinkers announced cultural pluralism as their supreme ideal. They were more concerned with American Jews than any other group, but their values have been appealed to eagerly by Latinos, Asians, Arabs, and Africans, especially the immigrants among them who yearn to form a community in diaspora rather than lead solitary lives as exiles. Their assertiveness has given pause to Anglo-Americans who were ensconced in their own identity and overlooked others' solidarity until they felt the former imperiled by the latter. The bold claim of the pluralist and the multiculturalist follows these lines: "We are a group, unlike other groups; we expect to be respected as they are respected."[28]

Both assimilation and multiculturalism have their merits, but neither is wholly satisfactory. Each has significant flaws which can be remedied only by blending the approaches. Neither assimilation nor multiculturalism is inherently and thoroughly good or evil. Both can become authoritarian, each obeying its own authorities. Assimilation and multiculturalism both have their leftist and rightist variations. Together, they place Asian Americans in a no-win bind between being "all-American" and being "gooks," being ordered one day along the lines, "You should just be an American," and being pitied another day with, "It's too bad you've lost your culture." If Asian Americans assimilate, we can never appease whites who appear to be the arbiters of the matter from above and whose whims dictate the trends from preppy to grunge. We will be awkward, social climbers striving to fit in. We also will be reviled as having sold out as "bananas"—yellow on the outside but white on the inside—to our Asian American peers who are embarrassed for us in our white pose. If we are multiculturalists, we will always be short of authentic to Asians who seem to judge the matter from afar and whose advice about how our shared ancestors would prefer matters we must accede to because we cannot know better about veneration of the spirits. We will be lost, coming to the city not just from the country but from the wrong country. We also will end up validating stereotypes held by non-Asian observers by being as Asian as we can be, as if it is foreordained.

The End(s) of Assimilation

Hector Saint John De Crevecoeur and Israel Zangwill's ambitions for American assimilation are preserved as the patriotic script that the old stock requires new arrivals to follow with dedication, if not enthusiasm. Their words have joined the collection of official documents that have become the canon of our unifying secular culture. They are taught to students as part of their initiation to civic rights and responsibilities, augmenting the Pledge of Allegiance, the Declaration of Independence, the Bill of Rights, the Gettysburg Declaration, and Emma Lazarus's inspirational words on the Statue of Liberty.

A French noble who immigrated to Canada and who later moved to upstate New York, Michel Guillaume De Crevecoeur was hopeful about the developing agrarian republic. Using the pen name Hector Saint John De Crevecoeur, he begins his dozen *Letters from an American Farmer* of 1782 with a question: "What then is the American, this new man?" In the guise of a plain-speaking yeoman chronicler, he answers, "He is neither a European nor the descendant of a European, hence that strange mixture of blood, which you will find in no other country," and he gives as an example "a family whose grandfather was an Englishman, whose wife was Dutch, whose son married a French woman, and whose present four sons have four wives of different nations." Therefore, Crevecoeur declares triumphantly, "he is an American who, leaving behind him all his ancient prejudices and manners, receives new ones from the new mode of life he has embraced, the new government he obeys, and the new rank he holds."[29]

Recalling that the American had been a lowly squatter in his homeland but became a gentleman freeholder of some stature in his adopted land by acquisition of property and through operation of law, Crevecoeur concludes by equating identity with work and progeny. He provides a prophecy, that "here individuals are melted into a new race of men, whose labours and posterity will one day cause great changes in the world."[30]

The remainder of Crevecoeur's legacy has been obscured. From among his recollections of killing a kingbird to free the bees it had eaten from their hive, meeting a party of Indians and sharing a supper of bear cub (their contribution) and brandy (his), and visiting whalers who hunted the leviathan for its oil, a single passage has been culled out of its context. His felicitous proverb—"from this promiscuous breed, that race now called Americans has arisen"—has been misread as an audacious signal for general assimilation.

Crevecoeur anticipates that Americans will "become as to religion, what they are as to country, allied to all," but by that he means all of the "various Christian sects." He expects that regional diversity within the various states "will grow more evident in time" with the effects of climate.[31] That vein of biological determinism has been always been a widely held hypothesis about the etiology of racial differences.

Crevecoeur's feelings about the slave trade were unclear, but are indicative of his sense of racial roles. He distinguishes between Northern blacks, who "are fat, healthy, and hearty . . . [and] think themselves happier than many of the lower classes of whites," and Southern slaves, one of whom he meets on the road chained in a cage and being eaten alive by birds. He regards them as capable of "feeling the spurs of emulation and the cheerful sound of encouragement" to become like whites, but after he dined with the masters who were killing the tortured slave he happened upon and to whom he'd given water, he says, "There I heard that the reason for this slave's being punished thus was on account of his having killed the overseer of the plantation. . . . [T]hey told me that the laws of self-preservation rendered such executions necessary."[32] He does not worry the reader with their exposition of the laws of self-preservation; the chapter ends abruptly.

Once an honorary member of the Oneida tribe, Crevecoeur thinks Native Americans have survival skills that surpass Europeans', but they stand outside the ambit of civilization: "There must be something very bewitching in their manners, something very indelible and marked by the very hands of nature." Even if you "take a young Indian lad, give him the best education you possibly can, load him with your bounty, with presents, nay with riches," he would still "on the first opportunity he can possibly find" sneak off to the woods of his father "which you would imagine he must have long since forgotten." Crevecoeur cares to learn from them, but he does not intend to regress to their level, as the domesticated pig does to the wild hog if we "excuse a simile," and he would "not wish to see either my wife or daughter adopt those savage customs." Even his glorious new Americans, if they were "backsettlers" in the frontier woods who mingled too much with the Indian, could exhibit "their depravity . . . greater or less, according to what nationality or province they belong."[33] Assimilation of Indians does not last; assimilation toward Indians is to be avoided.

A Tory loyalist, Crevecoeur fled from the United States during the Revolutionary War. In the false bottoms of botanical sample boxes, he hid the papers that he would turn into his masterpiece. After settling in his native Normandy and achieving literary notoriety in the salons of Paris, he returned to the United States as the French consul in New York City. When he came back, he discovered that his estate had been burned down and his wife murdered. In two further volumes of his work, he accuses "Low Illiterate Little Tyrants" of caring more for equality than liberty. Even for Crevecoeur, assimilation was not permanent.

Crevecoeur's rhetoric cannot be anything but a product of its time. He sees Americans as derived explicitly from Europeans. He was elated to find an Englishman with a Dutch wife and a French daughter-in-law, never mind envisioning people more completely intermingled as would happen if the white slaveowner released his black property and became engaged to a black wife. In his view, men alone qualify as founders of the race. Even if Crevecoeur's limitations are excused as anachronisms, they do not commend his counsel to us.

Learning more about Crevecoeur as a person only weakens his case. Crevecoeur invented his identity, being slightly suspect to his contemporaries for his prevarications. Much of the charm of his narrative is his personal story as we can adduce it from his fictional correspondence, because, as with the more renowned Alexis de Tocqueville, we Americans encourage a French reporter who flatters our country at its founding by interpreting its customs to its own citizens and thereby providing an object lesson for Europe. At least de Tocqueville was blunt about his doubts that America could contain both blacks and whites while maintaining a democracy.

If we realized Crevecoeur's notion of assimilation, none of us would be interested in such particulars about him or any other writer. We would not preface their ideas with their biographies as we prefer to do, as if the former are extensions of the latter and are equally important. We care to know who they are, by which we mean what their race and nationality are.

Israel Zangwill, a British Jew whose family was from Russia, expressed more cheerfulness than Crevecoeur did, borne of harsher conditions. He gave the title *The Melting Pot* to his third play, which opened on Broadway in 1908.[34] Although the script is not revived as part of the repertoire, the title has become part of the American vocabulary. Zangwill is credited with the term that has forever given a name to casting off the old and adopting the new, although Transcendentalist philosopher Ralph Waldo Emerson had earlier spoken of a similar "smelting-pot."

The protagonist of the melodramatic romance is David Quixano, a Jewish immigrant whose family was killed in a pogrom. When he moves to New York City to live with his uncle in—according to the stage directions—a "curious blend of shabbiness, Americanism, Jewishness, and music," he meets Vera Revendal, a Christian social worker who upon being mistaken for Jewish replies, "I, a Jewess, how dare you?"[35] His musical composition is to be underwritten by her settlement house as an act of charity, much as his assimilation will be brought about by her affection. As their work together proceeds, their courtship does as well.

Scarred on his left shoulder, where he rests the violin, from the brutality he witnessed and barely escaped, David does not attend Chabod services but instead works on his art. He intends it for the immigrant who "will not understand . . . with their brains or their ears, but with their hearts and their souls"—not the "same smart set" that patronizes Carnegie Hall.[36]

The couple soon finds out that the massacre of David's parents was led by Vera's father, the Baron, a cruel military officer. Uncle Mendel and David quarrel before realist Mendel evicts his young charge and idealist David forsakes his last remaining relative. David gets the better of the argument.

Uncle Mendel confronts David over Vera, claiming, "The Jew has been tried in a thousand fires and only tempered and annealed."[37] David replies, "Fires of hate, not fires of love. That is what melts." Mendel says, "You are mad already—your dreams are mad—the Jew is hated here as everywhere.— You are false to your race." David says, "I keep faith with America. I have faith America will keep faith with us. Flag of our great Republic, guardian of our homes, whose stars and—." Mendel interrupts, "Spare me that rigmarole. Go out and marry your Gentile and be happy."

In a subplot that allows for the author's commentary on capitalism and socialism, Quincy, the wealthy dilettante who is a friend of Vera's father and his new wife, torments David and harasses Vera.[38] Vera's father tells Quincy that Russia will solve its Jewish problem, as "1/3 will be baptized, 1/3 massacred, the other 1/3 emigrated here." The Baron is pompous about his incorruptible nature (he does not take the bribes available to him due to his position), but his new wife wishes that Vera would marry Quincy (who already has a wife) so she can have a rich son-in-law.

A gun appears, but it is never used. David and Vera give up their misbegotten affair because there is a "river of blood" between them. Each assumes that pursuing the other is futile.

They are surprised, however, by the success of David's music. They overcome their tragic past through the melody. As David's concerto is played on a rooftop beneath the Statue of Liberty, he speaks exuberantly of America as "God's crucible." What he had earlier called the "melting pot where all the races of Europe are melting and re-forming," he now extends to take in "Celt and Latin, Slav and Teuton, Greek and Syrian, black and yellow."[39]

At a Washington, D.C., performance of this play, President Theodore Roosevelt is said to have called out from his box, "That's a great play." Zangwill returned the compliment by dedicating later editions to Roosevelt.

Although the intimate relationship of David and Vera is made possible only by heroically focusing on what is yet to come, their heartrending forgiveness exceeds what can be asked of most people. In an afterword offering the author's explication for a morality play, Zangwill adds a caveat about the pairing of David and Vera that seems to counteract any consummation of their love.[40] "The action of the crucible is not exclusively physical," he states, for "the Jew may be Americanised and the American Judaised without any gamic interaction." His play includes for comic relief a thoroughly "Judaised" Irish maid, who in the opening act grumbles that she must stoop to labor for a Jewish family but by the closing act has started to mutter asides to herself in Yiddish and is able to debate whether riding up an elevator and riding down an elevator are equivalent violations of Chabod strictures.

Zangwill foresaw that "even the negrophobia is not likely to remain eternally at its present barbarous pitch."[41] He was pleased that his work was "universally acclaimed by Americans as a revelation of Americanism, despite that it contains only one native-born American character [Quincy], and that a bad one."[42]

At their most desperate, Asian Americans turned to assimilation. Facing loss of liberty, livelihood, and property during World War II based on unproven suspicions that they would be loyal to an enemy nation because of racial ties, Japanese Americans affirmed a creed that purposely echoed Crevecoeur and Zangwill. Well before the war, numerous individuals within the Japanese American communities of the West Coast had assimilated as best as they could. Although many of them had earned degrees in professional disciplines such as engineering, pharmacy, law, or medicine, most of them were unable to find work in their fields due to racial restrictions and ended up returning to family farms or opening small businesses. But they took up baseball, tennis, bowling, and other American sports, forming their own clubs when they were prevented from joining white leagues and associations.

The onset of war drove many of them closer to the United States rather than farther away from its ideals. Drafted hastily as tensions mounted before Pearl Harbor, the Japanese American Citizens League (JACL) creed was a hyperpatriotic testimonial. Spokesperson Mike Masaoka wrote it sincerely and without irony, and the words have been printed regularly in JACL programs and recited dutifully in unison at JACL events ever since.

A high school debate champion from Utah who served in the U.S. Army, as did all of his brothers, Masaoka penned a paean to the United States: "I believe in her institutions, ideals and traditions; I glory in her heritage; I boast of her history; I trust in her future . . . as a free man equal to every other man." His blithe adulation of the United States did not sit well with other Japanese Americans, who alleged that he was collaborating in the imprisonment of the people he was supposedly representing. (The lawyer for the nonconformists, Wayne Collins, pronounced the initials "JACL" as "jackal.") He wrote, "Although some individuals may discriminate against me, I shall never become bitter or lose faith, for I know that such persons are not representative of the majority of the American people." Even his metaphors respected middle-class sensibilities: "I am fair in my belief that American sportsmanship and the attitude of fair play will judge citizenship and patriotism on the basis of action and achievement, and not on the basis of physical characteristics." He ended with a vow to believe in America and "assume my duties and obligations as a citizen, cheerfully and without reservations whatsoever, in the hope that I may become a better American in a greater America."[43]

In the segregated military, many soldiers of the Japanese American 442nd Regimental Combat Team and 100th Infantry Battalion, man for man the most decorated units of the racially segregated army, died for their country on the battlegrounds of the European Theater in an extraordinary demonstration of becoming "better Americans in a greater America."[44] Their spirited motto, "Go for Broke," concealed the estrangement expressed by their unit song, "We Don't Give a Damn." Their insignia even read, "Remember Pearl Harbor." A startling sight wherever they went, Asian faces in American fatigues, carrying tommy guns and speaking English, they suffered the losses of suicide missions. Liberating the Texas "Lost Battalion" outside Bruyeres, France, in September 1944, they took 800 casualties to save 211 fellow Americans trapped by surrounding Germans.

The bravery of the Japanese American troops made for a novel story, which the press exploited in full. They were assimilated into their uniform with its regalia, under the command of white officers, even though their families remained behind barbed wire, within the sights of gun towers, and under the guard of fellow soldiers.

Yet the image of the Nisei superfighter they created has been regarded with an ambivalence that is not often mentioned. All Asian Americans appreciate the mortal sacrifices of the military veterans, which alleviated somewhat the enmity toward other Japanese Americans after the war and aided immensely the reparations movement much later. Some Asian Americans worry that the deserved exaltation of their magnificent deeds has the side effect of setting unfortunate expectations of deference rather than dissent, because of the implicit message that Asian Americans must be willing to march under a flag that does not fly for them. Admonished are the cousins of the soldiers, the "no-no" boys who were given that name because they had replied negatively to the pair of government questions administered to them during their detention, asking if they would swear allegiance to the United States and if they would serve in its armed forces. Their assimilation to the equally American norm of civil disobedience was unwelcome (although arguably that would be the case regardless of race).

More than a half-century after Masaoka wrote his creed, it once again became the center of discord.[45] Japanese Americans suffered an upsetting break in the consensus of the community. When the federal government authorized the construction of a memorial to Japanese American patriotism to be built in the nation's capital in 2000, the multimillion-dollar project became controversial because of plans to chisel the creed in stone. The JACL won out.

Before and after World War II, academics developed assimilation as the leading theory of race relations. Robert Park, who started as a journalist and Booker T. Washington's secretary-publicist, founded the discipline of sociology at the University of Chicago, and, with a multitude of disciples, produced the idea of an inexorable cycle in race relations: "contact, competition, accommodation, and eventual assimilation."[46]

The intellectual apex of the assimilation movement, however, came at the beginning of the civil rights era. University of Massachusetts sociologist Milton M. Gordon published *Assimilation in American Life: The Role of Race, Religions, and National Origins* in 1964.[47] His comprehensive study sets out seven related categories of assimilation that are still referred to. Most important, he distinguishes between acculturation and structural assimilation. Acculturation consists of a minority group acquiring the cultural practices of the host society. Structural assimilation concerns not cultural content but ordinary interactions. It is assessed not by whether a person behaves as his grandparents might have, but by whether his relationships are restricted to his cousins, and his family's to their ethnic cohort. Acculturation and structural assimilation are related but not the same. A person could be acculturated but not structurally assimilated, and vice versa.

Gordon delineates a variation on assimilation, Anglo-conformity, which provides a more specific model for conduct. He protects the sponsors of Anglo-conformity: "It would appear that all racists, in so far as they have conceded the right of any of their disfavored groups to be present in America . . . have been Anglo-conformists; but the converse is not true—all upholders of Anglo-conformity have not been racists."[48]

Like all conventions, assimilation suffered in the revolutions of the 1960s. Gordon published not a moment too soon. Black Power, and all the social movements that copied its confrontational stance, defied his Anglo-conformity, identifying it as repressive and impossible. "Black is Beautiful" encapsulated an outlook that refused to idealize blonde hair and blue eyes, instead imbuing its own aesthetics of the body with wide-ranging cultural ramifications and political corollaries.

In the cycle of history, as the 1960s have receded into memory, assimilation has enjoyed a resurgence. In its comeback, as before, it serves as both a description of how people behave and a prescription for how they ought to behave. Proponents of the melting pot want to throw everyone into it, with few regrets about the intensity of its dissolving operation. They would turn around the decline in assimilation, but in spite of their fervor they lack the poetry of Crevecoeur and Zangwill and the science of Park and Gordon.

Sometime presidential contender and syndicated columnist Pat Buchanan, who has assumed the mantle of reform, declares "there is only one race in this country, the American race," and "Third World" immigration is ruining the culture.[49] A charming isolationist who has revived the "America First" ideology, Buchanan resolves any contradiction with a revealing question; the pious preface is trivial next to his racial inquiry: "I think God made all people good, but if we had to take a million immigrants in, say Zulus, next year, or Englishmen, and put them in Virginia, what group would be easier to assimilate and would cause less problems for the people of Virginia?"[50] His comments are consistent, then; he equates citizenship with race, so that white Americans become the only real Americans; everyone else remains unassimilable outside the circle of belonging. Buchanan argues that "high rates of non-European immigrants" will "swamp us," especially the spectre of black-on-white crime, and implores, "is it not time to take America back?" Dispelling any doubt that may have remained about the "one race" of America, he mourned the trends that would mean "a majority of Americans will no longer claim Europe as their ancestral home."[51]

British immigrant Peter Brimelow takes the case for racial citizenship even farther, as discussed in Chapter 3. He stresses that "the only possible answer" to immigrants who will not assimilate as he has directed them to do is that "they'd better." In his book, he scoffs at historian Ronald Takaki's complaint that Asian Americans are not accepted as real Americans. Brimelow explains that for that to happen white Americans would be forced to give up their "sense of identity," a loss he loathes.[52] Although he describes the agonies of assimilation, he is not sympathetic. He regards them as another reason immigrants should just be excluded, as if the problem can be attributed to immigrants rather than the attitudes he espouses.

Author Richard Brookhiser, a defender of white Anglo-Saxon Protestant values, has greater confidence than Brimelow that the WASP can endure and co-opt others. In his 1991 book, *The Way of the Wasp*, he writes that it was the way of the WASP that made America great. He asserts, however, that "the fact is, there was no challenge that non-WASPs were capable of mounting that could have undermined the cultural hegemony of a group as large, as central, and as entrenched as the WASPs in America." He observes that non-WASPs were for the most part too busy trying to become like WASPs to exert themselves in bringing down WASPdom.[53]

Other writers—Arthur Schlesinger, Todd Gitlin, Peter Salins, Roy Beck, John Miller, Georgie Anne Geyer, and Richard Lamm among the more circumspect—have demanded assimilation while decrying anything else.[54] In book after book, they present the conventional wisdom. They promise that our society will receive all people regardless of race so long as they assimilate wholeheartedly. They deplore racial considerations for full membership in a shared culture, and they downplay the affinities between themselves and Brimelow and those of his ilk.

Schlesinger and Gitlin are proud of their liberal-left credentials, which they tout as if immunizing themselves against charges of bias. Salins preempts criticism similarly, discussing his family's assimilation. He argues in *Assimilation: American Style*[55] that assimilation is a "two-way street." His metaphor does not mean that the native culture changes as the immigrant changes. He means instead that the natives agree to admit the immigrant, and the immigrant agrees to assimilate. To the native belongs the right-of-way; the immigrant must acquiesce. Salins discounts the possibility that, since the arc of assimilation represents progress, it requires a relationship of superior to inferior, those who are assimilated to and those who must assimilate. The host society keeps the permanent authority to grant or withhold permission for cultural practices to the eternal guests, who are continually requesting approval for their way of life. Salins ignores the likelihood that host and guest can never switch their roles, because even if clothing and names are changed and accents flattened, assimilation can be questioned and lineage revealed. The native-born American who demands assimilation is saying to the immigrant, and, worse, to the immigrant's children, "I am better. Be like me."

However well-intentioned Schlesinger, Gitlin, and Salins are, their pledge is coupled with enough of an ultimatum to be menacing. Despite their goodwill, the racial fringe shadows them.

Throughout history, assimilation has been compulsory rather than voluntary. Benjamin Franklin feared that German immigrants would vie with English immigrants for control of the continent, but German Americans were defeated so thoroughly that they have all but disappeared as a cognizable group. Americanization programs had their heyday during the Red Scare era between the turn of the twentieth century and the Great Depression, as tremendous levels of immigration set off cultural alarms. Crusading organizations such as the American Protective Association and the National Americanization Committee, along with the Daughters of the American Revolution, the Native Sons of the Golden West, the National Security League, and various civic groups, led "I am An American Day" parades, mandatory flag salutes, purges of civil servants through loyalty oaths, and displays of piety in school prayer.

With the backing of no less than Presidents Theodore Roosevelt and Woodrow Wilson, who bemoaned the durability of ethnicity, these organizations sought to eliminate hyphenated Americans and form the "100% American" in their place. Roosevelt said that America had no room for hyphenated Americans. He adopted the slogan "America for Americans" and called hyphenation of identity "moral treason."[56] As he became convinced by warnings about "race suicide," he also became increasingly sure that Asian immigrants could not become real Americans because of their racial background: "no greater calamity could now befall the United States than to have the Pacific slope fill up with a Mongolian population."[57] Wilson said, even after the Great War, "I cannot say too often—any man who carries a hyphen about with him carries a dagger that he is ready to plunge into the vitals of this Republic whenever he gets ready" and "if I can catch any man with a hyphen in this great contest I will know that I have got an enemy of the Republic." He delivered this address on September 25, 1919, in Pueblo, Colorado, shortly before collapsing. His hatred of the hyphenated American was all the more strange, given that he was campaigning for the establishment of the League of Nations that was opposed by nativists who also were isolationists. Even though the great orator, one of the best educated presidents we have ever had, said during his remarks that "the beauty of all democracies is that every voice can be heard, every voice can have its effect, every voice can contribute to the general judgment that is finally arrived at," he also said, "when you hear an opinion quoted you do not count the number of persons who hold it; you ask, 'Who said that?'" He would avoid a tyranny of the majority, but in doing so he would exclude the hyphenated American from "the beauty of all democracies."[58] He had told Congress in an annual address a few years earlier that citizens of foreign birth "poured the poison of disloyalty into the very arteries of our national life." He declared that "such creatures of passion, disloyalty, and anarchy must be crushed out."[59]

It was during World War I that the nativists concentrated on the sizable German American population, which formed the largest white ethnic group, trying to close down thriving presses, successful language schools, and the other institutions that constituted the community. Meanwhile, they suspected that Catholics, Jews, and Jehovah's Witnesses would be undemocratic. Their excesses included denaturalization and expatriation of alleged communists, anarchists, and radicals, along with labor organizers and Mexican Americans—even those who were native-born—without regard for their families. At the same time, the assimilation of Native Americans was merciless in exterminating the adults and extinguishing the souls of their young. The rallying cry was "kill the Indian, save the child."

Hence many who would be subjected to assimilation distrust its offer. They are cynical about assimilation coming easily as well as that acceptance following perforce. The assimilationist tradition takes into account Protestants, Catholics, and Jews; the title of Drew University sociologist Will Herberg's 1955 study, *Protestant-Catholic-Jew*, indicated who was entitled.[60] Assimilationists who have faith that "this is a Judeo-Christian nation," as some still say from time to time, must be uneasy when they meet Buddhists, Hindus, and Muslims who would become Americans as well.

Cambridge professor George Steiner, in a dense and learned essay on Zionism, once argued that "the Socratic moment for modern Jewry is the Dreyfus affair," because "it compelled on the Jew the question of whether he could, even in an emancipated and assimilationist garb, ever obtain a secure citizenship in the city of the gentile." Yet when Steiner locates "our homeland" in "the text," rather than a physical place, he, too, has in mind the specific text of the Torah; not just any great text will do. As a modern Jew, he is a wanderer literally but not physically rooted in a culture that has become detached from geography.[61] Contrary to stereotype, Asian Americans are more likely to be adherents of Western faiths than Eastern ones, but there are many who would fall within the pejorative "pagan." Many African Americans who have assimilated find equality elusive.[62] The neighborhood in which they would like to and can afford to live will not let them buy a house, or if it does will abide only so many black families before reaching "tipping point" where whites flee. Whites often argue that their property values will be stable, and their real estate investments will pay off, only if the neighborhood stays "good," meaning "white."

Doubters further advise that integration is a coercive idol that will betray its beneficiaries because its universalism is a disguised form of the overriding particularism. In this respect, Asian Americans who are most assimilated are most apt to be disillusioned. They can assimilate aggressively and steadfastly disregard everything Asian—their parents might have decided, as many have done, that they would try to raise them as American as possible and without Asian influences—but they eventually will learn that they are not allowed to shed their skin. Both Ghandi and Malcolm X, before their nationalist and eventual humanist phases, were assimilationist.

Asian Americans who are native-born Americans as the children of immigrants and who have played Bach on the piano since the age of five may still be criticized as having only staggering technical prowess on the keyboard without the heartfelt soul of an artist. They do not have the Western repertoire in their blood. However much they rehearse the books of "Well-Tempered Klavier," they do not look like the musicians who can lay claim to the Goldberg Variations as part of their cultural heritage by birthright. It was superstar Isaac Stern who may have introduced the stereotype in his Oscar-winning documentary, "From Mao to Mozart," made from his 1979 tour of mainland China. The violinist said, "Their approach to Western music was somewhat limited. They were not accustomed to playing with passion and color. . . . They have not had the experience of living with Western music, as we have, for hundreds of years."[63] The Japanese make the same comment: One judge of piano competitions says, "we do not have to listen to all of them, because they are all the same; they have no individual character." The criticism cannot be explained entirely by the youthfulness of Asian performers, for it is said of mature adults as well and the same is not said of non-Asian prodigies such as pianist Yvgeny Kissin.[64] Yet without Asians and Asian Americans as talented amateurs trained by the Suzuki method, ardent listeners who buy season subscriptions, and eager consumers of audiophile recordings of classical music, symphonies, and recording companies would lack much of their contemporary audience. Maestro Zubin Mehta has asked, "where would the great American orchestras be without the Asian input?" At Juilliard, more than a third of the enrollment is Asian, about half Asian foreigners and half Asian Americans; in the pre-college division, more than half the students are of Asian descent.[65] Composer Tan Dun notes, "in Europe and even Japan, everyone thinks I'm an American composer. . . . But in America, I'm a Chinese composer."[66] As late as 1997, all of the 140 members of the Vienna Philharmonic were white men (only two of whom were Jewish). None of the many Asians studying in that capital of classical music had ever been invited to even audition for a seat.[67] Similar reactions greet all non-Europeans who approach the canon that they have been taught to be in awe of; ultimately it is not theirs. The African American who stars in Shakespearean drama in period costume; the Latino who paints in the style of the Impressionist school; the Arab American who dances *Swan Lake*—all are regarded as borrowers who are trying too hard, imitators who cannot be inventors.

Yet people of color profess to be taking part in the same ongoing cultural conversation as whites, even if the opposite is not often claimed. Poet Langston Hughes, the creator of Jesse B. Semple as the archetypal African American who migrated from the South to Harlem and dispensed his homespun wisdom as the central character in a regular column for the Chicago *Defender* newspaper, author of sixty-six short stories, two novels, and a total of more than forty books, once said it was French short story stylist Guy de Maupassant who inspired him to become a writer. Hughes also was influenced by Walt Whitman's *Leaves of Grass*.[68] Few modern white authors, however, cite Hughes in return. Even in a post-colonial era, as Ania Loomba, a professor at Nehru University in New Delhi who took her Ph.D from Sussex University, has written, more students read Shakespeare at the University of Delhi every year than do in all the universities in England.[69]

People of color cannot even be themselves convincingly. The star vaudeville performer Bert Williams, an African American with diction and enunciation that matched his white audiences', had to be taught poor elocution to play to them. Even with his comic abilities, he was not how whites pictured an African American male. African Americans such as Williams struggled to compete with whites in blackface costume, eventually donning blackface themselves in a preposterous turn of events. African Americans could not be more believable or well-liked than their stereotype. The Asian American detective Charlie Chan has been played by white men in all the movies made about him. Asian immigrant Bruce Lee pitched to studio executives the idea for the *Kung Fu* television series in the early 1970s, but white American David Carradine was picked by the producers to be the star. Asian Americans are less credible than whites pretending to be Asian Americans.

Even absolute integration may not be laudable. Through an effective form of assimilation, immigrants may come to oppose immigration. They have a right to do so if anyone does, but it is troubling that they would be encouraged toward unseemly self-interest as if their own full admission is hastened by closing the door behind them. They see themselves as attracted to America with pure motives and others as sullied by avarice. In the terms of assimilation, equality is sameness. African Americans who pursue what whites take for granted must assert their claims as the proposition that African Americans and whites are identical. They must leave behind their own African American identity as extraneous, however much they may wish to see it. The subordinate parties, as the guests or the inferiors, must give up distinctiveness—

their ethnicity—even if it is white ethnicity growing into a liability like an appendix, a biological vestige serving no useful function.

Asian immigrants are treated somewhat differently, although not better, than other people of color. They may be regarded as similar to white ethnics, relegating them to follow German Americans into oblivion. Brimelow scorns the African American and Hispanic crowds he encounters in New York City riding the subway, but he admires Asian Americans because "the young female students I see every morning entering the Parsons School of Design are very charming, and fashionable."[70] The Asian women who have caught his eye give him the idea that their "ethnic message . . . may be different" from that of other non-whites because they "seem to have graduated . . . in the era of segregation, to a sort of honorary white status" and "to an actual white status" as they "intermarry . . . and essentially vanish . . . from the Census returns."[71] Even more exasperating than Brimelow's perception that people of color graduate from segregation, as if they must earn a whiteness equivalency degree, is his implication that the only good Asian is the white Asian.

The Mean(s) of Multiculturalism

Like Crevecoeur and Zangwill, Horace Kallen depicted a New World founded on ideology rather than race. He held an utterly different set of convictions, emphasizing multiculturalism. Like them, he portrayed American society as heterogeneous in its national origins. Unlike them, he further glorified it as a mixture of cultural lineages. Kallen extolled immigration, writing that the country was "founded upon variation of racial groups and individual character; upon spontaneous differences of social heritage, institutional habit, mental attitude, and emotional tone; upon the continuous, free, and fruitful cross-fertilization of these by one another."[72]

A German Jew whose father was a rabbi, Kallen had come to the United States as a child. Although he entered Harvard as an individual who wished to be identified as an American rather than as a Jew, he changed his mind when he concluded that he could be both an American and a Jew and that his Americanism could be based on his Judaism. In his most productive period between 1915 and 1924, Kallen, then a philosophy professor at University of Wisconsin, wrote a series of essays for the *Nation*, giving a scientific structure to Walt Whitman's turn of phrase about the United States being "a nation of nations." Kallen transformed it into "the federal republic; its substance a democracy of nationalities, cooperating voluntarily and autonomously through common institutions in the enterprise of self-realization through the perfection of men according to their kind." He exhibited the same weakness as Crevecoeur, looking only toward Europe. He decreed that his American civilization had the potential for "the perfection of the cooperative harmonies of 'European civilization'—the waste, the squalor and the distress of Europe being eliminated—a multiplicity in a unity, an orchestration of mankind."[73] He made two insignificant references to African Americans in his extended work, *Culture and Democracy in the United States*, both for the purpose of suggesting that their benighted condition was what white immigrants might escape.

Kallen was emphatically anti-racist. But he was a racial anti-racist. He was afflicted with a racial fundamentalism, by which a person's many attributes are overwhelmed by race as the essential characteristic. Kallen wrote as if anthropologist Franz Boas were not establishing the influence of nurture on development. Kallen wrote, "Men may change their clothes, their politics, their wives, their religions, their philosophies, to a greater or lesser extent," but "men . . . cannot change their grandfathers." He added, "Jews or Poles or Anglo-Saxons, in order to cease being Jews or Poles or Anglo-Saxons would have to cease to be."[74] Race was immutable, for "intermarriage or no intermarriage, racial quality persists, and is identifiable . . . to the end of generations."[75]

"Yet the blood remains," Kallen quoted an earlier writer in explaining why even intermarriage cannot lead to racial assimilation. "He is not, he cannot make himself, altogether an American, divesting himself of the parental tendencies, of the emotional excitability of the Czech or the impulsiveness of the Italian," he said of the American-born children of Czech or Italian immigrant parents.[76] In a superb study, *The Metaphysical Club: A Story of Ideas in America*,[77] City University of New York English professor Louis Menand writes that Kallen "wanted each ethnic group to keep its proper place; he only wanted it to be honored for doing so . . . [His] pluralism was a formula for a kind of noninviduous segregation." Menand notes that "the ethnic groups in Kallen's pluralist vision were all European . . . and it is just as well, since a theory that celebrates socioeconomic stratification does not hold an obvious appeal for the group already consigned to the bottom rung."[78]

Like African Americans, Asian Americans fit uneasily into such pluralism. "Conceivably, a newborn Chinese child, brought up from its first cry in a loving Yankee family, might for all practical purposes be a Yankee," Kallen admitted. "The patterns of its behavior and the contents of its mind would certainly be Yankee. And if enough such infants could be brought up, they might compose a race of Mongolian Yankees. . . . If America be a melting pot, this is the thing that is done," he continued. "Only, the United States is no more, and no less, a melting pot than any other country in the world. . . . Birth, which we do not choose, carries with it simultaneously certain cultural acquirements of a nature so basic, so primary, as to be indistinguishable from inheritance."[79] The Chinese Yankee is a misnomer.

During the course of a lengthy career, Kallen continued to refine his arguments. In 1956, he wrote *Cultural Pluralism and the American Idea*, which excised some of his sense of racial fatalism. Nonetheless, Kallen's contentions suffer from the same dogmatism as his opponents'. His multiculturalism is as obligatory as is their assimilation. Whereas they insisted that the immigrant must assimilate on pain of maltreatment for disappointing them, he insists that even the immigrant's child could not possibly achieve the objective regardless of the effort invested. Like his archetypal counterpart of "the Negro" and "the Jew," an Asian American becomes "the Asian American," representative of a type.

For Kallen, someone such as Francis Fukuyama cannot be born or must be regarded as an inexplicable anomaly if he should turn up. The neoconservative author, who became internationally prominent with *The End of History and the Last Man*,[80] could be called, if semi-facetiously, an Oriental messenger of Occidental victory. Fukuyama has alluded to his Japanese background only infrequently, and it seems to have affected neither his cultural perspective nor the reception accorded his opinions. A Hegelian political theorist who has written several other best-selling treatises, he argues that Western democracies have secured their primacy once and for all. He has written that "the common American culture . . . is actually a sectarian Protestant Anglo-Saxon culture that was somehow detached from its ethnic roots."[81] Fukuyama has even claimed that "some groups, like Jews and Asians, might come to possess these values in abundance, while Wasps themselves might lose them and decay."[82] Even Fukuyama has rhapsodized, however, about his grandfather, who collected samurai swords during the Depression, and his own inheritance of a similar zeal for Japanese hand tools, forged with a Buddhist faith in the spirituality attained "through the perfection of the most common everyday tasks." In a short essay, he describes how his Japanese prized possessions in the basement workshop, like his German hand-plane, are different than the mass-produced American tools that have declined in quality over the years.[83]

Alongside Kallen, Randolph Bourne was the foremost dreamer of multiculturalism. As the United States was readying itself to enter the trenches dug by European powers, Bourne advanced an apostasy with his essay on "Trans-

National America," published in 1916 in *Atlantic Monthly* by Anglo-Saxon
editors who were themselves hesitant about attacking their own ascendan-
cy.[84] Bourne has profited from a deserved revival in recent years, due to his
rediscovery by academics during the Vietnam War. His "The Handicapped—
By One of Them" was recently chosen by Joyce Carol Oates for a collection
of the best essays of the twentieth century.

Although Bourne was descended from the Anglo-Saxon elite, as a hunch-
backed dwarf he was not one of them. He had been born disfigured, due to
complications and an accident with the physician's forceps used to deliver
him, and he became stunted as a child following a bout of spinal tuberculo-
sis. His family having lost its money, he had to take a job at a piano factory.
Only when at age twenty-three he won a scholarship to Columbia University was he able to start his higher education, becoming a protege of John
Dewey and publishing influential essays while still a student. A pacifist, he
broke with Dewey and reproached his mentor for counting on societal support for the war effort to be a unifying cause that could benefit liberals.
Decrying all intellectuals who wanted the United States to enter the fighting in Europe, he coined an anti-jingoistic jingle that made him famous but
resulted in his imprisonment for sedition: "War is the health of the state." He
died at the age of thirty-two in the worldwide flu epidemic that claimed 25
million just after the end of the Great War.

Bourne was among the writers who joined the staff of the liberal *New
Republic* magazine when it was founded, although he was offended that they
gave him only trifling assignments. His arch literary style is memorialized by
his own last words: Moments before he passed away, he asked for eggnog and
made a point of praising the paleness of the drink brought to him. Novelist
John Dos Passos memorialized Bourne in his afterlife as "a tiny twisted
unscarred ghost in a black cloak hopping along the grimy old brick and
brownstone streets still left in downtown New York, crying out in a shrill
soundless giggle: 'War is the health of the state.'"[85]

In his lively essay on transnational America, Bourne began, "No reverber-
atory effect of the great war has caused American opinion more solicitude
than the failure of the 'melting-pot."[86] Speaking of the "Germans, Scandina-
vians, Bohemians, and Poles" who refused to be melted, he applauded them
for retaining their own culture whatever the tests from overseas events. Pre-
figuring what would come much later, Bourne "urge[d] us to an investigation of what Americanism may rightly mean"[87] and he distinguished between
the deficiencies of Americanization and the defects of democracy.[88] "We act
as if we wanted Americanization to take place only on our own terms," he

wrote, "and not by the consent of the governed." He elevated the immigrant as someone who "will have a hand in making" the country as much as "a ruling class, descendant of those British stocks which were the first permanent immigrants."[89]

Using the prejudice of Northern Anglo-Americans against them (and counting himself among them), Bourne suggested that if they truly sought Americanization they would assimilate immigrants into "that region of the States which has remained the most distinctively 'American,' the South." He compared the industry and progress of the Midwestern states, with their substantial ethnic populations, with the complacency and stagnation of the Deep South, with its lack of any such invigorating influx. His objections were more than an insistence on the equality of the immigrant and the native. Indeed, he belittled the very notion of cultural uniformity as "tasteless" and "colorless" or a "tame flabbiness." Thus, he fretted that the white ethnic who had given up his spirit and adopted the standards of the mob was someone "who has made money and has got into ward politics."[90]

Bourne's conclusion was that we have, other than the South and New England, "which, like the Red Indian, seems to be passing into solemn oblivion,"[91] no national culture. He believed we will come to have, and ought to welcome, "a federation of cultures." In this manner, we will decrease rather than increase violence thanks to our contact with each other and the cross-cutting loyalties of our polity. For "out of these foreign peoples there has somehow been squeezed the poison,"[92] and in college we make friends with those who do not have our ancestry. His vision of the country that is ideal and the individual with integrity even recognizes dual citizenship and supports return migration in a constant revitalization of cosmopolitanism.

Bourne reworked his essay as "The Jew and Trans-national America" to highlight its observations with respect to one group. Bourne even spoke to the Harvard Menorah Society about transnationalism as "a Jewish idea." He told its members that Zionism was a modern transnationalism. "The Jew in America is proving every day the possibility of this dual life." Bourne did not give "the Jew in America" other choices.[93]

In his radicalism and his resolute belief that the young would change the country, Bourne foresaw what would happen a half-century after his death. His "transnational America" is filled with insights that were remarkable given the imminence of war and are still instructive today. Unlike Kallen, who regarded ethnic groups as bleakly fixed, Bourne treated them as elastically plastic, although even Bourne would make every Jew a Zionist. Together,

Kallen's and Bourne's views confirm that multiculturalism has been offered as an alternative to assimilation from the start. Whether or not such pluralism is viable, it cannot be summarily dismissed as a recent invention of political correctness.

Of course, pluralism has its costs. The principal objection to pluralism is that it recklessly destabilizes a common cultural core. The oddity of this claim is its historically false premise. Earlier writers, whether they were assimilationists or multiculturalists, recognized that the United States had numerous cultures jostling up against one another. At the founding, Crevecour saw them as eventually coming together, and by the time Zangwill wrote he too saw them as eventually coming together. Kallen and Bourne wanted to postpone any unification indefinitely. Kallen shrewdly observed that "what troubles" the Anglo-Saxon Americans who wished to restrict immigration "is not really inequality; what troubles them is difference."[94] Whether they liked it or not, all of them saw the process as still ongoing and not nearing completion. American Jews, African Americans, white ethnics, Asian Americans—all had their own ghettos, their own places of worship, their own nightclubs, their own civic associations, their own cemeteries, and their own cultures.

There could be no serious claim that all these communities were on equal terms with white Anglo-Saxon Protestants. Even within elite professions such as the ranks of the corporate bar, there were Protestant, Catholic, and Jewish law firms, whose clients tended to match up with their attorneys. In New York City it was not until the post-World War II era that a firm such as Paul, Weiss, Rifkind, Wharton & Garrison could come into being, maintaining its prestige and having Protestant, Catholic, and Jewish partners (although all white and all male). It is only through romanticized hindsight that we could believe we once had a cultural unity that has been compromised. It is not the appearance of minority cultures that is new, it is their power.

Pluralism does more than fragment society; it fractures individuals. In one of the many provocative passages of his work, W. E. B. Du Bois wrote profoundly about "dual consciousness." He said about African Americans that, "One ever feels his two-ness,—an American, a Negro; two souls, two thoughts, two unreconciled strivings; two warring ideals in one dark body, whose dogged strength alone keeps it from being torn asunder." In an age of official segregation, before the United States had assumed its place as a superpower, he started with the "unasked question . . . how does it feel to be a problem?"[95]

"The history of the American Negro is the history of this strife," Du Bois wrote in a key text that should be contrasted with Crevecoeur's accolades for assimilation and Kallen's testament to multiculturalism. He spoke of aspiring to assimilation, of "this longing to attain self-conscious manhood, to merge his double self into a better and truer self." But his absorption of the greater society and absorption into it is not to the point of obliterating either group solidarity or individual persona, for "in this merging he wishes neither of the older selves to be lost. He would not Africanize America, for America has too much to teach the world and Africa. He would not bleach his Negro soul in a flood of white Americanism, for he knows that Negro blood has a message for the world."[96] And Du Bois sets minimal requirements of tolerance, asking that his country "make it possible for a man to be both a Negro and an American, without being cursed and spit upon by his fellows, without having the doors of Opportunity closed roughly in his face."[97]

Much later, Stanford University English professor Shelby Steele updated Du Bois's eloquent message, again speaking to a recurring duality, the "very specific double bind" of middle-class blacks "that keeps two equally powerful elements of our identity at odds with each other."[98] The winner of a National Book Critics Circle Award for his essay collection, *Content of Our Character: A New Vision of Race in America*,[99] Steele's rendition of the theme is significant because he reveals the ambiguities of diversity. He is imprisoned by its mandate.

On the one hand, Steele writes, "the middle-class values by which we were raised—the work ethic, the importance of education, the value of property ownership, of respectability, of 'getting ahead,' of stable family life, of initiative, of self-reliance, et cetera"—were "raceless and even assimilationist" and these values push him "toward integration, toward a strong identification with society, and toward the entire constellation of values that are implied in the word individualism." He is self-aware that this class identity came "by means of positive images gleaned from middle- and upper-class white society and by means of negative images of lower-class blacks." He traces the habit back to "house slaves" who "mimicked" white masters and "held themselves above the field slaves."[100]

On the other hand, Steele continues, "the particular pattern of racial identification that emerged in the sixties and that still prevails today urges middle-class blacks (and all blacks) in the opposition direction" by pushing them to "an adversarial stance toward the mainstream and an emphasis on ethnic consciousness over individualism." He is conscious of this ethnic identity being imposed and manipulated by white stereotyping. He cites the example of a professor who informed him that he was "not really black" because he was "not disadvantaged."[101]

Promoting diversity in all its forms creates anarchy. Almost nobody really welcomes each and every existing form of rebellion and opposition. We confuse racial diversity and cultural diversity, as if their correlation were absolute rather than abstract. Each is conducive to the other, and the absence of one diminishes the other as well. But an institution can be multiracial without being multicultural, and vice versa. A company could accept employees of every skin color but demand submission to its buttoned-down protocol. A college could be predominantly black but encompass multiple national origins, geographic influences, class backgrounds, religious faiths, socioeconomic classes, and ethnic traditions.

Even so, diversity sounds too good to be true. People who love diversity in theory may not like it in practice. They presume that they can pick and choose which diversity is best. In other words, they would like to be discriminating about diversity. Kallen thought of only white ethnic groups, not people of color. Bourne believed that Southern culture would die out, a possibility that he did not much mourn. Those who renew their messages seem to reverse Kallen and do not appear eager to apply Bourne's preservationist pluralism to Southern culture. They are enamored of the happy faces of diversity, supposing implausibly that the benign elements of many cultures can be preserved without their malignant complements, and, equally fantastically, without conflict among them. (Ironically, tolerating all cultures also disrespects all cultures, because it requires rejecting the unique claim of each to the truth.) The followers of Kallen and Bourne are careless about the manner in which fostering that sense of time, place, and belonging for some depends on exclusion of others. They looked at the innocuous symbolic ethnicity of a limited list of oppressed groups that they had in mind, and they did not foresee the myriad substances that can be effortlessly inserted into the same label. Even though multiculturalism is meant as a response to rather than a cause of racial discrimination and should not be confused with the original problems, it can exacerbate them. Whites may be left wondering what multiculturalism holds for them.

Within the alternative canon of multiculturalist authors, for example, Michael Novak is absent. A Catholic Slovak-American who advised Presidents Gerald Ford and Jimmy Carter on the opening of a White House Office of Ethnic Affairs, Novak has used a faith-based perspective to critique capitalism and has been instrumental in bringing attention to the white ethnic electorate. The author of twenty-five books, Novak wrote *Unmeltable Ethnics: Politics and Culture in American Life* in the 1970s.[102] His book was a call for the empowerment of white ethnic Catholics—Irish, Italians, Polish,

Ukrainians, and the like—and a manifesto of political and cultural resistance to white Anglo-Saxon Protestant hegemony, but it did not make common cause with African Americans and other people of color. He would not give up whiteness, but he would reclaim ethnicity; he was not asking to enshrine whiteness, but to enrich society with ethnic cultures that are as foreign to Anglo-conformity as African American culture is. His new edition of *Unmeltable Ethnics*, released in 1996,[103] makes evident his resentment about what he regards as a misrepresentation of the pluralism he helped pioneer. He decries the multiculturalism that he sees as having taken over college campuses, which relies on (his list of "nine perversions"): anti-Americanism, victimology, ego-boosting, evasion, tactical relativism, censorship, group-think, egalityranny, and double standards.

Novak is right. He is a multiculturalist, and he was a multiculturalist before many multiculturalists were born. He just isn't the type of multiculturalist that most multiculturalists would subsidize with grants or place on recommended reading lists. He is not only white but also conservative. Therein lies the problem. Multiculturalists either must confess that Novak is as anathema to them as they are to him, or they must heed his demands for inclusion and share a modified multiculturalism with him.

Supporters of diversity, if they are to be true to the banner they fly, must acquiesce to the claims of the born-again Christian such as newspaper columnist Cal Thomas or Southern partisan such as University of Alabama history professor Michael Hill if they argue that evangelicals or neo-Confederates are minorities, too, who must be represented on the op-ed page and in front of the classroom. Thomas, one of the original leaders of the Moral Majority, responds to complaints about media bias against racial minorities by arguing that the press discriminates against the conservative faithful. Hill is president of the League of the South, which has revived a serious movement of secessionism for "the New Dixie" and which opposes the modernism of the North.[104] Stripped to its logical minimum, diversity means nothing more than difference. An advocate for diversity—real diversity—is an advocate for maximizing difference. If difference for the sake of difference by itself is actually a social good, then every variation is valuable. One person's difference cannot be another's damnation.

If diversity is the measure, Ku Klux Klan members or skinheads who ask why there are not more like themselves in Congress or the boardroom have the same gripe as anyone else if the numbers bear out a claim of lack of parity. The cause of diversity offers no foundation for disallowing a group as either ersatz or malicious. Whatever we may think of them, white supremacists are spawning their own subculture. Aided by the advent of the Internet, and through flags, books, music, clothes, accents, body language, religious sects, secret rituals, a code of honor, days of remembrance (memorializing Ruby Ridge and Waco)—all the trappings of any culture—they have sought to imbue their prejudices with a lineage borrowed from apocalyptic millennialism and Norse mythology. In their estimation that theirs is a lost cause and a last stand, "angry white males" have even appropriated some of the language used by the civil rights movement. No less an authority than C. Vann Woodward, one of the leading historians of the twentieth century, argued a century after the Civil War that Southerners could identify with the oppressed because of their defeat.[105] Pat Buchanan can use the same idiom of protest, even the same tone of virtue, substituting Christian white males as his protected group.

Matt Hale, the Pontifex Maximus of the World Church of the Creator, illustrates how demagogues can maneuver into a martyrdom that abuses multiculturalism. Hale is an admirer of Adolf Hitler who has called for a "holy war" of whites against non-whites. One of his followers, Benjamin Smith, killed two and wounded nine in a shooting spree over the Fourth of July weekend in 1999 in the Chicago area. Hale disavowed responsibility for the slaughter, the targets of which were all racial or religious minorities, but he eulogized Smith, who took his own life. Hale has been trying for years to become an attorney. Although he passed the bar exam, the state of Illinois has repeatedly denied him a license on the grounds that his character and morality render him unfit to be an attorney, as bar associations have long done to others who were unpopular. Hale's views are heinous, but the decision to prohibit him from practicing his profession is based on his beliefs, not his actions, as there is nothing linking him to Smith's carnage. Suppressing him has turned him into a celebrity rebel. After race riots in the Decatur, Illinois, schools in 2000, Hale arrived to lead a counter-protest as Jesse Jackson Sr. came to protest; he has become a sought-after public speaker as an anti-Jackson of sorts. Thanks to his adversaries, he has become stronger. He can claim truly that his First Amendment free speech rights have been violated by the government, because it has denied him entrance to the courtroom. A multiculturalist cannot desire diversity above all, then turn around and snub Hale because he is despicable.

The failure to engage Novak, an intelligent and thoughtful writer, is dishonest and shameful, as is the neglect of large segments of the population personified by Thomas and Hill, who are stereotyped because of their faith or their geographic origins as not part of the intellectual class. Novak, Thomas, and Hill have a legitimate grievance if they are excluded. The refusal to address outright racists such as Hale is understandable, to avoid giving them a platform and lending credence to their hate-mongering, but it is cowardly of the fan of the transgressive and the marginalized to abandon a group that is undoubtedly transgressing and arguably marginalized. Not contending with the many websites, publications, and organizations that span the spectrum from Novak, Thomas, and Hill to Hale and beyond would be a mistake. They can seize the opening. Their views fester underground.

Oklahoma City bomber Timothy McVeigh, who was executed for killing 168 people, shows how dangerous people can become if they are disaffected. In 1995, when the Oklahoma City federal building exploded in the worst act of domestic terrorism in U.S. history, the initial suspicion was that Arab immigrants must have been responsible. Once an all-American ex-G.I. became the suspect, most people (other than Arab immigrants) forgot the earlier prejudice and expressed shock at the identity of the perpetrator. He was not one of them, but one of us. Even as he prepared for a lethal injection, dieting to appear gaunt like a victim, the public speculation about his motives intensified. His protest against the federal government was emphasized, his ties to white supremacists de-emphasized. The relationship of the anti-government views and the white supremacist views was glossed over. The propaganda of white supremacists blames multiculturalism for societal malaise, implicitly suggesting that white supremacists are a reaction to multiculturalism. The reverse is more accurate, that societal malaise generated multiculturalism and that white supremacy prompted it.

The propensity to make multiculturalism moderate threatens to make it meaningless. In partisan politics, conservatives and liberals have agreed that the malevolent aspects of multiculturalism are aberrant. Conservatives are reluctant to admit that racists resemble them in the least. Liberals are relieved by their renunciation of the fringe.

For example, Louisiana politician David Duke has said that he is only saying what other white politicians don't dare to. When Duke, the former Ku Klux Klan Grand Dragon, came close to upsetting the establishment candidates in his bid for the U.S. Senate in 1992, the late Lee Atwater, chair of the Republican National Committee, disassociated himself and his party from the extremist. Atwater's Democratic counterparts praised his discretion. Duke has a point, however. His speeches paraphrase the oratory of many members of the Know-Nothing Party in the nineteenth century and more than a few Dixiecrats of the mid-twentieth century. He is not so far removed from their successors. He also is popular. He was elected to the state legislature, and in his repeated runs for higher office has consistently polled one-quarter to one-third of the electorate. His supporters would feel disenfranchised if they did not hold any seats in government.

Yet when the governor of Virginia found out in 2001 that the state commemoration of European American Heritage and History had been issued to Duke's National Organization for European American Rights, he quickly rescinded the proclamation.[106] The issuance of the press release observing the accomplishments of European Americans, such as founding the nation, shows how easy it is to package an agenda as multiculturalism and how embarrassing it becomes to all concerned if the package is opened up.

It would be too clever to say "every day is European American Heritage and History Day." That witticism is grossly insulting to Novak, who is neither a racist nor a WASP, even if it suffices to dispense with Duke, who is a racist and who doesn't make fine distinctions among whites. Diversity itself contains no principles for distinguishing between European American Heritage and History Month and African American Heritage and History Month. Diversity must be supplemented to provide a basis for the distinction.

The claim for recognition not of the supremacy of whiteness at a wholesale level but for the pride of white ethnic groups, such as Italian Americans, presents the problem in sharper relief. In Spike Lee's *Do The Right Thing*, the central conflict is between an Italian American pizzeria owner and his African American customers. It is Italian Americans in particular, not whites more generally, whose photographs are hung on the walls of the store, forming the montage that so maddens the African American protagonists. To gainsay the real discrimination faced by Irish Americans a century ago, by German Americans during World War I, or the stereotyping of Italian Americans and Polish Americans to this day, without at least some consideration of the matter, does not advance the cause of civil rights and needlessly angers members of those groups. Moreover, Southern culture may have become the dominant American culture. [107]

Diversity suffers another intractable drawback. A believer in cultural diversity must deal with a political conservatism within minority groups that cannot be challenged without some sort of cultural purchase. Relativism across time and space can be used to defend the reactionary as easily as it can be used to advance the radical. The most aggravating issues are cultural practices that turn out to harm either other groups, individuals within the group, or liberalism itself. However they are characterized, either cultural diversity or political liberalism can prevail, but not both. The problem is acutely apparent in the case of the minority group that mistreats the internal minority within its own ranks, all the more so if outsiders attempt to interfere.[108] Examples include the non-Western cultures that carry out female genital mutilation, people of color who abhor gays and lesbians, and religious persons who shun the disabled. The issue need not even be as dramatic as discrimination. Non-white Americans argue that they have different standards on daily decisions that are at once personal but of legitimate interest to society. For example, parents may argue that their corporeal punishment of children cannot be judged by the standards for abuse of whites. Labels such as "liberal" and "conservative" do not apply readily to situations; race is set against gender and sexual orientation. A woman who exercises her right to an abortion by selecting against female fetuses so she can bear a male heir can be pro-choice even as she succumbs to a sexist choice.

It was a feminist author, Melusina Fay Pierce, who wrote a book in 1918 arguing for immigration restrictions that included a bar against Asians with "the sole and all-sufficient and imperative reason being their attitude toward and treatment of their womankind as an inferior caste, and their unblushing polygamy, profligacy, and sodomy."[109] But it was multiculturalist conservatives who engaged in the following exchange about journalist Helen Zia when she was still in the closet in the 1980s: An African American community organizer in Boston worried that Zia was lesbian and would harm their progressive collaboration; he was reassured by an Asian American leader, "Homosexuality is not part of our community."[110] In any of these situations, Asian Americans and others are no worse than white Americans with similar views, except that under multiculturalist rules they gain recourse to special pleading.[111]

The *fatwah* against Salman Rushdie is the unintended consequence of our tolerance for intolerance. By publishing his 1989 novel *The Satanic Verses*, Rushdie—who is from a Muslim family—angered fundamentalist Muslims worldwide. The Ayatollah Khomeini issued a directive for his death, and India banned the India-born author's award-winning bestseller, which was greeted in the West with as much curiosity as condemnation. If our nation wishes to protect freedom of expression and reject capital punishment for blasphemy, we must build leeway into our multiculturalism. Otherwise, the minority group (including its American offshoots) who listened to Khomeini are within their rights at least as to censorship if not execution. Indeed, some of the most resentful reactions toward Rushdie came from non-Muslims offended by Rushdie's effrontery to Islam. Some fellow writers failed to defend Rushdie, not because he had failed to assimilate but precisely because he was not ethnic enough. He did not comport with their view of either the proper Englishman or the infidel Muslim. Auberon Waugh wondered how much "we should exert ourselves, as deeply stained white imperialists, to protect [Rushdie] from his own people" while Michael Dummett, a devout Catholic himself, published an open letter stating that Rushdie could never again denounce "white prejudice" because "you are one of us." But even as Dummett proclaimed him an "honorary white," Norman Tebbitt—of "the cricket test" fame, who would ask immigrants whether they cheered the English team in matches—called him a "villain." Tebbitt could not forgive Rushdie for remembering the taunts he had suffered throughout life, because "we mostly shrug them off."[112]

Beyond Assimilation and Multiculturalism

There are other possibilities. Assimilation says everyone must convert to Anglo-conformity and multiculturalism that nobody can do so. Racists combine those propositions to argue that people of color must follow a law they cannot keep: They cannot become whites. New York University sociologist Henry Pratt Fairchild, who was considered a liberal, argued in 1926 that the inassimilability of immigrants was the principal reason for excluding them. In his direct rebuttal of Zangwill's *Melting Pot* play, entitled *The Melting Pot Mistake*, he rejected the term "racism" and substituted "consciousness of kind."[113] Perhaps we can reconceptualize our predicament. Individual and group choices should be evaluated sympathetically. Individuals try to forge genuine lives and groups try to forge what University of California at Berkley sociologist Robert Bellah has aptly called "communities of memory."[114] Assimilation and multiculturalism are options falling along a spectrum, strategies that must be dynamic rather than roles that are assigned. Whether they work or not should be judged by results, and then only on a case-by-case basis. Our nation no longer starts utopian projects such as the nineteenth-century experiment of Brook Farm, but we have a new urbanism springing up to re-create the village and the town square, as well as a co-housing movement bringing together individuals who reconceive the family unit.

Both identities and communities arise from the relationships of individuals to individuals, individuals to groups, and groups to other groups. Rather than claiming that all of us "revert to type," as earlier writers on race supposed, it may be more accurate to say that each of us reverts to role, as social psychologists are finding.[115] Identities are, in the words of philosopher Charles Taylor, "dialogic."[116] As University of California at Berkeley philosophy professor Richard Rorty, one of the leading pragmatists writing today, has said, "the question, 'Do groups diminish or enhance individuality,' is as bad as the question 'Are parents good or bad for children?'"[117] Neither an identity nor a community is formulated by a single person deliberating in isolation from perfect rationalism, who will relate to others who have done the same, until the optimal program for a racial prisoners' dilemma emerges. The individual who glamorizes the egotistical project of self-invention is dangerous to the rest of us. The murdering usurper Richard III, the anti-hero who closes out Shakespeare's tetralogy on the Yorkist kings, is his own man most treacherously to everyone else—killing his brothers and the young nephews imprisoned in the Tower and wooing a woman whose husband he killed before dispensing with her—to gain the English throne.

Like everybody else, Asian Americans cannot fabricate their personalities out of whole cloth. They do what they can, within a specific context. A person who grows up Asian American in the Midwest or the South, for example, may be the only person who looks as she does in her high school graduating class. That situation is different than the person who grows up in Los Angeles or New York City, within a community. An Asian immigrant— and there are hundreds of thousands of them—cannot be expected to take Crevecoeur's prescriptions exactly and purge Asian traits wholly. But an adopted Asian child—and there are hundreds of thousands of such Asian Yankees as well—cannot be expected to live up to Kallen's predictions and flaunt Asian traits by reflex.

The choice may be between lives that are empty and lives that are fulfilling, which need not be related to race and ethnicity. An assimilation that holds out the prospect of an all-encompassing humanism is uninspiring to most of us, but cultural pluralism that counters with a return to clans is too hazardous for most of us. The rationalists of the French Revolution may have wanted to free themselves from the dead hand of history, but they gave us the terror of the guillotine. The philosopher Martin Heidegger may have called for all of us to cherish our organic past, but his writing was taken up by Hitler's Germany in its valorization of a distinctly race-based folklore.

The United States has tried to strike out on a different course than the Jacobins or the Nazis, hewing to the course of neither integration nor pluralism. Only through constant efforts is it possible to balance assimilation and multiculturalism in the vital effort to create identities and sustain communities, recognizing that what was is not what will be. The legal system of the United States is undeniably Anglo-American in its basics (except in Louisiana with its Napoleonic Code). A barrister from the Inner Temple would have recognized the use of precedent, the style of argument, and the formalities of the profession a century ago and would still be able to follow the course of proceedings today. But a British immigrant has no advantage as an attorney in a Los Angeles courtroom, and non-white Americans are not precluded from becoming expert trial lawyers. The respect we accord the former is due as well to the latter.

The past is more than incidental, but it is not all-important. Not all traditions ought to be terminated, but not every tradition should be continued. Among immigrant minority communities, some traditions are the very cause for departure. The Indian caste system should not be resettled here.

Harvard philosopher Kwame Anthony Appiah has identified a "rooted cosmopolitanism." University of California at Berkeley professor David Hollinger has published an influential book entitled *Post-Ethnic America*,[118] in which he argues that our voluntary identities can become as powerful as our involuntary identities in directing our lives. In the rooted cosmopolitanism of post-ethnic America, where race and culture correlate only approximately to the extent they do so at all, we can divorce race from culture and improve on rather than lose altogether the creations of what was once racial culture. In that society, races will recombine themselves as never before and culture will be reformed. We will still have group affiliations, but they will be neither racial nor rigid. Nor is this new. Although the Greeks may have invented the concept of the "barbarian," it was not a Greek but a Macedonian, Alexander the Great, who was responsible for the hegemony of Hellenism. Later, it was Muslim Arabs who rescued and interpreted Aristotle, while Europe was in its Dark Ages. Had it not been for their dedication to preserving what was then the leading body of scientific work, Thomas Aquinas could never have rediscovered it.

Our lives become meaningful because of substance rather than form. The contest of integration versus pluralism, assimilation versus multiculturalism, is a false dichotomy. It distracts from the real division between the substantial and the superficial, what is sublime and what is vulgar. The test is not whether we have a single common culture or many different cultures; it is whether our culture is educational, with each of us a creator, an active participant in living traditions, or entertainment, a virtual reality universe with only a few distant stars to be gazed upon, leaving the rest of us to be passive consumers of interchangeable commodities. The problem is less the literature of the Orient, which has always influenced the West, than it is our shared penchant for the lowest common denominator, the voyeuristic thrill of "reality television." People have stopped reading Homer and Plato, not because they have taken up Asian poets or philosophers, but because they have stopped reading altogether.[119] When the late University of Chicago humanities professor Allan Bloom wrote the book that started "the culture wars," *The Closing of the American Mind: How Higher Education Has Failed Democracy and Impoverished the Souls of Today's Students*, he confused the debauchery of pop culture with an onslaught of non-Western culture. The two are linked only through commercialism.[120] An Afrocentric curriculum that is rigorous may be preferable to one that is auctioned off for product placements.

Great music can belong to the traditions of opera, jazz, classical, rock and roll, blues, country and western, folk, and religious—but not the easy listening of the elevator. True music lovers, musicians themselves, do not allow any single genre to claim a monopoly on art. They are open to the possibilities of the ancient and the modern, the crowd pleasing and the avante-garde. They can take pleasure from a live period performance of Beethoven's Fifth as much as from a modern digital recording of the same composition. They can listen enraptured by the African American opera singer such as Jessye Norman as well as the white jazz pianist such as Dave Brubeck, conducted by an Asian American or accompanied by a Latino, or the collaboration of minimalist composer Philip Glass with the Indian sitar playing of Ravi Shankar. We will find unexpected beauty, if we have high standards and eclectic tastes.

Versatile film director Ang Lee, whose body of work is only beginning to develop, has shown excellence in multiple cultural contexts. Honored as the top director by the Directors Guild of America in 2001, Lee, who identifies as an Asian American, has been behind the lens for movies about such topics as a mythological China in the multiple-Oscar-winning *Crouching Tiger, Hidden Dragon* (which became a parody of itself when dubbed); modern Taiwan in the critical hit, *Eat, Drink, Man, Woman*; Asian immigrants in *Pushing Hands*; gay humor in *The Wedding Banquet*; the Civil War in *Ride with the Devil*; a Jane Austen novel in *Sense & Sensibility*; and 1970s suburban ennui in *The Ice Storm*. He is now wrapping up a science fiction remake of *The Incredible Hulk*.

Diversity presents us with the challenge of saying what we mean so we can mean what we say. Mere diversity is not enough. Substance matters.

In the next chapter, I take up intermarriage and the mixed race movement. They transcend assimilation and multiculturalism. A couple who come from different racial backgrounds and their child of multiple ancestries are both the product of assimilation and the producers of multiculturalism.

The Changing Face of America

Intermarriage and the Mixed Race Movement

I am a white American female. My husband is Chinese, born in Vietnam. He has a permanent resident visa. My question: What nationality does that make our children? Someone told me that they are white American, but to me that means that they are ignoring their Oriental heritage. My daughter says she is half-Chinese and half-American. Please straighten this out, as we never know how to fill out the forms when this question is asked.

—Letter to "Dear Abby"
advice column, *Chicago Tribune*, June 24, 1991

The Chinese Girl in the Sixth Grade

When I was a boy, I once asked my mother if she would love me if I married an American girl. She answered that she would love me if I married a foreigner. But she added that she would love me more if I married a Chinese girl.

I'm not sure how I would have avoided marrying somebody white, if I wanted to be married at all. In elementary school, there was only one grade in which an Asian American girl was in the same class as me. Everyone teased us that we were supposed to be married someday, but she avoided me. Without her, I was left with nobody. I had not learned it, but as much as boys and girls didn't play together as children, whites and non-whites didn't marry one another as adults.

When I was much older, I dated a woman who was white but spoke Chinese fluently. Her father was a Scottish immigrant; her mother was from the impeccable WASP milieu of mainline Philadelphia. She had studied Mandarin in college and Japanese in graduate school; lived in China, Taiwan, and Japan for extended periods of time; and earned advanced degrees with a concentration in Asian studies. Her accent was perfect; her vocabulary was extensive. She was literate. She could pass the "telephone test," meaning that a listener who could not see her would be fooled into believing that she was Chinese. She even had a job once as a radio broadcaster in Japan, using her similarly impressive Japanese. Her expertise with all matters Asian surpassed that of most Asian Americans, and she was better able than I to chat with my parents. She is an "egg": white outside, yellow inside.

I enjoyed more than she did surprising people at restaurants or overseas, who made assumptions about race and gender and expected me to communicate with them in Chinese only to find that she was in charge. There are enough whites who are fluent in Asian languages that in major cities abroad they are no longer even commended for having learned the native tongue, even though they are novel even now here at home.

Eventually, I married a Japanese American woman. On her paternal side, she is second generation (*nisei*); on her maternal side, she is third generation (*sansei*). As we started dating, I traveled with her to meet her mother in St. Louis. After we were introduced, my girlfriend's mother said to her, "He's good looking. . . . He looks Japanese."

By the time we were engaged, my parents had realized I would follow my own course in life. From their perspective, their prospective daughter-in-law might as well have been white. But they were relieved I would not end up an eccentric bachelor, never mind that the woman I had found was not Chinese.

Both my nieces by marriage have husbands who are white. Anybody familiar with Japanese Americans would find the family photographs shown off atop the mantelpiece to be quite ordinary. Japanese Americans can be distinguished from white Americans who lead otherwise similar lives, albeit only barely. My brother-in-law and sister-in-law have memories of the internment camp, but their children are as integrated as can be. The whiteness of their daughters' spouses is insignificant, in a good sense. The *hakujin* husbands have included themselves in the Asian American community, such as it is.

I remember a white friend I had in elementary school. (I only had white friends in elementary school, because there were no other Asian Americans or any people of color for that matter in any of my classes, other than that one girl.) Like many of my white friends whom I made and lost, a few of whose parents did not want them playing with me, he asked me what my nationality was. I can still recall it, because, although I had developed my vocabulary from almost no English when I'd enrolled in kindergarten, I did not know the word "nationality." Once I figured it out, I gave myself too much credit for being clever in returning the favor with the question, "Well, what nationality are you?" I was puzzled by his answer, which used a metaphor that was restricted to white mixtures, "I'm Heinz 57. . . . Like the ketchup, 57 varieties."

In just my lifetime, intermarriage has become the taboo that binds. Mixed race individuals are accustomed to hearing "what are you?" rather than "Who are you?" and being fixed in an unwelcome gaze, but the mixed race movement is informing others that the "What are you?" inquiry is inappropriate even if it cannot ensure that it becomes irrelevant.

The future of race relations is mixed, literally as well as figuratively. Gradually, interracial relationships have become normal rather than forbidden, and the progeny of such relationships are accepted for their varied ancestries rather than rejected as abominations whose very existence violates natural laws. Although Asian Americans as a group may challenge the prevailing black-white racial paradigm, mixed race persons as individuals confound the concept of such straightforward racial opposites. For better or worse, they personify ambiguities because they demonstrate that race is not always hereditary.

Because the families of America are changing, the self-conception of America itself is changing. The 1960 Census, taken at a time when intermarriage was criminal conduct in more than a dozen states, showed only 149,000 interracial marriages within a total population of 179 million. The 1990 Census, taken when the number of multiracial babies being born was growing at a higher rate than the number of monoracial babies being born, showed more than 1.46 million interracial marriages within a total population 281 million. Mixed marriages constituted about 3 percent of all marriages in 1980 nationwide and an estimated 5 percent in 1990. In California, which leads the mainland United States, about one out of six marriages now brings together couples of different racial or ethnic backgrounds. Among Asian Americans under the age of thirty-five who are married, half have found a spouse of a non-Asian background. Experts forecast that more than

20 percent of all marriages will be mixed by 2050. By 1990, more than 60 percent of Hawaiian babies were mixed race; by 2000, more than 20 percent of the Hawaiian population was mixed race. The 2000 Census counted about 6.8 million people of mixed race background, making up 2.4 percent of the population.

The transformation is recent. It was only in 1967 that the Supreme Court struck down legal bans on intermarriage in a case involving the aptly named Loving couple.[1] Since then, states have slowly repealed the bars that they had on the books. Alabama did not revise its statutes until 1999.[2] Local authorities reportedly were enforcing the rules in violation of the mandate from the highest court in the land. They did so by referring to the nullification doctrine of the antebellum era by which their predecessors had tried to ignore federal legislation against slavery by appealing to states' rights.

In the less than two generations since the *Loving* case, what social scientists have called "exogamy" or "outmarriage" has proliferated by an order of magnitude. Because of the personal nature of the relationships, the unions symbolize much more. Yet as with other demographic patterns, as a society we are only beginning to comprehend the complexities that they bequeath us. However sanguine we are about intermarriage and mixed race children, the success of all marriages and the future of any child depend on many factors. Intermarriage and the mixed race movement are positive, but they are no panacea. Both can reflect the effects of racial discrimination in the most intimate manner. Jeanne Wakatsuki Houston, author of a popular memoir about the internment, *Farewell to Manzanar*, writes that she saw her white husband as her "Anglo Samurai" who by "wielding his sword of integrity" would "slay the dragons that prevented my acceptance as an equal human being in his world."[3]

In this chapter, I begin by considering white opposition to interracial marriage and white attraction to people of color. I then turn to the ambivalence toward mixed marriages expressed by minority communities, both racial and religious. Finally, I consider the mixed race movement and its implications specifically for Asian Americans.

The Core of the Heart of the Race Problem

Both proponents and opponents of racial justice grasped that intermarriage was the culmination of racial equality. James Weldon Johnson, composer of the hymn "Lift Every Voice and Sing" (sometimes referred to as the black national anthem) and author of the novel *The Autobiography of an Ex-Colored*

Man,[4] once wrote, "in the core of the heart of the race problem the sex factor is rooted."[5] Gunnar Myrdal ranked "intermarriage" and in particular "sexual contacts with white women" as the area of greatest racial discrimination.[6]

When Abraham Lincoln signed the Emancipation Proclamation, his adversaries were fixated on the probability of legal equality leading to social equality.[7] When he ran for reelection in 1864, two pro-slavery writers sought to associate him with a fake Republican pamphlet purporting to endorse miscegenation, to inspire backlash. They coined the term "miscegenation" from Latin roots for mixture and race. Earlier, abolitionist Wendell Phillips actually had issued a similar call in earnest.[8] He preached "amalgamation" as the best means of uniting a divided nation.

A century later, as integration actually began in earnest, the paranoid fear that whites articulated again was the possibility that race mixing would proceed apace from the classroom to the bedroom. Foreseeing the impending upheaval of the old South, Theodore G. Bilbo, twice the governor of Mississippi and a three-term U.S. Senator, penned a book, *Take Your Choice: Separation or Mongrelization*,[9] in which he argued for "repatriation" of blacks to Africa specifically to avoid intermarriage. "The incontrovertible truths of this book and its sincere warnings," he wrote, "are respectfully inscribed to every white man and woman, regardless of nationality, who is a bona fide citizen of the United States of America."[10] He inveighed against what he believes to be false interpretations of democracy and Christianity, which would require recognizing African Americans as equal persons. He stated that intermarriage is "totally destructive to the white race" because "the Negro race is physically, mentally, and morally inferior."[11] Even if the mulatto might be the equal of the white man, "amalgamation must be condemned" because "it cannot be said to be a matter of trial and error . . . corrupted blood cannot be redeemed."[12] He concluded his book with his own bill for "voluntary resettlement" of African Americans on the African continent.[13]

The official end of racial segregation in public education, decreed by the Supreme Court decision in *Brown v. Board of Education*, was thought to be the harbinger of a sexual calamity. Congressman Jon Bell Williams of Mississippi called the issuance of the *Brown* decision "black Monday," and Judge Thomas Brady of the same state borrowed the phrase for the title of his pamphlet, issued by the white supremacist Citizens' Councils of Mississippi, in which he asserted that the Supreme Court is tending toward Communism and proposes either that a new state be created and blacks transported there for their own benefit or that all public schools be closed and African Americans left to their own devices. Insisting that he would like harmony between races,

Brady predicted that white Southern men would fight to the death to pre-serve racial purity, defined as whiteness and the honor of their women. "We say to the Supreme Court and to the entire world," he wrote, "'you shall not make us drink from this cup.'"[14] He warned, "those who do not believe this may try through force of arms to accomplish it. If this happens, then it will take an army of one hundred million men to compel it." He concluded, "You shall not mongrelize our children and grandchildren!"[15]

The defining occasion of desegregation came in 1957, as federal troops had to be ordered out to enable blacks to attend Little Rock Central High School.[16] State officials were heading the campaign of massive resistance to school integration. A list of seven questions circulated by white leaders in Lit-tle Rock at the time began with, "Would the Negro boys be permitted to solicit the white girls for dances at school-soirees?" It ended with, "When the script calls for the enactment of tender love scenes, will these parts be assigned to negro boys and white girls without respect to race and color in drama classes?"

Such segregationist propaganda, like the hoax perpetrated against Lincoln, was based on the premise that whites who backed racial integration would blanch at sexual contact between their white daughters and black men. A pop-ular line of reasoning was that segregationists were willing to abide integration, but integrationists would have to understand that their morality would neces-sitate Southern belles bedding black men indiscriminately. The presumption was that once such an abhorrent result became apparent, even self-proclaimed liberals would come to their senses. Novelist Norman Mailer explained that, "The white man fears the sexual potency of the Negro. . . . The white loathes the idea of the Negro attaining equality in the classroom because the white feels that the Negro already enjoys sensual superiority."[17]

In reply, African American men were reduced to pledging that, even as they sought to be admitted to all spheres of public life on equal terms, they would not aspire to the hands of white women, and to assuring whites that not all black men were superstuds. They did not wish to appear like Bigger Thomas, the African American male in Richard Wright's 1940 novel, *Native Son*. Thomas accidentally kills the wealthy young white woman for whom he works, and toward whom he is attracted, but Thomas also brutally kills his black girlfriend, the latter crime being both the more intentional and insignificant in the context of his wretched life.[18] They knew the strategic advantage of stopping short of intermarriage. Michael Lind, in *The Next American Nation: The New Nationalism and the Fourth American Revolution*,[19] argues that intermarriage is crucial to the future of a diverse democracy. He observes that "even Martin Luther King Jr. dared dream, at least in public, only of black and white children playing together in the red hills of Birmingham, Alabama, instead of dreaming of weddings of mixed-race couples in the churches of Birmingham." In 1971, Robert E. Kuttner (a leading racialist not to be confused with the liberal economist of the same name) published in the now-defunct *American Mercury* magazine a think piece entitled, "Race Mixing: Suicide or Salvation?" Kuttner left no doubt that he considered it the former: "Legalized pornography teaches that the height of sexual pleasure can be attained only with Negro partners. . . . Who has not seen teen-age girls with pale blond hair carrying Negro babies in Hippie settlements or in the drug communes around our elite universities?" He concluded, "Racial instincts in man deserve objective investigation by the methods of modern psychology" because white men prefer white women and "cannot be dismissed merely because womanless soldiers, explorers and colonizers mated with native women." In sum, "Race mixing between advanced and lower stocks is of no benefit to the higher type."[20]

Whites could be as upset by Asian Americans joining the family as they were by African Americans doing so. In the Western states, their dread of an Asian California was exceeded only by their horror at an Asian and Caucasian Pacific Coast. A white minister named Ralph Newman, living in Sacramento, said in 1931:

> Near my home is an eighty-acre tract of as fine land as there is in California. On that tract lives a Japanese. With that Japanese lives a white woman. In that woman's arms is a baby. What is that baby? It isn't white. It isn't Japanese. It is a germ of the mightiest problem that ever faced this state; a problem that will make the black problem of the South look white.[21]

Newman could have been confident that whites would back up his sentiments virtually unanimously. Whites from ardent segregationists to moderate integrationists opposed intermarriage. President Harry S Truman replied frankly to a reporter who asked whether intermarriage would become common, "I hope not; I don't believe in it."[22] Truman, who had taken incremental steps to dismantle segregation, was known to ask "Would you want your daughter to marry a Negro?"[23] In 1958, the Gallup organization reported that 96 percent of whites were against intermarriage.

With the civil rights movement, approval and disapproval of intermarriage have switched places in the polls, but the figures still show discrepancies by racial group. When the Gallup poll broke out separate figures for whites and blacks on this issue for the first time in 1972, the results were mirror images: 27 percent of whites approved of intermarriage and 73 percent disapproved of it; 76 percent of blacks approved of intermarriage and 24 percent disapproved of it. Since then, the attitudes of whites and blacks have converged, as have the attitudes in the North and the South and of the college educated and the non-college educated. By 1997, the last year for which data are available, a majority of respondents approved of intermarriage: 67 percent of whites approved of intermarriage and 33 percent disapproved of it; 83 percent of blacks approved of intermarriage and 17 percent disapproved of it. According to a survey published in 2001 by *The Washington Post*, Harvard University, and the Kaiser Foundation, approval of intermarriage is rising, but "nearly half of all whites—more than any other group—still believe it is better for people to marry someone of their own race."[24]

Among Asian Americans, intermarriage is as pervasive as resistance to it. A 1998 study by the Organization of Chinese Americans found that 69 percent of Chinese American parents strongly agreed or agreed with the statement "I prefer that my children marry someone in the same ethnic group."[25] Among children, only 50 percent agreed with that sentiment.

As salutary as the overall statistics may appear, they are likely to be inflated.[26] Social science data are often distorted by preference falsification. Interviewees give answers they suppose will be acceptable to society or pleasing to the interviewer, tending not to disclose their true outlook. In any event, attitudes and behavior are not the same. Intermarriage rates are well below what they would be if people acted on their stated willingness to intermarry, and progress has come slower than appearances would suggest.

In high culture, William Shakespeare's *Othello* has long been the foremost portrayal of mixed race marriages. One of the Bard's mature works, traditionally listed with *King Lear, Hamlet,* and *Macbeth* as the "Big Four," the play has been among the most frequently staged of his canon. The eponymous Moor general was a hero of the first order until he wed the fair Desdemona, the daughter of an influential senator. Theatergoers have wondered for centuries what induced his lieutenant Iago to harass the couple. His fatal obsession was not motivated by plain jealousy. The tragedy has been a hit even without any rationale for his actions. Iago carried out the vengeance of society even if he was not goaded on by anything else. President John Quincy Adams—an opponent of slavery—wrote that the "moral lesson of *Othello* is that black and white blood cannot be intermingled without a gross outrage upon the laws of Nature; and that, in such violations, Nature will vindicate her laws."[27]

Two hundred years later, a "photo negative" production by the outstanding Shakespeare Theatre of Washington, D.C., in its 1999–2000 season starred Patrick Stewart, the white Englishman best known for his television performances as Captain Jean-Luc Picard in *Star Trek: The Next Generation*, with an all-black supporting cast. Having a white Othello accentuated the racial elements of the script, but it did not quite reverse them. The lead couple stands out as unusual, and their fate is inevitably death. Othello must murder Desdemona, then kill himself.

Nor is Othello the only black suitor from Shakespeare's pen. There are only two other adult male roles with distinct racial identities in his canon, out of more than a thousand dramatis personae. The skin color of each of them is integral to his role as lover. Aaron the Moor plots with Tamora, the Goth Queen, in the vicious melodrama *Titus Andronicus*. Aaron is defiant even as he is tied to stakes and buried up to his head in the ground to die of dehydration and starvation, asking only that his son be spared although the baby's birth to Tamora had indicted them both. The Prince of Morocco is comic relief as a failed suitor to Portia in the *Merchant of Venice*, which is already disturbing for the anti-Semitic maltreatment of the moneylender Shylock. As the Prince departs in the flamboyance of his traditional garb, having banked on the wrong casket in the lottery to win Portia, she states, "let all of his complexion choose me so." The utmost insult of Hermia, the young woman spurned by her lover in the forest of *A Midsummer Night's Dream*, is that she is an "Ethiope" who will be rejected for her dark skin and her short stature. Only in *Love's Labour's Lost*, where the friends of the King of Navarre swear off women while they are occupied by their studies, is there an exception. One of the fellows, Berowne, falls for the Princess's lady-in-waiting, who is dark-hued.

Color blind casting of classic plays has not always fared well when it involves romance. In 1998, black Briton Ray Fearon appeared in the Royal Shakespeare Company's first-ever cross-racial *Romeo & Juliet*.[28] While the company was on tour, a racially motivated assault in Brussels left his arm broken.

Popular culture has defined "mixed marriage" in circumscribed terms. As late as the 1950s, the term "mixed marriage" referred to couples who came from different ethnicities that were white and not to couples who came from different racial heritages. A husband who was Greek and a wife who was English were regarded as having a "mixed marriage." The triple melting pot was envisioned as operating on Catholics, Protestants, and Jews, separately. Catholics would marry Catholics: German Catholics, Italian Catholics, Polish Catholics, French Catholics, and Irish Catholics would merge together; Protestants and Jews would do the same. All of the participants in the triple melting pot were assumed to be Caucasian, and the Catholics, Protestants, and Jews were not expected to cross religious lines.

The norms were not to be transgressed. The late entertainer Sammy Davis Jr., who was African American, jeopardized his popularity by courting May Britt, who was Swedish, in the 1960s. As a member of the famous Rat Pack, with Frank Sinatra, Dean Martin, Peter Lawford, and Joey Bishop, crooner Davis was inundated with death threats after he and Britt were wed. Each of them was called upon repeatedly to justify the marriage. Entertainer Lena Horne and her second husband, bandleader Lennie Hayton, kept their marriage secret for years because they anticipated a negative reaction. Together, Horne, who is African American, and Hayton, who was an American Jew, faced racial discrimination against African Americans in addition to anti-Semitism. Even though Horne had endured prejudice from other African Americans on the basis of her light skin, she also was criticized for choosing Hayton.

Although that kind of public hostility on the part of whites has receded, its private vestiges persist. University of California at Santa Barbara historian Paul Spickard began his 1989 study of intermarriage with an anecdote.[29] He was visited by a white woman from South Dakota, whose daughter was enrolled in Spickard's class. The mother confronted him: "Don't you feel ashamed, promoting mixed marriage like this?" In fact, the students were examining the phenomenon with academic impartiality.

In 1998, Edgar Bronfman, former chair of the Seagram Company, wrote in his memoirs that he had objected to his son marrying an African American woman. She offered to convert to Judaism, and the grandchildren later were raised Jewish, but the elder Bronfman said that religion "was not the point." Identifying himself as a "closet liberal" who "respected the optimism of youth," he said that he was motivated by kindness. Marriages were hard enough to sustain without racial issues, and he was worried that his grandchildren "would have problems being accepted by either Black or White society."[30] With due respect for Bronfman *pere*, he contributes to the problems he is concerned about; the very people who ask "won't the children suffer" of a mixed race marriage are the ones who make it so. It is because of parents like him that interracial marriages become hard to sustain, and it is because of grandparents like him that youngsters have problems being accepted. He would protest that it is unnamed others and not himself who are recalcitrant about their racial animosities. But he would acquiesce to those who will whisper about his daughter-in-law rather than welcome her.

However they are phrased, the arguments against interracial marriages are disquieting. If nothing else, our love of liberty should be enough to protect our love. Both Sidney Poitier himself and the physician character he played, in the 1967 film *Guess Who's Coming to Dinner*, should be enough to shame the undecided. Even in the movie, extolled for its daring and lambasted for its simplifications, the new couple eases their ordeal by moving abroad.

Integration and intermarriage are mutually reinforcing, but the former will not have occurred as long as the latter is noticed. Integration will remain incomplete unless intermarriage is allowed.

Yet those of us who value integration should strive for more than tolerating intermarriage. We ought to foster true intermarriage and not some idealized form of renegade romance. Admirers of intermarriage should be alert to the possibility that individuals who are involved are more than lovers following their heart to their partner across the color line while disregarding both social convention and parental dictates. A serious analysis of intermarriage suggests that some people have a wider variety of choices, and some combinations are regarded more favorably than others.

Even though interracial couples might, like any other couple, become livid at the suggestion that their mutual attraction was the effect of anything other than their own feelings, intermarriages collectively are conspicuously color conscious and gender-specific. Individuals may adore their sweethearts in individual cases, but society selects the "all-American" look.

Psychologists and economists, especially those who are trying to apply evolutionary theory to human behavior, have new means of explicating our marital decisions.[31] They posit that competition to produce offspring induces our actions. *Homo sapiens*, no different than other animals, evaluate their companions based on coded signals of their likely biological status and their own market power. Each of us seeks out the smells of sweat that is not like our own and covets the mate who is too good for one's self. The geneticists who borrow from game theory may be somewhat reckless in their conjectures that monogamy is unnatural and gender roles are hardwired, so that philandering husbands and mean stepmothers are natural, but it has not been long since many societies openly arranged marriages for dynastic pacts, the bounty of dowries, and other concrete advantages.

Race alters the terms of the bargain.

Yellow Fever and Trophy Boyfriends

Inequality runs as a theme through the literature of mixed race liaisons. Poet Langston Hughes wrote a poem, entitled "Cross," about mixed parentage, ending with the stanza:

> My old man died in a fine big house.
> My ma died in a shack.
> I wonder where I'm gonna die,
> Being neither white nor black?[32]

The most famous such relationship in American history involved a white man and a black woman; he was as powerful as she was not.[33] As was rumored in the press in his time and verified by genetic testing in ours, founding father Thomas Jefferson carried on a long-term affair with his slave Sally Hemings.[34] Until the genetic testing resolved the matter, as Mount Holyoke College historian Joseph Ellis has noted, the Jefferson-Hemmings relationship was rejected as a scurrilous rumor by the mostly white academic community as much as it was repeated as common knowledge in the black oral tradition.[35] The relationship between the future president and the woman who was his late wife's half-sister probably began when she was an adolescent serving as a nanny in his household. They may have been passionate and devoted. It is inspirational to imagine that they worked out a semblance of parity through mutual commitment. The truth may be disheartening.

Whatever their private personas, their public roles were grossly unequal. When Jefferson demanded that Hemings return from France, where he was serving as ambassador, to Virginia and his Monticello estate, both of them knew that she was free overseas but would be held in bondage once back home. Jefferson owned her. The children born to them were his chattel property, too.

Intermarriage still occurs in distinct configurations, and not all individuals have the same ability to engage in it. Races come together asymmetrically. Intermarriage may reinforce rather than break down the color line that separates whites from blacks, because intermarriage has risen primarily due to alliances among whites, Asian Americans, and Latinos, not African Americans. White-black intermarriage lags behind as the least frequent. Whites are much more likely to marry Asian Americans than African Americans. The Asian American intermarriage rate is triple the African American rate.

Asian Americans generally marry up. Just as the idea of "marrying up" is an admission of socioeconomic hierarchy, so is "marrying up" interracially an acknowledgment of racial hierarchy. For most Asian Americans, a white spouse ranks higher than a black spouse. Whites and blacks may both be "foreign devils," but whites are the more sought-after foreign devils. Halford Fairchild, a noted psychologist who is of African American and Hawaiian Japanese descent, has said that "the black community, in general, has been a lot more accepting of racial differences than other communities."[36] His Japanese American mother's family disowned her for marrying a black man, cautioning her that when they returned to his home in California, she would find "he has nothing."

In 1990, thirty times as many intermarried Asian Americans had white spouses as had black spouses, even though years ago intermarriage between Chinese Americans and African Americans in Harlem was not unheard of. The 1992 independent movie *Mississippi Masala* by director Mira Nair, about a South Asian woman from Uganda who falls in love with an African American man who owns a carpet-cleaning business (essayed by Denzel Washington, whom women of all races have pursued to the box office), is abnormal even within the atypicality of interracial romances. The 1997 Disney remake of Rodgers and Hammerstein's *Cinderella*, starring African American television actress Brandy in the title role and Asian American stage actor Paolo Montalban as Prince Charming, is anomalous in the opposite direction.

White Americans also rank above other Asian Americans. Although Asian Americans are marrying across Asian ethnicities more often than before—as my wife and I did—they are more likely to intermarry with white Americans than with Asian Americans of a different ethnicity. Few fail to grasp that it is the white look, not the Asian look, that is in demand. In John Updike's short story, "Metamorphosis," the white male protagonist is naïve in his infatuation with his Asian American female doctor. Fantasizing that he can capture her attention, he asks for reverse eyelid surgery to give himself almond eyes. In the O. Henry-style surprise ending, however, once he has undergone the painful operation, he spies on her desk her family photograph showing her husband "not old, exactly, probably younger than [him] by some years, but craggy, Caucasian, grinning, big-nosed, rather monstrously bumpy and creased." As he leaves the office, he ponders "how foolish he must look!" and he is grateful that he still has his right tear duct.[37]

The various pairings also exhibit the mutual influence of race and gender. Among African American-white married couples, an African American husband with a white wife remains more widespread than a white husband with an African American wife. According to the 1990 Census, 72 percent of African American–white couples consist of an African American male and a white female. It appears that the African American man who marries a white woman is exchanging his higher economic status for her higher social status. He is augmenting his material success with a woman who is regarded as belonging to a superior class; she is acquiring access to his affluence.

Terry McMillan's best-selling novel *Waiting to Exhale*[38] chronicled the love lives of a quartet of African American women. Among them was Bernadine Harris, whose trauma of being left by her African American husband was aggravated by the identity of the "other woman." Bernadine and her friends list the problems with black men: "with white women" comes second in the litany, after "scared to make a damned commitment," before "gay," and well ahead of ugly, stupid, and in prison.[39] After Bernadine had supported him as he struggled through his career, her husband left her for a younger white woman once his business became profitable. In the book, Bernadine reviews her mistake of trusting him: "Kathleen the bookkeeper, who was fresh out of some two-year college and California pretty" was "not at all a threat because, number one, she was white and you knew [he] would never look at a white girl and number two, he loved you and the kids."[40] In the movie, Angela Bassett in the role of Bernadine was cheered by audiences as she acted on her anger: she visited her husband's office, slapped her rival, and confronted her husband, before returning home, clearing out the contents of his closet, dumping his fancy shirts and expensive suits into his luxury car, and setting it all ablaze.

The modern white–black intermarriage that prompted record outcry, from whites and blacks alike, was the 1949 marriage of Walter White and Poppy Cannon.[41] White, the long-time secretary of the NAACP, divorced his African American wife to take up with Cannon, a white businesswoman. Many whites found in the two of them proof of the conspiracy of black men to steal their women. Some black women deplored the dumping of a black woman for a white woman, treating the divorce and remarriage as an exercise in crass racial upward mobility. What White and Cannon should have made apparent was the fabrication of race. When they traveled, they were regarded as an interracial couple, but people made assumptions that reversed their racial roles.[42] White fit his name: He was light-skinned, blonde, and blue-eyed; both of his parents could have passed as white and his daughter was so light she had problems pursuing an acting career because she could not credibly play a black person but could not be cast as a white person.[43] Cannon was darker all-around, blacker in a physical sense.

Shortly thereafter, the widower Thurgood Marshall wed Cecile "Cissy" Suyatt. Known as Mr. Civil Rights for his courtroom victories against racial segregation, Marshall served for many years as the general counsel for the NAACP Legal Defense Fund prior to his historic appointment to the U.S. Supreme Court. Suyatt was a Filipina secretary at his office. She initially turned down his proposal for fear of the likely reactions. She reported whispers against her that she was a "foreigner," and she worried about what her family would say about an African American husband. Like White's marriage, Marshall's met the censure of some Southern whites. In response to the newspaper editorial that called him a racist for marrying a white woman, Marshall said, "I just think you ought to be accurate. . . . I've had two wives and both of 'em are colored."[44] In 1995, *Ebony* magazine listed the Marshall-Suyat wedding among its fifty "best" of the past half-century.[45]

In a reversal of the black–white interaction, 72 percent of Asian American–white couples consist of an Asian American wife and a white husband. Writing in *American Demographics* magazine, journalist Roberto Suro reported that Asian women are intermarrying at twice the rate of Asian men.[46] In a 2000 California survey of Asian–white intermarriages, Filipina–white intermarriages were the most common. In the Golden State throughout the 1990s, there were 16,503 births of children to Filipina mothers and white fathers and only 5,556 births to white mothers and Filipino fathers. The former occurred almost three times as often as the latter.

The data produce a puzzle, however: Unless there are many more Asian American women than there are Asian American men, there must be enormous numbers of single Asian American men compared to single Asian American women. The solution to the conundrum of uneven rates of out-marriage is immigration. It appears to be foreign-born Asian women who are intermarrying as much as it is Asian American women.

In other words, Asian women are being imported. There have always been war brides throughout human history, part of the victor's booty; there have not been war husbands.[47] Following World War II, some 20,000 Japanese women came to the United States as newlyweds accompanying their American soldier husbands. From 1950 until the immigration reform of 1965, the majority of the 17,000 Korean immigrants were women coming over with husbands who had been servicemen fighting in the Korean war. The very circumstances of their marriage made some Asians and some Americans alike stereotype them as what was euphemistically called "business girls" in Korean or "loose women" in the American vernacular. Other Asian immigrant women disdain them as likely to have come from the "camptowns" of vice surrounding U.S. military bases throughout Asia.[48]

There are now many mail order brides but few mail order husbands.[49] The trade relies on the economic desperation of ethnic women in poor countries. The brokers supply purchasers who are by and large white American men looking for the antithesis of a liberated woman. The images of subservient Asian women are so desirable that they were used by a con artist convicted in 1993 of creating a bogus dating service to bilk more than 400 men, most of whom were white, out of a total of $280,000. Posing as the fictitious "SAF" (Single Asian Female) Velma Tang in personal ads, Christopher Eugene Barnes attracted thousands of correspondents, to whom s/he described her body as 37-23-35, her desire to meet a nice American man, her erotic fantasies, and her upbringing that taught her the role of submissiveness.[50]

Beyond war brides and their mail order cousins, particular gender stereotypes attach to interracial relationships. Race and gender together, not separately, explain why it is easier for Asian women to incorporate themselves into white society.[51] Asian women are supposed to integrate themselves into white society. Seldom are the white men bothered about integrating into Asian society. The classic question about interracial relationships, asked by racial skeptics who suppose others are only hiding their racial reactions, is gender specific: "Yes, but would you let one marry your daughter?" It is not: "Yes, but would you let your son sleep with one?"

The literature of an earlier time is replete with references to white men who could not help themselves when they were tempted by the lewdness of black Jezebels, although their advances were often violently imposed. Nineteenth-century New Orleans boasted quadroon balls where mulatto women could offer themselves as concubines to white men.[52] Illinois State University sociologist F. James Davis reports that whites used to joke "that a white boy doesn't become a man until he has had sexual relations with a black girl."[53] University of Cincinnati professor Patricia Hill Collins, in *Black Feminist Thought*,[54] argues that "freedom for Black women has meant freedom from white men."[55] As in William Faulkner's 1936 masterpiece *Absalom! Absalom!*, a planter who raped his slave produced the hazard that further miscegenation would be incest if his white children sought out their black half-siblings.

The laws on intermarriage were part of the problem. The 1691 Virginia legislation that proscribed mixed marriages said nothing about white men having illicit relations with black women, even if they produced children out of wedlock, but white women who had illicit relations with black men and gave birth to an illegitimate child committed a crime. The regulation was meant to defend the sanctity of whiteness. Contrary to claims of evenhandedness in barring all interracial relationships, the drafters of the prohibitions were indifferent to race mixing among people of color.

Even the suggestion of a white woman with a black man was anathema, however, and the charge of sexual assault could be the reaction to a whistle or simply made up, with imprisonment or lynching the potential consequence. Poet Hughes wrote another poem, "Silhouette" about the ardor of the prosecution; it reads in part:

> Southern gentle lady,
> Do not swoon.
> They've just hung a black man
> In the dark of the moon.
> For the world to see
> How Dixie protects
> Its white womanhood.[56]

Emmett Till and the Scottsboro boys were only the most prominent examples of this attitude. Till was a fourteen-year-old black youth from Chicago who, due to polio, had a speech impediment that resulted in his making whistling noises. When he visited relatives in Money, Mississippi, in 1955, he was said to have "wolf-whistled" at a white woman in a public square. He was abducted and murdered. When his corpse was found, it showed that he'd been stabbed and shot, his eyes gouged out, and his head split open with an ax. His killers were acquitted by an all-white jury. The Scottsboro boys were nine black teenagers who rode the rails as hobos. A group of white hobos with whom they had fought thought they would have their retribution by invoking the specter of black on white rape. They found two white women, also vagrants who occasionally prostituted themselves, who said they'd been assaulted, although their stories were thoroughly discredited. When the boys emerged from a boxcar in Paint Rock, Arkansas, in 1931, a posse carried them off to be tried for their lives in the county seat of Scottsboro. White women eventually formed the Association of Southern Women for the Prevention of Lynching to disavow any complicity in the carnage and campaign for its curtailment.

Today, black-white couples report a recurring experience while driving their cars of being stopped by police. Their humiliation is not lessened by the sincere alarm of the officers; their cars are pulled over so the cops can check that the black man in a black-white couple is not a rapist or that the black woman in a black-white couple is not a prostitute.

With Asian Americans, another set of stereotypes enhance the beauty of Asian women and the beastliness of Asian men.[57] White interest in Asians can be a fetish (just as its opposite can be), but white male interest in Asian women—"yellow fever"—seems to be more acceptable than perverse. Its distaff counterpart is unusual and kinky. The most famous Asian American male-white female couple of recent years were Vili Fualaau and Mary Kay Letourneau of Washington State, the thirteen-year-old student and his lonely teacher, the daughter of a prominent congressman, who had two children together. After the teacher went to prison, they wrote a book and cooperated in the making of a television movie about their illicit relationship. Her Caucasian husband, cuckolded by not only a child but an Asian, had suspected the affair all along. One of his relatives ultimately turned in Letourneau as a sexual predator.

The onset of geek chic generated by high-tech fortunes and entrepreneurial values prompted *Newsweek* magazine in 2000 to pronounce in a more wholesome mode that Asian American men were "trophy boyfriends" or "the fashion accessory of the moment."[58]

From the Puccini opera *Madame Butterfly* and the James Michener 1954 bestseller *Sayonara* to movies such as *Love Is a Many-Splendored Thing* and *The World of Suzie Wong*, the West knows that Asian women are exotic erotics, alluring coquettes hiding behind their fans. The China Doll or Geisha Girl possesses Oriental sex secrets that make her aggressive in bed, but she also is trained to be obedient around the house. She is available for white men to release from oppressive boredom, eager to be dominated. Japanese author Shoko Ieda borrowed the name of the familiar taxi company, Yellow Cab, to connote an easy woman who "can be ridden anywhere, anytime."[59] Powerful African American men can avail themselves of accommodating Asian and Asian American women as well. In 2001, Archbishop George A. Stallings of Washington, D.C., asked the Reverend Sun Myung Moon to find him a Japanese bride. Reverend Moon provided Stallings, an excommunicated Catholic priest who had started his own breakaway African American congregation, with Okinawa native Sayomi Kamimoto. Stallings angered the African American women in his congregation by remarking on his bride's inclination to "do things with me and for me" and "take care of the kids" and "not party all the time," implicitly in contrast to black female personalities. They were wed in a mass ceremony in New York City, angering other black clergy who did not approve of the bond between Reverend Moon and Archbishop Stallings.[60]

From pulp fiction criminal mastermind Fu Manchu and movies such as *Rising Sun*, we learn that Asian men are sexual predators, asexual eunuchs, or, improbably, somehow both. They all lust after the blonde, blue-eyed cheerleader, whom they would like to steal off into white slavery, but they are impotent in their efforts to do so. They yearn to violate the chastity of white women, who may be duped into welcoming them. French novelist Margeurite Duras immortalized one of the few images of the virile Asian man in *The Lover*, her 1984 Prix Goncourt-winning autobiographical account of an innocent schoolgirl being seduced by a pedophiliac playboy in colonial Indochine.[61] She also wrote the screenplay for *Hiroshima, Mon Amour*, the 1960 movie about the trysts between a French woman and a Japanese man.

When Julie Su, a staff attorney at the Asian Pacific American Legal Center in Los Angeles, won a dramatic modern-day slave labor lawsuit on behalf of Thai workers who were held captive in a California sweatshop throughout the 1990s, movie producers approached her about doing a script. One of them asked her, however, if it would be possible to add an "American" hero. She explained that she was an American. The producer then suggested maybe an "American" love interest for her character. After she raised the racial and gender implications of these suggestions, the producers dropped the project entirely.[62]

The images can be juxtaposed to show how ridiculous they are:

> Consider it this way: what would you say if a blonde homecoming queen fell in love with a short Japanese businessman? He treats her cruelly, then goes home for three years, during which time she prays to his picture and turns down marriage from a young Kennedy. Then, when she learns he has remarried, she kills herself. Now, I believe you would consider this girl to be a deranged idiot, correct? But because it's an Oriental who kills herself for a Westerner—ah!—you find it beautiful.[63]

The passage is from David Henry Hwang's visionary play *M. Butterfly*, based on the true story of Bernard Boursicot, a French diplomat who carried on an affair with Shi Pei Pu, a Chinese opera singer who turned out to be not only a man but also a spy. Shi's deception was so elaborate that s/he even presented Boursicot with a son.

Hwang won the 1988 Tony Award for his queer deconstruction of *Madame Butterfly*. In his retelling, the character Song Liling, based on Shi, is blasé about the success of the ruse. S/he says that when the character Gallimard, based on Boursicot, "finally met his fantasy woman, he wanted more than anything to believe that she was, in fact, a woman." Song is confident s/he knows why s/he was able to fool him, even if his/her Communist handler persecutes him/her for the vice of sodomy. S/he continues, "I am an Oriental. And being an Oriental, I could never be completely a man."

Song was convincing. Audiences always exclaimed their shock when actor B. D. Wong—the actors who have played Song on Broadway and on tour have used only their initials in their stage name to preserve the mystery—disrobed and bared himself.

Despite Hwang's hit, during the next season on the Great White Way the London import *Miss Saigon* was much anticipated.[64] An updated musical rendition of *Madame Butterfly* set on the eve of the fall of Saigon, featuring the gimmick of a full-sized helicopter landing on stage, it was ready to open with the highest ticket prices and most lucrative advance sales ever for a Broadway production. It reiterated the plot that Hwang had turned inside out so effectively. It had, however, an Asian character (later revised to a Eurasian character), the Engineer, as the male lead. A pimp who dealt in the flesh trade of Vietnamese streetwalkers catering to American servicemen, the Engineer sang of transporting himself and his entrepreneurial operations overseas to realize a lurid parody of the American dream.

Hwang and Wong led a protest of the production, especially the casting of a white actor, Jonathan Pryce, as the Engineer. The perception that activists were seeking to remove Pryce from a coveted role because of his race arises only because Asian American actors, even equally well-trained, were never originally considered for the opportunity. Reprising his award-winning run on the West End, Pryce performed in "yellowface," using prosthetics and makeup to give himself an Asian guise. Hwang and Wong initially persuaded the Actors Equity union to block Pryce, who, as a foreigner, needed its permission to perform. Their cause was lost when audiences demanded that the show go on. The producers made a conciliatory promise to hire more Asian American actors, noting that by doing so they were becoming the largest employers of Asian American actors. They were oblivious to the damage caused by perpetuating the stereotype of sexily submissive Asian women and lasciviously devious Asian men. Nor did they seem to realize that using a multitude of Asian American actors in the parts does not improve offensive images.

After the show had ceased to be the most talked-about production in town, an Asian American actor eventually replaced Pryce as the Engineer. Pryce had by then become the pitchman in television advertisements for a line of Japanese luxury automobiles. More daring would have been Asian American actors among the American soldiers.

In part due to these perceptions, Asian American women have surpassed Asian American men professionally only in broadcast journalism. Critics have dubbed this the Connie Chung syndrome after the CBS news anchor, who shared her responsibilities with Dan Rather from 1993 to 1995.[65] Certainly Asian American women are talented and deserve opportunities, but although every major market boasts an Asian American woman reporter, few stations have ever had an Asian American male counterpart. Asian American women in other occupations face racial discrimination and gender discrimination, but their very ubiquity on television suggests another form of racial prejudice fused with gender prejudice. Asian American women are eye candy on the six o'clock news. The white men with whom they are paired are the headliners of the team, possessed of gravitas. Asian American men are ominous rather then enticing. Experienced journalists who are Asian American males, such as Ti-Hua Chang, have been told by white producers that white audiences just don't like looking at them because they resemble the enemy. Chang related that comment in 1987 at the first-ever Asian American Journalists Association convention, held in Los Angeles. Although he has since become an award-winning broadcaster in New York City, he remains a rarity in the business.

Not everyone is troubled that interracial marriages are skewed toward African American men with white women and white men with Asian and Asian American women. Steve Sailer, a writer for the *National Review*, recommends that African American women and Asian American men start dating one another instead of being angry about racialized rejections from African American men and Asian American women, respectively. He believes that interracial marriages prove that human beings inhabit "a landscape rich with fascinating racial patterns" and not the "racial uniformity" of "fashionable philosophies." He puts forward biological reasons that "make blacks more masculine-seeming and Asians more feminine-seeming," an innate diversity that he praises. He points out that Asian American men are shorter than white and black men, and taller is preferable. African American women have shorter hair than white and Asian American women, and longer hair is preferable.[66] Although Sailer is right to call on African American women and Asian American men to reject their own prejudices, which may prevent them from finding each other, he would have all of us capitulate to an array of prejudices as facts of life. Given his views, it would be hypocritical for him to endorse color blindness, but his color consciousness would compel individuals to look away from their own race. In any event, his recommendations are not being followed. Fay Yarbrough, a college student of Korean and African American background, told *Time* magazine in 1997 that even though she speaks Korean and has lived in Korea, "Asian men don't date women who look like me."[67]

Grandchildren Who Look "Like Us"

All of us can improve ourselves. Doing so would require sensitivity along with a willingness to take controversial stands. Opposition to a proposed mixed marriage is none the better if it comes from the Asian side of the aisle than from the white side. City College of New York sociologist Betty Lee Sung, who has studied intermarriage, said that for some Asian immigrant parents, intermarriage is "the worst thing that could happen" and hurts them "terribly."[68] Each set of would-be in-laws may want grandchildren who "look like us," but invocations of filial piety cannot redeem racial exclusion.

In his memoir, *The Accidental Asian: Notes of a Native Speaker* (1998),[69] Eric Liu—a graduate of Harvard law school, a high-level advisor to Bill Clinton, and a television commentator, all before he was thirty-five, the sort of man with whom many parents would want their daughters to stand at the altar—ends with a defense of his own interracial marriage that is not defensive in the least (nor should it be). It is written as much for Asian immigrant parents as for white parents. He felt he had to explain, but his explanation aims to rid itself of that necessity. "It wasn't as if I had a plan," he recounts. "I wasn't trying to prove a point." People of different races marry for the same reasons that "they go to school together, live together, travel together, work together: because they can." Above all, he was adamant that the choice was his insofar as any choice about love is anybody's; it was not cultural factors that made him "fight all [his] life against the stereotype of the emasculated Asian male"; it was not that he "needed to have a white wife to set things right."[70]

Nonetheless, although efforts by communities of color to encourage dating among their own and white efforts to discourage miscegenation may not be different in the abstract, they may be in practice. The situations of people of color and of whites are not identical, so the lament of the former about a sense of betrayal is different than the diatribes of the latter about corrupting the good name of the family. Pan-Africanist Marcus Garvey repudiated intermarriage (and the "near-white" leaders of the NAACP) with the same fervor as the Ku Klux Klan leaders with whom he met to agree that separation would be best for blacks and whites. But his rhetoric need not obscure reality.

As a matter of numbers, even without considering the segregated nature of our society, whites are likely to associate with other whites, and it takes no effort for whites to develop relationships with other whites. As is true for any cognizable minority, if Asian Americans would like to be introduced to other Asian Americans, we must take steps to make it likely. Especially if we live in areas where ours is the only Asian American family, we will be much more likely to meet non-Asian Americans than Asian Americans. Furthermore, we are living within a culture that takes white features as the aesthetic standard and where the people of color who most resemble whites thereby become beautiful people.

We can neutralize such isolation and overwhelming influences only if we consciously organize social functions that are predominantly Asian American. If we do not bother, we are likely to befriend and prefer whites over Asian Americans. Under such conditions, the prevalence of intermarriage with whites may indicate the constraints of minority status.

For a minority group, intermarriage presents an age-old problem. American Jews have given the matter great consideration. To the extent that a minority community such as that of Judaism has maintained its own culture, our aspirations toward diversity leads us into the same quandary. In some sense, a mixed race individual stands for our diversity at the individual level, if he is to be treated as a token. In another sense, the minority community is the essence of American diversity at the group level. The mixed race individual and the minority community potentially destroy each other. The mixed race individual can decimate the minority community because he is likely to be born outside the community, and he, like his minority parent, may be destined to exit the community.[71] The loss of a single child from a faith is more demoralizing for a minority community than it is to the majority. Judaism may be weakened as a faith with half-hearted members. A minority community that was insular and that hindered mixed race marriages, whether or not by design, can prevent the mixed race individual from ever coming into being. The ultra-orthodox are not likely to yield mixed race persons.

The tension between individual and group level diversity is evident within American Judaism, which undergoes occasional paroxysms of identity conflict.[72] Some American Jews complain that they are being embraced out of existence, that they are suffering attrition through affection, that emancipation has been too good. Provocateurs make a macabre comparison, arguing that American assimilation is doing what Hitler's Nazism could not do, annihilating Judaism. Yeshiva University philosopher Sol Roth said in 1980 that intermarriage was "a Holocaust of our own making," and his phrase became popular among the Orthodox as "the Silent Holocaust."[73] Because of past bigotry and their minority status, American Jews already must struggle to keep their faith. Maddeningly, declining discrimination and rising opportunities worsen the predicament. It is not just zealots who may hesitate before blessing an interfaith couple who decorate a Christmas tree and exchange presents. More progressive Jewish movements have tried to attract the interfaith couple and their children. Those who champion intermarriage may want to cheer as that couple forms their own religious sensibilities and stands against the lingering animosity of their extended families, but we also must concede that the couple is leaving behind at least one set of traditions that cannot survive without its communal context.

What may be required is more diversity at both the individual and group levels. If Asian Americans are forced toward neither whites nor Asian Americans, so that some end up with whites and others with Asian Americans, and with the constant renewal of immigrants arriving, both intermarriage and Asian American communities should continue to thrive.

A New Face for Betty Crocker

Mixed race individuals have existed since before the nation was founded, but the mixed race movement is new. In 1896, Homer Plessy challenged state-sanctioned racial segregation before the Supreme Court.[74] When he lost his case, the decision established the legality of the Jim Crow system. What started as open white supremacy remade itself through the falsehood of the phrase "separate but equal" until that fiction could no longer be sustained. The ruling against Plessy is all the more remarkable because Plessy himself was an "octoroon," who had seven great-grandparents who were white and only one great-grandparent who was black. But Plessy would have to ride in the "colored" compartment of the train, and, eventually, his descendants would be relegated to the back of the bus and the decrepit schoolhouse.

Mixed race individuals were formerly shunned. They were especially despised if their mothers were white. Under the rule of white supremacy, mixed race children took the subordinate race as theirs. Thus, a white woman could give birth to a black baby, but a black woman could not give birth to a white baby. The arrival of neither mixed race child would be celebrated. (As African American novelist James Baldwin once said to a white segregationist about these unstated rules, "You're not worried about me marrying *your* daughter." He explained, "You're worried about me marrying your *wife's* daughter. I've been marrying your daughter ever since the days of slavery."[75])

Because they engender confusion about categories, mixed race individuals destabilize a universal order in which all know their place and stay there. White attitudes toward mixed race individuals have oscillated between extremes, with animal husbandry providing the analogy in both cases. Expert dog breeder Leon Fradley, who wrote *The Complete Book of Dog Care*, was also a eugenicist who wrote *The Case for Sterilization* and praised Adolf Hitler for carrying out sterilization on a wide scale.[76] Philanthropist Elroy Stock had his gift to Augsburg College returned in 1988 after he was discovered to be the author of thousands of unsigned letters sent to strangers in a campaign targeting people in mixed marriages and who had adopted children of other races; one of his primary arguments to the strangers whom he terrified was, "A dog breeder would not think of producing mongrel dogs, so why should the human race be mongrel?"[77] The depictions of mixed race individuals have been contradictory, but all contained a monstrous aspect. They were commonly looked upon as the incarnation of crossbred degeneracy, the exemplars of dangerous tendencies toward racial amalgamation. Less often they were viewed as the embodiment of hybrid vigor, experiments in propagating the best of two types. In any event, they were frightening because they could lead to the extinction of the white race, but they also were rumored to be sterile like mules.

Even sympathetic accounts presented them as "the tragic mulatto." Mulatto souls were at war with themselves in a tragedy born of their breeding rather than society. The men were militant, the women ravishing, but both were doomed. Carnegie Institute eugenicist Charles Benedict Davenport wrote during World War I that "one often sees in mulattos an ambition and push combined with intellectual inadequacy which makes the unhappy hybrid dissatisfied with his lot and a nuisance to others."[78] Skidmore College professor Everett Stonequist, a disciple of Robert Park and product of the Chicago school of sociology, detailed what he presumed to be the thoughts of "the mulatto" as "the marginal man": "After all, does not the blood of the white man flow in his veins? Does he not share the higher culture in common with the white American? Is he not legally and morally an American citizen? And yet he finds himself condemned to a lower caste in the American system!"[79] Asian American followers of the same school of thought argued that Asian Americans who felt "marginal" also could blame the "culture conflict" within themselves. Roosevelt University sociologist Rose Hum Lee wrote in 1956 that among Chinese Americans, "when the 'culture gaps' are closed, so to speak, the cultural hybrid no longer poses a problem to himself and others."[80]

White Asian scoundrels have been staples of pulp fiction. Dr. No of the first James Bond movie, for example, torments others because he is tormented himself over his mixed identity. His henchmen are "Chigroes," Chinese Negroes. Even among mixed race Asians, the part-white Asian is the brains of the operations and the part-black Asians are the brawn. As British historian and Bond fan James Chapman comments in his academic study of the most successful film franchise in history, its initial installment "does seem explicitly racist." By saving the "colonial outpost" of Jamaica from the villains who are mostly mixed-race people of color, 007 reaffirms "white, British superiority at a time when, in reality, Britain was beating a hasty retreat from empire" as Jamaica became independent.[81]

The 1973 premier issue of Marvel Comics' *Shang-Chi, Master of Kung Fu*, introduced "the most fantastic, most fascinating hero of this or any other year . . . born to be the world's most fearsome fighter, yet also born to carry the cruelest curse in mankind's memory—because his father is the most infamous villain of all time, Fu Manchu." His mother was Russian. Readers were promised, "You've never seen anything like this before. We guarantee it."[82] As University of Akron law professor Brant Lee—an avid comic book collector who owns all 125 issues of *Shang-Chi*—notes, "the running story line is that Shang-Chi is fighting both his father and Western authorities because no one will believe that the son of Fu Manchu is actually fighting rather than defending his father. They believe it is a trick."[83]

Sociologists who have studied the matter are confident that one-quarter to one-third of African Americans are of mixed heritage, not to mention many whites who have never doubted their own absolute whiteness. Frederick Douglass, Booker T. Washington, W. E. B. DuBois, Philip Randolph, Martin Luther King Jr., Malcolm X, Kwame Anthony Appiah, and Lani Guinier all had white parents or grandparents. Alex Haley's family history, *Roots*, was a best-selling book and one of the first television mini-series. Novelist Ishmael Reed has said of Haley's account of his slave ancestry, "If [he] had traced his father's bloodline, he would have traveled twelve generations back to, not Gambia, but *Ireland*."[84] Gregory Howard Williams, dean of the Ohio State University law school, believed he was white and his father was Italian, until he was ten years old. His book, *Life on the Color Line: The True Story of How a White Boy Discovered He Was Black* (1995),[85] is one of three recent autobiographies penned by law professors about their mixed race status, part of a new genealogical specialty in race relations literature that attests to our sudden willingness to discuss, to borrow the title of journalist Edward Ball's National Book Award-winning work, "slaves in the family."[86]

A century after *Plessy* and in imitation of the 1963 March on Washington of the civil rights movement, the mixed race movement gathered in 1996 at the nation's capital to demand equality. Organized by *Interracial Voice* magazine, the rally attracted only a few hundred people despite the burgeoning numbers of mixed race individuals. According to the 2000 Census, there are about 1,655,830 mixed race individuals who are part Asian. They make up almost one in seven of the total number of Asian Americans and about one quarter of all mixed race persons.

The mixed race movement, with advocacy groups such as Reclassify All Children Equally (RACE), has had a much stronger political effect than the numbers of those directly involved might suggest. Its rhetoric is based more on personal liberty and human dignity than on scientific precision or historical accuracy. Central to its crusade are photographic portraits of mixed race people and personal stories about busybodies asking "How did you come by that name?" demanding to know, "Which are you more of?" or being told by white cousins, "You're so normal," or, for light-skinned individuals "You're no more black than I am." The principal claim of the mixed race movement is that individuals should be allowed to define themselves, either by designating themselves as belonging to as many official classifications as each person wishes or by refusing to participate in the classificatory scheme altogether. It has appropriated the term "hapa haole," a Hawaiian word for "half white," which has had derogatory connotations and made "hapa" more dignified.

The mixed race movement won a partial victory with the 2000 Census. The query to the "Dear Abby" advice columnist, given as the epigraph to this chapter,[87] was answered at last. Mixed race persons were not asked to accept their place in an arbitrary taxonomy by bureaucratic mandate or for a rigid consistency with a black and white worldview. The Office of Management and Budget worked out a compromise. As another indication of the illusory quality of race, the Census has modified racial classifications regularly, never using the same system for any two consecutive decades. This time, although the Census form did not include a new multiracial category, people could check off as many boxes as they wished and they would not be assigned to a race by surveyors. The several boxes produced sixty-three permutations.

Defying expectations, as it grew the mixed race movement found few allies among established community organizations such as the National Association for the Advancement of Colored People (NAACP). The Congressional Black Caucus conducted a forty-two-city tour urging African

Americans to "check the black box."[88] They enlisted Black Entertainment Television host Tavis Smiley, radio personality Tom Joyner, and black preachers to remind African Americans that they were once counted as only three-fifths of a person and suggested that only by checking a single box would they be accorded their full status as a person. The director of the effort, Kristen Haggins, explained, "Checking more than one box on the Census could prove to dilute our count and also dilute our potential for receiving money for our communities and impact how boundaries are drawn politically."[89]

Although the plea of mixed race individuals for self-determination is easy to accept, the NAACP also can hardly be faulted for having subverted the white tenet that any black ancestry turns a person black. The NAACP is turning this tenet into an organizing principle for the benefit not of whites but of blacks. The very people of mixed race backgrounds whom whites refused to accept as their own could be enlisted among blacks, each addition being another voter in democratic elections. But the tactic has an uncertain future, because it depends on people of mixed race backgrounds continuing to lack autonomy.

The unintended consequences of the mixed race movement are already apparent. There are broader and deeper issues at stake. Former House Speaker Newt Gingrich supported the multiracial category, but only because he wanted to purge all racial counting. Conservative leader Ward Connerly has mounted a California initiative campaign in an attempt to accomplish that very goal. Even Connerly has admitted that people laugh at him if he claims to be Irish based on his three-eighths Irish blood, which constitutes the largest proportion of his background. Whatever his ideology, Connerly is perceived of as black.

It would be regrettable if the progressive aims of the mixed race movement led to the elimination of all racial data. Ironically, efforts to determine the effects of racial discrimination must label individuals by race. Racial data can ameliorate the feelings of coercion by allowing self-definition. The opposition to compiling racial data of any type is misguided at best and misleading at worst. Connerly implies that the racial problem is the data rather than the reality and that eradicating information will eradicate problems. Others offer an inflammatory but inappropriate comparison of Census requirements with the Nazi Nuremberg laws or the South African apartheid regime, drawing a parallel that is plausible only if racism and its remedies are rendered equivalent.

Paradoxically, color blindness requires color consciousness. Racial numbers substantiate racial disparities. Without numbers, it becomes impossible to measure if a society has progressed toward integration or to corroborate the existence of racial discrimination. For example, it would become difficult to present objective evidence that African Americans are underrepresented among state government employees compared to their proportions within the general population or compared to the qualified pool of job applicants, or that African Americans and other people of color are the victims of disparities in the criminal justice system that can be explained by nothing other than racial factors. Statistics cannot prevent people from making decisions based on race, but they make it possible to prove that people have done so. Without data, however imperfect, issues of race cannot even be analyzed intelligently. Nobody would suggest a similar strategy in any other context. If the National Weather Service stopped tracking tornadoes, they would not stop touching down.

If nothing else, the mixed race movement has won over companies that would like to please a wide range of potential consumers. In 1996, the General Mills conglomerate unveiled a new face for its Betty Crocker brand name.[90] Using a computer, designers gave the iconic homemaker a painstaking makeover by using the profiles of 75 women of various races to generate a composite.

Tiger, Keanu, and the Passing of Asian Americans

Support for the mixed race movement can be blended with caution about its implications. As compelling as the desire to define oneself may be, the mixed race movement poses the risk of increasing rather than decreasing the invidious forms of color consciousness. A range of color categories expands the reach of prejudice. By a Creole or mestizo sensibility, half-white may come to look better than all-black. Just as African Americans straighten their hair, Asian Americans perm theirs; just as African Americans have cosmetic surgery for a "classical" nose and Asian Americans do so for round eyes, the mixed race movement may promote, even if inadvertently, the practices of whitening.

University of North Carolina professor Jon Michael Spencer, who happens to be mixed race himself, argues against the ambitions of the mixed race movement in his 1997 book, *The New Colored People: The Mixed-Race Movement in America*.[91] Spencer believes that race can bring together oppressed peoples. He notes that historically and even at present, in areas with large numbers of individuals who are both black and white, such as nineteenth-century New Orleans, apartheid South Africa, or contemporary Hawaii and

Brazil, the gradations among hues can be much finer in distinction than black and white but no less odious as discrimination against the darker skinned. None of the places whose populations have multiplied creatively have become racial nirvanas. The various methods of classifying people according to pedigree—for example, by the moons of fingernails—have in common the placement of whites at the top and the ordering of everyone else from swarthy to tawny in descending order. The expressions for every ancestral assortment are no better for being archaic. In addition to the official terms allocating with false precision the admixture of heredity, from "mulatto" to "quadroon" to "octoroon," were slang terms that could be decidedly uncomplimentary, such as "Sambo," which originally meant three-quarters black, and "high yellow" or "yella."

As much as some of us might proclaim enthusiastically, "There is only one race, the human race," few of us live up to the belief through our actions. Among African Americans, the colorism of "lighter is righter" has copied white prejudice.[92] Under slavery, white owners might choose lighter-skinned slaves for household duties instead of the toil of field work, and white men might take the lighter women as mistresses. Light-skinned mulattos, many of whom were freed through the wills of their white fathers, could have contempt for their darker brethren. Some of them even became slaveholders themselves, occupying a middle position between black and white. One of the most scathing attacks on black culture, *The American Negro*, was written a century ago by William Hannibal Thomas about his darker fellows. His vitriolic comments were scarcely distinguishable from those of white supremacists.[93] Even up to the civil rights era, an emphasis by some "blue veined" mixed race individuals on their white derivation can harken back to the "paper bag" test. A few "bougie"—"bougie" is a vernacular derivation of "bourgeois"—social clubs within African American communities, such as the Bon Ton Society of Washington, D.C., were said to employ a "paper bag" test for membership: Successful applicants had to be as light as the pallid brown of a paper bag.

The practice of passing, or "crossing over," bears out the pecking order. People of color who have the requisite skin tone and facial features are able to pretend that they are exclusively white so that they can enjoy the tangible advantages. They may even become white permanently, leaving behind their family, friends, and community, as they follow the excruciating path of forsaking their identity for their livelihood.

Passing usually occurs in only one direction. People who are white rarely try to disguise themselves as people of color and would have few reasons to do so. There are only a handful of people who became what was dubbed a "voluntary Negro": Morehouse College founder William Jefferson White, who had black ancestors and was raised within the black community; turn-of-the-century novelist Charles W. Chesnutt, who used the honorific "FMC," an antebellum term for "free man of color"; Adam Clayton Powell, who was virtually blonde and blue-eyed, but as a minister and Congressman was an advocate of black power; and jazz musician Mezz Mezzrow, nee Milton Mesirow, the Russian Jewish author of an autobiography, *Really the Blues.*[94]

The opposite is much more common. Whites even sued to avoid being classified as black. Until recently, it was considered libel of the worst form to call a white person black. It was an offense because it offended; black was decidedly inferior. In 1982, a well-to-do woman named Susie Guillory Phipps filed suit as an anonymous "Jane Doe" to challenge a Louisiana statute that made anyone with black ancestry automatically black.[95] She wanted to be white, not black or multiracial. Snubbing some of her relatives, she maintained she had had no idea she was even remotely black. Recalling her devastation at the revelation, she said she took sick for three days. "I was brought up white, I married white twice," she said. She lost. But publicity about her case prompted the state to amend its laws so that parents were allowed to list the race of newborns and an individual could adjust her birth certificate upon a showing that she was white by a preponderance of the evidence.

In the nineteenth and early twentieth centuries, the Asian population would have been driven out of existence by a combination of the rules on immigration and those on intermarriage. Immigration laws made it difficult for Asian women to come to the country. The ratio of Chinese men to Chinese women exceeded one hundred to one. Anti-miscegenation laws passed by states prevented Asian men from marrying white women. The Cable Act passed by Congress stripped non-Asian women of their citizenship if they married Asian men. Asian-black children were black. The government argued against granting of birthright citizenship to the few native-born children of Asian parents. If the mutually reinforcing public policies had been fully effective, Asian Americans could not have reproduced themselves.

Nowadays, Asian Americans are melting away voluntarily. Even as Asian Americans are continuing to appear through immigration, we are constantly disappearing through intermarriage. Japanese Americans, who have out-married in the highest proportions, are joined by very few new arrivals from Japan. The Yasui family of Hood River, Oregon, is typical. The subject of Lauren Kessler's *Stubborn Twig: Three Generations in the Life of a Japanese-American Family,*[96] only one of eighteen third-generation cousins of the clan married another Japanese American (and then only in a second marriage). As go the Yasuis's children, so go Japanese Americans. They are likely to vanish as a distinctive ethnic group within another generation unless large numbers of mixed race individuals in the fourth and fifth generations choose an Asian American identity rather than a white identity. Some have said that Japanese American integration was hastened by the internment, but other Asian American ethnic groups also are intermarrying at high rates.

So for Asian Americans, passing presents a dilemma. Few are as unique as sculptor Isamu Noguchi, whose father was Yone Noguchi, a Japanese (not Japanese American) poet, and whose mother was Leonie Gilmour, a white American. Noguchi grew up in Japan and the United States; lived in Paris, where he was an apprentice to sculptor Constantin Brancusi; worked with choreographer Martha Graham while also designing the lamps for which he is best known; and became an internationally renowned artist representing the United States at the Venice Biennial and being recognized as a national treasure by Japan. Many Asian Americans are forced toward whiteness or blackness as two extremes along a spectrum with a preferred pole. Tiger Woods and Keanu Reeves show the effects of such dispersion.

Golf sensation Tiger Woods has become a reluctant poster child for the mixed race movement. (The unsuccessful legislation that would have required the Census to include a multiracial category was dubbed the "Tiger Woods bill.") As an athlete who has revitalized his sport as no other single competitor has ever done for any game, Woods can hardly be considered average in any terms. Just as it is inappropriate to make an individual the representative of everyone else of his specific racial background, it is unseemly to turn a single person into a symbol for everyone of mixed race background. He may be the product of the fusion of diverse cultures, but it would be absurd to give him the mixed man's burden of leading us to racial reconciliation.

Indeed, Woods reveals the contradictions of the mixed race movement. Even for international celebrities whose lives are known in every detail by total strangers, private and public racial identities do not align neatly.

In 1997, the twenty-one year-old Woods became the youngest player ever to win the Masters Tournament as he began his ascent toward legendary status. Having left Stanford University as the top-rated amateur golfer, he defeated the professional field with a seemingly invincible superiority. Again and again, he defeated all comers while drawing a swelling crowd of spectators, many of whom would not have idolized Arnold Palmer or Jack Nicklaus as they putted on the links of exclusive country clubs. Shoal Creek in Birmingham, Alabama, was excluding blacks as late as 1990. Its rules prompted the PGA to adopt an anti-discrimination policy. In response, some clubs decided to give up their affiliation with the PGA.

Woods was different from his seniors. Poised and telegenic, he thrilled spectators by coming back to win even if he had had a poor start well over par. He graded himself after he played his rounds, to the irritation of his peers. His "C" game beat everybody else's "A" game. He was extraordinary even when he wasn't bothering to try too much. His most spectacular television advertisement used footage that was filmed accidentally. Before he was about to shoot the scripted material, he was goofing off by bouncing a ball on his club head two dozen times in a row without dropping it, before hitting it into the air and sending it flying several hundred yards.

Immediately, the story of his life introduced his fans to the mixed race movement. The son of Earl Woods, an African American Green Beret lieutenant colonel, and Kultida Punsawad, a well-to-do Thai secretary who was raised as a devout Buddhist near the bridge on the River Kwai (as in the movie of that title), Eldrick Woods was nicknamed Tiger in honor of Phong Nguyen, a Vietnamese officer who had saved his father's life more than once.

Woods was imitating his father's golf swing before he was a year old. By the time he was three, he had won against a club professional and appeared on television with Bob Hope. He shot his first hole in one when he was six. Because his mother wanted him to develop academically as well, she allowed him to play golf only if he had finished his homework.

From time to time, Woods has returned to his mother's homeland as a conquering hero. There he is said to be Asian "from the eyes up." He has even led a Thai national golf team in Asian regional contests. He also believes in most of the principles of Buddhism. But Woods is not simply African American some of the time and Asian American the rest of the time. His background is more complicated, and societal reactions to it more problematic, than that.

Appearing on Oprah Winfrey's television program just after his record victory at the Masters, Woods talked about his lineage at length. He told a nationwide viewership that he had invented a term for himself, "Cablinasian," to unify verbally his Caucasian, Black, Indian, and Asian heritage. To be precise, if it is possible to be precise in these matters, his father is half black, one-quarter Native American, and one-quarter Chinese; his mother is half Thai, one-quarter Dutch, and one-quarter Chinese. Woods said, "I just am who I am." Asked whether it bothered him to be labeled as an African American, he said, "It does." He checked off the official boxes on forms for both African American and Asian American, because, "Those are the two I was raised under, and the only two I know."

Winfrey christened him "America's son." But the episode proved controversial. As soon as Tiger became a precious commodity, Asian Americans and African Americans began an unbecoming dispute over who would claim him as one of their own. Asian Americans noted that technically, as half Thai and one-quarter Chinese, Woods was three-quarters Asian, and that was the largest portion of his makeup. African Americans were dismayed that someone who paid homage to black golfers of the past and alluded to continuing racial segregation seemed to be disowning his blackness when presented with the chance and selecting a paler self.

The tension between Asian Americans and African Americans was made superfluous, even if it was not quite resolved, thanks to the intervention of a white observer. Notwithstanding the intense publicity over Woods's compound bloodlines, in most people's eyes, Woods turned out to be effectively black.

The pivotal incident came when Fuzzy Zoeller, a veteran of the PGA tour who happens to be white, made remarks about Woods to a television crew. Referring to the winner's prerogative of setting the dinner menu for the festivities at the Masters, Zoeller referred to Woods's race in a nonchalant remark. Calling Woods "that little boy," Zoeller said he should be told not to serve fried chicken or collard greens "or whatever it is they serve."[97] Even aside from the use of "that little boy," Zoeller was undoubtedly talking about race by referring to stereotypical Southern black cuisine.

Released by his major sponsor, K-Mart, as a spokesperson, Zoeller then delivered a tearful explanation about his penchant for being "a jokester"; he added, "I just didn't deliver the line well."[98] He even withdrew temporarily from the professional tour.

Woods accepted Zoeller's apology. But giving Zoeller the benefit of the doubt and treating him as a decent man acting in good faith only makes the mistake of his perception worse. It is as if he cannot help himself: When he looks at Woods he sees race; he sees blackness. He is cued to talk about soul food. He does not bring up curry chicken or lemongrass soup. That would have been equally (in)apt.

Woods may be one of the most well-known people on the face of the earth. He may even be renowned for his mixed race status and acquainted personally with the observer who is engrossed with race. Whatever Woods declared for himself and however Asian Americans and African Americans calculated their fractions, the real test of his race is how he is treated by strangers on the street who don't recognize his celebrity status. Woods himself has said, "I am 90 percent Oriental, more Thai than anything." But he also has said that while he was in college, "What I realized is that even though I'm mathematically Asian—if anything—if you have one drop of black blood in the United States, you're black."[99]

The one drop rule to which Woods referred was a legal rule. On the theory that a single drop of black blood would contaminate white virtue, any person whose ancestry could be traced back to a black person was deemed to be black no matter how distant the relationship. The one drop rule, which has no basis in biology, has been abolished legally but not culturally. Somebody who is like Woods but who is not instantly identifiable from shoe advertisements is for practical purposes black. In a recent anthology of essays on being "half and half," one writer said of Woods, "'When the black truck comes around, they're going to haul his ass on it.'"[100]

Movie actor Keanu Reeves provides a contrasting example. He played the epitome of a clueless Californian in the teen favorite *Bill and Ted's Excellent Adventure*. He has been the Buddha and the son of the Devil in other films. He earned raves for his Hamlet on stage and he turned in an admirable Don Juan in Kenneth Branagh's cinematic version of Shakespeare's *Much Ado About Nothing* (with Denzel Washington as his better brother). He emerged as an action superstar with the thriller *Speed*, one of the highest-grossing movies of the 1990s.

Billed by *Vanity Fair* as "Hollywood's hottest heartthrob," Reeves was born in 1964 in Beirut. His father was a wealthy geologist of Hawaiian-Chinese extraction. His mother was a British showgirl who became a costume designer for rock musicians. Readers of sensational accounts of his life know that his father was estranged from the family and imprisoned for drug possession and that his mother raised him in Toronto with a series of stepfathers. His first name is based on a Hawaiian term for the wind over the mountains. He was a high school hockey player of some talent. A serious motorcyclist, he rides a vintage Norton Commando even after two accidents. He has opted to tour with his band, Dogstar, in obscure venues instead of taking on lucrative but unsatisfying acting roles.

Reeves is a closeted Asian American. He has become a Caucasian Asian. To most moviegoers, he is an average white guy. He is an archetypal dude. He can easily be accepted as white. There is no reason for him to publicize that he is anything else. Only a fanatical devotee of tabloid news would even know his paternity. Neither his facial features nor his family name are obviously Asian. His father, however, can be readily identified as Asian from the few published photographs. He peers out from the shadows as an enigmatic figure.

There would be no reason other than excessive ethnic pride for Reeves to out himself as Asian. But the ease with which he has adopted whiteness is fascinating. To the extent that he has chosen to be white and has consciously selected his whiteness, he confirms that whiteness is beneficial. Other than Reeves, whose martial arts exploits were enhanced by "bullet time" special effects in the science fiction blockbuster *The Matrix*, Asian men are leading men and heroes only in the kung fu chop socky genre; unless Reeves is regarded as Asian American, the highest-grossing movie ever made without a white male lead is the Jackie Chan–Chris Tucker buddy flick *Rush Hour*. To the extent that Reeves has not selected whiteness but has stumbled into it, he indicates how whiteness is the default mode. Unless he deviates blatantly from the norm, he is assumed to be white.

Even though Reeves is essentially white, the uniformly negative commentary of film critics on his work unwittingly echoes the classic line about Asians. To many reviewers, ironically, he is inscrutable. Reeves himself once said about his skills as thespian, "I don't know anything, man."

It should give us pause that Woods is black and Reeves is white and neither is Asian. They are not even Eurasian or Amerasian. The terms have become antiquated exactly as they were on the cusp of becoming commonly applicable.

In the Mississippi Delta, where a few thousand Chinese laborers were brought during Reconstruction, many of their descendants intermarried long ago.[101] Families with Chinese roots came to have both white branches and black branches. With successive intermarriage, the Chinese roots have been forgotten, and the white branches and the black branches have grown apart. The same has happened to the little-known community of Punjabi Mexican Americans in California.[102]

Mixed race individuals do not leave race behind. A study conducted using 1980 Census data showed wide divergences in the racial identity of mixed race children. Among children with white mothers, only 35 percent of those with Chinese fathers were identified by their parents as white, but 74 percent of those with Asian Indian fathers were; conversely, among children with white fathers, about 62 percent of those with Chinese mothers were identified by their parents as white but 93 percent of those with Asian Indian mothers were.

Although the research on these topics is just beginning, the only summary that can be made thus far is that matters seem to be complicated and dynamic. The point should not be some sort of futile effort to make Woods and Reeves, along with the groups in Mississippi and California, into Asians through the dubious transmogrification of racial alchemy. In truth, they are no more Asian than they are black or white. They cannot be reduced to race with any coherence. Darby Li Po Price, a comedian with a doctorate in ethnic studies, tells the following opening joke: "I am of Chinese descent from my mother, and Scots-Irish, Welsh, and Cherokee descent from my father, so in the United States that means I'm Latino."[103] Yet as mixed race people take on their own identities, their cumulative choices create a new identity, such as Japanese, white, and Jewish combined.

As mixed race status becomes hip, however, individuals start to make superficial claims to be part this or part that, without any actual appreciation of the minority culture or acceptance of the consequences of affinity with it. The Native American population is growing much faster than its birthrate (and, needless to say, it has no immigration), thanks to people who are outsiders to Indian culture suddenly discovering their Indianness. When Disney released its animated movie *Pocahontas,* it inspired many such superficial Indians to fantasize about identity.[104]

Many Native Americans have contempt for ersatz Native Americans who are not enrolled in a tribe who casually say that they had a great-grandparent who was an Indian brave or an Indian maiden, some of whom seem to be doing nothing more than trolling for government benefits or speculating that they can cash in on the exaggerated riches of casino gambling. Most Native Americans grant that it is possible to be a bona fide Indian without being a pureblood, but they have had more than enough experience, largely catastrophic, with outsiders defining who is an Indian and what it means to be an Indian.[105]

The wannabees who announce that they are Native Americans but who have no actual experience as a Native American have not grappled with the alcoholism, poverty, and suicide of reservations.[106] They know nothing of the difficulty of enforcing treaty rights or the humiliation of seeing skeletons of their ancestors displayed in museums and caricatures of themselves as sports mascots. (They are not like the "black Seminoles," African Americans who more than a century ago took on the customs of neighboring Native Americans, part of the largely neglected integration of African Americans and Native Americans.)

Among Asian immigrants, the poignant case of children fathered by U.S. military personnel in Vietnam shows how the standing of mixed race individuals depends on the situation.[107] From their birth, they were snubbed as *bui doi,* the dust of life. Their mothers were considered prostitutes. With passage of the Homecoming Act by Congress in 1987, allowing them and their families to come here, they became *con van*, golden children. They could be the ticket to the United States for the relatives who rushed to claim them.

Our expectations of the mixed race movement should not be naïve. The mixed race movement can conceal a pessimistic message, namely that American society is most likely to flourish if it is monoracial rather than if it is multiracial. Few of its current adherents state their belief this way, but earlier enthusiasts of intermarriage candidly doubted that any culture could be sustained with numerous races. For them, intermarriage was the only hope and not the best hope. Cultural critic (then on the left, now on the right) Norman Podhoretz wrote that the "Negro problem" would not be solved unless we "let the brutal word come out—miscegenation."[108] Podhoretz would have been mortified if "a daughter of mine" were " 'to marry one'," and he "would rail and rave and rant and tear my hair." However, he would hope to "have the courage to curse myself for raving and ranting, and to give her my blessing."[109] Political philosopher Hannah Arendt once made the same recommendation. Even though Arendt's argument was implicit rather than explicit, according to Harvard professor Werner Sollors, "she had a hard time getting her views published and generated a venomous debate." Even *Dissent* magazine, where the essay originally appeared, published a disclaimer and two separate rebuttals.[110] Intermarriage was the means of achieving a single racial identity. Native Americans, for example, could be rescued only if their cultures were destroyed and they were absorbed into white society. The Reverend Jedidiah Morse, an orthodox Calvinist, could try to save Indian souls by ensuring that they become "literally of one blood with us."[111]

The mixed race movement could bring about an unfortunate rediscovery: The most bitter enemies are your kin. Cousins can hate one another with an intensity not summoned against the unfamiliar. The great tragedies are family tragedies. Blood is the proper metaphor for race, even if it does not comport with biological fact.[112] Whites and blacks of the old South, masters and slaves, were often ill-fated relations. The world has witnessed, in the vengeful repetitiveness of divisive ethnic conflicts that emerge repeatedly, that people who know history can be damned to repeat it, as groups who seem to be the same to outsiders become all the more fierce for their similarity in their avowal that they are special and each is better than the other. It was their fellow Greeks, the Spartans, and not their foreign enemies, the Persians, who demolished the Athenian democracy; the hubris of the Athenians themselves hastened their downfall in the Peloponnesian War. Veteran political consultant Kevin Phillips argued in *The Cousin's Wars: Religion, Politics, and the Triumph of Anglo-America* that it was fratricide of the English Civil War, the

American Revolution and the Civil War, that formed our national spirit.[113] The latest research has turned up intriguing hints that the Japanese and the Korean royal families may once have been the same; their enmity becomes a feud like that of the British and the French.[114]

Our familiarity with other races also should not lead us to premature self-congratulation.[115] The clichéd rejoinder "many of my friends are black" is not persuasive, because that very friendship may mislead a person into treating those who are close to them as exceptions who prove the rules of race. Marrying someone of a different race provides no immunity from prejudice, as exposed by the ongoing case involving serial rapes of Asian American women in the Chicago area, the suspect in which was arrested in the Philippines when he visited his Filipina wife. Dating someone of a different race does not even grant a license to take liberties, as actor Ted Danson found out when he was dating comedian Whoopi Goldberg and he performed an embarrassing skit in blackface at the 1993 Friars Club roast in her honor. Having children who were of mixed racial background did not much move most of the white masters of slaves, other than to perform the gesture of manumitting them in a will.

At its best, the mixed race movement makes us think. Race may be fictional, but racism is real.[116] Although most of us may be reluctant to blame people who yearn for the benefits of passing, seeking privileges that many whites are not even aware of, we also may be hesitant to receive them as people of color, if they can conceal their identities when it is convenient.

The mixed race movement and passing give to some individuals who were assumed to be members of a stigmatized group the wherewithal to disassociate themselves from the group. It would be better if society recognized their right to belong to the groups of their choosing rather than coercing them into groups with whom they may have nothing in common. But it would be best if we stopped subjugating whole groups to the point where those who can would rather leave them. We will know we have achieved genuine racial equality when people who could claim to be white if they wanted to would rather stand up to say that they are proud to be black and they will lead lives within black communities. If everyone makes the same choice—white—then it is clear that there is no meaningful choice.

Perhaps the mixed race movement can be of lasting importance not by elevating some individuals out of the darker boxes but by persuading us that racial classifications in general are pernicious. If intermarriage and the mixed race movement are to live up to the optimistic claims that they are the future of race relations, they must hold out a greater promise than that some individuals can make a good match and a few individuals are able by themselves to ascend to whiteness. We will have accepted the mixed race movement as another form of our manifest diversity only when we know in our bones that "they" are "us."

In the final chapter, I discuss coalitions. Intermarriage and the mixed race movement can form the nucleus of coalitions, enabling all of us to transcend artificial categories altogether. Only through coalitions can we do the work of a diverse democracy, but the best coalitions are more fragile than facile.

The Power of Coalitions

Why I Teach at Howard

A lawyer's either a social engineer or . . . a parasite on
society. . . . A social engineer [is] a highly skilled, percep-
tive, sensitive lawyer who [understands] the Constitution of
the United States and how to explore its uses in the solving of problems of local communities and in bettering
conditions of the underprivileged citizens.

—CHARLES HAMILTON HOUSTON,
FORMER DEAN, HOWARD UNIVERSITY LAW SCHOOL

Leaving China

My parents were once Chinese. My parents came here from China and Taiwan. Both my father and my mother had been born on the mainland, in
small villages within the same province as the commercial metropolis of
Shanghai. Their families fled the advance of the Communists as part of the
exodus that accompanied the retreat of the Nationalists. The Communists
were familiar to Americans as Mao Ze Dong of his little red book and gar-
ish caricatures by pop artist Andy Warhol; the Nationalists through the personalities of Generalissimo and Madame Chiang Kia-Shek in regal formal
wear visiting the United States to solicit its military support.

So my parents grew up in what was then called "Formosa"—meaning "beautiful island"—in its time as a Dutch colony. But they dreamed about leaving for the United States, "mei guo" or "beautiful country" in Mandarin Chinese. Formosa belonged to the Third World. It had been until recently a Japanese colony. It possessed few natural resources. Its only strategic advantage was its dangerous proximity to a giant nation that regarded it as a renegade province. The United States was renowned. It was rich, powerful, and glamorous. Anyone who lived overseas in the immediate aftermath of World War II, when the United States had vanquished the Axis and saved both Europe and Asia, knew from Hollywood movies or heard through friends of friends of friends with first-hand knowledge that everything good in life could be found across the ocean and that prosperity was infinite.

My parents were lucky. They had excelled in school. They secured sought-after invitations to continue their education in the United States in the late 1950s. My father moved to Iowa City, Iowa, following his older brother in studying at the University of Iowa, home of the "fighting Hawkeyes." In the snowy plains of the bucolic Midwest, he rented a house with a half-dozen other male students. They were a network of Chinese from Taiwan; all of them had attended the same high school or college or had a brother or a sister who had done so. They crowded together in their living quarters by choice and circumstance. They could not have afforded anything better, and they would have had some difficulty finding another landlord who would open doors to them even if they'd had the money to spend on the luxury of space. They had no refrigerator, so they were able to buy perishable foods only when it was cold and they were able to store the items outside.

My mother moved to Cleveland, Ohio, an only child who had already earned a college degree in English literature and then taught high school. She attended what was then Western Reserve University, studying library science as did so many other Chinese women. She met my father there, after he started research toward his doctorate in engineering at the neighboring Case Institute of Technology.

My parents arrived in the United States just as the celebration of the post-World War II era was ending and the uneasiness of the Cold War was beginning, before the civil rights movement had developed momentum. The economy was still expanding, but the cultural confusions of the 1960s lay just ahead.

They were sure of their identity. They would have had to be obstinate to harbor any doubts. They would not have cared about postmodern deconstructions of identity or the academic argot of referents, signifiers, tropes, racial hegemony, or bourgeoisie nationalism that has engulfed identity. The matter was straightforward. They were Chinese through and through; their Chineseness was their race, their ethnicity, their nationality, their culture, and their language. They knew who they were. Others recognized them just as easily. There was no being bashful about race. To themselves, they were Chinese people, as my mother would have told anyone who asked—and many often did ask. To others, they were Orientals, as my father's collegiate intramural basketball team was known, its victories announced in the collegiate newspaper under the headline "Orientals Win Another."

White people referred to my parents by racial epithets now and again. They were not initially familiar with the terms. They eventually inferred from the tone, the context, and other actions that they were being condescended to as inferior. They always could take pride, nonetheless, that they were descended from ancestors whose revered traditions dated back far longer than the memories of the foreigners among whom they found themselves. Although they were a conspicuous minority who were reviled here, they were the dominant majority back home where their hearts remained and their hearths lay. What they were not allowed to forget, they would remember with their preferred interpretation. They could take solace in the careers that they could conceive for themselves. With their confidence not yet tried, they would be able to work harder and thus would be compensated for their talent and their effort, enjoying what revenge there is in success. They possessed the necessary daring of the immigrant.

They did not believe that they had common cause with other Asian immigrants, much less other people of color. There was no pan-Asian identity in Asia, other than the evils springing from imperial ambitions and conquests and the resulting resentments and revolts. They did not even liken themselves to other Chinese immigrants, such as the Chinese Americans who washed dishes at the restaurants and toiled in the sweatshops, remaining behind in the lurid tourist traps that ethnic ghettos had become as the downtown around them decayed. After all, my parents were Mandarin-speaking, and although they were not much more than peasant stock, they held themselves above the Cantonese, Fujian, and Toisan whose grandparents had come before them. They had few friends who were not also like them, Chinese and from Taiwan.

The few Japanese Americans they encountered they would not have been fond of because of the unhappy relationship of Japan and China. Other Asian foreigners—a Korean or an Indian—were too uncommon to spend much time thinking about.

As for blacks, it was readily apparent that they were pariahs who could not command a status even as good as the Asian foreigners in a white American society, no matter that their folk had arrived long ago. Asian immigrants, whatever their own feelings before arriving in America, learned that blacks bore the ignominy of their skin color. They were blacks, not necessarily Americans, and even if they were Americans they could vie with aliens to be the least liked.

My parents were conscious of racial issues beyond their own ethnic group. They knew that Americans regarded them as looking like any other Chinese, Japanese, or Koreans. They were more benevolent than malevolent toward African Americans. But because they could barely cope with the pervasive bias against them, they were left empathetic but paralyzed as to other issues and other peoples. They were not active in assisting other Asian Americans or African Americans, but neither was anyone else making an effort to reach out to them.

Over time, my parents decided to stay. Together, they started to put down roots in this country. With children and jobs, then a house and friends, they were settling into a different identity that was as unusual to them as the course was familiar to an immigrant nation. My father was an engineer; my mother was a librarian, later a full-time housewife and mother, and after that, a real estate agent. We moved around, never quite satisfied with the community. My parents were able to budget every penny and take out mortgages that required that they continue to skimp. My father drove a used economy car lacking air conditioning and riddled with rust holes that he would repair painstakingly with Bondo putty, and he would spend weekends doing all the yardwork around the house. My mother clipped coupons and diluted the orange juice from concentrate with extra water so it would last longer, and she was constantly sewing clothes for our wardrobes from McCall's patterns to accompany the hand-me-downs from our cousins. My parents eventually were able to buy a ranch house with a walkout basement on country property past the end of the subdivision tracts, far enough away from city lights that the paved roads stopped. The fields, which were still tall with corn in the summer, became frozen expanses in the winter. We were on a rural route for mail delivery, and teenaged drivers in fact did speed by in cars knocking down mailboxes and trailing a cloud of dust. My parents never turned on the air conditioning in the summer, and they dialed the thermostat down to 58 degrees in the winter (we wore plenty of layers).

So my parents became Chinese Americans. They naturalized and were sworn into a new status as U.S. citizens. Their hyphenated condition said as much to themselves as to others that they were both Chinese and American, blending their heritage with their own initiative. Like Neil Armstrong's declaration as he touched down on the moon, it was one small step for man and a giant leap for mankind (albeit with man and mankind amended to human and humanity).

Our lives were segregated, however, belying the duality of the label. My parents worked with whites, and my brothers and I attended school with whites. We had almost no day-to-day interaction with other Asian Americans, and we certainly had no contact with African Americans. We lived among whites, shopping, playing, and doing everything else whites did, mimicking them as we would if we had to figure out which fork to pick up at a fancy dinner and wanted to follow their lead. But we were rarely invited into the homes of whites, and my parents never asked a white adult into our home unless it was a teacher. When my friends came over, my parents were awkward even as they tried to take an interest in meeting their neighbors' children. Even if we were close, my friends' parents did not become my parents' friends.

My parents formed their own social circle instead. Their friends would come over for weekend dinner parties, potluck meals that had Chinese dishes for the adults and American options for the children. The guest list consisted of other Chinese Americans like my parents, mostly couples with husbands who worked in technical occupations with one of the domestic automobile manufacturers, wives who stayed at home, and children who were perpetual contestants in a parental competition for bragging rights. Their friends extended slightly over time, as they made new acquaintances from the Saturday morning Chinese school where they'd enrolled us, to include Chinese Americans from other ethnic, linguistic, religious, class, professional, and political backgrounds. There were Chinese immigrants who were Cantonese-speaking, Catholic, more or less well-to-do, employed in non-engineering occupations, and contentious on homeland matters. There were Chinese immigrants from other countries; it was not unheard of for Chinese to come to the United States from Germany or the Philippines.

Yet my parents were becoming less Chinese. They may have worried about their children becoming too American, but the hazards of assimilation were as great for them as the prospect was inescapable for us. They were avid readers of Chinese newspapers published in the United States. My uncle and aunt rolled up the thin back issues into a self-contained tube and sent them on a regular basis. They subscribed to glossy magazines from Taiwan. We always had a stack between the easy chairs in the family room, next to a canister of whole peanuts and a bag of roasted watermelon seeds. But we all spent more time listening to baseball on the radio, becoming fans of Ernie Harwell calling the Detroit Tigers' games especially in rookie pitcher Mark "The Bird" Fydrich's one and only All-Star season during the Bicentennial, and watching American television sitcoms, such as the top-rated *Happy Days* with the Fonz. We followed the trends as best as we could. In the 1970s, we bought an eight-track cassette player, a CB radio, and polyester jogging suits. While their children were growing up, my parents lacked the funds to travel to Taiwan more than once a decade, and they did not even place international phone calls unless there was a death in the family. With their modest efforts, even though they wrote letters regularly to my grandparents in well-practiced Chinese calligraphy, they were losing touch with an Asia that they had left as young adults, an Asia that itself was modernizing.

In the remainder of this chapter, I discuss the transitions of my own family and the course of my career. I consider in sequence how I became an Asian American and a civil rights activist, while realizing that in some sense I remain very much an Asian as well. I close with examples of people, institutions, and efforts who have undertaken the true work of coalition-building.

Coming to Asian America

My brothers and I became Asian Americans. As much as our parents struggled to become Chinese Americans and to form Chinese American associations, we were relieved to declare ourselves to be Asian Americans and join Asian American organizations. We were attempting with the proclamation to wrest control for ourselves and away from others, so that we could avoid the imposition of a stereotype and define ourselves. The quaint term that was used during our childhood, "Oriental," is more appropriate for rugs than for people. As Columbia University professor Edward Said, a Palestinian exile, has argued influentially, "Oriental" conjures up the exotic, the "Other."[1] In 2001, under the leadership of Governor Gary Locke, the first Chinese American to be elected as a state executive in the continental United States, the Washington legislature decided to replace the word "Oriental" throughout its laws.

Asian Americans are made, not born. Lyric poet Rainer Maria Rilke once wrote, "We are born, so to speak, provisionally, it doesn't matter where; it is only gradually that we compose, within ourselves, our true place of origin, so that we may be born there retrospectively."[2] Asian Americans invent ourselves collectively and individually in the United States; our true place of ori-

gin nowhere to be found on a map. Our race, like anybody else's, is an accident of birth. We are threatened, unlike most whites, by efforts to use our race
against us. Alone among whites, an Asian American is on the verge of being
a freak. But instead of searching for an escape from our own race, rejecting
it as an irritating irrelevance or a distracting digression, we can find an affirmative adaptation in Asian American-ness, allowing us to accept ourselves.
We always knew we were something different, but we were not able to say
for ourselves what that something was in positive language until we heard of
"Asian Americans." With that idea, we make ourselves whole.

Like many Asian Americans, I had to learn what it meant to be Asian
American. Ka Ying Yang, the director of the Southeast Asian Resource Action
Center in Washington, D.C., recalled in an interview as vividly as if it were
yesterday being punched and kicked, having her hair pulled, even being spat
upon, not to mention being taunted by slurs, on an almost daily basis in
school after being rescued as a refugee with the other Hmong who had
fought at exorbitant cost to themselves on behalf of the United States in the
covert war in Southeast Asia. She said, "I wondered what was wrong with
me." It was not until she was in college, taking courses on Asian Americans,
that she saw she had done nothing wrong to bring upon herself such tor-
ment; the courses made it possible for her to respond to the problem. "I
learned," she said, "that there was something called 'racism.'"[3]

Most Americans are ignorant of the heroic role of the Hmong, recruited
to fight for the United States in Southeast Asia in the late 1960s and early
1970s. As essayist Anne Fadiman recounts, the Hmong pilots were treated differently than American flyers in every respect. Their pay was lower; their
rations worse. The double standards were fatal: The Hmong veterans were
regarded as more expendable than the American boys. They were sent on
missions until they died ("fly till you die" was the motto); they had no rest
and recreation and no end to their mission other than being shot down.[4]

When University of Rochester historian Christopher Lasch published his
Culture of Narcissism: American Life in an Age of Diminishing Expectations,[5]
decrying the American malaise, I was coming to my knowledge as an Asian
American through books, but it was through self-study, because all of my
teachers, even in quality public schools, had neglected to mention any facet
of Asian American experiences. When I started to come across Asian Americans in college, I was shocked by what had been omitted or distorted. It was
as if all of our accomplishments were trivial, as if we had participated in no
significant events. I had read little about, much less by, Asian Americans, not
even episodes that have a proper place in any thorough survey of American

history or contemporary social science, not even in gifted and talented programs that had more than one Asian American student enrolled. There was nothing about the Chinese Exclusion Act, which initiated immigration regulation; the Japanese American internment, which set the constitutional standards for government references to race; the 1965 Immigration Reform Act, which has remade the population; the Korean War and its effects on migration; the Vietnam War and the refugees it produced; or the Asian American small businesses, predominantly Korean-owned, in inner cities.

Asian Americans and other Americans alike were shown an Asia that was a fantasy, in mystical parables set in the Far East of Cathay and Nippon. Hans Christian Andersen's tale "The Nightingale" is a typical children's story. The extraordinary singing bird in the Chinese Emperor's palace is replaced by a mechanical toy sent by the Japanese Emperor. It returns when the ruler is on his deathbed. It releases him from mortality with its wondrous character. The movie *Chinatown*, an updated film noir starring Jack Nicholson, Faye Dunaway, and John Houston, transfers the same mysteries to Los Angeles. The Asian Americans are bit players in the background, more plot devices and scenery than characters. They have nothing to do with the machinations at the core of the interlocking detective story and romance involving the theft of precious water from the Owens Valley and the relationship between Faye Dunaway and her sister/daughter. Yet their home is the metaphor that gives everything meaning, because anything can happen there.

The literature that features Asians—think of the daughter of missionaries, Pearl S. Buck, writing on China, or Nazi SS explorer Heinrich Harrar on Tibet—is not meant for Asian eyes. Neither P. J. O'Rourke nor Bill Barich would likely have offered their anti-Asian work to periodicals where they knew Asian Americans were in charge.

Satirist J. O'Rourke's scurrilous 1988 "Seoul Brothers" article for *Rolling Stone* is a prime example. He claims that looking over a multitude of Koreans with their "pie-plate" faces made him realize "oh, no, they really *do* all look alike." He describes their cuisine as strong enough that with one meal "you could have used your breath to clean your oven"; and he ridicules them as "a hive of worker bees" and "a whole nation of people who did their homework on Friday night."[6] Even though the magazine, whose long-time editor had been Ben Fong-Torres, an Asian American (whose father added the "Torres" surname to enter America disguised as a Filipino), issued an apology, O'Rourke was unrepentant. He later told an interviewer, "I know people feel that way, that I'm making fun of funny looking foreigners. What can I say. It's a comic technique that's been used from time immemorial. I do mind being called racist, but I don't mind being called xenophobic. Everyone's scared of strangers. And I suppose I'm a culturalist of some kind. Everybody thinks his own culture is best."[7] Thus, Asians are "funny looking foreigners" to O'Rourke. Furthermore, if Asians are "funny looking foreigners," Asian Americans probably are "funny looking Americans" at best and "funny looking foreigners" at worst, because there is not much of a distinction apparent to O'Rourke. Asians may be foreigners to Asian Americans as well, but they are not "funny looking foreigners." And although we all may be scared of strangers and think our own culture is best, Asian Americans are less likely to be scared of Asians or to belittle their culture. By the logic of O'Rourke's distinction between racism and xenophobia, there can be no Asian Americans; if by speaking about the "pie-plate faces" that all look alike, he is not racist but only xenophobic, then none of those faces can belong to Americans and all of them must be aliens. In defending himself as he did, he only worsened his position.

Author Bill Barich was not writing for the Hmong when he penned an essay about them (confusing them, incidentally, with Cambodians) that caused a furor when it was reprinted in the magazine of the California State Automobile Association.[8] The 2.5 million subscribers to *Motorland* were told in winter 1996 that the Hmong "grew backyard poppies for personal-use opium and dealt in child brides." According to Barich, they "wore clothes as though they'd been set free on a shopping spree at K-Mart." "Evidence" of the bad driving of the Hmong, who "might run down our children," was one who crouched "behind the wheel in white-knuckled terror over the horsepower at his command."[9] If the Hmong "might run down our children," then they are not among the "us" who belong to the automobile association and read its magazine. The Hmong demanded an apology. After they were rebuffed, they organized a protest and received an apology and full-page advertisements in state newspapers praising the Hmong for their service to the U.S. military, work ethic, thrift, and ability as farmers.

When I started browsing the library bookshelves, there were no more than a handful of volumes on Asian Americans. I could read them all easily even when cramming to write a term paper. Since then, I have built a library of my own with more than a hundred titles. I could not make enough time even to skim through all the excellent additions to the literature, even if I devoted myself to the endeavor.

The general absence of Asian Americans and the stereotyping of Asians were not to the detriment of Asian Americans and Asians alone. They affect our society and are related to other problems. My white classmates failed to learn about the people around them, and I was not introduced to African Americans, Latino/as, American Jews, Arab Americans, and others. We knew one another as nothing but shadows, without substance.

By definition, Asian Americans do not exist in Asia. Overseas Asians as often as white Americans regard Asian Americans as only temporarily absent from the homeland, errant kin who will come home none the worse for their peculiar experiences. The Chinese will say, as if it were a verity not subject to doubt: "You're always Chinese, no matter where you are."[10]

Yet there is nothing like visiting Asia to persuade most native-born Asian Americans that, whatever we are back in the United States, we are not identical to Asians overseas; we are like African Americans touring Africa and white Americans in Europe.[11] Asian Americans traveling in Asia look at both Asian natives and white tourists as kindred spirits, but Asian natives and white sightseers are oblivious to them. Asian Americans can be ugly Americans abroad if they insist, but they submit to a reversal of their situation in America when they just go about their own business: They suddenly look like everyone else but don't know the way of life. They are incognito, but only until their heavy accents betray them as American, or simply the pace of their walk, the crossing of their legs, or a careless gesture marks them as uncouth.

Asian Americans are uniquely American. Our concerns about self-realization, racial dynamics, minority status, and the related matters arising from our status arise here; they do not bother Asians overseas. Asian Americans were created in the abstract from the unlikely convergence of radical activism and official bureaucracy.[12] The student protests of the late 1960s, especially the Third World Liberation Front strikes on the San Francisco State College and University of California, Berkeley, campuses in 1968 and 1969, launched the militancy of Black Power amid unrest across the country and the assassinations of Bobby Kennedy and Martin Luther King Jr. Inspired, Asian American students started a Yellow Power counterpart to demand self-determination. A few years later, the federal Office of Management and Budget issued its Directive No. 15 requiring that government agencies maintain statistics on racial groups, including an "Asian or Pacific Islander" category, as post-Watergate reformers tried earnestly to remake the government and restore trust in its abilities. Starting in 1977, Asian Americans found ourselves assigned to the same box in what David Hollinger has called "the ethnoracial pentagon" of black, white, Native American, Asian, and Hispanic.[13]

Directive No. 15 required difficult decisions. According to MIT professor Melissa Nobles in her study, *Shades of Citizenship*,[14] the committee charged with developing its details, for example, "debated whether persons from India should be categorized under the 'Asian or Pacific Islander' category or under the 'White/Caucasian' category, since they were purportedly Caucasians, 'though frequently of darker skin than other Caucasians.'" Nobles reported that "in the trial directive, they were classified as Caucasian, but they were reclassified as Asian in the final version (most likely in response to Asian Indian lobbying efforts to ensure racial minority status)."[15] In contrast, in another demonstration of both the fictitiousness and the power of race, South Asian immigrants in England are generally considered "black." That designation has made all the difference in the possibility of Asian-black cooperation between the United States and the United Kingdom.[16]

Since the advent of Yellow Power and Directive 15, organizations such as the Asian American Studies Association, Asian American Journalists Association, and Asian Pacific American Bar Association have made the idea operational by emphasizing a pan-Asian American basis for their activities in academic and professional settings. The Asian Pacific American Institute for Congressional Studies encouraged nonpartisan political empowerment.[17] The 80–20 Initiative, organized in response to the 1996 campaign fundraising imbroglio, tried to deliver a bloc vote of Asian Americans to a presidential candidate in the 2000 elections, after its board—one-third Democrat, one-third Republican, and one-third independent—convened to select the candidate who would be best for Asian Americans. The Asian Pacific American Labor Alliance, part of the AFL-CIO, promotes unionization among Asian immigrants. Numerous other umbrella groups have worked to be both broad in their Asian American outreach and deep in their commitment to the grassroots. They represent a tense marriage of the dual origins of Asian American identity: the revolutionary and the status quo. Organizations devoted to specific ethnicities persist, but they, too, are brought together by the same array of internal impetus aligned with external forces. Asian American, Asian Pacific American, Asian Pacific Islander, and the abbreviations "APA" or "API" have become the preferred names Asian Americans give ourselves as a group.

Asian American identity encompasses Filipinos, Vietnamese, Indians, Pakistanis, Thai, Hmong, Korean, Japanese, Hawaiians, Samoans, and others. The grandparents of Asian Americans would not have embraced this diversity. We did not come by it instinctively.

Asian Americans have become Asian Americans without losing the remainder of our identity. My parents never stopped being Chinese. They just added being American. It is absurd to state absolutely which aspect of our identity is the most central, and it is senseless to ask. Every aspect of it is integral to the whole, what has been ascribed as well as what we have claimed for ourselves. I am a man, a son, a husband, a lawyer, a professor, a writer, a dog lover, a motorcyclist, a Unitarian Universalist, and many other things besides. Which of these becomes paramount depends on the circumstances. Asian Americans can be Democrat or Republican, Communist or Libertarian. Some are culturally conservative but politically liberal, just as some are culturally liberal but politically conservative. Some Asian Americans were raised in Hawaii, where Asian Americans are a majority; others in California, where we are a plurality in some areas; and still others on the East Coast, in the Midwest, or in the South, where here and there we are concentrated in pockets, whereas elsewhere we are a minority that is so small it can hardly be counted.

Yet Asian American narratives share a family resemblance across ethnicities, generations, time periods, and geographic regions; these Asian American experiences also distinguish us from other Americans. Individual Asian Americans usually have an anecdote about how they became Asian Americans. Something happened to them, or a series of events repeated themselves, that impressed on them that they are Asian Americans. They conclude that they may not be Asian Americans first and foremost, but neither are they Asian Americans last and least.

Asian Americans who tell our life histories are sometimes surprised by the déjà vu reaction from Asian American audiences. We find that although we may have been the only one in the room as a child who felt what we felt, others across the country were simultaneously leading parallel lives. We were undergoing the same glare of unfair blame as the teacher lectured about Pearl Harbor, the Korean War, or the Vietnam War, and were feeling the same anger well up whenever the stranger on the street accosted us with some slur. The similarities are uncanny. Asian Americans can joke about it uneasily among ourselves.

As an Asian American, I have become an accidental plagiarist and a hesitant exhibitionist.[18] When I read an account by David Mura about "turning Japanese"[19] in his thoughtful book of that title or Amy Tan's breakthrough novel *Joy Luck Club*,[20] I assimilate it into my own experience. I know I am no more Mura than he is me and that none of the quartet of characters who play mah-jongg in the *Joy Luck Club* are my mother, but I recognize his life and their lives—it could still be my life and it might have been my mother's life. They and others among the burgeoning number of memoirists and authors of an intensely personal fictional genre know my secrets. I read filmmaker Desmond Nakano's remembrance of playing war with his brother, and his brother yelling "kill 'em, kill 'em, kill the Japs!" before they realized "we're

Japanese to white people but we're both American" and they were saying, in effect, "kill us! Kill us!" and I feel as if I am Nakano's brother.[21] My ethnic experiences are freely available. I am chagrined that they have made public my own private shames, telling the world on my behalf what I would have preferred to keep to myself.

In turn, I do the same. I reveal my own humiliations in the hope that I can alleviate the anguish through humor, despite my distaste for portraying my own childhood as an unmitigated series of racial encounters. Asked whether I faced racial discrimination by a stranger, I have no desire to reply that I grew up miserable any more than people typically return the greeting "how are you?" with a melancholy account of the wretchedness of daily life. It isn't true; even if it were, most people would like to believe that they have more command over their lives and few of us like to divulge the mistreatment that only shows our inability to affect what is happening around us. Because I refrain from charging people with "racism" in all but the most extreme cases, I am appalled by unfounded accusations that writers about race such as myself are pretending that there is discrimination because we would be out of work if we admitted there was not. It is not as if I have no interests besides making up incidents of bias and have nothing better to do.

We lead ourselves astray if we suppose that we are best served by hearing the rote recitation of our lives played back to ourselves. Much of what we as individuals and as a society need to figure out, we can know only if we critique ourselves and what we believe we know. If any of us, however thoughtful, looks at race through the lens of our own lives without additional perspectives, we will distort our understanding and impair our vision, the minority no less than the majority. We are all of us unreliable narrators of our own lives, in which our egos have the better of the facts.[22] As individuals we confuse our meager experience with a supreme truth, extrapolating from a story to a stereotype. We also impose a fictional order on the contingencies and the messiness of ordinary life, which further misleads us. If autobiography substitutes for argument, any rebuttal cannot help but seem like a personal attack. Everything becomes subjective, and disclosures of intimate details of childhood become mandatory. Our accepted wisdom on race will be abridged in dreary yarns about the bad old days, which make us nostalgic for a shared misery. We can be dismissed as too sensitive or patronized for having hurt feelings, as if the best comeback is, "lighten up," or "get over it."

Taking action on issues is more important than sitting in an audience hearing stories, but the one may come about only after the other. The stories give us the impetus to act. They are not public therapy.

Exactly because "Asian American" is an artificial concept, Asian Americans are a natural group for coalition movements. The charge that Asian Americans have made up "Asian American" is accurate, but the ability of Asian Americans and all of us to make up racial categories and imbue them with significance should be recognized and such self-determination be encouraged. Armenians, Persians, Khazaks, Filipinos, Asian Indians, Pacific Islanders, and numerous others have been Asians and not Asians as well. The latest change, created by and not merely reflected in the 2000 Census, resulted in Asian/Pacific Islanders being broken up into Asian American and Pacific Islander. The evolution of Asian Americans exemplifies why and how diverse peoples can synthesize new communities. Asian Americans are not Asia added to America. In the very invention of a race, we are forging something new that cannot be given the simplistic summary of "the best of Asia and the best of America." The world knows from the tragedy of history that the opposite claim, that a "folk" is organic, is treacherous. Contrary to what its detractors might suppose, "Asian American" is less and not more ethnic than what existed before.

The effort to bring together Asian Americans is in its preliminary stages. It requires much work. Asian America is dynamic rather than static. It is flourishing. Asian American student groups are always arguing among themselves about whether it is even appropriate that they should exist. Theirs is a healthy skepticism. Only people in a collaborative venture that is strong, who do not regard themselves as ossified into institutions, can ask themselves if they should proceed.

Ironically, pan–Asian American identity can be strongest where Asian Americans are weakest. As high numbers of Asian immigrants continue to arrive, they may decide that they will be both more Asian and more ethnic than American and pan-Asian American. In Chicago, for example, Asian American community groups work together regularly across ethnic lines. The groups recognize that they must form alliances because each discrete group is too small to sustain itself. In California, by contrast, Asian American community groups fragment into those catering to specific ethnic groups. The groups are confident, even foolhardy, in believing that each by itself can thrive.

The key step I have taken is to care about race without caring exclusively about my race. Over time, I became involved with progressive causes. On every issue, it is obvious that I alone cannot effect change, and even a solid bloc of Asian Americans cannot effect change. In a diverse democracy, that is as it should be. No single person or single group should be capable of dominating the political processes. Asian Americans must be united as Asian Americans, but we must be united with whites, African Americans, Latino/as, Native Americans, and others who have the same commitments and passions. Each of us has an individual role, but together we have the greater role in the pursuit of racial justice. The great Western thinkers, if they were idealists, have regarded public life as the highest life; if they were realists, as a necessary one. In both traditions, they are unlike their Eastern counterparts, who believed the public life to be neither valuable nor obligatory. The teachings of Confucius and other Eastern sages were not meant to cultivate democratic participation. In a democracy, Asian Americans as Asian Americans must hew closer to the West and not the East.

Yet the integration of Asian Americans should further integration, not Asian Americans personally. Our empowerment cannot be for our sake alone, to acquire power and install Asian faces in political office. We must have a principled agenda if we are to be a moral group. The substance of Asian American political identity cannot be raw self-interest if we are to be legitimate at all. Asian Americans must heed the admonition of Rabbi Hillel, "If I am not for others, what am I?" and we should coalesce around what Cornel West has called an ethics of ethnicity. He argues that "the black freedom struggle" is not "an affair of skin pigmentation and racial phenotype but rather . . . a matter of ethical principles and wise politics."[23] Without principles, we should not be a group. In that the critics of "balkanization" are correct.

Accordingly, I would no sooner vote for or endorse candidates whose promises I doubted or whose policies I opposed if they were Asian American than I would if they were of any other racial background. The Asian Americans are even worse for me, because they may seem to be like me. Former Peruvian President Alberto Fujimori, a military dictator of Japanese descent known as El Chinito ("little Chinaman"), should not be a hero to Asian Americans just because he is Asian.

Lessons from School

As a law professor at Howard University in Washington, D.C., I am reminded of the importance of race every morning when I walk to work.[24] In the leisurely stroll down five blocks between my home and my office in the nation's capital, I move from a mostly white residential neighborhood that is quite affluent to a predominantly black institution that is economically mixed. The switch is more than physical, but it cannot be reduced to easy terms.

Howard University has been for more than a century the leading school in the nation for the training of black lawyers. Its legendary dean of the

World War II period, Charles Hamilton Houston, as quoted in the epigraph to this chapter,[25] once said that every lawyer was either a social engineer or a parasite on society. A perfectionist who concurred with Supreme Court Justice Oliver Wendell Holmes Jr., that the law was "a jealous mistress," Houston devoted himself to preparing the social engineers. Graduates during his watch included such giants as Thurgood Marshall, who would use the law to produce racial desegregation by achieving the moral victory of *Brown v. Board of Education* before the Supreme Court in 1954. The tradition they started continues to this day, giving the school a mission that most others cannot claim.

I am privileged to be the first Asian American on the Howard law faculty, and yet there seems to be something remarkable about a person of Asian heritage being associated with a historically black college. Strangers may not be sure what it is that is so surprising to them, but their uncertainty induces them to wonder aloud. Since becoming a member of the academy, I have lost count of the number of times people have asked, "Why are you at Howard?" or been impressed because they thought I taught at Harvard. They ask, "What is it like to be a minority among minorities? How does it feel?" Sometimes, "Do black people accept you? Or do they discriminate against you?" They ask, "What are they like? Are they good students?" Or, "Are you trying to make an ideological statement? Are you rebelling?" They add, "Couldn't you find a job anywhere else? Do you want to stay?" Even, "Did you grow up in a black neighborhood?" On more than one occasion, a person has looked me over carefully, paused, and then stammered, "Are you— are you actually black?"

The people who ask these questions casually but constantly in various combinations are almost all good-hearted. Most are white, some are black, and a few are Asian American themselves. Despite their diverse backgrounds, they share the same curiosity. Within a moment of meeting me and finding out what I do—or more precisely, where I do what I do—whether it is during a professional conference, while I am at a television station appearing as a guest, visiting a campus to speak, at a social gathering such as a dinner party, or in striking up a new acquaintance through an introduction by friends, they pull me aside to confide their surprise. It doesn't matter what I may have been doing or talking about—trying to learn to play tennis or chatting about politics—and I need not make any effort to provoke any racial issue. People raise their eyebrows when I mention my employer.

After awhile, the questions started me mulling over race itself. Speculating about an Asian American teacher with mainly African American students is not offensive, although I admit I am exhausted by the tedious interrogations. I toyed with having a sarcastic retort printed on the back of my business cards, but they are looking for more than cursory answers. They are looking for something, they know not what, but it is directly in front of them. More than might be intended by the people who are inquiring, their inquisitiveness reveals the invisible influence of racial judgments on our everyday perceptions. All of us see race inevitably, without even being awake to what is on our minds. Race is the elephant in the room, in the exercise of trying not to think about the elephant in the room; the harder we try to pay no attention to race, like the elephant, the larger it looms.

When I was pondering where to embark on my life as a scholar, nobody thought to ask, "Well, what will it be like to be the only Asian American at a white school? How does it feel?" or "What are whites like? Are they good students?" I am bemused that Asian Americans now and then suggest that I have taken a position to curry favor with blacks, because I work at a predominantly black institution. They don't seem to realize that if such an assumption can be made about me without any other basis, they must be ingratiating themselves to whites by the same reasoning. Nobody ever bothers my wife, an Asian American who happens to teach at another fine but predominantly white law school across town, about why she has chosen that place of employment or expects her to be an expert on whiteness.

Becoming the only Asian American at a white school was an option available to me. I was fortunate enough to have been invited to interview with many law schools. I would have ended up every bit as much the minority at any of them. None of the law schools with which I interviewed had ever had an Asian American professor. The majority of the 175 accredited law schools in this country did not then and had never had a person of Asian descent in a tenured position teaching any subject. After they hire one, who knows whether they will hire another. There is no place where my wife and I could be among a majority of Asian Americans; even in Asia, we would be out of place as Asian Americans.

Even so, I suspect that not many people who are white—or for that matter Asian American—consider as a "white" law school one that boasts an overwhelmingly white enrollment, a totally white alumni until recently, a mostly white faculty, or an all-white administration; or where the framed photographs of judges and lawyers displayed with pride on the walls include no black faces (or needless to say, Asian faces), where a lone person of color has recently become a professor while a corps of racial minorities have always been janitors. Those African Americans who call a school "white" are likely to be chided for having imagined a problem for themselves. I doubt that anybody would suppose that joining the faculty at such a white law school represents a political choice as much as a politic one.

My hypothesis is that many of us are afflicted with a partial color blindness. We cannot see clearly, and our would-be color blindness conceals the subjectivity of our own vantage point from ourselves. Through this filter, Asian Americans see that being in the company of white Americans is accepted as assimilating into the mainstream, a sign of upward mobility. Someone who is neither black nor white observes that given a choice, it would be smart to try to become white because that status brings tangible benefits. Asian Americans follow whites, not blacks, in trying to become American, and we disregard the dictum that it is blacks who are the most authentic Americans. The alternative, intentionally associating with African Americans, is weird, some sort of naïve error or purposeful subversion. As soon as Asian Americans deviate from the rule that we should prefer to be white rather than black, we will be gently corrected.[26]

Perhaps all of us regardless of race have an unconscious tendency to accept white culture as the majority culture as well as the favored culture. White is normal. Whiteness is desirable. Our world has more than racial categories, so transparent as to be invisible. It has racial hierarchies, both blatant and subtle.

Many whites and Asian Americans do not have enough contact with African Americans to have formed a sense of any individual African American as a human being. For them, I am an interpreter. I can expound on my experience as pompously as John Howard Griffin did poignantly in his 1961 book, *Black Like Me*, in which he recounted his travels throughout the Deep South as a white man disguised through chemicals to look like a black man. As much as I try to resist it, by talking to whites about African Americans I sometimes suspect that I become more white to them. It is as if I am a nineteenth-century adventurer who has explored the Dark Continent and returned as an authority to regale my audience. Or I am an outsider between worlds and thus momentarily an insider in each world. For the same reason, I am a more credible source for a letter of recommendation than an African American colleague, with the authority of independence. I seem to be vouching for students as if I can say that they can fit into a white environment, without racial allegiance toward them.

So I am not sure whether to be flattered or insulted that people consider my current position a form of personal charity or an experimental phase of life. They do not see that, even acting solely out of calculating self-interest, being at Howard has been good for my career. Thanks to them, there probably is a certain cachet to being the Asian guy at the black school. An Asian American law professor is rare enough, to be sure; an Asian American law professor in a black school is *sui generis*.

Every autumn, as the year begins with another set of students on the far side of the podium, I realize again how race is in the details of our daily lives. Race is unyielding and manifests itself in the discrepancy in our respective power to discount its effects. In one of the best articles on whiteness, Wellesley College professor Peggy McIntosh gave a personal account of grasping the advantages of her own skin color. Writing in 1988 from a feminist standpoint, she listed more than fifty conditions of her life she could count on, unlike people of color. They ranged from "I can go shopping alone . . . pretty well assured that I will not be followed or harassed" and "I can talk with my mouth full and not have people put this down to my color" to "I can worry about racism without being seen as self-interested or self-seeking" and "I can chose blemish cover or bandages in 'flesh' color and have them more or less match my skin," "I can talk about the social events of a weekend without fearing most listener's reactions," and "I will feel welcomed and 'normal' in the usual walks of public life, institutional and social."[27] Washington University law professor Barbara Flagg, a critical race theorist, borrowed the lines from the hymn *Amazing Grace* to illustrate how whiteness envelopes: "was blind, but now I see."[28] As anti–affirmative action activist Clint Bolick has said, "I almost never think about my 'whiteness.'"[29] White Americans can choose to stop thinking about race (or to never start), unless they are trapped and cannot avoid an altercation or if they have decided that they will join with Asian Americans or become a scholar studying Asian Americans.[30] Their erstwhile ethnicity is for the St. Patrick's Day parade.[31]

Comic Eddie Murphy spoofed white privilege as a member of the cast of the *Saturday Night Live* television show in 1984. He showed himself being made up in whiteface, donning a suit, and learning how to walk. He says as he rehearses, "their butts are real tight. . . . I gotta remember to keep my butt real tight when I walk." He reads Hallmark greeting cards out loud to learn clichés and practice his enunciation. With his camouflage and his new name, "Mr. White," he learns that, when only white people are around, everything is free; once the last black man exits the bus, a party breaks out; loan officers at banks give out money without requiring collateral or even identification. He closes the skit by saying, "I've got a lot of friends, and we've got a lot of makeup." So he warns whites the next time they meet a fellow white, "don't be too sure."

African Americans cannot disregard race, except when they are among a crowd of African Americans. The very act of congregating in a group, which allows them such an escape, only provides white Americans with another negative visual cue. Paradoxically, it takes the race conscious act of forming a group to beget the color blind ideal of being judged on one's merits. When people of color are numerous enough, we form a critical mass. We cease to bear the burden of being representative, and we can relax as our race recedes into latency. We do not generate a stereotype with our every action, because we are not uniform except in the superficial sense of skin color. Yet when African Americans come together, they risk the accusation of self-segregation, as if African Americans could be segregated without whites also being segregated.[32]

Although the means and the ends may contradict, race can be eliminated as an element in decision making. The race conscious act of presenting a list of finalists for a job, all of whom were African American, would ensure that an employer behaved in a color blind fashion in hiring one of them. When the same list of finalists for a job has several whites and a single African American, no selection whether of a white or an African American can be free of reservations that it is tainted by some prejudice.

Ambitious African Americans must leave behind their background, but ambitious white Americans only become more fixed in theirs. The same career path leads them to divergent lives. African American professionals almost certainly always will be the only people of their racial background in the room at meetings at their law firm, investment bank, major corporation, or university department, becoming more isolated from other people of color as they become more successful, unless they make a deliberate and costly choice to work within minority communities.[33] They must become intimately familiar with the details of WASP culture; wearing clothes ordered from the Abercrombie & Fitch catalog is not enough if they are invited to Thanksgiving dinner and do not recognize aspic. When in public, they must speak with the diction, enunciation, and accent of white people.

Conversely, white professionals equally certainly never will be the only ones of their racial background in the room at meetings at their law firm, investment bank, major corporation, or university department, and even if they do not try to avoid African Americans they will encounter few African Americans who are their social and economic peers or betters. They can consume black culture as radical chic; buying the latest hip-hop album at the mall outlet suffices without any need for knowledge of the origins of jazz. They need never adopt the speech patterns of blacks and in private can even ridicule the sophisticated verbal play on the street corner—a bard's facility with words that converts "salty" into a synonym for "sad" as an allusion to tears, before it is replaced in a few months by another coinage—as ignorant and boorish.

Even white professionals who work among Asians and Asian Americans are not likely to live among Asians and Asian Americans. They have an ability to exit. They may answer to an Asian American boss at a high-tech company, but after business hours they can return home to a suburb that is white. They will not be ostracized if they cannot use chopsticks; they are not expected to study Japanese or Korean. They are held to a standard so low and unlike that applied when the roles are reversed that Asians are charmed when their Caucasian friend knows how properly to proffer a business card with both hands and a slight bow and delighted if they can mutter, "Hello, how are you?" in an Asian language. Few white American expatriates living in Asia would be pleased to see their children "go native."

Asian Americans are deceived if we believe we escape these effects. We all must make choices.

I was no different. Until I started at Howard, I would not have been accustomed to finding myself the only Asian American in a room of African Americans. Growing up in what I did not know was the most segregated major metropolitan area in the country,[34] I knew only whites and no blacks. I attended a suburban high school that shared a campus with another high school. The two schools together had an enrollment of more than 4,000, among which was one African American. Scarcely less rare were Asian Americans. There were no faculty, no administrators, and no staff who were African American, and not more than one or two who were Asian American. There may have been a few Latino/as. There were only a few Jews.

Since coming to Howard, I have become so used to being there that I am startled to be the only Asian American in a roomful of whites—or, for that matter, an Asian American among other Asian Americans.

Here is a thought experiment about the minor symbols of racial double standards. When I began teaching, a street vendor who had set up operations near the Howard University Law School was selling fake leather goods. Likely manufactured in Asia, his bargain wares were emblazoned with the logo Eurosport. Many incoming students bought his backpacks to carry their heavy loads of casebooks back and forth. If a sizable number of first-year students at Harvard Law School passed by advertising Afrosport with their bookbags, it would prompt a double-take. Eurosport on blacks is fashionable; Afrosport on whites would be puzzling.

In many ways, Howard's law school resembles Harvard's. Students are similarly apprehensive about whether they have made a terrible choice in volunteering themselves for the Socratic method. They have the same delusions about legal practice, gleaned from television shows such as *Ally McBeal* and *Judge Judy*. They undergo the same pre-exam panic over distinguishing hypothetical fact patterns from the relevant precedent. They aspire to comparable professional goals of lucre and rank. The field of law has its own culture, with specialized jargon; elaborate ceremonies; and methods of delineating insiders, outsiders, and the ranks of the bar and bench. For this reason, it would be a mistake to treat the law schools at Howard and Harvard as representative of black culture or white culture, respectively. Non-lawyers of any sort would object with good reason if they were measured against lawyers. Some Howard students, even if they come from backgrounds that are not especially privileged, are socialized just as other students from backgrounds of privilege are socialized into having contempt for their clients as unworthy if they are indigent.

In other ways, however, Howard is quite unlike Harvard. Howard students agree that racism still affects their lives, but they disagree on what to do about it. They have first-hand experience with gun violence and economic despair, even if they come from a middle-class upbringing. A relatively high proportion of students have to testify at criminal trials or cope with the day-to-day exertions of being a single mother. The cafeteria has grits for breakfast and greens at lunch. There is an active choir that gives concerts in our chapel. Many students say "sir" and "ma'am," and some staff call me Mister Frank.

Howard is no more perfect than Harvard. There is some grumbling about the number of non-blacks and acceptance of discrimination by black as the "flip side" of white racism elsewhere. An excessive number of students want to become sports or entertainment lawyers. An occasional poster announces a boycott of an Asian American-owned business in derogatory racial terms. I am saddened that, from time to time, when students are understandably frustrated at the seeming Catch-22 ineptitude of the institution that manifests itself here and there, they will remark, "What do you expect from black folks?"

Black schools and white schools are not mirror images. Their origins, their purposes, and their meaning to society are not alike. Black institutions of higher learning came about because blacks were denied the chance to study elsewhere. White institutions barred blacks by law or by custom.

Black institutions are one of the complicated legacies of racial segregation, which ended only during the lifetimes of people alive today. They have a specific function of ingathering, which creates a special community without insinuating that others are inferior. Black students seek out black schools because they are welcoming. White students self-select themselves away from black schools with only a few exceptions. They are absent because they believe the schools are beneath them, not vice versa. Black schools seem immune from the backlash against affirmative action, even though black schools are undeniably not color blind but institutions that are wholly color conscious. The implications are that color consciousness is acceptable if it tends toward racial segregation but not if it is aimed at racial integration, and black institutions either are too important or too inconsequential to be subjected to a stern edict of color blindness. In contrast, many white schools tend to be faceless way stations leading toward a coveted credential. Students matriculate anonymously at the best school that has accepted them, without any connection to it.

Black schools enhance diversity. They do so at another level than is conventional. They ensure that even as institutions become integrated internally, so that African Americans fit in as equals at Stanford University or the University of Michigan—where I taught as a fellow and graduated from law school, respectively—institutions continue to differ from each other. African Americans ought to have a choice to be more than a token or an anomaly, even if white Americans are not eager to gain first-hand knowledge of minority status. If every place were identically integrated, African Americans (not to mention Asian Americans) would end up always alone among whites. Whites might feel differently about the allure of color blindness if they knew that each individual white person would be alone among African Americans in order to satisfy the goal. A white person might not feel quite as reassured by a solemn pledge of color blindness if she were the only white person in a roomful of African Americans.

An institution perceived as wholly black can be more integrated than institutions that are thought to be quite ordinary. Howard University, which has always opened its doors to everyone, has had its share of deans, professors, and students who were white.[35] Established after the Civil War, it is named for a white Union general who became the director of the Freedman's Bureau. (This is not to suggest, as sometimes seems to be implied, that a predominantly black institution is only as good as the number of whites it can attract.) It has an annual enrollment of more than 10,000 students, serving as a Mecca for black intellect spanning cultures and transcending politics, drawing to it an African diaspora from well beyond American borders. Its openness has been the basis for a rooted cosmopolitanism rather than an immutable parochialism.

When I looked out at my classroom during my first year, looking back at me were a half-dozen white faces among the fifty students. When I showed up for faculty meetings, around the table sat that same number of whites among my two dozen or so colleagues. These numbers of whites are equal to if not greater than the representation of blacks at other schools. Our faculty is more diverse than that of other law schools. The professors display a range of opinions that matches that found at any other school.

Nor am I unique. Two generations ago, many Asian immigrants could be found teaching at historically black colleges. After they received their doctorates, they found it easier to obtain employment there than at segregated white campuses. They staffed the math, science, and engineering departments of the dozens of historically black colleges. Many of them have retired, but some are still there as the senior faculty.

I have become convinced that there is a value, and not for African Americans alone, to having a place where people of color can be in the overall majority and hold most of the leadership positions. The cumulative effect of being a permanent minority is a demoralizing stress. It is only from the outside—or if the state of affairs is reversed to the extent possible—that the identity of whites as a group is even discernible. Paul Igasaki, the first Asian American to serve as chair of the United States Equal Employment Opportunity Commission, is fond of noting that a white male manager whose team consists of only other white men, who may be unmindful of the message he conveys just by introducing his colleagues at a meeting, cannot help but take notice if Igasaki were to do the same and surround himself with Asian American men. It wouldn't be right if Igasaki's office included only Asian Americans, even if each was eminently qualified.

Nor can the pernicious effects of being in a racial minority be rationalized as a byproduct of numbers. People of color cannot be a minority in any substantial sense, unless their status as people of color is perceptible as a means of differentiating them from the majority. Left-handers are a minority, but not a minority group. The 90 percent of us who are right-handed have historically discriminated against left-handers, and we have built the world to suit us. Southpaws were literally "sinister." They were cured forcibly. A major study, *The Left-Hander Syndrome: The Causes and Consequences of Left-Handedness*,[36] by University of British Columbia psychologist Stanley Coren, documents continuing statistical disparities in everything from life expectancy to mental illness rates based on handedness. According to Coren, left-handedness may be a consequence of prenatal trauma. However, handedness is not a basis for organizing society. Left-handed products may exist, both serious and novelty, and left-handed third basemen may be exceptional on the baseball diamond, but left-handedness is neither used for purposes of segregation and subjugation nor does it divide people. Skin color and handedness are not the same because they do not have the same effects.

On issues of race, I have learned as much as I have taught. My personal opinions on race have been transformed through a series of events, which have in common that I have defied my own as well as others' expectations. All of these events required the purposeful decision on my part to insert myself into places where I would never have found myself by chance. But they also required that I overcome my own confines of identity.

I am convinced that this approach is more generally applicable: By becoming more conscious of our own perceptions, as a society we will be able to neutralize racial prejudice. The necessary but not sufficient threshold is acknowledging that race operates in our lives, relentlessly and pervasively. Working in multiracial coalitions of equal members, united by shared principles, we can create communities that are diverse and just. Together, we can reinvent the civil rights movement.

And that possibility is why I teach at Howard.

Becoming the English Butler

My parents recently returned to Taiwan to see if they might like it there. They are not certain about their future. It took them a year to sell their house in the United States and to pack their furniture. Their friends and their social lives did not move as easily, and they are still wondering if they can go home again.

Their transition has made me realize that they are more transnational than I am. As a child, I always secretly thought I was more sophisticated than they were. My conceit was not too much off the mark, for I am at ease with American culture at a level that they never will be. I speak without an accent, and on the surface I have overcome everything else that an accent represents. I am likely to be better accepted than they were, albeit because of changes in society more than anything about me personally.

Now, I appreciate what they have done. My parents have lived in two cultures, whereas I cannot visualize living elsewhere even briefly. They could manage in the United States, doing well enough to nurture me to take better advantage of the opportunities. They are literate in two languages, but I can write only my name in sloppy Chinese ideograms. I could not follow in their venture, and I do not have the courage even to want to try. I would have to become a dot-com billionaire in Australia to match the proportions of their triumph.

When writing this book, I had an epiphany: In the end, it turns out I am actually more Asian than I ever supposed I was. I mean more than that I keep a few pairs of slippers in the hall closet and never wear shoes in the house. Social scientists are busy studying whether it is true, as many suppose, that first-generation Asian immigrants and their second-generation Asian American children are more likely to esteem harmony than are white or black Americans.[37] Researchers led by University of Michigan psychologist Richard Nisbett are even venturing toward the hypothesis that Asians and Caucasians think differently in the most basic sense, conceptualizing reality with different categories.[38] Nisbett has confronted directly the discredited racial suppositions of the past as well as the similar racial contentions of *The Bell Curve* today, accepting the use of racial classifications but attempting to rebut what he calls the "scurrilous" arguments about black intellectual inferiority. His most famous experiment involves digitally animated scenes of fish in their aquatic environments: When asked to describe the scenes they had observed, on average Japanese made twice as many comments about inanimate objects in the background and Americans noted little else besides the biggest fish. Nisbett says, "If it ain't moving, it doesn't exist for an American."[39] Although his work on the holistic and interdependent styles of reasoning used by Asians compared with the analytic and independent styles used by Caucasians is only beginning and does not appear to consider either Asian Americans or mixed race individuals, it is intriguing and deserves consideration. He can sound like a radical, not a reactionary, in acknowledging the limits of research. At the end of one of his recent papers, he admits that his best-known book, on human inference, may be not universal but ethnically specific because of its lack of cross-cultural comparisons.[40]

As reluctant as I am to stereotype myself, much less others, there seems to be some support for the notion that Asian Americans are more likely to evaluate ourselves deprecatingly, blaming ourselves for not having done enough work, and denigrating others for the same fault, rather than self-inflating, taking credit for work and telling others theirs' was a job well done. Asian American employees will be loyal to a company whether such steadfastness will be reciprocal, confusing a society of personal relationships with one of impersonal rules. We also are more likely to be emotionally undemonstrative, expect kids to concentrate on schoolwork, consider an absence of punishment to be adequate reward, and suppose that play is worthless. And I would add that we draw more of a line between public roles and private lives.

Racial discrimination aggravates the generation gap and is a factor in the estrangement of parents from their children. Immigrant parents already are hampered by their reliance on their children in an unbecoming role reversal that has the youngsters advising their elders about the realities of the world. They are uncomprehending more than they are unsympathetic about race matters. They would like to protect their children from prejudice, but they are aware that it is not feasible for them to do so. They believe they can keep a low profile, thus evading racial matters. They don't instigate anything with whites because it cannot help but be racial, and they put up with what they cannot avoid. They come around to the attitude that their children must have it much easier than they have had, because the youngsters have been born into the culture. Immigrant parents may believe despondently that the discrimination they face is their own fault, because they are not fluent in the English language and familiar with American culture. They also may be willing to endure discrimination here, because they are more concerned with oppression in Asia. So immigrant parents tend to side with the teacher and the majority rather than with their own children, with respect to complaints of racial discrimination. If their American-born children report even an undoubtedly racial problem at school, their response is the reprimand, "You should try harder to fit in." Asian immigrant parents stress that, above all, a child should not dishonor the family. By doing so, they play directly into stereotyping. They assume that one must always behave as if one's actions reflect on all Chinese (or Japanese, Korean, Vietnamese, and so forth). Yet Asian American children dishonor the family in their assimilation. That many of them become ashamed of their own parents is one of the primary lessons they take home from school. The more Asian Americans try to work hard and be quiet and ignore tensions, the worse they make matters. They seem to be all the more competitive and clannish.

All these statements are generalizations, which suffer the flaws of their kind. But as approximations and averages, they are informative and helpful. Without decreeing that one behavior pattern is better than another, it is possible to consider the contrasts.

I am different from my white and black colleagues. I am following a different set of principles about everything from obeying authority and gender roles to picking up the check when dining out with friends and asking for favors. None of my white or black friends know the code of honor govern-

ing the exchange of gifts. Even when we are on the same page, we are reading different books.

I do not even know the Asian rules all that well, because they were taught
to me by parents, who were young themselves when they left an Asia that is
no longer there as they remember it. I have been enamored of the Asian rules
in toto, especially insistence on unquestioning conformity, kowtowing to
seniority, and fidelity to tradition.

I know the American rules, from growing up awkwardly and violating the
etiquette. I have learned to make prolonged eye contact with strangers. I try
not to smirk like the Cheshire cat when I mean to be submissive (although
even in Western culture, it is relatively recently that a full-toothed grin openly shown has been taken as a friendly salutation rather than a sign of idiocy.)

There is not a single set of American rules. Georgetown professor Deborah Tannen, author of several popular books on linguistics, has explained that
there are wide cultural differences on basic rules such as interrupting a person who is talking or raising your voice to make a point.[41] Such actions can
mean that you are engaging in spirited conversation with somebody, or they
can mean that you are disrespecting her. New York University history professor Robin D. J. Kelley, in *Yo Mama's Disfunktional! Fighting the Culture Wars
in Urban America*,[42] likewise explained the misinterpretation of the African
American vernacular practice of "playing the dozens." Also known as "capping," "snapping," "ranking," or "busting," playing the dozens is an of exchange
of insults that can be profane and outrageous, but the verbal interplay is
good-humored and the means of social bonding—the jokes about "yo'
mama" have crossed over to white America.

Yet I have become self-conscious, and I realize that, however they might
work in Asia, some strategies for life are not adapted to America. I berate
myself spontaneously; I am astonished at my non-Asian friends' lack of con-
trition or shame.

As a manager, I am vulnerable to manipulation. I end up acquiescing to
avoid conflict. In Asia, presumably I would benefit from my position in the
social order. My employees would be mortified if they created problems. We
would be able to labor together, because any of us disrupting the calm would
be antithetical to our collective values. In America, unfortunately, the Asian
trait of preferring cooperation is regarded as passive aggressive, even worse
than plain aggressive because it is somehow devious. Here, few people set
their sights on being a good subordinate.

As a worker, I can be exploited because I don't believe in complaining or
making excuses, and I harm my own likelihood for promotion by doubting

my work, accepting responsibility even for problems that are not my doing, and automatically agreeing with my boss while conveying my doubts only as subtle hints. I make myself look like an insecure incompetent and sound like a sycophant. In Asia, everyone would understand that admitting fault was the performance of a ritual. They would approve of the less blunt style of argument. Here, stars are advanced to the top while other members of the team are left behind.

As a lawyer, I am not as strong an advocate as my clients have a right to expect. I am very good at arguing to a court, but I am averse to arguing with opposing counsel because too many attorneys seem to enjoy rudely shouting and even using obscenities. Asians may swear this way on the street, but not in the office. Among attorneys, my desire to be conciliatory is a character flaw.

As a teacher, I am not as effective as I would like to be because I come across as unduly harsh. I offer only negative feedback. Again, in Asia, that might be enough. My students would understand that compliments were supposed to be rare. They would learn from me regardless, because their motivation would come from self-discipline rather than my applause. In a grade-inflated world of undergraduates as consumers, honest evaluations ruin morale.

We do not all need to follow the same rules. But we all need to have a better understanding of the multiple sets of rules that are in operation. We could follow any one of several reasonable models without surrendering to relativism, but whether we like it or not individuals tend to be better off if they are consistent with the culture.

I was not surprised to find out that psychologists who study Asian Americans find a high level of anxiety and mental illness. Some problems are no different than those of anyone else, but some problems also can be attributed to the internal struggle to be Asian and American, compounded by the external strain of racial prejudice.

Their research reminds me of Kazuo Ishiguro's 1989 novel *Remains of the Day*,[43] winner of the British Whitbread Book of the Year citation. The Anglo-Asian author depicts the restrained protocols that epitomized Stevens, an English butler, before and after World War II. The servant was courteous even as he was asked for his opinion on foreign policy by the gentlemen upon whom he was waiting, in their private game of mocking him and thereby democracy. As they belittle him, he is gracious if blank in replying, "I'm sorry, sir, but I'm unable to be of assistance in this matter." His impeccable training enabled him to pass for the one of them (they would have called themselves his betters) when he found himself traveling alone through the countryside in a borrowed car that he normally would drive as a chauffeur, but it also prevented him from expressing emotion at his father's death or being able to articulate his love for any woman.

Reading *Remains of the Day* and watching the Merchant-Ivory movie, starring Anthony Hopkins, I thought I understood how its author could have an intimate grasp of English society but feel alienated from it. It was not at all odd to me that Ishiguro, who moved to London at the age of six and became a British subject, would have chosen to write about the all-but-extinct breed of the English butler. The immigrant shares with the servant the task of learning to act like the master. They may know the house rules of behavior better because they must follow them more strictly.

Like Ishiguro's protagonist, I sometimes feel schizophrenic in my duties. My balance is bad. I alternate between striving for peace and tranquillity and being just as aggressive and unruly as the next person. I am quiet when I should be loud and loud when I should be quiet. I believe that reconciliation among my many personalities may be possible, that I can blend the best of Asian serenity with the best of American commotion. Coalition must start with inner equilibrium.

Re-Forming the Civic Society

Asian Americans have been involved in coalitions as long as we have been Asian Americans. Even before Cesar Chavez did his magnificent work, Asian American farmworkers were striking in solidarity with Chicano farmworkers. The Unity conferences of journalists, the latest of which brought together thousands in Seattle in 1999, are the largest gatherings in the profession. They are organized by the African American, Hispanic, Asian American, and Native American media organizations. Notwithstanding the massive size of the Unity programs and the impressive roster of attendees, media outlets remain overwhelmingly owned and managed by whites.

Asian American racial identity, and any empowerment of people of color, is often condemned as a divisive force. Once it is set in context as a point along a continuum—as a means to an end rather than an end in itself—it becomes easier to accept such a group and its work as a cohesive influence that brings about greater loyalties. But the Asian Americans who have built bridges can be disquieting to whites, because each of them has chosen to be allied with other people of color. They speak up and stand out.

Yuri Kochiyama, a Japanese American woman, was an associate of Malcolm X. She can be seen in the photographs of his assassination, cradling him in her arms after he had been shot. *The New York Times* called her "Harlem's

Japanese sister." She had befriended Malcolm X a few years earlier, telling him she respected him for the direction he was giving to his people but disapproved of his stand on integration. In later life, she wrote and spoke about Asian-Black "linkages" globally, recalling W. E. B. DuBois's high regard for Mao and Mao's support for "the just struggles" of urban riots such as Watts. One need not be a Maoist to agree with her "sincere hope . . . that Asian Americans will continue to side with the oppressed."[44]

Grace Lee Boggs, a Chinese American woman, has been a union organizer in Detroit from the 1960s to the present day. She and her late husband, James Boggs, an African American, wrote revolutionary tracts arguing that urban centers could be the base for black liberation. Identified by the FBI as most likely a mixed-race "Afro-Chinese" Marxist, the Bryn Mawr Ph.D. was proposed to by the first president of Ghana but wed a self-taught migrant from Alabama who worked on an automobile assembly line. After she became a widow, she carried on their life's work in *Living for Change*,[45] in which she details her efforts in the Motor City, whose burnt-out office buildings have been icons of racial problems ever since the "people's rebellion" of 1967.

Bill Lann Lee, the first Asian American to serve as assistant attorney general for civil rights, was a lawyer for the NAACP Legal Defense Fund and head of its West Coast office. Lee is a Chinese American whose father, a U.S. military veteran, operated a series of hand laundries in Harlem, where the family lived above their small business. Known for resolving cases through compromise, Lee was even commended by his adversaries. His race was not held against him, but his affiliation with African Americans was. The Senate refused to confirm him in the nation's highest civil rights job, citing his work with the NAACP. He served for more than two years in an "acting" capacity, before receiving a controversial presidential appointment during a congressional recess.

Yale professor Harold Hongju Koh is an excellent example of the type of leader who exceeds ethnic expectations. The lone lawyer facing the U.S. Department of Justice with only a team of students, he represented hundreds of Haitians in testing the legality of government policies toward Haitian refugees. He litigated on behalf of clients with no other hope, up to the Supreme Court. Because he set such a high standard for coalition building, the case is worth describing in detail.

In September 1991, a military coup in Haiti deposed popular President Jean-Bertrand Aristide. Civil society disintegrated, as violence, malnutrition, and disease became rampant. In the United States, a presidential race was taking place. Incumbent George Bush was dismayed that the 40,000-strong

Haitian migration might affect his reelection chances, as twelve years earlier Jimmy Carter had been harmed by the Cuban Mariel boatlift. Carter had to cope with another crisis that seemed beyond his control as more than 125,000 Cubans floated to Florida. This added to his tribulations and his eventual defeat by Ronald Reagan.

Alarmed by the influx of Haitians, Bush ordered "interdiction." United States gunships would forcibly stop Haitian boats on the high seas. Only a few of the Haitians who feared death amid the chaos in their country, where people were being executed or vanishing, had their requests for asylum considered on the merits. The overwhelming majority lost without judicial review and therefore could not remain in America. Bush stated that people fleeing persecution were still welcome but those who wanted economic advantages were not. The Congressional Black Caucus claimed that the Cubans had been favored over the Haitians either because of their generally lighter color or due to U.S. hostility toward the Castro regime.

Presidential candidate Bill Clinton promised that if elected, he would reverse the Bush administration policy, which he characterized as cruel and inhumane. Once he won the White House, he reneged and continued to turn away the refugees. Shortly before he was sworn in, he gave a Voice of America radio speech declaring, "leaving by boat is not the route to freedom." He preferred to process claims for refugee status from applicants still in Haiti itself, not from those who had fled. In addition, he sought to restore democracy there and ordered an invasion of the island. He later expedited processing of asylum cases before finally deciding to divert Haitians to other countries, such as Panama, until the crisis in Haiti could be resolved.

Many died while fleeing. In one incident in August 1995, authorities discovered that 100 of the 600 Haitian passengers aboard a stopped vessel had been thrown overboard to drown. Others were held in indefinite detention by the U.S. government, crowded into camps on Guantanamo Bay. To the officials deciding their fate, the reputedly high incidence of HIV infection among them rendered them even more unwanted.

It was this situation that Koh, like the civil rights lawyers who were his predecessors, was dedicated to changing. In 1993, the Asian Law Caucus of San Francisco honored Koh for his work. In a moving speech amplifying his commitment to his clients, he described himself as "the worst kind of Asian: an uptight, buttoned-down, Ivy-league, ivory tower East Coast Asian academic," so different from the "West Coast Asians raised in the mellow multiculturalism of the Bay Area." Because he was still engaged in the high-stakes battle to overturn the Haitian blockade, which he called "a floating Berlin

Wall," he wanted to tell other Asian Americans why he had come to have such passion for the cause.

His father, he told the audience, had landed by boat in the United States from Korea in 1949, "carrying all of his belongings in a small suitcase, here without family or friends." Due to discrimination against him, which prevented his finding work, and out of "desperation" for the family he was raising he would tell his son to study physics, "because in a profession where you work with numbers and not words, they can't discriminate against you."

When Koh went to college and took a year abroad in Korea, there was an attempted coup there as Richard Nixon resigned following the Watergate scandal back home. Delineating the difference between "the most powerful nation in the world" making a transition from one man to another man "without tanks rolling in the streets" while "a tiny country could not do the same thing without violence and bloodshed," Koh's father told him why: "In Korea, if you control the military you become president; in the United States, when you become president you control the military." Your existence is proof that the dream is . . . stronger than the pain," Koh's father told him. Those words guided Koh when he accepted the case of the Haitian refugees.

The story of "one Asian American lawyer's journey" is the same as the story of the Haitians. From "the dashed hope of democracy, the search for refuge, the clash between principle and power, a belief that there is a rule of law and not a rule of individuals," to "their pain and their dreams," Koh saw his father in the Haitians.[46]

Recalling the voyage of the *St. Louis*, a ship fleeing Nazi Germany with Jewish refugees, whose passengers were returned to Hitler and their eventual deaths, Koh said that his "whole life" had been brought together "in a single [legal] argument." The needs of national sovereignty, which had been called upon to exclude Chinese immigrants and intern Japanese Americans, and his scholarly research on presidential prerogative, international human rights, and civil procedure, were all important.

At the conclusion of his after-dinner speech, Koh received an emotional standing ovation. His final words reiterated the highest ideals of Asian Americans and indeed all Americans:

> As I prepared for the oral argument [before the Supreme Court], I realized that this is a case about We and They. And that the reason the government had been so successful so far is because they've been able to convince all of us that the Haitians are they, not us. Because after all, if the Haitians, those sick people on

Guantanamo . . . are somebody else, then they are not our problem, and, after all, don't we have enough problems?

If you've ever been a refugee, or if your parents have ever been refugees, then you're a Haitian. If you've ever been in an internment camp or know anyone who's ever been in an internment camp, then you're a Haitian. If you've ever been discriminated against or know someone who has been discriminated against because they have HIV, then you're a Haitian. If you've ever believed for a second that what it says on the Statue of Liberty is not just words, but, as my father said, a sacred promise, then you're a Haitian. If you've ever believed that this is a nation of laws, and not individuals, then you're a Haitian.[47]

Even though the United States was violating a treaty it had signed, the Supreme Court ruled in favor of the government and against the Haitians. After Koh finished his work on the Haitian case, President Clinton asked him to join his administration. When Koh was formally nominated to be assistant secretary of state for human rights, he had strong support from Haitian immigrants but was practically unknown to Asian Americans.

African Americans have invited Asian Americans into other campaigns for racial equality. In an artistic vein, Anna Deveare Smith, an African American actress who presents a one-woman show based on transcripts of actual interviews with ordinary people, has incorporated Asian Americans. Smith had developed and starred in *Fires in the Mirror* (1993), based on incidents in the Crown Heights section of Brooklyn, New York, when in August 1991 a rabbi's motorcade accidentally killed an African American child, and a Jewish student was killed by African Americans evidently as a retaliatory act. The next year, the MacArthur "genius" award winner was commissioned to come up with a show about the riots following the Rodney King beating verdict.

Working with a diverse dramaturgical team whose Asian American and Latino members were the most vocal, Smith refined her 200-plus interviews into *Twilight: Los Angeles, 1992 on the Road: A Search for American Character* (1994).[48] She thought it was "a call to the community," and she sought to evoke the many characters of all races affected by the disturbance. In the published version of her script, which contains only the words and fails to record the power of the performance, she cautioned that the frequently asked question "Did you find any one voice that could speak for the entire city?" was not the right question. "In order to have real unity," she thought, "all voices would have to first be heard or at least represented."[49]

The National Asian Pacific American Legal Consortium, a legal advocacy organization, honored Smith in 1999 at its fundraiser in Washington, D.C.

Before offering excerpts from her stage work, Smith said that the Korean immigrant liquor store owner whose role she played was the person in the drama who was the least like her. Although Smith had been criticized for her use of a Korean accent and Korean phrases, her rendition of Mrs. Young-Soon Han was astounding in its accuracy. She used her talent to become another person on stage, making that person larger than life. Hitting the table for emphasis with a drum-like rhythm, with the gestures, enunciation, and pauses that could have convinced anybody who suspended their disbelief that they were witnessing the testimony of a Korean shopkeeper, she repeated the syncopated words of "swallowing the bitterness"[50]:

> *Until last year*
> *I believed America is the best*
> *I still believe it*
> *I don't deny that now*
> *because I'm a victim . . .*
> *I really realized that*
> *Korean immigrants were left out*
> *from this*
> *society and we were nothing*
> *What is our right? . . .*
> *Many Afro-Americans*
> *who never worked*
> *they get*
> *at least minimum amount*
> *of money*
> *to survive*
> *We don't get any! . . .*
> *Where do I finda [sic] justice? . . .*
> *What about last year?*
> *They destroyed innocent people.*
> *And I wonder if that is really justice*
> *to get their rights*
> *in this way.*
> *I waseh swallowing the bitternesseh,*
> *sitting here alone*
> *and watching them . . .*
> *and I have a lot of sympathy and understanding for them*
> *Because of their effort and sacrificing,*

other minorities, like Hispanic
or Asians,
maybe we have to suffer more
by mainstream . . .
I wish I could
live together
with eh [sic] Blacks
but after the riots
there were too much differences.
The fire is still there -
How do you call it? -
Igni . . .
igniting fire.
Dashi yun gi ga nuh
It's still dere.
It canuh
burst out anytime.

Coalitions also must become partnerships. Cynical individuals who consider themselves part of the civil rights movement sometimes privately observe that it has an informal hierarchy that inverts the racial hierarchy: African Americans are on top, whites are on the bottom, and everyone else is assigned to their place in reverse order compared to the general population—except that, even within this alternate universe, whites cannot be at the bottom because of their majority status in reality. Asian Americans do not wish to relegate ourselves to junior status in coalitions, forever conceding that African Americans have a virtual monopoly on the civil rights franchise.[51] But Asian Americans also should not assume that we will take over as the leaders of coalitions just by showing up, expecting that African Americans will concede the central role out of gratitude or permit Asian Americans to take advantage of them.

Asian Americans are not usurpers, but we ought to understand how we can appear to be such to African Americans who feel that they have been waiting for their turn interminably. Nobel laureate Toni Morrison accused Asian immigrants of having made it "on the backs of blacks," and the animosity is understandable.[52] When Asian Americans help African Americans, we cannot have a sense of noblesse oblige, as if we are selfless in lending aid. When Asian Americans help African Americans, we also help ourselves, by confronting mutual enemies.

If for no other reason, Asian Americans and African Americans can be pragmatic. The white supremacists who went on shooting sprees in Chicago, Los Angeles, and Pittsburgh over the past few years went after African Americans, Asian Americans, Latinos, and Jews. At a minimum, these groups have common interests in mutual defense. Neither Asian Americans nor African Americans would benefit if the other group disappeared in the inner city neighborhoods where ill will is greatest between them. Asian American shopkeepers would not have customers; they could not readily substitute anyone else. African American consumers would not have stores; they would not inherit the businesses. Rodney King is remembered not only for the beating he suffered at the hands of police officers but also for his televised prayer: "Can we all get along?" In his hometown of Los Angeles, that plea is an imperative.[53] Asian Americans and African Americans there have worked, before the King case and since then, on the project of interracial reconciliation.

Our coalitions are best if they are complete. Coalitions also must be crosscutting and changing: Individuals and groups should value their multiple commitments, and their combinations should shift depending on principles. Some supposedly Asian American groups are dominated by Chinese Americans and Japanese Americans. By claiming to be Asian American, such groups leverage the vast numbers of that title to the benefit of a few. To be legitimately Asian American, an organization must be more inclusive, with Vietnamese Americans, Filipinos, South Asians, and Pacific Islanders participating and taking leadership positions. Otherwise, it replicates the very discrimination it is meant to fight and betrays its cause.

William Tamayo, a longtime civil rights lawyer who heads the Equal Employment Opportunity Office in San Francisco, gave a speech in June 2000 at a conference in Hawaii arguing that "our historic responsibility requires that we not presume unity." He recalled that his Filipino mother responded to his historic work in overturning the convictions of Japanese Americans who resisted the internment by saying, "You know, that's war." Although she did not mean to equate Japanese Americans who were imprisoned by their own government with the Japanese Army that savaged the Philippines, neither did she feel that the Japanese American internment defined her Asian American experience. South Asians (Indians and Pakistanis) also feel as if they have been scorned by other Asian Americans, marked by color and the "subcontinental" designation as if the geographical prefix implied a racial status. There are, too, Asian immigrants who have come here as transients from other places that have shaped their identities during their interim stay there: Chinese, Japanese, Koreans, Filipinos, and South Asian refugees have made their expeditions via Africa, Europe, the Middle East, the Caribbean, or Latin America.[54]

Nor is adding Asian Americans alone enough. Latino/as, Native Americans, American Jews, Arab Americans, and others must be included.

Coalitions have their limits, of course. Coalitions of Asian Americans, African Americans, and Latino/as can try to respond to the diminishing stock of affordable housing, the deplorable state of public schools, rampant crime or a perception of the loss of neighborhood safety, a shortage of good entry-level employment opportunities, and global economic uncertainties, but not even the most robust joint efforts of Asian Americans, African Americans, and Latino/as can cure the root causes of such myriad ills. We must recruit whites. The electorate that will support public policies and the private sector that will contribute can be won over.

White support for coalitions is essential. As Farai Chideya, an ABC News correspondent specializing in youth and race, writes in *The Color of Our Future* (1999),[55] "Even more important than forming coalitions among different nonwhite groups is changing the often antagonistic politics between the racial majority (whites) and racial 'minorities.'"[56] The earliest leaders of the civil rights movement were astute enough to have enlisted whites, welcoming them whether as patrons or compatriots. Revolutionary John Brown and other white abolitionists were crucial to the cause. The NAACP was founded by whites as well as blacks. The activists of the 1960s, from leaders and volunteers to Freedom Riders and martyrs, formed a multiracial front.

One of the top children's movies in 2001, *Spy Kids*, represents the future: The ethnic has become mainstream. The story of an ordinary boy and girl whose parents turn out to be secret agents has a Latino nature so obvious as to be taken for granted. The Latino background of the lead characters is as important yet as invisible as is the Anglo identity of white heroes in most instances. The movie was directed by Robert Rodriguez; it stars Antonio Banderas as a character named after the principal in one of the earliest Chicano movies, *The Ballad of Gregorio Cortez* (He tells his youngsters to remember they are "Cortezes"); longtime Latino comic Cheech Marin, as their uncle, reveals the secret identity of the father and the mother to their children; there are English subtitles when Spanish is spoken; the music has a mariachi beat; the sets are inspired by Catalan architect Antonio Gaudi; much of the action takes place in South America; and, incidentally, the villain is Anglo. These aspects of the movie are so pervasive as to imbue it with a distinctive identity, but its fast pacing, clever plot, and adventure clichés also make the movie utterly Hollywood.

A heartfelt effort at coalition work also can react to white nervousness about their displacement.[57] John Tanton, the founder of the leading anti-immigrant group and the English-only movement, is infamous for having written an internal memorandum for discussion in 1986 asking, "As whites see their power and control over their lives declining, will they simply go quietly into the night? Or will there be an explosion?" Tanton feared Latino immigration, especially because of the influence of Catholicism.[58] An anti-immigrant group put it more nervously in a report issued in 2001: "Each group in the new minority-majority country has longstanding grievances against whites."[59]

This is a tough topic. Talking about it requires that whites forthrightly own up to misgivings about becoming a racial minority in a color conscious society, which doubles as an admission that it is better to be in the racial majority in that color conscious society, because in a truly color blind culture whites logically could not entertain any qualms about being a minority. It also requires that people of color generously allow that whites are not just yearning to retain their own privilege, even if they construe the sentiment as whites dreading that people of color will take retribution by treating whites as whites have long treated them. Whites ought not to feel besieged to begin with, because they still occupy the upper strata of society to a far greater extent than people of color, whether measured by high offices in the government, management positions in the leading companies, or sheer wealth. But people of color must know that they can exacerbate the tensions if they suggest that they intend to bring the downfall of whites. All of us must be able to give and receive mutual assurances that together we can rise above our checkered history, that those who know the past are not doomed to repeat it. Just as Asian Americans can identify with whites, we may be able to coax whites into identifying with us.

Coalitions also make us reconsider our objectives. As people of color approach equality, it becomes even more elusive. Reconstruction always ends unfinished. Racial minorities approach the point of diminishing returns, where the additional expenditure of effort produces a lower level of benefit. The progress that has been made affects the potential for further change, and momentum loses to the odds.

At least middle-class African Americans have achieved some semblance of equality in formal terms. They undoubtedly continue to suffer in comparison to their white peers, but they may appear to be better off than whites who are poor. As a consequence, arguments about racial disparities—even disparities that can be proven—lose some of their moral force along with most of their practical effect. The majority is no longer sympathetic toward a minority, because the problem is no longer glaring and thus beyond denial. The bar against African Americans at a private country club is reprehensible, but even if it reinforces the bar against African Americans at a public school, it does not seem quite as wrong. An African American who has an income equivalent to a white who is relatively wealthy (or an Asian American who is presumed to be equal to whites more or less) but who complains that he is still discriminated against, however justified the claim, cannot make himself seem compelling. Even if he is believed, he is not persuasive. His argument exposes the increasing significance of socioeconomic class. African Americans who have amassed enough capital to be petitioning for abolition of the estate tax are right to be offended that they cannot transmit their status as readily as whites, because for racial reasons they have had far fewer generations than whites to accrue property.[60] But in their desire to bequeath all of their assets, they accept the inherited privilege of a few if they can pass it on to their children, too.

Whites who are less well-to-do may resent a claim by a racial minority whom they believe, albeit wrongly, to be better off, that they are not yet respected as are the white rich. The minority also has less reason to protest, for the same reason that the problem is no longer glaring and can even be tolerated. An African American (or an Asian American) who lags behind the white who is identical with her can be satisfied at the modicum of gains she has achieved. Some reckon that the matter is no longer a life-and-death struggle for themselves, even if it is for others. It may be that they cannot acquire more even if the system is improved, although others may be able to do so. Once the minority and the majority overlap, by whatever measure, so that some members of the minority are above some members of the majority, it becomes more difficult to deny the importance of addressing other forms of discrimination. There also is just less incentive to fight, even for those disadvantaged by racial prejudice, if they can advance however modestly without a fight.

There are white Americans who are different in their own way. There are white American Buddhists who have assimilated themselves as thoroughly as I have, but along a path running opposite mine. I know only the pop versions of Zen from perusing the overviews to it written by self-styled "trickster guru" Alan Watts of the Beat generation, the author of books in the 1950s such as *The Meaning of Happiness, The Wisdom of Insecurity,* and *The Way of Zen,* and Robert Pirsig, the author of *Zen and the Art of Motorcycle Maintenance.* I am not interested in shaving my head, donning robes, and chanting in a monastery, but neither am I likely to make fun of that life choice. I need white American Buddhists as much as they need me.

Coalitions make us realize the scope of our challenge. Even if elite institutions become racially integrated, most people of all backgrounds will still be excluded by them. But once elite institutions are racially integrated, they show that many distinctions are arbitrary at best and invidious at worst.

Coalitions that start with race need not end at race. Race can be supplemented without being subsumed. The greatest honor I have received was the invitation to join the Board of Trustees of Gallaudet University. I was humbled to be asked to become a part of the institution, the only liberal arts college for the deaf in the nation. In 1988, the "Deaf President Now!" Movement brought about the end of the patronizing manner in which the school had been operated.[61] Whether it was deliberate, the dominance of hearing administrators and faculty at a school for the deaf and hard-of-hearing suggested that they were incapable of independence and the institution was only nominally for its students. Whenever I am on the campus, I am struck by how deafness is not disabling in the least, within the context of a deaf community. It is I, the hearing individual, who is dumb, at a loss and able to communicate only through interpreters.

The disability rights movement may be the future of the civil rights movement.[62] The disability rights movement, which had its great success with passage of the American With Disabilities Act in 1990, has improved the civil rights movement in many respects. Disability rights activists point out that any of us may, and if we are fortunate to lead a long life are likely to, join their ranks; it only takes an accident or the natural consequences of aging to make us realize that the ramp, the curb cut, and the handrails are there for our benefit, too. They also have argued persuasively that it is not the physical aspects of a disability but rather the social constructions of prejudice and patronizing attitudes that are disabling. The best examples are people who are disfigured, who are widely assumed to be in some sense disabled and are pitied for their condition, even though they are not likely to be in any manner incapable and it is the very compassion that creates stigma.[63] But even those who are handicapped to some extent by nature often find that what is debilitating to a far greater extent is culture. Even though most of us no longer believe that the disabled deserve their condition, many of us continue to feel that they are more deserving if they are superheroes striving to overcome their bodies; our goal is to cure them, so that they will be more like us. Our pity for them establishes our own superiority. In insisting that dignity should not be denied a person because of difference, the disability rights movement rejects the idea that civil rights are bestowed as charity.

I confess, however, that I have dropped issues of gender, sexual orientation, and other bases of discrimination from my speeches, writings, and activism. Sometimes, I have done so out of misguided strategy, as if my cause is stronger if I have fewer supporters. At other times, my neglect has not been as benign, because I also suffer the same sorts of bias as anyone else. My error leads me to ignore the intersectionality of these problems; by referring to racial minorities, women, the deaf, gays and lesbians, and so on, each as if it were a discrete group, I overlook the individuals who are women of color, or deaf and gay, and so forth. I am complicit in discriminating against them— a majority of the populace—as abnormal and reinforcing false dichotomies.

It is the young, however, who will lead. Youth culture should be applauded for its gift for overcoming the faults of earlier generations. Asian American hip-hop artists and African American martial arts black belts are only the most visible personifications of enriching trends. They embody the vitality of diverse cultures. Their dynamism can take on a life of its own. There are many other subcultures that are both more genuine and more sensitive to their own created identities than to racial categories. The subcultures of academe and the military are as different from each other as they can be, but they also are similar in their separation from society at large.[64] The subculture of hunting, fishing, living off the land, and self-sufficiency has fallen out of favor; sportsmen, even bowhunters who kill game to provide food for their family's table, are maligned when they should be admired. Subcultures have arisen around professions and avocations ranging from practicing medicine and acting to ballroom dancing and the board game Scrabble. They infuse society with a diversity that finally divorces race and culture but respects the value of difference.

Civil society either founders on factions or is founded on coalitions. We all share a stake in the healing of the body politic. We must keep the faith.

Epilogue

Deep Springs

Nothing can bring you peace but the triumph of principles.

—RALPH WALDO EMERSON, "SELF-RELIANCE"

I finished this book while spending a week as a teacher at a distinctive institution, Deep Springs College, located in California at the edge of Death Valley. I realized while I was there that this book is about more than Asian Americans and more than race relations; it is about self-consciously creating a true community that allows for personal autonomy.

Deep Springs is such a community. Its enrollment consists of twenty-six men whose academic records are among the finest to be found; who are given full scholarships; and who commit themselves to a rigorous courseload, operating an actual ranch, and governing themselves while living for two years under a strict pledge to give up television and alcohol and not to leave the isolation of their desert campus. After they complete the two years without a summer vacation, the overwhelming majority transfer to the type of school they had been considering as competition to Deep Springs: Harvard, Yale, the other Ivy League institutions, Chicago, and Berkeley. Sixty percent eventually earn doctorates.

I had never been any place like Deep Springs. One of the other instructors who was Asian American, however, remarked that it was the most American place she had ever been.

The founder of Deep Springs was L. L. Nunn, a self-taught and slightly eccentric entrepreneur, who made his fortune in the nineteenth century as the first person to transmit alternating current electricity on a commercial basis and the one who brought power to Niagara Falls. A short man who admired Napoleon, he began to train engineers for his mines because he was unable to find anybody who already had the necessary qualifications. With respect for academic work but disdain for the lack of practical skills offered by colleges, he tried several educational endeavors before establishing Deep Springs College in 1917.

The campus is nestled within mountain ranges, at an elevation of about 5,500 feet above sea level. There is no habitation for thirty miles in any direction. The hour's drive from the Cottontail brothel to the school gate is among the loneliest stretches of highway in the country.

Each student at Deep Springs has finished high school within the top 10 percent of his class and scored on standardized tests within the top few percent of the population. In the morning, the students study physics, Plato, and psychology, at a level equivalent to graduate seminars. In their botany and zoology courses, they tour the rugged environment surrounding them. For a painting class, they hike out with their easels and pigments to depict the same landscape.

The key feature of Deep Springs is the ranch. The ranch trains students to do everything from branding and castrating the calves to milking the cows to slaughtering them. In the afternoons, students ride horses, irrigate and plow fields, feed animals, and clean stables and pens.

The students are responsible for everything: cooking, stocking supplies, planting. At a Friday evening student body meeting, they deliberate over policy. Separate committees, which reverse the usual faculty committee composition by consisting of several students with a single faculty representative, are charged with selecting the incoming students, hiring the new faculty, and managing the agricultural business.

Making the most of their knowledge on even daily routines, they must sort the garbage into the slop that can be fed to the pigs, the materials that can be recycled, and what can be burned. They are smart and talented but neither pedantic nor pretentious. They are mature in some respects, as judged by their ability to discuss Nietzsche with sensitivity, but they are eighteen-year-old boys in other respects, with typical disarray in their dorm rooms. This is no *Lord of the Flies.*

With favorable media coverage from journalists, whose visits must be approved by the students in advance, the extraordinary school has attracted plenty of applicants. Up to 200 young men vie for admission by writing a set of seven lengthy essays for consideration by their peers. The students themselves select a group of finalists, who are invited for a one-week working visit. Almost all of the students they ultimately invite to come accept the offer, foregoing the idle pleasures of taking the summer off and showing up just days after their high school commencement ceremonies.

At once radical and reactionary, Deep Springs is based more on self-selectivity than on elitism. Its pedagogical method not only produces critical thinkers capable of manual labor but also ensures that these students grow into leaders who dedicate themselves to service. Everyone is on a first-name basis. The students, along with the faculty and the staff, who include the customary Ph.D.s and a vice-president who is a cowboy, share their meals in the Boarding House, summoned by a bell when the buffet fare is ready. After eating, anyone with an announcement to make bangs on a metal napkin dispenser with his spoon to call for attention, then stands up to speak. While I was there, one of the students interrupted dinner to tell us that there was a double rainbow in the hills. Everyone ran outside into the sun shower, as some of the students raced toward the terrestrial foundations of the brilliant twin arcs.

It would be easy to idealize Deep Springs, which has its share of problems, ranging from the mundane complications of its multifaceted program to the occasional student who fails as spectacularly as his colleagues are succeeding. Deep Springs is not a model for society; it is all-male and highly selective, among other differences that cannot and should not be emulated. But the success of Deep Springs suggests that our multiple aspirations to diversity can be reconciled and realized. It also reveals, however, how artificial culture really is: It requires thoughtful planning to create the possibility of spontaneous camaraderie.

Most obviously, Deep Springs is very much a community with all the benefits and disadvantages that concept entails. It is a real community, not an imagined one. The communal nature of its activities enhances the passage of time and the purity of personal space. Days, weeks, months, and years all have their rhythms, but the pace is set by study, work, and community, with only the natural hurry of livestock to be fed or an accident to be tended to and without the temptations of becoming a couch potato channel-surfing through sitcom reruns, drinking to excess, or, for that matter, pursuing romance. In the vastness of the distances, a car can be glimpsed ten miles away as it slowly makes its way down the highway. The concentrated housing, arranged in a circle around the Main Building, offers both the reassuring and claustrophobic insularity of the surrounding busyness of people in close quarters and a much-needed but overwhelming sense of solitude in occupying a building all to yourself.

Students must live, work, play, and study together. Breaks from their fellows allow them to escape only into seclusion. They quickly recognize that they are dependent on one another for their physical sustenance, even as each of them becomes more self-confident of his intellectual abilities. Their emotions can be extreme, but they are tempered.

In a time and at a place with everyone sharing the same mission, which is so unlike that of any other school, the Deep Springs students bond and appreciate what they have in common even as they develop and welcome what makes them dissimilar. Each of them possesses his own identity, and together they share a singular purpose. Both the individuals and the group are impressively unique: It would be as impossible to confuse a Deep Springer for another college student elsewhere as it would to confuse them with each other. The opposed meanings of the word "cleave" capture the spirit aptly: Deep Springs cleaves the students from society at large, but the students cleave to one another. There is neither orthodoxy nor anonymity.

The rest of us lack the benefits of direct guidance from professors, farmers, cooks, and alumni, not to mention the classes in great literature, the projects of the laboratory, the day-to-day interaction with a herd of cattle, and mandatory participation in civic life. We do not often ask that our lives change in the manner that young men expect will occur when they leave home. We may not be eager for the intensity of the experience.

The issues that must be dealt with to sustain Deep Springs and those that must be dealt with to sustain our culture are the same except for their scale. They may be amenable to similar philosophies. Just as the Founders believed that patriotism could be committed to cosmopolitanism even as it was loyal to the United States of America too, I believe that by containing the world our nation can find its strength. In so doing, our country can become moral without being self-righteous. We also can be an exemplary power, not an imperial one. We can celebrate a fusion of ritual and dissent. Our lives are nourished by many sources.

As is true at Deep Springs, each of us alone and all of us together must face the challenges of universalism and individualism. The universalism is abstract and thin; the individualism is applied and thick; together, they are the means and the ends of meaningful lives.[1] The balance is exemplified by Ralph Waldo Emerson, the sage from Concord, whose essays I re-read in the appropriate setting of the Deep Springs reading room. Emerson's Transcendentalist aphorisms are the perfect argument for a combination of universalism and individualism in their equipoise of the Oversoul with the self-reliant man. In his essay on the "American Scholar," which announced the birth of a new intellectual epoch, Emerson asserts, "It is one soul which animates all men," but "in self-trust all the virtues are comprehended," and "help must come from the bosom alone."[2] With a mysticism that required a receptive attitude even then, in his essay on the "Oversoul" he speaks of "within man . . . the soul of the whole; the wise silence; the universal beauty, to which every part and particle is equally related, the eternal ONE." In his essay on "Self-Reliance," he writes that "imitation is suicide" and "I am ashamed to think how easily we capitulate to badges and names, to large societies and dead institutions."[3] He is adamant that "what I must do is all that concerns me, not what the people think." These thoughts may be contradictory—it is no wonder that Emerson declares, "a foolish consistency is the hobgoblin of little minds"—but they still resonate.

As I observed at Deep Springs, a genuine universalism understands traditions, combines them, and generates something new as the core while inventing a structure that allows multiple subcultures to flourish; the only requirement being the toleration of others. Such a universalism offers procedural liberty, setting out the general rules under which everyone can pursue their own visions of the good life. Universalism can overcome our tendencies toward self-interest, group-interest, and the meanness of bigotry. It may be the only treatment for the conceit from which almost all of us suffer, which causes us to prize our ancestry as if our name by itself gave us the claim to superiority. Asian Americans need an antidote to this arrogance as much as anyone else.

This universalism cannot be a particular agenda masquerading as the absolute truth nor a bland homogeneity. It may be impossible to insist that we become fluent in Esperanto as the synthetic language of awkward compromise. It is possible instead to allow all who have adopted English to adapt it as well. If English is to be respected as the lingua franca, none of its speakers can be denigrated. The master's accent and diction should be surpassed, rather than copied. The universal cannot be imposed through conquest even if metaphorical. Universalism also cannot be too intangible, vanishing into vagueness and losing all appeal.

A genuine individualism is creative, producing new ideas that are dynamic and unconventional, perhaps lacking even the value of humility in their passion. Such an individualism provides substantive equality if it succeeds, but whether we can achieve the good life through the principles we have devised can be tested only on a case-by-case basis. Asian American individuals give "Asian American" meaning as they define it to suit themselves. One cannot become an individual by categorically avoiding Asian Americans in favor of following others, for that individualism would be a farce.

But as I also saw at Deep Springs, this individualism can be neither imitative nor imitated; it cannot be parochial. It cannot be the product of either coercion that forces a conception of ethnicity upon a person or a contrary compulsion that induces a rejection of ethnicity in a person. It cannot be assimilation of an ordinary type, demanding uniformity with an external set of norms, any more than it can be multiculturalism of a crude type, insisting on submission to an inherited set of customs. Individualism also cannot be too egotistical, retreating into narcissism and solipsism.

All people yearn to belong and to be comforted with the absolute affection we enjoyed when we were children, but we also strive to stand out as important and deserving in our own right. We seek each of these feelings within a context: if not at school or at work, then among family and friends, perhaps at church or within a political organization, and at a level above that of the charge card advertising slogan, "membership has its privileges." As persons and as a people, we ought to make choices that allow us to lead lives of integrity whether we prefer the universal or the individual. If we are to lead lives that are active and contemplative, the options are more similar than they are different. They are bound up affirmatively through the cultivation of mutual respect and the encouragement of independence, negatively in the rejection of materialism and superficiality. At this level, Asian Americans are identical to everyone else.

The experiment of Deep Springs is the experiment of our democracy. As a nation to surpass nations, we have promised ourselves liberty and equality. Over time, we have extended civil rights to an ever-greater range of people while reducing the invidious distinctions among us. We still have work to do to fulfill our potential. All American dreams depend on optimism and perpetual rejuvenation. Americans were idealists once and we can become idealists again. We must approach perfection even if we cannot reach it. Our journey begins anew.

References

Chapter 1

With respect to Asian Americans in general, I recommend Ronald Takaki, *Strangers from a Different Shore: A History of Asian Americans*, rev. ed. (Boston: Little, Brown, 1998), as the standard work. Other important volumes are Karin Aguilar San Juan, ed., *The State of Asian America: Activism and Resistance in the 1990's* (Boston: South End Press, 1994); Sucheng Chan, *Asian Americans: An Interpretative History* (Boston: Twayne, 1991); Roger Daniels, *Asian America: Chinese and Japanese in the United States Since 1850* (Seattle: The Washington University Press, 1988); Jeffery Paul Chan et al., eds., *The Big Aiiieeeee! An Anthology of Chinese American and Japanese American Literature* (New York: Meridian, 1991); Frank Chin et al., eds., *Aiiieeeee! An Anthology of Asian-American Writers* (Washington: Howard University Press, 1974); Timothy P. Fong and Larry H. Shingawa, eds., *Asian Americans: Experiences and Perspectives* (Upper Saddle River, N.J.: Prentice Hall, 2000); Timothy P. Fong, *The Contemporary Asian American Experience: Beyond the Model Minority* (Upper Saddle River, N.J.: Prentice Hall, 1998); Jessica Hagedorn, ed., *Charlie Chan Is Dead: An Anthology of Contemporary Asian American Fiction* (New York: Penguin Books, 1993); Min Zhou and James V. Gatewood, eds., *Contemporary Asian America: A Multidisciplinary Reader* (New York: New York University Press, 2000); and Helen Zia, *Asian American Dreams: The Emergence of an American People* (New York: Farrar, Straus & Giroux, 2000).

An important early resource is Amy Tachiki et al., *Roots: An Asian American Reader* (Los Angeles, Calif.: UCLA Asian American Studies Center, 1971). A valuable reader on women, gender, and feminism is Asian Women United of California, ed., *Making Waves: An Anthology of Writings By and About Asian American Women* (Boston: Beacon, 1989).

The leading academic journals concerning Asian Americans are *Amerasia Journal,* published by the UCLA Asian American Studies Center, and *Asian American Policy Review,* published by the Kennedy School of Government at Harvard University and the new *Journal of Asian American Studies,* published by Johns Hopkins University Press. The papers presented at the Association of Asian American Studies conferences, which are published by Washington State University, and the reports of Leadership Education for Asian Pacifics, also are important resources. The leading Asian American-interest popular periodicals are *A. Magazine* and *Asian Week*; more specialized magazines such as *Giant Robot* and *Yolk*, which target a younger demographic, also may be useful for information on the latest trends.

An especially helpful resource for researchers is a bibliographic essay by Sucheng Chan, "Asian American Historiography," in Franklin Ng, ed., *The History and Immigration of Asian Americans* (New York: Garland, 1998).

Also useful are the five reports of the United States Commission on Civil Rights regarding Asian Americans. U.S. Commission on Civil Rights: *Briefing on Civil Rights Implications in the Treatment of Asian Pacific Americans during the Campaign Finance Controversy* (Washington, D.C.: U.S. Commission on Civil Rights, 1998); U.S. Commission on Civil Rights, *Civil Rights Issues Facing Asian Americans in the 1990s* (Washington, D.C.: Government Printing Office, 1992); U.S. Commission on Civil Rights, *Voices Across America: Roundtable Discussions of Asian Civil Rights Issues* (Washington, D.C.: Government Printing Office, 1991); U.S. Commission on Civil Rights, *The Economic Status of Americans of Asian Descent: An Exploratory Investigation* (Washington, D.C.: Government Printing Office, 1988); U.S. Commission on Civil Rights, *Recent Activities Against Citizens and Residents of Asian Decent* (Washington, D.C.: Government Printing Office, 1986).

The numerous scholarly and mass media articles that were reviewed for background but not directly quoted have not been cited, with only a few exceptions.

Chapter 2

Among the most important books and articles on the model minority myth are the following: Herbert R. Barringer et al., *Asians and Pacific Islanders in the United States* (New York: Russell Sage Foundation, 1993); Jayjia Hsia, *Asian Americans in Higher Education and at Work* (Hillsdale, N.J.: Lawrence Erlbaum Associates, 1988); Stacey J. Lee, Unraveling the "Model Minority" Stereotype New York: Teachers College Press, 1996); United States Civil Rights Commission, *The Economic Status of Asian Americans: An Exploratory Investigation* (Washington, D.C.: U.S. Civil Rights Commission, 1988); Deborah Woo, *Glass Ceilings and Asian Americans: The New Face of Workplace Barriers* (Walnut Creek, Calif.: Alta Mira Press, 2000); Amado Cabezas and Gary Kawaguchi, "Empirical Evidence for Continuing Asian American Income Inequality: The Human Capital Model and Labor Market Segmentation," in Gary Y. Okihiro et al., eds., *Reflections on Shattered Windows: Promises and Prospects for Asian American Studies* (Pullman: Washington State University Press, 1988); Cliff Cheng and Tojo Joseph Thatchenkery, ed., "Asian Americans in Organizations," *The Journal of Applied Behavioral Science* 33, no. 3 (1997): 270–406 (special issue on Asian Americans); Lucie Cheng and Philip Q. Yang, "The 'Model Minority' Deconstructed," in Min Zhou and James V. Gatewood, eds., *Contemporary Asian America: A Multidisciplinary Reader* (New York: New York University Press, 2000), 459–82; Diane Divoky, "The Model Minority Goes to School," *Phi Delta Kappan* 70, no. 3 (1988): 219–22; Morrison G. Wong, "The Education of White, Chinese, Filipino and Japanese Students: A Look at 'High School and Beyond,'" *Sociological Perspectives 33* (1990): 335–74; Morrison G. Wong, "Model Students? Teachers' Perceptions and Expectations of Their Asian and White Students," *Sociology of Education* 53 (1980): 236–46; Charles Hirschman and Morrison G. Wong, "The Extraordinary Educational Attainment of Asian-Americans: A Search for Historical Evidence and Explanations," *Social Forces* 54, no. 1 (1986): 1–27; Charles Hirschman and Morrison G. Wong, "Socioeconomic Gains of Asian Americans, Blacks, and Hispanics: 1960–1976," *American Journal of Sociology* 90, no. 3 (1984): 574–607; Charles Hirschman and Morrison G. Wong, "Trends in Socioeconomic Achievement Among Immigrant and Native-Born Asian-Americans, 1960–1976," *Sociological Quarterly* 22 (1981): 495–513; Won Moo Hurh and Kwang Chung Kim, "The 'Success' Image of Asian Americans: Its Validity and Its practical and Theoretical Implications," *Ethnic and Racial Studies* 12 (1989): 512–38; Harry H. L. Kitano, "Japanese Americans: The Development of a Middleman Minority," in Norris Hundley, Jr., ed., *The Asian American: The Historical Experience* (Santa Barbara, Cal.: Clio Books, 1976); Gilbert Kwok-

Yiu Ko and Clifford C. Clogg, "Earnings Differential between Chinese and Whites in 1980: Subgroup Variability and Evidence for Convergence," *Social Science Research* 18 (1989): 249–70 ; Donald T. Mizokawa and David B. Ryckman, "Attributions of Academic Success and Failure: A Comparison of Six Asian-American Ethnic Groups," *Journal of Cross-Cultural Psychology* 21, no. 4: 434–51; Victor Nee and Jimy Sanders, "The Road to Parity: Determinants of the Socioeconomic Achievements of Asian Americans," *Ethnic and Racial Studies* 8 (1985): 75–93; Victor Nee & Herbert Y. Wong, "Asian American Socioeconomic Achievement: The Strength of the Family Bond," *Sociological Perspectives* 28, no. 3 (1985): 281–306; Samuel S. Peng and DeeAnn Wright, "Explanation of Academic Achievement of Asian American Students," *Journal of Educational Research* 87, no. 6 (1994): 346–52; Paul Ong and Suzanne J. Hee, "Economic Diversity," in Paul Ong, ed., *The State of Asian America: Economic Diversity, Issues and Policies* (Los Angeles: LEAP, 1994); Paul M. Ong, Lucie Cheng and Leslie Evans, "Migration of Highly Educated Asians and Global Dynamics," *Asia and Pacific Migration Journal* 1, nos.3–4 (1992): 543–67; Doobo Shim, "From Yellow Peril Through Model Minority To Renewed Yellow Peril," *Journal of Communication Inquiry* 22, no. 4 (1989): 385–409; Stanley Sue and Sumie Okazaki, "Asian-American Educational Achievements: A Phenomenon in Search of an Explanation," *American Psychologist* (August 1990): 913–20; Bob H. Suzuki, "Asian Americans as the 'Model Minority:' Outdoing Whites? Or Media Hype," *Change* (November-December 1989): 12–19 (special issue on Asian Americans); Bob H. Suzuki, "Education and Socialization of Asian Americans: A Revisionist Analysis of the 'Model Minority' Thesis," in Russell Endo, Stanley Sue and Nathaniel N. Wagner, ed., *Asian-Americans: Social and Psychological Perspectives* 2 (1980): 155–75; Elizabeth S. Ahn Toupin, "Preliminary Findings on Asian Americans: 'The Model Minority' in a Small Private East Coast College," *Journal of Cross-Cultural Psychology* 22 (1991): 403–17; Morrison G. Wong, "Post–1965 Asian Immigrants: Where Do They Come From, Where Are They Now, and Where Are They Going?," *Annals of the American Academy* 487 (1986): 150–68; Morrison G. Wong & Charles Hirschman, "Labor Force Participation and Socioeconomic Attainment of Asian-American Women," *Sociological Perspectives* 26, no. 4 (1983): 423–46; Paul Wong et al., "Asian Americans as a Model Minority: Self-Perceptions and Perceptions by Other Racial Groups," *Sociological Perspectives* 41, no. 1 (Spring 1998): 95–118; Deborah Woo, "Bibliographic Essay: Asian Americans in Mainstream Corporate Management: Barriers Despite Educational Achievement," *Sage Race Relations Abstracts* 21, no. 2 (May 1996): 3–33; Deborah Woo, "The Socioeconomic Status of Asian American Women in the Labor Force: An Alternative View," *Sociological Perspectives* 28, no. 3 (1985): 307–38; Keiko Yamanaka and Kent McClelland, "Earning the Model-Minority Image: Diverse Strategies of Economic Adaptation by Asian-American Women," *Ethnic and Racial Studies* 17, no. 1 (January 1994): 79–114; Albert H. Yee, "Asians as Stereotypes and Students: Misperceptions That Persist," *Educational Psychology Review* 4 (1992): 95–132; Won Yong-Kin, "'Model Minority' Strategy and Asian Americans' Tactics," *Korea Journal* 34, no. 2 (Summer 1994): 57–66; Chuanshen Chen and Harold W. Stevenson, "Motivation and Mathematics Achievement: A Comparative Study of Asian-American, Caucasian-American, and East Asian High School Students," *Child Development* 66 (1995): 1215–34; Chuanshen Chen and Harold W. Stevenson, "Homework: A Cross-Cultural Examination," *Child Development* 60 (1990): 551–61; Robert D. Hess et al., "Cultural Variations in Family Beliefs About Children's Performance in Mathematics: Comparisons Among People's Republic of China, Chinese-American, and Caucasian-American Families," *Journal of Educational Psychology* 79 (1987): 179–88; Barbara Schneider and Yongsook Lee, "A Model for Academic Success: The School and Home Environments of East Asian Students," *Anthropology & Education Quarterly* 21 (1990): 359–77; Naomi Fejgin, "Factors Contributing to the Academic Excellence of American Jewish and Asian Students," *Sociology of Education* 68 (1995): 18–30; Valeria Ooka Pang, "The Relationship of Test Anxiety and Math Achievement to Parental Values in Asian-American and European-American Middle School Students," *Journal of Research and Development in Education* 24 (1991): 1–10.

I have discussed these issues previously in Theodore Hsien Wang and Frank H. Wu, "Beyond the Model Minority Myth," George E. Curry, ed., *The Affirmative Action Debate* (Reading, Mass.: Addison-Wesley, 1996), 191–207.

Chapter 3

Both of the leading works on immigration history cover primarily European immigrants; they are John Higham, *Strangers in the Land: Patterns of American Nativism 1860–1925* (New Brunswick: Rutgers University Press, 1998) and Oscar Handlin, *The Uprooted: The Epic Story of the Great Migrations that Made the American People*, 2d edition (Boston: Little, Brown, 1951). Two useful works on the immigration history of Asian Americans are Bill Ong Hing, *Making and Remaking Asian America Through Immigration Policy, 1850–1990* (Stanford, Calif.: Stanford University Press, 1993) and Lisa Lowe, *Immigrant Acts* (Durham, N.C.: Duke University Press, 1996). An important discussion of the perpetual-foreigner syndrome is Neil Gotanda, "Asian American Rights and the 'Miss Saigon' Syndrome," in Hyung-Chang Kim, ed., *Asian Americans and the Supreme Court: A Documentary History* (Westport, Conn.: Greenwood Press, 1992) For information about immigration generally, I have relied on James Smith and *The New Americans: Economic, Demographic, and Fiscal Effects of Immigration* (Washington, D.C.: National Academy Press, 1997); Alejandro Portes and Ruben G. Rumbaut, *Immigrant America: A Portrait*, 2d ed. (Berkeley: University of California Press, 1996); and David M. Reimers, *Unwelcome Strangers: American Identity and the Turn Against Immigration* (New York: Columbia University Press, 1998). I have discussed some of these issues previously in Frank H. Wu, "The Limits of Borders: A Modest Proposal for Immigration Reform," *Stanford Law & Policy Review* 7 (1996). 35-73 and Frank H. Wu and Francey Lim Youngberg, "People from China Crossing the River: Asian American Political Empowerment and Foreign Influence," in Gordon H. Chang, *Asian Americans and Politics: Perspectives, Experiences, Prospects* (Washington, DC.: Woodrow Wilson Center/Stanford University Press, 2001): 311-53.

Chapter 4

With respect to Asian Americans and affirmative action, there are only a few studies extant. The most important are Teresa Chi-Ching Sun, *The Admission Dispute: Asian Americans Versus University of California at Berkeley* (Lanham, Md.: University Press of America, 1997); Don T. Nakanishi and Tina Yamano Nishida, eds., *The Asian American Educational Experience: A Source Book for Teachers and Students* (New York: Routledge, 1995); and Dana Y. Takagi, *The Retreat from Race: Asian-American Admissions and Racial Politics* (New Brunswick, N.J.: Rutgers University Press, 1992). Additional sources are cited in Gabriel J. Chin, et al., *Beyond Self-Interest: Asian Pacific Americans Toward a Community of Justice* (Los Angeles: UCLA Asian American Studies Center 1996) and Frank H. Wu, "Neither Black Nor White: Asian Americans and Affirmative Action," *Boston College Third World Law Review 15*, no. 2 (1995): 225–84.

I have discussed these issues previously in Theodore Hsien Wang and Frank H. Wu, "Beyond the Model Minority Myth," George E. Curry, ed., *The Affirmative Action Debate* (Reading, Mass.: Addison-Wesley, 1996), 191–207.

Chapter 5

To present the narrative of the Wen Ho Lee case, I reviewed all articles about him published in the following periodicals: *L.A. Times, New York Times,* and *Washington Post.* I also have reviewed those materials prepared by his defense counsel that are available.

Chapter 7

In addition to texts cited specifically below, I have found the following works especially helpful in understanding intermarriage and the mixed race movement: Katya Gibel Azoulay, *Black, Jewish, And Interracial: It's Not the Color of Your Skin, but the Race of Your Kin,* (Durham, N.C.: Duke University Press, 1997); Jack D. Forbes, *Black Africans and Native Americans: Color, Race and Caste in the Evolution of Red-Black Peoples* (Oxford: Basil Blackwell, 1988); Martha Hodes, ed., *Sex, Love, Race: Crossing Boundaries in North American History* (New York: New York University Press, 1999); Rachel F. Moran, *Interracial Intimacy: The Regulation of Race and Romance* (Chicago: University of Chicago, 2001); Paul C. Rosenblatt, *Multiracial Couples: Black and White Voices* (Thousand Oaks, Calif.: Sage, 1995); Maria P. P. Root, ed., *The Multiracial Experience: Racial Borders as the New Frontier* (Thousand Oaks, Calif.: Sage, 1996); Maria P. P. Root, ed., *Racially Mixed People in America* (Newbury Park, Calif.: Sage, 1992); Werner Sollors, ed., *Interracialism: Black-White Intermarriage in American History, Literature, and the Law* (Oxford: Oxford University Press, 2000); Werner Sollors, *Neither Black Nor White Yet Both: Thematic Explorations of Interracial Literature* (Cambridge: Harvard University Press, 1997); Paul Spickard and W. Jeffrey Burroughs, eds., *We Are a People: Narrative and Multiplicity in Constructing Ethnic Identity* (Philadelphia: Temple University Press, 2000); Paul R. Spickard, *Mixed Blood: Intermarriage and Ethnic Identity in Twentieth-Century America* (Madison: The University of Wisconsin Press, 1989); Charles Herbert Stember, *Sexual Racism: The Emotional Barrier to an Integrated Society* (New York: Elsevier, 1976); Teresa Williams-Leon, *The Sum of Our Parts: Mixed Heritage Asian Americans* (Philadelphia: Temple University Press 2001); Joel Williamson, *New People: Miscegenation and Mulattoes in the United States* (New York: New York University Press, 1984); Naomi Zack, ed., *American Mixed Race: The Culture of Microdiversity* (Lanham, MD: Rowman and Littlefield, 1995); and Naomi Zack, *Race and Mixed Race* (Philadelphia: Temple University Press, 1993).

Epilogue

For information about Deep Springs College and its founder, L. L. Nunn, I have consulted the following sources: Robert B. Aird, *Deep Springs: Its Founder, History and Philosophy, with Personal Reflections* (Dyer, Nev.: Deep Springs College, 1997); Michael A. Smith, *The Students of Deep Springs College* (Revere, Penn.: Lodima Press, 2000); Jim Doherty, "The Cattle Ranch That Doubles as a School for Doers," *Smithsonian* (April 1995): 114; Sally Johnson, "A Free Bachelor's. No Kidding," *New York Times,* January 4, 1998, 4A-17; Ben Wildavsky, "Isolated College's Unusual Allure; School, School on the Range," *San Francisco Chronicle,* July 29, 1993, A1. My understanding of Ralph Waldo Emerson has been shaped by, in addition to Emerson's own writings, most especially Robert D. Richardson, *Emerson: Mind on Fire* (Berkeley, Calif.: University of California Press, 1995).

Notes

Chapter One

1. Jeff Yang et al., *Eastern Standard Time: A Guide to Asian Influence on American Culture, from Astro Boy to Zen Buddhism* (Boston: Houghton Mifflin, 1997); Olivia Barker, "The Asianization of America; But Eastern Influences Do Not Mean Asian-Americans Are Insiders," *USA Today,* March 22, 2001, A1.

2. Arthur Golden, *Memoirs of a Geisha* (New York: Knopf, 1997).

3. Elaine H. Kim, *Asian American Literature: An Introduction to the Writings and Their Social Context* (Philadelphia: Temple University Press, 1982), xix.

4. "Miss Manners," the advice columnist, has addressed this issue, but she prefers to assume that these incidents are not racial. See Judith Martin, "Anger, Fear and Loathing at Airport and at Dinner," *Washington Post,* July 22, 1998, D16.

5. Ralph Ellison, *Invisible Man* (New York: Random House, 1952); bell hooks, *Killing Rage: Ending Racism* (New York: Henry Holt, 1995), 8–10.

6. Ellis Cose, *The Rage of a Privileged Class: Why Are Middle Class Blacks Angry? Why Should America Care?* (New York: Harper Collins 1995); Lena Williams, *It's the Little Things: The Everyday Interactions That Get Under the Skin of Blacks and Whites* (New York: Harcourt, 2000).

7. Lee Ross and Richard E. Nisbett, *The Person and the Situation: Perspectives of Social Psychology* (Philadelphia: Temple University Press, 1991). For a review of the social psychology literature, I also have relied on Susan T. Fiske, "Stereotyping, Prejudice, and Discrimination," and Marilynn B. Brewer and Rupert J. Brown, "Intergroup Relations" in Daniel T. Gilbert et al., eds., *The Handbook of Social Psychology,* 4th ed., vol. 2 (Boston: McGraw-Hill, 1998), 357–414, 554–94. See also Gordon W. Allport, *The Nature of Prejudice, 25th anniversary ed.* (Reading, Mass.: Perseus, 1979).

8. Matt Dietrich, "WQLZ Makes Bad Call With Chinatown Bit," *State Journal-Register* (Springfield, Illinois), April 15, 2001, 43; Marsha Ginsberg, "Crisis Inflames Bias Against Asians; Ethnic Stereotypes in Broadcast, Print Media Prompt Protests," *San Francisco Chronicle,* April 14, 2001, A1; Lynette Kalsnes, "Some Asians Fear Film Fallout," *Chicago Tribune,* May 26, 2001, B20; Chisun Lee, "Fun With China," *Village Voice,* May 1, 2001, 50.

9. *Seeing Calvin Coolidge in a Dream* (New York: St. Martin's Press,, 1996); "Thinking About Internment," *Chronicles,* January 2000, 42–44.

10. See Philip A. Pan, "China Convicts Scholars: AU Researcher Sentenced to 10 Years on Spy Charges," *Washington Post,* July 25, 2001, A1; Elisabeth Rosenthal, "For China-Born U.S. Citizens, Visiting Homeland Has Risks," *New York Times,* May 1, 2001, A1; John Pomfret, "Another Academic Detained by China," *Washington Post,* April 10, 2001, A16; Michael E. Ruane, "Plane-Collision Furor Worries Husband of Detained Scholar: Man Fears Wife Will Remain in Chinese Prison Even Longer," *Washington Post,* April 8, 2001, C1; Erik Eckholm, "Beijing Agents Detain Another Chinese-Born American," *New York Times,* March 31, 2001, A7.

11. A "race man" is someone who, because racism has forced him to adopt race consciousness, uses race as a source of pride rather than shame. St. Clair Drake and Horace R. Cayton, *Black Metropolis: A Study of Negro Life in a Northern City* (New York: Harcourt Brace & World, 1945).

12. The Committee of 100, American Attitudes Toward Chinese Americans & Asian Americans, Including Conversations with Americans About Chinese Americans and Asian Americans (New York: Committee of 100, 2001); see also Thomas B. Edsall, "25% of U.S. View Chinese Americans Negatively, Poll Says," *Washington Post,* April 26, 2001, A4.

13. The change in racial attitudes is documented in Howard Schuman, *Racial Attitudes in America: Trends and Interpretations, rev. ed.* (Cambridge, Mass.: Harvard University Press, 1997) and Donald R. Kinder and Lynn M. Sanders, *Divided by Color: Racial Politics and Democratic Ideals* (Chicago: University of Chicago Press, 1996). The ongoing reports released by the *Washington Post*, Harvard University, and the Kaiser Foundation also provide useful information. See Richard Morin, "Misperceptions Cloud Whites' View of Blacks," *Washington Post*, July 11, 2001, A1; Malcolm Gladwell, "Personal Experience, the Primary Gauge," *Washington Post*, October 8, 1995, A26; Richard Morin, "A Distorted Image of Minorities; Poll Suggests That What Whites Think They See May Affect Beliefs," *Washington Post*, Oct. 8, 1995, A1. The problems of denial and preference falsification are discussed in Michael A. Milburn and Sheree D. Conrad, *The Politics of Denial* (Cambridge, Mass.: MIT Press, 1996) and Timur Kuran, *Private Truths, Public Lies: The Social Consequences of Preference Falsification* (Cambridge, Mass.: Harvard University Press, 1995). See also David O. Sears et al., *Racialized Politics: The Debate About Racism in America* (Chicago: University of Chicago Press, 2000).

14. John F. Dovidio and Samuel L. Gaertner, "On the Nature of Contemporary Prejudice: The Causes, Consequences, and Challenges of Aversive Racism," in Jennifer L. Eberhardt and Susan T. Fiske, eds., *Confronting Racism: The Problem and the Response* (Thousand Oaks, Calif.: 1998); Samuel L. Gaertner and John F. Dovidio, "The Aversive Form of Racism," in Samuel L. Gaertner and John F. Dovidio, *Prejudice, Discrimination, and Racism* (Orlando, Fla.: Academic Press, 1986), 61–89.

15. One of the few places the essay can be readily found is S. T. Joshi, *Documents of American Prejudice: An Anthology of Writings on Race from Thomas Jefferson to David Duke* (New York: Basic, 1999), 439–44.

16. Philip S. Foner, *Jack London: American Rebel* (New York: The Citadel Press, 1964), 59; see also Andrew Sinclair, *Jack: A Biography of Jack London* (New York: Harper & Row, 1977), 105–8.

17. Joan London, *Jack London and His Times: An Unconventional Biography* (Seattle: University of Washington Press, 1968), 212; Robert Baltrop, *Jack London: The Man, the Writer, the Rebel* (London: Pluto Press, 1976), 87.

18. Jack London, *Novels and Social Writings* (New York: Literary Classics of the United States, 1982). Foner also omits it from his American Rebel edition.

19. Lawson Fusao Inada, *Only What We Could Carry: The Japanese American Internment Experience* (Berkeley, Calif.: Heyday Books, 2000), 123.

20. The document is reprinted as Samuel Gompers and Herman Gutstadt, "Meat vs. Rice: American Manhood Against Asiatic Coolieism," in Joshi, *Documents of American Prejudice*, 436–38.

21. Bernard Mandel, *Samuel Gompers* (Yellow Springs, Ohio: Antioch Press, 1963), 186.

22. Alexander Saxton, *The Indispensable Enemy: Labor and the Anti-Chinese Movement in California* (Berkeley, Cal.: University of California Press, 1971), 273.

23. Tomas Almaguer, *Racial Fault Lines: The Historical Origins of White Supremacy in California* (Berkeley, Cal.: University of California Press, 1994), 201.

24. Samuel Gompers, *Seventy Years of Life and Labour, vol. 2* (New York: Augustus M. Kelley, 1967), 161.

25. Florence Calvert Thornton, *Samuel Gompers—American Statesman* (New York: Philosophical Library, 1957), 87.

26. A brief mention of the case can be found in Karl Olson and Erin Daly, "Hyperbole, Epithets, Fiery Rhetoric and Other Strong Words Are Still Protected in the Arena of Robust Speech," *The Recorder*, June 18, 1991, 8.

27. Mari J. Matsuda et al., *Words That Wound: Critical Race Theory, Assaultive Speech, and the First Amendment* (Boulder, Colo.: Westview, 1993).

28. See Amy Gutmann and Dennis Thompson, *Democracy and Disagreement* (Cambridge, Mass.: Harvard University Press, 1996); George Lakoff, *Moral Politics: What Conservatives Know That Liberals Don't* (Chicago: University of Chicago Press, 1996); Michael Lerner, *The Politics of Meaning: Restoring Hope and Possibility in an Age of Cynicism* (New York: Perseus, 1997).

29. Gary Y. Okihiro, *Margins and Mainstreams: Asians in American History and Culture* (Seattle: University of Washington Press, 1994), 31–63.

30. Chang-Lin Tien, "Affirming Affirmative Action," Perspective on Affirmative Action . . . and Its Impact on Asian Pacific Americans (Los Angeles: Leadership Education for Asian Pacifics, 1996), 19.

31. *Gong Lum v. Rice*, 275 U.S. 78 (1927).

32. Michael Lind, "To Have and Have Not: Notes on the Progress of the American Class War," Harper's, June 1995, 35. See also, e.g., Michael Kelly, "Test Results Illustrate Racial Divide That Can't Be Ignored," *National Journal*, April 16, 2001, A11. Dan Walters, *The New California: Facing the 21st Century* (Sacramento: California Journal Press, 1986), 20.

33. Roi Ottley, *New World A-Coming: Inside Black America* (New York: Arno Press, 1968).

34. Spike Lee, *Do The Right Thing* (New York: Fireside, 1989), 250–51.

35. Harry H. L. Kitano, *Japanese Americans: The Evolution of a Subculture* (Englewood Cliffs, N.J.: Prentice-Hall, 1969), 3.

36. Cornel West's collection of essays by that title has been an important influence on discussions of race. Cornel West, *Race Matters* (Boston: Beacon, 1993).

37. Joann Lee, "Mistaken Headline Underscores Racial Presumptions," *Editor & Publisher*, April 25, 1998, 64.

38. Howard Chua-Eoan, "Profiles in Outrage; America Is Home, But Asian Americans Feel Treated as Outlanders with Unproven Loyalties," *Time*, September 25, 2000, 40.

39. See Cindy Rodriguez, "No Longer Classified As Minorities, Asians Fear," *Boston Globe,* November 1, 1999, C6; Cindy Rodriguez, "Reclassified, Asians Fear Cuts in School Assistance," *Boston Globe,* October 25, 1999, A1. Asian Americans successfully persuaded the Gates Millennium Scholars program, one of the largest ever, to include promising students of Asian descent, along with other people of color.

40. Al Kamen, "The Honeymoon Sinks in the East," *Washington Post,* May 25, 2001, A37.

41. See "Lynn Minton Reports Fresh Voices: A Racial Slur Opened My Eyes," *Parade,* July 16, 2000, 15.

42. Edward G. Carmines and James A. Stimson, *Issue Evolution: Race and the Transformation of American Politics* (Princeton: Princeton University Press, 1989); Thomas Byrne Edsall and Mary D. Edsall, *Chain Reaction: The Impact of Race, Rights, and Taxes on American Politics* (New York: Norton, 1991).

43. William Claiborne, "Immigration Foes Find Platform in Iowa; National Groups Fight Governor on Recruiting Workers From Abroad," *Washington Post,* August 19, 2001, A3.

44. Fiske, "Stereotyping, Prejudice, and Discrimination," in Gilbert et al., *Handbook of Social Psychology,* 359.

45. Yolanda Woodlee and Eric Lipton, "Mayoral Aide Has a New Assignment," *Washington Post,* February 11, 1999, J1; Yolanda Woodlee, "Mayor Acted 'Hastily,' Will Rehire Aide; D.C. Official's Use of 'Niggardly' Prompted Controversy and Resignation," *Washington Post,* February 4, 1999, A1; Linton Weeks, "Caught in a Verbal Vortex; One Word Leaves a Lot Still to Be Said About Former D.C. Official David Howard," *Washington Post,* January 29, 1999, C1; Yolanda Woodlee and Vanessa Williams, "Aide's Quitting Spurs Review by D.C. Mayor," *Washington Post,* January 28, 1999, B1; Yolanda Woodlee, "Top D.C. Aide Resigns Over Racial Rumor," *Washington Post,* January 27, 1999, B1. See also John McWhorter, *Losing the Race: Self-Sabotage in Black America* (New York: Free Press, 2000), vii–xv.

46. Andrew Hacker, *Two Nations: Black, White, Separate, Hostile, Unequal* (New York: Scribner's, 1995). Recently a few writers have published books that are more inclusive. For example, journalist Scott Malcolmson, *One Drop of Blood: The American Misadventure of Race* (New York: Farrar, Straus & Giroux, 2000), has extensive sections on both Native Americans and African Americans historically and includes some material on Latinos and Asian Americans today.

47. Lise Funderberg, *Black, White, Other: Biracial Americans Talk About Race and Identity* (New York: William Morrow 1995).

48. W.E.B. DuBois, *Writings* (New York: Literary Classics of the United States, 1986), 372. I have consulted the definitive biography of DuBois, David Levering Lewis, W.E.B. DuBois: *Biography of a Race, 1868-1919* (New York: Henry Holt, 1993) and David Levering Lewis, *W.E.B. DuBois: The Fight for Equality and the American Century, 1919-1963* (New York: Henry Holt, 2000).

49. DuBois, Souls, 363.

50. "Blacks Versus Browns: African-Americans and Latinos," *Atlantic Monthly* (October 1992): 41–68. This essay is reprinted in Nicolaus Mills, *Arguing Immigration: The Debate Over the Changing Face of America* (New York: Touchstone, 1994), 101–42.

51. John Bowring, ed., *The Works of Jeremy Bentham,* vol. 4 (London: Simpkin, Marshall & Co. 1843), 37.

52. Michael A. Omi, "The Changing Meaning of Race," in Neal J. Smelser et al., eds., *America Becoming: Racial Trends and Their Consequences* (Washington, D.C.: National Academy Press, 2001), 252–53.

53. Asian refugees, like any refugees, qualify for federal cash assistance (but, in many instances, not state cash assistance). The programs for refugees, however, are not race based and provide a lower level of benefits. Asian American-owned banks have had trouble with community reinvestment regulations, which require that they lend to economically disadvantaged borrowers. Although they have a heavily Asian American clientele, they lack African American and Latino borrowers and are loathe to reach out to them.

54. Bernard Weinraub, "Turning the Tables on Race Relations," *New York Times,* February 6, 1995, C11.

55. As an example, see Barbara Amiel, "Gender, Race, and O.J.," *Wall Street Journal,* March 9, 1995, A18. Amiel describes Ito as "a suitable race-neutral judge of Japanese ancestry." *See also* Cynthia Kwei Yung Lee, "Beyond Black and White: Racializing Asian Americans in a Society Obsessed with O.J.," *Hastings Women's Law Journal* 6 (1995): 165–208.

56. Lawrence Van Gelder, "D'Amato Mocks Ito and Sets Off Furor," *New York Times,* April 6, 1995, B1.

57. "One America in the 21st Century: The President's Initiative on Race," Commencement Address, University of California at San Diego, 33 *Weekly Comp. Pres. Docs.* 876, 877 (June 14, 1997). The project was criticized by conservatives for lacking opponents of affirmative action. *See* Steven A. Holmes, "Conservatives' Voices Enter Clinton's Dialogue on Race," *New York Times,* December 18, 1997, A24; Steven A. Holmes, "Clinton Panel on Race Relations Is Itself Biased, Gingrich Says," *New York Times,* November 21, 1997, A30; Steven A. Holmes, "Race Panel Excludes Critics of Affirmative Action Plans," *New York Times,* November 20, 1997, A24. It was criticized by progressives for its moderation in Chester Hartmann, *Challenges to Equality: Poverty and Race in America* (Armonk, N.Y.: M.E. Sharpe, 2001).

58. John Hope Franklin and Alfred A. Moss, *From Slavery to Freedom: A History of African Americans,* 8th ed. (New York: Knopf, 2000).

59. Gunnar Myrdal, *An American Dilemma: The Negro Problem and Modern Democracy* (New York: Harper & Row, 1944). Myrdal does not discuss Asian Americans, other than to remark that "only Orientals and possibly Mexicans among all separate ethnic groups" have "as much segregation as Negroes." Ibid., 620. He does not note it, but his distinction aligns all people of color together.

60. Thomas Kuhn, *The Structure of Scientific Revolutions*, 3d ed. (Chicago: University of Chicago Press, 1996).

61. *See* William Powers, "Oh My!," *The New Republic*, August 11-18, 1997, 9; Peter Baker, "A Splinter on the Race Advisory Board: First Meeting Yields Divergent Views on Finding 'One America'," *Washington Post*, July 15, 1997, A4. For more detailed information, *see* "Meeting of the Advisory Board to the President's Initiative on Race and Reconciliation" (July 14, 1997).

62. Mary Frances Berry, "Pie in the Sky? Clinton's Race Initiative Offers Promise and the Potential for Peril," *Emerge* (September 1997): 68. A few commentators agreed with Oh that Latinos and Asian Americans, among others, should be included in discussions of race. Joe Hicks, "The Changing Face of America: In the Next Century, Latinos Will Replace African Americans as the Nation's Largest Minority, and the Asian Population Will Almost Triple; What Will 'Integration' Mean Then?" *Los Angeles Times*, July 20, 1997, M1; Richard Delgado and Juan F. Perea, "Racism Goes Beyond Black and White," *Rocky Mountain News*, November 3, 1997, A39.

63. Gerald Horne, "America's New Racial Divide Is East-West, Not North-South," *Los Angeles Times*, August 24, 1997, M1.

64. Orlando Patterson, "Racism Is Not The Issue," *New York Times*, November 16, 1997, D15.

65. In addition to the U.S. Census, I have relied on Smelser, *America Becoming*. Of the many books on demographic change, I have found helpful Dale Maharidge, *The Coming White Minority: California's Eruptions and America's Future* (New York: Times Books, 1996) and Michael S. Teitelbaum and Jay Winter, *A Question of Numbers: High Migration, Low Fertility, and the Politics of National Identity* (New York: Hill & Wang, 1998). *See also* Antonio McDaniel, "The Dynamic Racial Composition of the United States," *Daedalus* 124, no. 1 (January 1995): 179–98.

66. Derrick Bell has written an excellent essay on the "superstanding" that such individuals acquire to speak on racial matters. Derrick Bell, *Faces at the Bottom of the Well: The Permanence of Racism* (New York: Basic Books, 1992), 109–27.

Chapter Two

1. Richard Hofstadter, *Anti-Intellectualism in American Life* (New York: Knopf, 1963), 6.

2. "Success Story: Outwhiting the Whites," *Newsweek*, June 21, 1971, 24.

3. David Grogan, "Brain Drain Boon for the U.S.: Students of Asian-American Families with Rare Genetic Gifts and a Reverence for Learning Sweep a Science Contest for the Nation's High-Schoolers," *People*, April 21, 1986, 30; Mary Shaughnessy, "When the Westinghouse Talent Scouts Dealt Out Their Awards, They Gave the Kuos a Full House," *People*, June 8, 1987, 149.

4. Stephen G. Graubard, "Why Do Asian Pupils Win Those Prizes?," *New York Times*, January 29, 1988, A35.

5. "Minestrone, Ratatouille and Strudel," *Washington Post*, June 14, 1983, A18.

6. David Brand, "The New Whiz Kids: Why Asian Americans Are Doing So Well, and What It Costs Them," *Time*, August 31, 1987, 42; Martin Kasindorf, "Asian Americans: A Model Minority," *Newsweek*, December 6, 1982, 39.

7. Anthony Ramirez, "America's Super Minority," *Fortune*, November 24, 1986, 148.

8. Daniel A. Bell, "The Triumph of Asian Americans: America's Greatest Success Story," *New Republic*, July 15, 1985, 24; Louis Winnick, "America's 'Model Minority'," *Commentary* (August 1990): 23.

9. Fox Butterfield, "Why Asians Are Going to the Head of the Class: Some Fear Colleges Use Quotas to Limit Admissions," *New York Times*, August 3, 1986, Educational Supplement, 18.

10. Spencer Rich, "Asian Americans Outperform Others in School and at Work: Census Data Outlines 'Model Minority'," *Washington Post*, October 10, 1985, A1.

11. Peter I. Rose, *Tempest-Tost: Race, Immigration, and the Dilemmas of Diversity* (New York: Oxford University Press, 1997).

12. Richard Rodriguez, "Asians: A Class by Themselves; A Formal Model for Minority Education," *Los Angeles Times*, October 11, 1987, E1. Among William Raspberry's several articles on Asian Americans are "Asian Americans—Too Successful?" *Washington Post*, February 10, 1990, A23; "The Curse of Low Expectations," *Washington Post*, March 4, 1988, A25; and "When White Guilt Won't Matter," *Washington Post*, November 4, 1987, A23.

13. Alice Z. Cuneo, "Asian Americans: Companies Disoriented About Asians: Fast-Growing But Diverse Market Holds Key to Buying Power," *Advertising Age*, July 9, 1990, S2.

14. Rose, *Tempest-Tost,* 4.

15. Ron K. Unz, "Immigration or the Welfare State: Which Is Our Real Enemy?" *Heritage Foundation Policy Review* (Fall 1994): 33.

16. William McGurn, "The Silent Majority: Asian Americans' Affinity With Republican Party Principles," *National Review*, June 24, 1991, 19. Stuart Rothenberg and Williem McGurn, "The Invisible Success Story: Asian Americans and Politics," *National Review*, Sept. 15, 1989. 17. After the 2000 Presidential elections, in which Asian Americans supported Gore over Bush, the editor of *National Review* changed his mind about the prospects of Asian Americans belonging to the conservative "investor class" rather than representing the liberal "impact of immigration." John O'Sullivan, "Following the Returns: Investor Class or Immigrant Tide?" *National Review*, Dec. 18, 2000, 30.

17. Philip E. Vernon, *The Abilities and Achievements of Orientals in North America* (New York: Academic Press, 1982).James Flynn, a political science professor at University of Otago in New Zealand, has written a monograph showing that Vernon has overstated any IQ advantage on the part of Asians. James R. Flynn, *Asian Americans: Achievement Beyond IQ* (Hillsdale, N.J.: Lawrence Erlbaum Associates, 1991). Flynn also has done some of the most significant work in refuting the validity of IQ testing, showing a massive rise in IQ now known as "the Flynn effect." James R. Flynn, "Massive IQ Gains in 14 Nations: What IQ Tests Really Measure," *Psychological Bulletin* 101, no. 2 (1987): 171–91. See Sharon Begley, "Are We Getting Smarter?" *Newsweek*, April 23, 2001, 50.

18. Vernon, *Abilities and Achievements,* 273–74.

19. Ibid., 16.

20. Ibid., 271.

21. Norman De Bono, "Ex-UWO Student Defends Research," *London Free Press*, October 1, 200, A4; Norman De Bono, "Skull Size Theory Renews Furore," *London Free Press*, September 27, 2000, A1.

22. Ibid., 273–74.

23. Ibid., 273, 275.

24. Jean Stefancic and Richard Delgado, *No Mercy: How Conservative Think Tanks and Foundations Changed America's Social Agenda* (Philadelphia: Temple University Press, 1996), 24-26, 37-44. For information about the Pioneer Fund, see John Sedgwick "Inside the Pioneer Fund" and Adam Miller, "Professors of Hate," in Russell Jacoby and Naomi Glauberman, eds., *The Bell Curve Debate: History, Documents, Opinions* (New York: Times Books, 1995), 144–61, 162–78.

25. Julian C. Stanley, "Do Asian Americans Tend to Reason Better Mathematically Than White Americans?" *Gifted Child Today* (March/April 1988): 32.

26. Nathan Caplan et al., "Indochinese Refugee Families and Academic Achievement," *Scientific American* (February 1992): 36–42; Nathan Caplan et al., *The Boat People and Achievement in America: A Study of Family Life, Hard Work, and Cultural Values* (Ann Arbor: University of Michigan Press, 1989).

27. Jo Ann M. Farver et al., "Cultural Differences in Korean- and Anglo-American Preschoolers' Social Interaction and Play Behaviors," *Child Development* 66 (1995): 1088–99 .

28. Benjamin Franklin once said, "A leopard can't change its spots. The Jews are Orientals; they are a menace for the country that lets them in, and they should be excluded by the Constitution." Geoffrey Hartman, "Blindness and Insight: Paul de Man, Fascism, and Deconstruction" *New Republic*, March 7, 1988, 26.

29. Martin Peretz, "Cambridge Diarist," *New Republic*, February 10, 1992, 41.

30. Garry Trudeau, *Recycled Doonesbury: Second Thoughts on a Gilded Age* (Kansas City, Kans.: Andrews McMeel, 1990)(unnumbered pages).

31. Butterfield, "Why Asians Are Going to the Head of the Class," 18; Jay Mathews, "Asian Students Help Create a New Mainstream," *Washington Post*, November 14, 1985, A1; Brand, "The New Whiz Kids," 42.

32. Herbert R. Barringer, *Asians and Pacific Islanders in the United States* (New York: Russell Sage Foundation, 1993), 265.

33. Ibid., 266–67. *See* U.S. Department of Labor, Federal Glass Ceiling Commission, *A Solid Investment: Making Full Use of the Nation's Human Capital* (Washington, D.C.: Government Printing Office, 1995) and Federal Glass Ceiling Commission, *Good for Business: Making Full Use of the Nation's Human Capital* (Washington, D.C.: Government Printing Office, 1995).

34. The work of Queens College sociologist Joyce Tang offers strong substantiation. *Doing Engineering: the Career Attainment and Mobility of Caucasian, Black, and Asian-American Engineers* (Lanham, Md.: Rowman and Littlefield, 2000), Joyce Tang, "Earnings of Academic Scientists and Engineers: A Comparison of Native-Born and Foreign-Born Populations," in Randy Hodson, ed., *Research in the Sociology of Work*, vol. 6. (Greenwich, Conn: JAI Press 1997), 263-91. Joyce Tang, "The Model Minority Thesis Revisited: (Counter)Evidence from the Science and Engineering Fields," *The Journal of Applied Behavioral Science* 33, no. 3 (1997): 291–315; Joyce Tang, "The Glass Ceiling in Science and Engineering," *Journal of Socio-Economics* 26 (1997): 383–406; Joyce Tang, "Differences in the Process of Self-Employment Among Whites, Blacks and Asians: The Case of Scientists and Engineers," *Sociological Perspectives* 38 (1995): 273–309; Joyce Tang, "The Career Attainment of Caucasian and Asian Engineers," *Sociological Quarterly* 34, no. 3 (1993): 467–96.

35. With respect to social stratification, *see* Kenneth Arrow et al., eds., *Meritocracy and Economic Inequality* (Princeton, N.J.: Princeton University Press, 2000); Thomas D. Boston, *Race, Class & Conservatism* (Boston: Unwin Hyman, 1988); Peter M. Blau and Otis Dudley Duncan, *The American Occupational Structure* (New York: John Wiley & Sons, 1967); William Domhoff, *Who Rules America Now?: A View for the 80s* (New York: Simon & Schuster, 1983); Dennis Gilbert, *The American Class Structure: In An Age of Growing Inequality*, 5th ed. (Belmont, Calif.: Wadsworth, 1998); Christopher Jencks et al., *Inequality: A Reassessment of the Effect of Family and Schooling in America* (New York: Basic Books, 1972); Donald M. Levine and Mary Jo Bane, *The "Inequality" Controversy* (New York: Basic Books, 1975); C. Wright Mills, *The Power Elite* (New York: Oxford University Press, 1956); Daniel P. Moynihan, *On Understanding Poverty: Perspectives from the Social Sciences* (New York: Basic Books, 1968); Charles Tilly, *Durable Inquality* (Berkeley: University of California Press, 1998).

36. Julian C. Stanley, "Family Background of Young Asian Americans Who Reason Extremely Well Mathematically," *Journal of the Illinois Council for the Gifted* 7 (1988): 11.

37. Richard L. Zweigenhaft and G. William Domhoff, *Diversity in the Power Elite: Have Women and Minorities Reached the Top?* (New Haven, Conn.: Yale University Press, 1998), 140–57.

38. Deborah Woo, *Glass Ceilings and Asian Americans: The New Face of Workplace Barriers* (Walnut Creek, Calif.: Alta Mira Press, 2000), 26–30.

39. U.S. Civil Rights Commission, *The Economic Status of Asian Americans* (Washington, D.C.: Government Printing Office, 1988), 86.

40. Arthur Sakamoto and Satomi Furuichi, "The Wages of Native-Born Asian Americans at the End of the Twentieth Century," *Asian American Policy Review* 10 (2002): 17–30. See also Arthur Sakamoto et al., "The Declining Significance of Race Among Chinese and Japanese American Men," *Research in Social Stratification and Mobility* 16 (1998): 225–46.

41. See Katherine S. Mangan, "Professor's Comments on Affirmative Action Inflame a Campus," *Chronicle of Higher Education*, September 26, 1997, A33; John U. Ogbu, "Immigrant and Involuntary Minorities in Comparative Perspective," and "Low School Performance as an Adaptation: The Case of Blacks in Stockton, California," in Margaret A. Gibson and John U. Ogbu, *Minority Status and Schooling: A Comparative Study of Immigrant and Involuntary Minorites* (New York: Garland, 1991), 3–36, 249–86; John U. Ogbu, *Minority Education and Caste: The American System in Cross-Cultural Perspective* (New York: Academic Press, 1978); John U. Ogbu, "Overcoming Racial Barriers to Equal Access," in John I. Goodland and Pamela Keating, eds., *Access to Knowledge: An Agenda for Our Nation's Schools* (New York: College Entrance Examination Board, 1990), 59–90; John U. Ogbu, *The Next Generation: An Ethnography of Education in an Urban Neighborhood* (New York: Academic Press, 1974); and John U. Ogbu and Herbert D. Simons, "Voluntary and Involuntary Minorities: A Cultural-Ecological Theory of School Performance with Some Implications for Education," *Anthropology & Education Quarterly* 29, no. 2 (1998): 155–88. See also Signithia Fordham and John U. Ogbu, "Black Students' School Success: Coping with the Burden of 'Acting White'," *Urban Review* 18, no. 3 (1986): 176–206.

42. Robert Fullilove and Philip Uri Treisman, "Mathematics Achievement Among African American Undergraduates at the University of California Berkeley: An Evaluation of the Mathematics Workshop Program," *Journal of Negro Education* 59, no. 3 (1990): 463–78; Uri Treisman, "Studying Students Studying Calculus: A Look at the Lives of Minority Mathematics Students in College," *College Mathematics Journal* 23, no. 5 (1992): 362–72. See also William Raspberry, "Integrating Identities," *Washington Post*, February 12, 1999, A35; Mary Ann Roser, "UT Professor on Far-Reaching Path with Math; After Mistake on Test," *Austin-American Statesman*, March 12, 2000, A1. See also Freeman A. Hrabowski III, et al., *Beating the Odds: Raising Academically Successful African American Males* (New York: Oxford University Press, 1998).

43. Cheng and Yang, "The 'Model Minority' Deconstructed," in Min Zhou and James V. Gatewood, eds., *Contemporary Asian America: A Multidisciplinary Reader* (New York: New York University Press, 2000), 464.

44. Frank Chin and Jeffrey Paul Chan, "Racist Love," in Richard Kostelanetz, ed., *Seeing Through the Shuck* (New York: Ballantine, 1972), 65; Sumi Cho, "Redeeming Whiteness in the Shadow of Internment: Earl Warren, Brown, and a Theory of Racial Redemption," *Boston College Law Review* 40 (1998): 120; Claire Jean Kim, "The Racial Triangulation of Asian Americans," in Gordon H. Chang, ed., *Asian Americans and Politics: Perspectives, Experiences, Prospects* (Washington, D.C.: Woodrow Wilson Center/Stanford University Press, 2001), 39–78; Mari Matsuda, "We Will Not Be Used: Are Asian Americans the Racial Bourgeoisie?," in *Where Is Your Body* (Boston: Beacon Press, 1996), 149–79. Matsuda delivered the talk at the 1990 dinner of the Asian Law Caucus in San Francisco, California, where she first used the phrase.

45. Michael S. Greve, "The Newest Move in Law Schools' Quota Game," *Wall Street Journal*, October 5, 1992, A12. Recognizing the divisive role Asian Americans were being inserted into, the Japanese American Citizens League withdrew its support for proposed legislation attacking affirmative action in 1989. One of the sponsors of the bill had said of the effort: "So, in a way, we want to help Asian Americans, but at the same time we're using it as a vehicle to correct what we consider to be a societal mistake on the part of the United States." Robert W. Stewart, "'Merit Only' College Entry Proposal Failing: Opposition by Japanese Americans to Admissions Policy Change Frustrates GOP Sponsor," *Los Angeles Times*, December 9, 1989, B12.

46. Dawkins's ideas are elaborated upon in Susan Blackmore, *The Meme Machine* (Oxford: Oxford University Press, 1999).

47. Michael Lind, *The Next American Nation: The New Nationalism and the Fourth American Revolution* (New York: Free Press, 1995), 210.

48. Lisbeth B. Schorr, "Hope for Blacks from Broken Families,'" *New York Times*, March 12, 1988, A31.

49. Tomas Almaguer, *Racial Fault Lines: The Historical Origins of White Supremacy in California* (Berkeley, Calif.: University of California Press, 1994), 160. Greeley was anti-black as well as anti-Asian; once an abolitionist, he turned into an advocate for white supremacy.

50. Eric Foner, *Reconstruction: America's Unfinished Revolution: 1863-1877* (New York: Harper & Row, 1988), 419.

51. Lucy M. Cohen, *Chinese in the Post Civil-War South: A People Without A History* (Baton Rouge, La.: University of Louisiana Press, 1984), 124.

52. Ronald Takaki, *A History of Asian Americans: Strangers from a Different Shore*, rev. ed. (Boston: Little, Brown, Back Bay Books, 1998), 198. For a general account of the Chinese exclusion movement, I have relied on Stuart Creighton Miller, *The Unwelcome Immigrant: The American Image of the Chinese, 1785-1882* (Berkeley, Calif.: University of California Press, 1969).

53. Miller, *Unwelcome Immigrant*, 186–87.

54. Ibid., 241 n. 84, 199–201.

55. Roger Daniels, *Asian America: Chinese and Japanese in the United States Since 1850* (Seattle: Washington University Press, 1988), 317.

56. William Petersen, *Japanese Americans: Oppression and Success* (New York: Random House, 1971).

57. William Petersen, "Success Story, Japanese American Style," *New York Times*, January 9, 1966, 21.

58. Ibid.

59. "Success Story of One Minority in the U.S.," *U.S. News & World Report*, December 26, 1966, 73.

60. Richard J. Herrnstein and Charles Murray, *The Bell Curve: Intelligence and Class Structure in American Life* (New York: The Free Press, 1994). The *Bell Curve* is analyzed in Claude S. Fischer et al., *Inequality By Design: Cracking the Bell Curve Myth* (Princeton: Princeton University Press, 1996); Steven Fraser, ed., *The Bell Curve Wars: Race, Intelligence, and the Future of America* (New York: Basic Books, 1995); Joe L. Kincheloe, Shirley R. Steinberg, and Aaron D. Gresson III, eds., *Measured Lies: The Bell Curve Examined* (New York: St. Martin's Press, 1996); Jacoby and Glauberman, eds., *Bell Curve Debate*. With respect to genetics and race, L. Luca Cavalli-Sforza, Paolo Menozzi and Alberto Piazza, *The History and Geography of Human Genes* (Princeton: Princeton University Press, 1994) is helpful. With respect to Social Darwinism generally, the following also place the *Bell Curve* in perspective: Carl N. Degler, *In Search of Human Nature: The Decline and Revival of Darwinism in American Social Thought* (New York: Oxford University Press, 1991); Stephen Jay Gould, *The Mismeasure of Man* (New York: W. W. Norton, 1981); Richard Hofstadter, *Social Darwinism in American Thought* (Philadelphia: University of Pennsylvania Press, 1944).

61. Herrnstein and Murray, *Bell Curve*, 526.

62. William Safire, "Of I.Q. and Genes," *New York Times*, October 20, 1994, A27.

63. Bob Secter, "A New Bigotry Ripples Across U.S. Campuses; Incidents in the Last Two Years Suggest Colleges Are No Longer Enlightened Havens from Racism," *Los Angeles Times*, May 8, 1988, A1.

64. Spike Lee, *Do The Right Thing* (New York: Fireside, 1989), 174.

65. Daryl Michael Scott, *Contempt and Pity: Social Policy and the Image of the Damaged Black Psyche, 1880–1996* (Chapel Hill: University of North Carolina Press, 1997).

66. See *generally* Lee Ross and Richard E. Nisbett, *The Person and the Situation: Perspectives of Social Psychology* (Philadelphia: Temple University Press, 1991), 126–28, 153, 195, 227–28.

67. *See* Mary C. Waters, *Black Identities: West Indian Immigrant Dreams and American Realities* (Cambridge, Mass.: Harvard University Press, 2000).

68. James M. Washington, *Testament of Hope: The Essential Writings and Speeches of Martin Luther King, Jr.* (New York: HarperCollins, 1991), 259–67. Academics such as Henry Louis Gates Jr., however, promote high standards of scholarship and do not hesitate in criticizing—publicly and assiduously—work that is problematic. *See* Henry Louis Gates Jr., "Black Demagogues and Pseudo-Scholars," *New York Times*, July 20, 1992, A11, for just one example. John McWhorter's book, *Losing the Race*, is among the more zealous of recent works in this vein.

69. The effect is difficult to document, but a former U.S. Labor Department official remarked to a reporter, "I can tell you by experience in certain industries, when there's availability of Asian Americans, companies have sought to improve their (affirmative action) profile by hiring those they would have hired anyway." Bruce D. Butterfield, "Minority Hiring Programs No Longer Focus on Blacks: Affirmative Action Under Fire," *Boston Globe*, October 20, 1991, A33. In a similar vein, the central point of Jack Miles's famous *Blacks versus Browns* essay, discussed in Chapter 1, was the displacement of African Americans by Latino immigrants.

70. Karl Zinsmeister, "Asians and Blacks: Bittersweet Success," *Current* (February 1988): 9.

71. James J. Treires, "The Dark Side of the Dream," *Newsweek*, March 20, 1989, 10.

72. Ibid.

73. Ibid.

74. Jennifer Toth, "Race Relations: Asian Americans Find Being Ethnic 'Model' Has Downside," *Los Angeles Times*, May 21, 1991, A5.

75. Lynette Clemetson, "The New Victims of Hate," *Newsweek*, November 6, 2000, 61.

76. Daniel Seligman, "Up From Inscrutable," *Fortune*, April 6, 1992, 120.

77. News accounts are inconsistent; some refer to Dingell having said "little yellow men" and others to his having said "little yellow people." *See, e.g.*, Hobart Rowen, "Trans-Pacific Fury," *Washington Post*, April 1, 1982, A29.

78. Helen Zia, *Asian American Dreams: The Emergence of an American People* (New York: Farrar, Straus & Giroux, 2000).

79. I have relied on Nancy Abelmann and John Lie, *Blue Dreams: Korean Americans and the Los Angeles Riots* (Cambridge, Mass.: Harvard University Press, 1995); Mark Baldassare, ed., *The Los Angeles Riots: Lessons for the Urban Future* (Boulder, Colo.: Westview, 1994); Lou Cannon, *Official Negligence: How Rodney King and the Riots Changed Los Angeles and the LAPD* (Boulder, Colo.: Westview, 1999); Robert Gooding-Williams, ed., *Reading Rodney King, Reading Urban Uprising* (New York: Routledge, 1993); Ronald N. Jacobs, *Race, Media, and the Crisis of Civil Society: From Watts to Rodney King* (Cambridge: Cambridge University Press, 2000). Toni Morrison and Clauda Brodsky Lacour, eds., *Birth of a Nation'hood: Gaze, Script, and Spectacle in the O.J. Simpson Case* (New York: Pantheon, 1997); Staff of the Los Angeles Times, *Understanding the Riots: Los Angeles Before and After the Rodney King Case* (Los Angeles, Calif.: Times Mirror, 1992).

80. Quoted in Jacobs, *Race, Media, and the Crisis of Civil Society*, 1.

81. Staff of the Los Angeles Times, *Understanding the Riots*, 77.

82. H. Khalif Khalifah, ed., *Rodney King and the L. A. Rebellioin: Analysis & Commentary by 13 Best Selling Black Writers* (Hampton: U. B. & U. S. Communications Systems, 1992).

83. Lawrence Bobo et al., "Public Opinion Before and After a Spring of Discontent," in Baldassare, ed., *The Los Angeles Riots*, 103–33.

84. In-Jin Yoon, *On My Own: Korean Businesses And Race Relations in America* (Chicago: University of Chicago Press, 1997), 209.

85. Claire Jean Kim, *Bitter Fruit: The Politics of Black-Korean Conflict in New York City* (New Haven, Conn.: Yale University Press, 2000).

86. John Hoberman, *Darwin's Atheletes: How Sport Has Damaged Black America and Preserved the Myth of Race* (New York: Houghton Mifflin, 1997).

87. Reed Ueda, "False Modesty: The Curse of Asian-American Success," *New Republic*, July 3, 1989, 16.

88. Korean immigrants, for example, are obsessed with gaining admission to Harvard College. *See* K. Connie Kang, "Korean Americans Dream of Crimson. The Lure of Harvard Is Irresistible to Many Immigrant Parents. Some Go to Great Lengths to Prepare Their Children for What They See As an Automatic Key to Success," *Los Angeles Times*, September 25, 1996, A1.

89. Federal Glass Ceiling Commission, *Good for Business*, 103.

Chapter Three

1. This apparently happened to Wu at Brown University in 1997 the week before I appeared there for the debate discussed in this chapter, according to several students who had witnessed the protests.

2. The *Time* article, dated December 22, 1941, is reproduced in its entirety in David L. Eng, *Racial Castration: Managing Masculinity in Asian America* (Durham, N.C.: Duke University Press, 2001), 107. Another article appeared in *Life* magazine, with a similar diagram; it is reproduced in Lawson Fusao Inada, *Only What We Could Carry: The Japanese American Internment Experience* (Berkeley, Calif.: Heyday Books, 2000), 52. Among other similar articles, Milton Caniff drew a cartoon, "How to Spot a Jap." Ibid., 21.

3. Isaiah Berlin, *The Proper Study of Mankind* (New York: Farrar, Straus & Giroux, 1997), 2.

4. Peter Brimelow makes this argument, but he is principled in making the argument to everyone irrespective of race. Peter Brimelow, *Alien Nation: Common Sense About America's Immigration Disaster* (New York: Random House, 1995), 250–54.

5. Robert S. Boynton, "The New Intellectuals," *Atlantic Monthly* (March 1995): 53–70. *See also* Russell Jacob, *The Last Intellectuals: American Culture in the Age of Academe* (New York: Basic, 1987).

6. The examples of Asian racism are legion. There was a riot on Christmas Eve 1988, for example, in mainland China, with Chinese students shouting "kill the black devils" and attacking visiting African students. Even in the early 1990s, it was possible to find racist stereotypes such as Little Black Sambo dolls in Japan. "Darkie" toothpaste, with a grinning minstrel as the mascot on the tube, is a top-selling brand in Asia; its name was eventually changed to "Darlee" and its logo lightened but retained. Anti-Semitism remains a problem in Asia. However, Asians probably harbor the worst forms of prejudice toward other Asians, especially those to whom they are most closely related.

7. Frank Dikotter, *The Discourse of Race in Modern China* (Stanford: Stanford University Press, 1992); Frank Dikotter, ed., *The Construction of Racial Identities in China and Japan* (Honolulu: University of Hawaii Press, 1997).

8. The movie is true to the novel in this respect. Helen Fielding, *Bridget Jones' Diary* (New York: Penguin, 2001), 11. *See also* Richard Corliss, "Geishas and Godzillas; Which Is Odder—The Image of Japan in Hollywood Movies or the Image of Japanese in Its Own Films?" *Time*, April 30, 2001, 30.

9. Rooney's commentary, "Buy, Buy, Rockefeller Center," was distributed by Tribune Media Services on November 4, 1989.

10. Robert Reich, "Who Is Us?" *Harvard Business Review* (January/February 1990): 53–64.

11. Steven W. Mosher, *Hegemon: China's Plan to Dominate Asia and the World* (San Francisco, Calif.: Encounter Books, 2000); Bill Gertz, *The China Threat: How the People's Republic Targets America* (Washington, D.C.: Regnery, 2000); Pat Choate, *Agents of Influence: How Japan's Lobbyists Manipulate America's Political and Economic System* (New York: Knopf, 1990); Clyde V. Prestowitz, *Trading Places: How We Allowed Japan to Take the Lead* (New York: Basic, 1988).

12. *See* Bill Kaufman, *America First! Its History, Culture, and Politics* (Amherst, N.Y.: Prometheus Books, 1995) and Dana Frank, *Buy American: The Untold Story of Economic Nationalism* (Boston: Beacon Press, 1999).

13. Jay Mathews, "Economic Invasion by Japan Revives Worry About Racism," *Washington Post*, May 14, 1982, A26. When Dingell eventually met with Japanese negotiators, he made light of his racial mode of thinking, saying, "I am a Pole. . . . We learn to take a lot of things, as long as they are said with a smile. We know that such things are only said

about one's good friends." David Maraniss, "Backlash; Trade Bill Pushed as Signal to Japan," *Washington Post*, June 12, 1983, A1.

14. Brimelow, *Alien Nation*, 10.

15. Ibid., 211.

16. Ibid., 59.

17. Ibid., 11, 203.

18. Ibid., 125.

19. Ibid., 10–11.

20. *The Chinese Exclusion Case*, 130 U.S. 581, 606 (1889).

21. *Fong Yue Ting v. United States*, 149 U.S. 698, 741 (Field, J., dissenting) (1893).

22. Brant T. Lee, "Liars, Traitors, and Spies: Wen Ho Lee and the Racial Construction of Disloyalty," *Asian American Policy Review* 10 (2000): 8.

23. William R. Tamayo, "When the 'Coloreds' Are Neither Black Nor Citizens: The United States Civil Rights Movement and Global Migration." *Asian Law Journal* 2 (1995): 1.

24. Ronald Takaki, *A Different Mirror: A History of Multicultural America* (Boston: Little, Brown, 1993), 79; Lawrence H. Fuchs, *The American Kaleidoscope: Race, Ethnicity, and the Civic Culture* (Hanover, N.H.: Wesleyan University Press, 1990), 6.

25. Ian F. Haney Lopez, *White By Law: The Legal Construction of Race* (New York: New York University Press, 1996).

26. Ibid., 80–86.

27. Ibid., 86–92.

28. Sidney Blumenthal, "He's Ba-a-ck!," *New Republic*, October 19, 1992, 14.

29. Maya Lin, "As American as Anyone Else—But Asian, Too," *Washington Post*, May 12, 2000, B3; see Maya Lin, *Boundaries* (New York: Simon & Schuster, 2000), 4:15.

30. The internment is the most extensively documented aspect of Asian American experiences. I have relied on the following leading studies: Roger Daniels, *Concentration Camps, North America: Japanese in the United States and Canada During World War II* (Malabar. Fla.: Kreiger Publishing, 1993); Roger Daniels, *The Politics of Prejudice: The Anti-Japanese Movement in California and the Struggle for Japanese Exclusion* (Berkeley: University of California Press, 1999); Bill Hosokawa, *JACL in Quest of Justice: The History of the Japanese American Citizens League* (New York: William Morrow, 1982); Peter Irons, *Justice at War: The Story of Japanese American Internment Cases* (New York: Oxford University Press, 1983); Michi Nishiura Weglyn, *Years of Infamy: The Untold Story of America's Concentration Camps* (Seattle: University of Washington Press, 1996); United States Commission on Wartime Relocation and Internment Civilians, *Personal Justice Denied: Report of the Commission on Wartime Relocation and Internment of Civilians.* (Washington, D.C.: United States Commission on Wartime Relocation and Internment Civilians, 1983). Also invaluable is the collection of primary documents, showing the government's deliberations over internment, gathered in Roger Daniels, *American Concentration Camps: A Documentary History of the Relocation and Incarceration of Japanese Americans, 1942–1945*, vols. 1-9 (New York: Garland, 1989). The first textbook on the internment is Eric K. Yamamoto et al., *Race, Rights, and Reparation: Law and the Japanese American Internment* (New York: Aspen, 2001).

31. Bill Hosokawa, *Nisei: The Quiet Americans* (New York: William Morrow, 1969), 103.

32. Daniels, *Asian America*, 200–1.

33. John W. Dower, *War Without Mercy: Race and Power in the Pacific War* (New York: Pantheon, 1986).

34. United States Commission on Wartime Relocation and Internment Civilians, *Personal Justice Denied*, 66.

35. Cited in Daniels, *Concentration Camps*, 62.

36. Frank J. Taylor, "The People Nobody Wants," *Saturday Evening Post*, May 9, 1942, 24, 66.

37. *See* Daniels, *Politics of Prejudice*, 85–88; United States Commission on Wartime Relocation and Internment Civilians, *Personal Justice Denied*, 364–65.

38. *Regan v. King*, 49 F. Supp. 222 (N.D. Cal. 1942).

39. Daniels, *Concentration Camps*, 61; *see also* Goeffrey Smith, "Racial Nativism and Origins of Japanese American Relocation," in Roger Daniels et al., eds., *Japanese Americans: From Relocation to Redress*, rev. ed. (Seattle: University of Washington Press, 1986), 85.

40. Weglyn, *Years of Infamy*, 55.

41. Daniels, *Concentration Camps*, 33.

42. Ibid., 68–69. The Lippmann piece was his "Today and Tomorrow" syndicated column of February 12, 1942.

43. Ronald Steel, *Walter Lippmann and the American Century* (Boston: Little, Brown, 1980), 394.

44. Maya Angelou, "Excerpt from I Know Why the Caged Bird Sings," in Inada, *Only What We Could Carry*, 53–54.

45. *See* Samuel Walker, *In Defense of American Liberties: A History of the ACLU* (New York: Oxford University Press, 1990), 136–60.

46. *Korematsu v. United States*, 323 U.S. 214 (1944).

47. United States CWRIC, *Personal Justice Denied*, 66.

48. John Armor and Peter Wright, *Manzanar*, (New York: Vintage, 1989), xx.

49. Irons, *Justice at War*, 71–72.

50. Intelligence Officer, "The Japanese American Problem: The Problem and the Solution," reproduced in S.T. Joshi, *Documents of American Prejudice: An Anthology of Writings on Race from Thomas Jefferson to David Duke* (New York: Basic, 1999), 497.

51. The Munson report is reproduced in Daniels, *American Concentration Camps*, vol. 1 (unnumbered pages).

52. Irons, *Justice at War.*

53. Ibid., 288.

54. "Justice Black, Champion of Civil Liberties for 34 Years on the Court, Dies at 85," *New York Times*, September 26, 1971, 76. Likewise, columnist Lippman persisted, even while "frail and failing" and troubled by his role in encouraging the internment, to believe "it was the right thing to do at the time." Steel, *Walter Lippmann*, 395.

55. United States Commission on Wartime Relocation and Internment Civilians,, *Personal Justice Denied*, 8.

56. Toshio Welchel, *From Pearl Harbor to Saigon: Japanese American Soldiers and the Vietnam War* (New York: Verso, 1999), 103.

57. Quang X. Pham, "Many Are Called, But Few Are Chosen to Be Officers in the Marines," *Washington Times*, March 25, 1994, A23.

58. Ted W. Lieu, "'Are You in The Chinese Air Force?'" *Washington Post*, June 19, 1999, A19.

59. This material is adapted from Frank H. Wu and Francey Lim Youngberg, "People from China Crossing the River: Asian American Political Empowerment and Foreign Influence," in Gordon H. Chang, ed., *Asian Americans and Politics: Perspectives, Experiences, Prospects* (Washington, D.C.: Woodrow Wilson Center Press, 2001), 311–53, where complete citations are provided.

60. Wu and Youngberg, "People from China," 320.

61. Ibid., 322.

62. Ibid., 323–26.

63. Ibid., 327

64. "Asian Connection," *Washington Post* cited in Ibid., 328.

65. Brian C. Mooney, "Silber Draws Fire on Welfare Remarks," *Boston Globe*, January 26, 1990, B1.

66. Michael Kranish, "Policy Shift over Fund-Raiser Is Denied," *Boston Globe*, Jan. 17, 1997, A1; Michael Kranish, "Clintan Policy Shift Followed Asian-American Fund-Raiser," *Boston Globe*, Jan 16, 1997, A1.

67. Federation for American Immigration Reform, "Hollow Denial from White House About Immigration About-Face," Jan. 17, 1997 (available on Lexis-Nexis, P.R. Newswire).

68. The positive role of ethnic Americans in international relations is discussed in Yossi Shain, *Marketing the American Creed Abroad: Diasporas in the U.S. and Their Homelands* (Cambridge: Cambridge University Press, 1999).

69. Howard Chua-Eoan, "Profiles in Outrage; America Is Home, But Asian Americans Feel Treated as Outlanders with Unproven Loyalties," *Time*, September 25, 2000, 40.

70. *See, e.g.,* John B. Judis, "Sullied Heritage: The Decline of Principled Conservative Hostility to China," *New Republic*, April 23, 2001, 19.

71. Laurie Kellman and E. Michael Myers, "Tight Race, Tough Fight: Dole Insists He's Gaining, But Covers a Possible Setback," *Washington Times*, February 18, 1996, A1.

72. William F. Buckley Jr., ed., *In Search of Anti-Semitism* (New York: Continuum, 1992).

73. The essay is reprinted as "The Day the American Empire Ran Out of Gas," in Fred Kaplan, ed., *The Essential Gore Vidal* (New York: Random House, 1999), 754–62.

74. Ibid.

75. Gore Vidal, "The Empire Lovers Strike Back," *Nation*, March 22, 1986, 350. This essay is not reprinted in *The Essential Gore Vidal.*

76. Ibid.

77. Kaplan, *Essential Gore Vidal*, 755–56, 762.

78. Huntington's book-length version of his work is Samuel Huntington, *The Clash of Civilizations and the Remaking of World Order* (New York: Simon & Schuster, 1996). Three other important recent works on inevitable conflict within the new world order are Benjamin R. Barber, *Jihad Vs. McWorld: How Globalism and Tribalism Are Reshaping the World* (New York: Ballantine, 1996); Robert D. Kaplan, *The Coming Anarchy: Shattering the Dreams of the Post Cold War* (New York: Random House, 2000); and Robert D. Kaplan, *The Ends of the Earth: A Journey at the Dawn of the 21st Century* (New York: Random House, 1996).

79. Madison Grant, *The Passing of the Great Race, or the Racial Basis of European History* (New York: Charles Scribner's Sons, 1918). (I have relied on the reprint edition produced by Arno Press in 1970.); Lothrop Stoddard, *The Rising Tide of Color Against White World-Supremacy* (New York: Charles Scribner's Sons, 1920). (I have relied on the reprint edition produced by Negro Universities Press in 1971.)

80. Grant, *Passing*, 11.

81. Stoddard, *Rising*, xxxi.

82. Ibid., 229.

83. Ibid., 274.

84. F. Scott Fitzgerald, *The Great Gatsby* (New York: Charles Scribner's Sons, 1925), 13.

85. Lynn Pan, ed., *The Encyclopedia of the Chinese Overseas* (Cambridge, Mass.: Harvard University Press, 1999).

86. Ibid., 14.

87. Ibid., 118–19.

88. Martha Nussbaum et al., *For Love of Country: Debating the Limits of Patriotism,* ed. Joshua Cohen (Boston: Beacon, 1996), 6.

89. Ibid.

90. Ibid., 14.

91. The leading work in this school of thought is Gunther Barth, *Bitter Strength: A History of the Chinese in the United States, 1850–1870* (Cambridge: Harvard University Press, 1964).

92. Takaki, *Strangers from a Different Shore,* 11.

93. Mark Wyman, *Round-Trip to America: The Immigrants Return to Europe, 1880-1930* (Ithaca, N.Y.: Cornell University Press, 1993).

94. Joseph H. Carens, "Aliens and Citizens: The Case for Open Borders," *Review of Politics* 49 (1987): 251–73. The essay is reproduced in Will Kymlicka, *The Rights of Minority Cultures* (New York: Oxford University Press, 1995): 331–49. Carens also was one of the first to analyze the inverse relationship of open migration with public entitlements, in Joseph H. Carens, "Immigration and the Welfare State," in Amy Gutmann, *Democracy and the Welfare State* (Princeton, N.J.: Princeton University Press, 1988), 207–30. I am indebted to Carens for his framing of the issues. The notable exception to bounded conceptions of ethical obligations is Peter Singer, "Famine, Affluence, and Morality," 1 *Philosophy & Public Affairs,* 229-243 (1972); Peter Singer, "The Singer Solution to World Poverty," *N.Y. Times Sunday Magazine,* Sept. 5, 1999, 60.

95. Patrick J. McDonnell, "Thanks to an Obsession with Immigration, Glenn Spencer Has Ended Up on a List of Hate Groups. Is His a Courageous Voice in the Wilderness—or the Whine of a Hatemonger?," *Los Angeles Times Magazine,* July 15, 2001, 14.

96. Joseph J. Ellis, *American Sphinx: The Character of Thomas Jefferson* (New York: Knopf, 1997), 131.

97. Michael Walzer, *Spheres of Justice: A Defense of Pluralism and Equality* (New York: Basic, 1983), 40, 43, 48–51. Incidentally, Walzer recognizes the analogy between "strangers in political space (immigrants) and descendants in time (children)," but he does not make much of it. Ibid., 34–35.

98. Ibid., 61. The priority in time in argument is not usually extended consistently. If group seniority were regarded as properly establishing group entitlement, African Americans would have a dispositive argument along the following lines: because their forebears arrived prior to white ethnic immigrants, they ought to have a higher status than the white ethnics' descendants. Few of the proponents of immigration who control by virtue of group status also make this claim about African Americans, though.

99. Ibid., 38.

100. Bruce A. Ackerman, *Social Justice in the Liberal State* (New Haven, Conn.: Yale University Press, 1980), 4. Like Walzer, Ackerman recognizes the "tremendous fact of temporal priority" in practical terms, but he does not accept it as automatically having any normative significance. Ibid.

101. Ibid., 89–95.

102. Ibid., 95.

Chapter Four

1. Andrew Hacker, *Two Nations: Black, White, Separate, Hostile, Unequal,* Revised edition (New York: Ballantine, 1995).

2. Ibid., 102.

3. Ibid.

4. Correspondents of *The New York Times, How Race Is Lived in America: Pulling Together, Pulling Apart* (New York: Times Books, 2001).

5. Ibid., 23–40.

6. Melvin L. Oliver and Thomas M. Shapiro, *Black Wealth/White Wealth: A New Perspective on Racial Inequality* (New York: Routledge, 1997).

7. *See* Douglas S. Massey and Nancy A. Denton: *American Apartheid: Segregation and the Making of the Underclass* (Cambridge, Mass.: Harvard University Press, 1993). An explanation of residential racial segregation that emphasizes factors that are not expressly racial can be found in Ingrid Gould Ellen, *Sharing America's Neighborhoods: The Prospects for Stable Racial Integration* (Cambridge, Mass.: Harvard University Press, 2000).

8. Howard Schuman, *Racial Attitudes in America: Trends and Interpretations,* rev. ed. (Cambridge, Mass.: Harvard University Press, 1997); Donald R. Kinder and Lynn M. Sanders, *Divided by Color: Racial Politics and Democratic Ideals* (Chicago: University of Chicago Press, 1996); Michael A. Milburn and Sheree D. Conrad, *The Politics of Denial* (Cambridge, Mass.: MIT Press, 1996); Timur Kuran, *Private Truths, Public Lies: The Social Consequences of Preference Falsification* (Cambridge, Mass.: Harvard University Press, 1995); David O. Sears et al., *Racialized Politics: The Debate About Racism in America* (Chicago: University of Chicago Press, 2000). The lingering problems of race, coupled with attitudes of denial,

produce an illusion of integration. See Leonard Steinhorn and Barbara Diggs-Brown, *By the Color of Our Skin: The Illusion of Integration and the Reality of Race* (New York: Dutton, 1999).

9. It is important not to exaggerate the differences, as UCLA sociology professor Lawrence Bobo has argued. *See* Lawrence Bobo, "Race and Beliefs About Affirmative Action: Assessing the Effects of Interests, Group Threat, Ideology, and Racism," in Sears et al., *Racialized Politics*, 137–64.

10. *See* Gavin de Becker, *The Gift of Fear: Survival Signals That Protect Us from Violence* (Boston: Little, Brown, 1997).

11. Derrick Bell, *Faces at the Bottom of the Well: The Permanence of Racism* (New York: Basic, 1992).

12. James M. Washington, *Testament of Hope: The Essential Writings and Speeches of Martin Luther King, Jr.* (New York: HarperCollins, 1991), 295. King's remarks echo Edmund Burke's famous line that "the only thing necessary for the triumph of evil is for good men to do nothing" and Martin Niemoller's poem about failing to speak out when "they came for the Jews" and ending with nobody left to speak up when they came for the narrator.

13. Tom Wolfe, *Radical Chic and Mau-Mauing the Flak Catchers* (New York: Farrar, Straus & Giroux, 1970), 105–7.

14. Andrew Hacker, "Affirmative Action: The New Look," *New York Review of Books*, October 12, 1989, 64. There were numerous other articles asking or answering the same question. *See, e.g.,* James Gibney, "The Berkeley Squeeze," *New Republic*, April 11, 1988, 15 and Harold Johnson, "Model Victims," *National Review*, July 20, 1992, W7.

15. Jerry Kang, "Negative Action Against Asian Americans: The Internal Instability of Dworkin's Defense of Affirmative Action," *Harvard Civil Rights-Civil Liberties Law Review* 31 (1996): 1–47

16. The diversity arguments—for example, geographic diversity—used to limit the numbers of Jewish students were similarly disingenuous. They were not established to achieve diversity but as a surreptitious means of excluding Jews.

17. *See also* Stephen S. Fugita and Marilyn Fernandez, "Asian American Admissions to an Elite University: A Multivariate Case Study of Harvard," *Asian American Policy Review* 5 (1995): 45–62.

18. *Ho v. San Francisco Unified School District*, 965 F. Supp. 1316 (N.D. Cal. 1997).

19. Andrew Hacker, *Two Nations: Black and White, Separate, Hostile, Unequal* (New York: Ballantine, 1992), 152. In the immigration context, "diversity" has already become a rationale for favoring whites. The impetus for creating "diversity" visas that are distributed through a lottery system was the outlandish argument that the immigration system discriminates against European immigrants. The line of reasoning is as follows. Because the immigration policies expressly discriminated against Asians in the past, there are more Asians who are recent arrivals now. Thus, European immigrants have fewer immediate relatives than Asian immigrants, and thus cannot obtain as many visas allotted to a family reunification as can Asians (or Latinos). As Washington University law professor Stephen Legomsky has noted, however, a Swede and a Mexican, both of whom have a U.S. citizen spouse, are treated identically. Moreover, because of the per-county limits on visas, the Swede "is in fact treated far *better* than the Mexican . . . even without the diversity program, the Swede may jump ahead of the Mexican in the queue." Stephen H. Legomsky, *Immigration and Refugee Law and Policy*, 2nd ed. (New York: Foundation Press, 1997), 209. Nevertheless, in its early years, the diversity program had a rigid quota that 16,000 or 40% of its visas would be given to Irish nationals. *See* Public Law No. 101-649, sec. 132(c), 104 Stat. 4978, 5000.

20. Jeno F. Paulucci, "For Affirmative Action for Some Whites," *New York Times*, November 26, 1977, A21.

21. Patrick J. Buchanan, "Our Christian Dispossession," *New York Post*, November 28, 1998, 19.

22. Buchanan had been inspired by an earlier op-ed. Ron K. Unz, "Some Minorities Are More Minor Than Others," *Wall Street Journal*, November 16, 1998, A38 *See, e.g.,* Dante Ramos, "Losers: White Minorities Get Shafted," *New Republic*, October 17, 1994, 24. *See* A. Kenneth Ciongoli, "Discriminating Against Middle-Class Ethnic Americans," *USA Today* magazine, November 1, 1999, 32.

23. *See* Linda Matthews, "When Being Best Isn't Good Enough: Why Yat-Pang Au Won't Be Going to Berkeley," *Los Angeles Times Sunday Magazine*, July 19, 1987, 22; Grace W. Tsuang, "Assuring Equal Access of Asian-Americans to Highly-Selective Universities," *Yale Law Journal* 98, no. 2 (1989): 676 n.117.

24. Vincent Sarich, "Making Racism Official at Cal," *Cal Monthly* (September 1990): 17.

25. U.S. Department of Justice, *Discrimination Against Asian Americans in Higher Education: Evidence, Causes, and Cures* (Washington, D.C.: U.S. Department of Justice, 1988).

26. *Plessy v. Ferguson*, 163 U.S. 537 (1896).

27. Gabriel Chin, "The Plessy Myth: Justice Harlan and the Chinese Cases," *Iowa Law Review* 82 (1996): 151–82.

28. Terry Eastland, *Ending Affirmative Action: The Case for Colorblind Justice* (New York: Basic, 1996), 27–35.

29. Richard A. Epstein, *Forbidden Grounds: The Case Against Employment Discrimination Laws* (Cambridge, Mass.: Harvard University Press, 1992), 3.

30. Clint Bolick, *The Affirmative Action Fraud: Can We Restore the American Civil Rights Vision?* (Washington, D.C.: Cato Institute, 1996), 41.

31. Dinesh D'Souza, *The End of Racism: Principles for a Multiracial Society* (New York: Free Press, 1995). There are other books presenting cultural arguments of this nature; see Lawrence E. Harrison and Samuel P. Huntington, eds., *Culture Matters: How Values Shape Human Progress* (New York: Basic Books, 2000) and Gertrude Himmelfarb, *One Nation, Two Cultures* (New York: Knopf, 1999). Joel Kotkin, *Tribes: How Race, Religion, and Identity Determine Success in the New Global Economy* (New York: Random House, 1993).

32. Michael Levin, *Why Race Matters: Race Differences and What They Mean* (Westport, Conn.: Praeger, 1997), 11. J. Philipe Rushston, *Race, Evolution & Behavior* (Brunswick, N.J.: Transaction, 1995).

33. Richard A. Wasserstrom, "Racism and Sexism," in Bernard Boxill, *Race and Racism* (New York: Oxford University Press, 2001), 312. An important empirical account of the development of racial thinking is Lawrence A. Hirschfeld, *Race in the Making: Cognition, Culture, and the Child's Construction of Human Kinds* (Cambridge, Mass.: MIT Press, 1996).

34. *See* K. Anthony Appiah and Amy Gutmann, *Color Conscious: The Political Morality of Race* (Princeton, N.J.: Princeton University Press, 1996).

35. David Chambers et al., "Michigan's Minority Graduates in Practice: The River Runs Through Law School," *Law & Social Inquiry* 25 (Spring 2000): 395–504.

36. The expert reports are available in the public record of the litigation and the trial court opinion, which is *Grutter v. Bollinger*, 137 F. Supp. 2d 821 (E.D. Mi. 2001), and they are on file with the author.

37. Joseph Gannon, "College Grades and LSAT Scores: An Opportunity to Exmaine the 'Real Differences' in Minority-Nonminority Performance," in David M. White, ed., *Towards a Diversified Legal Profession* (San Francisco: Julian Richardson Associates, 1981); William C. Kidder, "Does the LSAT Mirror or Magnify Racial and Ethnic Differences in Educational Attainment? A Study of Equally Achieving 'Elite' College Students," *California Law Review* 89 (2001): 1055–1124.

38. C. M. Steele and J. Aronson, "Stereotype Threat and the Intellectual Test Performance of African-Americans," *Journal of Personality and Social Psychology* 69 (1995): 797; C. M. Steele, "A Threat in the Air: How Stereotypes Shape the Intellectual Identities and Performance of Women and African Americans," *American Psychologist* 52 (1997): 613; J. Aronson et al., "When White Men Can't Do Math: Necessary and Sufficient Factors in Stereotype Threat," *Journal of Experimental Social Psychology* 35, (1999): 29; S. J. Spencer et al., "Stereotype Threat and Women's Math Performance," *Journal of Experimental Social Psychology* 35 (1999): 4.

39. Claude M. Steele, "Thin Ice: 'Stereotype Threat' and Black College Students," *Atlantic Monthly* (August 1999): 44–54.

40. Nicholas Lehman, *The Big Test: The Secret History of the American Meritocracy* (New York: Farrar, Straus and Giroux, 1999). *See also* Robert L. Hayman, Jr., *The Smart Culture: Society, Intelligence, and Law* (New York University Press, 1997).

41. This point was made by the inventor of the term "meritocracy," in Michael Young, *The Rise of Meritocracy, 1870–2033* (London: Thames and Hudson, 1958). It has recently been re-argued in Mickey Kaus, *End of Equality* (New York: Basic Books, 1992). John Rawls has presented a progressive alternative to such a meritocracy in *A Theory of Justice*, rev. ed. (Cambridge, Mass.: Harvard University Press, 1999).

42. Peter Brimelow, *Alien Nation: Common Sense About America's Immigration Disaster* (New York: Random House, 1995).

43. Peter Brimelow, "Immigration Reform Laws: Redefining Who Belongs: Transcript: Dissolving the American People," *Rutgers Race and Law Review* 1 (1998): 143.

44. 8 U.S.C. § 1182(a)(5).

45. I have relied on the following: Leon F. Bouvier and John L. Martin, *Foreign-Born Scientists, Engineers and Mathematicians in the United States* (Washington, D.C.: Center for Immigration Studies, 1995); Todd M. Davis, ed., *Open Doors 1997/98: Report on International Educational Exchange* (New York: Institute of International Education, 1998); Anthony DePalma, "Drop in Black Ph. D.'s Brings Debate on Aid for Foreigners," *N.Y. Times*, April 21, 1992, A1. Anthony DePalma, "Graduate Schools Fill With Foreigners," *New York Times*, November 29, 1990, A1; Paul Desruisseaux, "2 Year Colleges at Crest of Wave in U.S. Enrollment by Foreign Students: Economic Turmoil and Increased Competition Spur Recruiting Efforts," *Chronicle of Higher Education*, December 11, 1998, A66; Lisa Ko, "The Asian American Doctor Debate," *A. Magazine* (October/November 1997): 44–46; Scott Stossel, "Uncontrolled Experiment: America's Dependency on Foreign Scientists," *New Republic*, March 29, 1999, 17–22; Robin Wilson, "Ph.D. Programs Face a Paucity of Americans in the Sciences: In Lab Without American Students, a Professor Urges Assimilation," *Chronicle of Higher Education*, May 14, 1999, 14–15; Robin Wilson, "A University Uses Quotas to Limit and Diversify Its Foreign Enrollments," *Chronicle of Higher Education*, May 14, 1999, 15–16.

46. Richard D. Kahlenberg, *The Remedy: Class, Race, and Affirmative Action* (New York: Basic, 1996), 234 n.75. I have relied on the following sources for information about alumni preferences: Jessica Burlingame, "All in the Family," *Lingua Franca* (November 1996): 8–9; Jerome Karabel and David Karen, "Go to Harvard; Give Your Kid a Break," *New York Times*, December 8, 1990, 23; John D. Lamb, "The Real Affirmative Action Babies: Legacy Preferences at Harvard and Yale," *Columbia Journal of Law and Social Problems* 26 (1993): 491–521; John Larew, "Why Are Droves of Unqualified, Unprepared Kids Getting into Our Top Colleges? Because Their Dads Are Alumni," *Washington Monthly* (June 1991): 10.

47. Barbara Bergmann, *In Defense of Affirmative Action* (New York: Basic, 1996).

48. *Hopwood v. Texas*, 861 F. Supp. 551, 581 (W.D. Tex. 1994).

49. *See, e.g.,* Theodore Cross and Robert Bruce Slater, "Why the End of Affirmative Action Would Exclude All But a Very Few Blacks from America's Leading Universities and Graduate Schools," *Journal of Blacks in Higher Education* (Autumn 1997): 8–17. Linda F. Wightman, "The Threat to Diversity in Legal Education: An Empirical Analysis of the Consequences of Abandoning Race as a Factor in Law School Admission Decisions," *N.Y.U. Law Review,* v. 72, pp. 1-53 (1997).

50. Nathan Glazer, "Affirmative Action Is Bad. Banning It Is Worse," *New Republic,* April 6, 1998, 20; Glenn C. Loury, "Admit It," *New Republic,* December 27, 1999, 6. *See also* Steven A. Holmes, "Re-thinking Affirmative Action," *New York Times,* April 5, 1998, D5.

51. Cass Sunstein, *Free Markets and Social Justice* (New York: Oxford University Press, 1997), *especially* 151–66; Kenneth J. Arrow, "What Has Economics to Say About Racial Discrimination?," *Journal of Economic Perspectives* 12 no. 2 (1998): 91–100.

52. William Julius Wilson, *When Work Disappears: The World of the New Urban Poor* (New York: Knopf, 1996).

53. Lyndon Johnson, "To Fulfill These Rights," in George Curry, ed., *The Affirmative Action Debate* (Reading, Mass.: Addison-Wesley, 1996), 16–24.

54. John David Skretny, *The Ironies of Affirmative Action: Politics, Culture, and Justice in America* (Chicago: University of Chicago Press, 1996).

55. Charles Moskos and John Sibley Butler, *All That We Can Be: Black Leadership and Racial Integration the Army Way* (Princeton, N.J.: Princeton University Press, 1998).

56. William Bowen and Derek Bok, *The Shape of the River: Long-Term Consequences of Considering Race in College and University Admissions* (New York: Basic, 1996).

57. William Julius Wilson, "Class Consciousness," *New York Times Book Review,* Jul 14, 1996, 11.

58. Gordon W. Allport, *The Nature of Prejudice,* 25th anniversary ed. (Reading, Mass.: Perseus, 1979); Daniel T. Gilbert et al., eds., *The Handbook of Social Psychology,* 4th ed., vol. 2 (Boston: McGraw-Hill, 1998), 576–79.

59. The Supreme Court decision was *Wards Cove Packing Co. v. Atonio,* 490 U.S. 642 (1988). Justice John Paul Stevens said that the company's practices "bear an unsettling resemblance to aspects of a plantation economy." The statutory exemption which is not codified, can be found at 105 Stat. 1099, Title IV, sec. 402 (1991). *See also* Congressional Quarterly, Almanac, v. XLVII (Washington, D.C.: Congressional Quarterly, 1991), 259–61. The 1991 Civil Rights Act involved anti-discrimination protections, not affirmative action, making the exception of Asian Americans and Native Americans even worse. But Asian Americans also have been subjected to discrimination, but left out of remedies. In a 1987 case, for example, the U.S. Court of Appeals for the Ninth Circuit reversed a lower court decision finding a defendant guilty of racial discrimination against a wide range of groups, including "Asians generally," but imposing affirmative action for African Americans only. *Shimkus v. The Gersten Companies, Inc.,* 816 F.2d 1318 (9th Cir. 1987).

Chapter Five

1. Lars-Erik Nelson, "Reports of the Select Committee on U.S. National Security and Military/ Commercial Concerns with the People's Republic of China," *New York Review of Books,* July 15, 1999, 6.

2. For a summary of the report, *see* Walter Pincus, "Hill Report on Chinese Spying Faulted; Five Experts Cite Errors, 'Unwarranted' Conclusions by Cox Panel," *Washington Post,* December 15, 1999, A16.

3. Robert Scheer, "No Defense: How the New York Times Convicted Wen Ho Lee," *Nation,* October 23, 2000, 11.

4. Bob Drogin, "How FBI's Flawed Case Against Lee Unraveled; Investigators Pursued Questionable Tactics in Their Zeal to Prosecute a Los Alamos Scientist as a Spy. Careers Are Ruined, and Still No One Knows How China Obtained Nuclear Secrets," *Los Angeles Times,* September 13, 2000, A1.

5. Robert Scheer, "The Times & Wen Ho Lee," *Nation,* February 26, 2001, 6.

6. Vernon Loeb, "Nuclear Weapons Expert Urges Bail for Lee," *Washington Post,* August 17, 2000, A4.

7. Scheer, "No Defense."

8. Matthew Purdy and James Sterngold, "The Prosecution Unravels: The Case of Wen Ho Lee," *New York Times,* February 5, 2001, A1.

9. Bob Drogin, "Science Academies Decry Lee's Treatment; Justice: Nation's Most Prestigious Institutes, While Not Saying Defendant Is Innocent, Protest His Jailing," *Los Angeles Times,* September 1, 2000, A1.; Drogin, "How FBI's Flawed Case Against Lee Unraveled."

10. Matthew Purdy, "The Making of a Suspect: The Case of Wen Ho Lee," *New York Times,* February 4, 2001, A1.

11. Scheer, "No Defense."

12. Drogin, "How FBI's Flawed Case Against Lee Unraveled."

13. These statements are all contained in Vrooman's sworn affidavit, filed by defense lawyers.

14. Vernon Loeb and Walter Pincus, "Espionage Whistleblower Resigns; Energy's Trulock Cites Lack of Support as Debate About His Tactics Grows," *Washington Post,* August 24, 1999, A1.

15. Lawrence Spohn, "Renowned Los Alamos Scientists Says Wen Ho *Lee* Case Is a 'Tragedy'," *Albuquerque Tribune,* December 23, 1999, A6.

16. Bob Drogin, "Science Academies," A1.

17. Theodore Hsien Wang and Frank H. Wu, "Singled Out, Based on Race," *Washington Post,* August 30, 2000, A25; Purdy, "The Making of a Suspect."

18. Drogin, "How FBI's Flawed Case Against Lee Unraveled."

19. Vernon Loeb, "Whistleblower or Demagogue? Trulock's Critics Say He Hyped Flimsy Chinese Spying Case," *Washington Post*, August 29, 1999, A6.

20. Vernon Loeb, "Physicist Lee Freed, with Apology; U.S. Actions 'Embarrassed' Nation, Judge Says," *Washington Post*, September 14, 2000, A1.

21. Plato Cacheris and John L. Martin, "Anatomy of a 'Spy' Case; Lessons Attorneys Can Learn from This Espionage Prosecution Gone Awry," *Legal Times*, October 30, 2000, 36.

22. "The Times and Wen Ho Lee," *New York Times*, September 26, 2000, A2; "An Overview: The Wen Ho *Lee* Case," *New York Times*, September 28, 2000, A26.

23. Neil A. Lewis, "The Nation: Searching Only in Profiles Can Hide a Spy's Face," *New York Times*, September 17, 2000, D6.

24. *See* Dan Eggen, "More Blunders by FBI in Lee Probe Detailed," *Washington Post*, August 27, 2001, A1; Dan Eggen and Ellen Nakashima, "U.S. Probe of Nuclear Scientist Assailed," *Washington Post*, August 14, 2001, A2; Dan Eggen and Ellen Nakashima, "Lee Probe Not Racist, Report Says; Investigation Still Called Flawed," *Washington Post*, August 8, 2001, A1.

25. Thomas W. Joo, "What, If Not Race, Tagged Lee," *Los Angeles Times*, August 15, 2001, B13.

26. Purdy and Sterngold, "The Prosecution Unravels."

27. The issue of clemency for Jonathan Pollard, an American Jew convicted of spying for Israel and given a life sentence, has divided mainstream Jewish organizations. Although some have argued that his activities benefited an ally and did not harm the United States, others have not been effusive in their support for his cause because it compromises their insistence that there should be no fear of "dual loyalties" directed toward Jews as a group. *See* Seymour M. Hersh, "The Traitor: The Case Against Jonathan Pollard," *New Yorker*, January 18, 1999, 26–33. The *Lee* and *Pollard* cases are not the same, however, because Lee was neither convicted nor even accused of transferring secrets to a foreign government.

28. *See, e.g.*, U.S. General Accounting Office, *Report to the Honorable Richard J. Durbin, United States Senate, "U.S. Customs Service: Better Targeting of Airline Passengers for Personal Searches Could Produce Better Results,"* GAO/GGD-00-38 (Washington, D.C.: Government Printing Office, 2000); David A. Harris, *Driving While Black: Racial Profiling on Our Nation's Highways, an American Civil Liberties Union Special Report* (New York: American Civil Liberties Union, 1999); Patrick A. Langan, et al., U.S. Department of Justice, Office of Justice Programs, Bureau of Justice Statistics, *Contacts Between Police and the Public: Findings from the 1999 National Survey*, (Washington, D.C.: Government Printing Office, 2001). *See also* David Kocieniewski and Robert Hanley, "An Inside Story of Racial Bias and Denial; New Jersey Files Reveal Drama Behind Profiling," *New York Times*, December 3, 2000, A53.

29. Werner Sollors, "Foreword: Theories of Ethnicity," in Werner Sollors, ed., *Theories of Ethnicity: A Classical Reader* (New York: New York University Press, 1996), x. *See also* Werner Sollors, *Beyond Ethnicity: Consent and Descent in American Culture* (New York: Oxford University Press, 1986). For a critique of the ethnic revival, *see* Stephen Steinberg, *The Ethnic Myth: Race, Ethnicity, and Class in America*, rev. ed. (Boston: Beacon, 1989).

30. Walter Lippmann, *Public Opinion* (New York: Free Press, 1965), 63–64.

31. Ibid., 63.

32. Jody Armour, *Negrophobia and Reasonable Racism: The Hidden Costs of Being Black in America* (New York: New York University Press, 1997).

33. Randall Kennedy, "Racial Profiling Usually Isn't Racist. It Can Help Stop Crime. And It Should Be Abolished," *New Republic*, September 13, 1999, 30. Kennedy makes another important point: Racial profiling usually incorporates race as only one factor; it isn't so crude as to rely on race alone.

34. J. Michael Kennedy, "Sheriff Rescinds Order to Stop Blacks in White Areas," *Los Angeles Times*, December 4, 1986, A18; Keith O'Brien, "Harry Lee Inducted Into La. Political Hall of Fame; Sheriff Gives Thanks, Takes Shots at Critics," *Times-Picayune*, January 28, 2001, 1.

35. Mike Clary, "Unusual Dinner Tab Brings Outcry Over Stigma of 'Dining While Black'," *Los Angeles Times*, November 14, 1999, A33.

36. Jeffrey Goldberg, "The Color of Suspicion," *New York Times Sunday Magazine*, June 20, 1999, 51.

37. Steven A. Holmes, "Black and Middle Class: Both a Victim of Racial Profiling—And a Practitioner," *New York Times*, April 25, 1999, D7.

38. Richard Cohen, "Closing the Door on Crime," *Washington Post Magazine*, September 7, 1986, 13.

39. *See* Marilyn Halter, *Shopping for Identity: The Marketing of Ethnicity* (New York: Schocken, 2000); Jim Taylor and Watts Wacker, *The 500-Year Delta: What Happens After What Comes Next* (New York: HarperBusiness, 1997); Joseph Turow, *Breaking Up America: Advertisers and the New Media World* (Chicago: University of Chicago Press, 1997); David Rieff, "Multiculturalism's Silent Partner: It's the New Globalized Consumer Economy, Stupid," *Harper's* (August 1993): 62.

40. "The Jeweler's Dilemma: How Would You Respond," *New Republic*, November 10, 1986, 18.

41. Marjorie Kagawa-Singer and Nadereh Pourat, "Asian American and Pacific Islander Breast and Cervical Carcinoma Screening Rates and Healthy People 2000 Objectives," *Cancer* 89 (2000): 696–705.

42. Richard Nadeau, "Innumeracy About Minority Populations," *Public Opinion Quarterly* 75 (1993): 332–47 . *See also generally* Daniel Kahneman et al., eds, *Judgment Under Uncertainty: Heuristics and Biases* (Cambridge: Cambridge University Press, 1982).

43. The leading books on race and criminal law are David Cole, *No Equal Justice: Race and Class in the American Criminal Justice System* (New York: New Press, 1999) and Randall Kennedy, *Race, Crime , and the Law* (New York: Random House, 1997); Katheryn K. Russell, *The Color of Crime: Racial Hoaxes, White Fear, Black Protectionism, Police Harassment and Other Macroaggressions* (New York: New York University Press, 1999).

44. Michelle N-K Collison, "In Rush to Help the Police, a College Enrages Its Black Students," *Chronicle of Higher Education*, April 14, 1993, A36.

45. Lisa Guernsey, "Court Clears SUNY Official Who Gave Local Police a List of Black Male Students," *Chronicle of Higher Education*, February 28, 1997, A44.

46. Petula Dvorak, "Black Officer's Beating Again Raises Bias Issue," *Washington Post*, March 25, 2001, C1.

47. Economist Gary Becker, whose work is relied on by advocates of racial profiling, also argued that criminal activity could be subjected to the same cost-benefit analysis. Gary S. Becker, "Crime and Punishment: An Economic Approach," *Journal of Political Economy* 76 (March-April 1968): 169–257. I have relied on the leading account of law and economics for an overview of its analysis of criminal behavior. Richard A. Posner, *Economic Analysis of Law, 5th edition* (New York: Aspen, 1998), 237–70.

48. *See* Iris Chang, *Thread of the Silkworm* (New York: Basic, 1996).

49. Toni Morrison, "Talk of the Town," *New Yorker*, October 15, 1998, 31.

50. David Mills, "Bootleg Black Bart Simpson, The Hip-Hop T-Shirt Star," *Washington Post*, June 28, 1990, D1.

51. Randall Kennedy, "Bias and Safety: Society Should Deal With Non-Racist Racial Discrimination," *Nieman Reports* (Fall 1995): 30.

52. John Stuart Mill, "Considerations on Representative Government," in *On Liberty and Other Essays* (Oxford: Oxford University Press, 1991), 428.

53. J. .S. Mill, *Utilitarianism*, Roger Crisp, ed. (New York: Oxford University Press, 1998), 55. I have benefited from Amartya Sen and Bernard Williams, eds., *Utilitarianism and Beyond* (Cambridge: Cambridge University Press, 1982).

54. Mill, *Utlitarianism*, 57.

55. Ibid., 81.

56. Robert William Fogel, *Time on the Cross: The Economics of American Negro Slavery* (Boston: Little, Brown, 1974).

57. "Winner of Nobel Prize in Economics Credits Wife of 44 Years for Her Role," *Jet*, November 1, 1993, 5.

58. R. M. Hare, "What Is Wrong with Slavery," *Philosophy & Public Affairs* 8 (1979): 103–21 .

59. The notion of traffic regulation as a mundane part of the social contract comes from the introductory essay by Charles M. Sherover to Jean-Jacques Rosseau, *Of the Social Contract*, translated by Charles M. Sherover (New York: New American Library, 1974), 13. For a pessimistic view of a racial contract tht harms people of color, see Charles W. Mills, *The Racial Contract* (Ithaca, N.Y.: Cornell University Press, 1997).

Chapter Six

1. Roland Barthes, "Toward a Psychosociology of Contemporary Food Consumption," in Carole Counihan and Penny Van Esterik, eds., *Food and Culture: A Reader* (New York: Routledge, 1997), 24.

2. Jessica Kuper, ed., *The Anthropologists' Cookbook*, rev. ed. (London: Kegan Paul International, 1997),: xii. For general information on food taboos and dog-eating, I recommend Frederick J. Simoons, *Eat Not This Flesh: Food Avoidances from Prehistory to the Present*, 2d ed. (Madison: University of Wisconsin Press, 1994), 200. I also have consulted the following sources: Alan Davidson, *The Oxford Companion to Food* (New York: Oxford University Press, 1999), 252; Stanley J. Olson, "Dogs," in Kenneth F. Kiple and Kriemhild Conee Ornelas, eds., *The Cambridge World History of Food* (Cambridge: Cambridge University Press, 2000), 508. To understand the role of food in culture, I have consulted Donna R. Gabaccia, *We Are What We Eat: Ethnic Food and the Making of Americans* (Cambridge, Mass.: Harvard University Press, 1998); Carolyn Korsmeyer, *Making Sense of Taste: Food and Philosophy* (Ithaca, N.Y.: Cornell University Press, 1998); Richard Pillsbury, *No Foreign Food: The American Diet in Time and Place* (Boulder, Colo.: Westview, 1998); and Waverly Root and Richard de Rochemont, *Eating in America: A History* (New York: The Ecco Press, 1981).

3. Among her many books, however, M. F. K. Fisher did write *How to Cook a Wolf* (New York: North Point, 1988), which exhibits her usual open-mindedness and great talent.

4. John Gardner, "The Art of Living," in John Gardner, *The Art of Living and Other Stories* (New York: Knopf, 1981), 302–3.

5. Paul Auster, *Timbuktu* (New York: Henry Holt, 1999).

6. Ibid., 5.

7. Linda Allardt, ed., *The Journals and Miscellaneous Notebooks of Ralph Waldo Emerson*, vol. 12 (Cambridge, Mass.: Harvard University Press, 1976), 237. For a recent account, *see* Craig S. Smith, "Peixian Journal: Local Treat Angers World Pet Lovers," *New York Times*, July 7, 2001, A4.

8. Jerry Hopkins, *Strange Foods: Bush Meat, Bats, and Butterflies: An Epicurean Adventure Around the World* (Hong Kong: Periplus Editions 1999), 4–9.

9. Ibid., 62–63.

10. David Haldane, "Judge Clears Cambodians Who Killed Dog for Food," *Los Angeles Times*, March 15, 1989, B1.

11. "Man Bites Dog," *Jet* (January 20, 1992), 19.

12. John Tierney, "The Big City: Falling for It," *New York Times*, July 17, 1994, F16.

13. Anne Fadiman, *The Spirit Catches You and You Fall Down: A Hmong Child, Her American Doctors, and the Collision of Two Cultures* (New York: Farrar, Straus & Giroux, 1997), 190.

14. May-Lee Chai, "When the Old Order in China at Last Changes: Dog's Place in History," *New York Times*, August 26, 1994, A28.

15. Jessica Hagedorn, *Dogeaters* (London: Pandora, 1991).

16. *See* Claude Levi-Strauss, *The Raw and the Cooked: Introduction to a Science of Mythology*, translated by John Weightman and Doreen Weightman (Chicago: University of Chicago Press, 1983).

17. George Engebretson, *Poi Dogs and Popoki: Animals and Pets in Hawaii* (Hong Kong: Hawaiian Humane Society, 1997), 97.

18. Katherine Bishop, "California Journal: U.S.A.'s Culinary Rule: Hot Dogs Yes, Dogs No," *New York Times*, October 5, 1989, A22. Some African Americans have objected to the animal rights movement for a related reason. They have suggested that comparisons of the treatment of animals in research laboratories to the enslavement of blacks in this country's history are demeaning and represent priorities that are not appropriate. Louis W. Sullivan, "Creatures' Rights: Comparisons to Civil Rights Era Are Insulting, Irresponsible," *Atlanta Constitution*, June 26, 1999, A9.

19. Yi-Ling Pan, "Asian Students Change Their Eating Patterns After Living in the United States," *Journal of the American Dietetic Association* 99, no. 1 (January 1999): 54–58.

20. Ellen Ruppel Shell, "New World Syndrome," *Atlantic Monthly* (June 2001): 50–53.

21. James Serpell, In the Company of Animals: A Study of Human-Animal Relationships (Cambridge: Cambridge University Press, 1996). I also have relied on James Serpell, The Domestic Dog (Cambridge: Cambridge University Press, 1995).

22. Serpell, *In the Company of Animals*, 45.

23. Upton Beall Sinclair, *The Jungle* (New York: Penguin, 1989).

24. Erik H. Erikson, *Childhood and Society*, 2d ed. (New York: Norton, 1963).

25. Ibid., 282.

26. For a discussion of American exceptionalism, I have relied on Seymour Martin Lipset, *American Exceptionalism: A Double-Edged Sword* (New York: W. W. Norton, 1996). An invaluable early reference work on assimilation and multiculturalism is Stephan Thernstrom, ed., *Harvard Encyclopedia of American Ethnic Groups* (Cambridge, Mass.: Harvard University Press, 1980). An influential book that combines empirical work with reflective analysis that also has been influential is Robert N. Bellah et al., *Habits of the Heart: Individualism and Commitment in American Life* (Berkeley: University of California Press, 1985). Another work that is helpful is William C. Fischer, *Identity, Community, and Pluralism in American Life* (New York: Oxford University Press, 1997). The importance of "imagined communities" is discussed creatively and encompassing a global scope in R. Benedict Anderson, *Imagined Communities: Reflections on the Origin and Spread of Nationalism* (New York: Verso, 1991). Two thoughtful contemplations on identity are Judith N. Shklar, *American Citizenship: The Quest for Inclusion* (Cambridge, Mass.: Harvard University Press, 1991) and Michael Walzer, *What It Means to Be An American* (New York: Marsilio, 1992).

27. This is the classic interpretation of the Fourteenth Amendment offered in Joseph Tussman and Jacobus tenBroek, "The Equal Protection of the Laws," *California Law Review* 37 (1949): 341–81.

28. One of the leading discussions of group rights theories is Owen M. Fiss, "Groups and the Equal Protection Clause," *Philosophy and Public Affairs* 5, no. 2 (Winter 1976): 107–77.

29. J. Hector St. John De Crevecoeur, *Letters from an American Farmer*, ed. Susan Manning (New York: Oxford University Press, 1997), 43–44. I have consulted Gay Wilson Allen and Roger Asselineau, *St. John de Crevecoeur: The Life of an American Farmer* (New York: Viking, 1987).

30. Ibid., 44.

31. Ibid., 48.

32. Ibid., 151–65.

33. Ibid., 202–3, 53.

34. Israel Zangwill, *The Melting Pot* (New York: Arno Press, 1975). I have found the following helpful: Elisa Bonita Adams, *Israel Zangwill* (New York: Twayne, 1971), 110–14 and Maurice Wohlgelernter, *Israel Zangwill* (New York: Columbia University Press, 1964), 175–86.

35. Zangwill, *The Melting Pot*, 11.

36. Ibid., 141.

37. Ibid., 96–98.

38. Ibid., 112.

39. Ibid., 33, 184.

40. Ibid., 207.

41. Ibid., 204. He added, however, that "in view of all the unpleasantness, both immediate and contingent, that attends the blending of colors, only heroic souls on either side should dare the adventure of intermarriage," and he urged mulattos to make Liberia a success, build a Negro state, or stay in the South. Ibid., 207.

42. Ibid., 215–16..

43. Mike Masaoka with Bill Hosokawa, *They Call Me Moses Masaoka: An American Saga* (New York: William Morrow, 1987), 50.

44. For information about Japanese American soldiers, I have relied primarily on Chester Tanaka, *Go For Broke: A Pictorial History of the Japanese American 100th Infantry Battalion and the 442nd Regimental Combat Team* (Richmond, Calif.: Go for Broke, 1982). I also have consulted Edwin M. Nakasone, *The Nisei Soldier: Historical Essays on World War II and the Korean War*, 2d ed. (White Bear Lake, Minn.: J. Press, 1999) and *Japanese Eyes, American Hearts: Personal Reflections of Hawaii's World War II Nisei Soldiers* (Honolulu: University of Hawaii Press, 1999).

45. The self-published institutional history of the memorial contains a detailed account of the controversy. National Japanese American Memorial Foundation, *Patriotism, Perseverance, Posterity: The Story of the National Japanese-American Memorial* (Washington, D.C.: National Japanese American Memorial Foundation, 2001).

46. Robert E. Park, *Race and Culture* (Glencoe, Ill.: Free Press, 1950), 150.

47. Milton M. Gordon, *Assimilation in American Life: The Role of Race, Religion, and National Origins* (New York: Oxford University Press, 1964). Another important work of the era is Nathan Glazer and Daniel Patrick Moynihan, *Beyond the Melting Pot: The Negroes, Puerto Ricans, Jews, Italians, and Irish of New York City*, 2d ed. (Cambridge, Mass.: MIT Press, 1970).

48. Gordon, *Assimilation in American Life*, 103.

49. Patrick Buchanan, "Looking Back with Longing," *Washington Times*, October 30, 1991, D1.

50. "In Buchanan's Words," *Washington Post*, February 29, 1992, A2. Paul Gigot, a columnist for the *Wall Street Journal*, retorted, "The Zulus . . . would probably work harder than the English." Peter Brimelow, *Alien Nation: Common Sense About America's Immigration Disaster* (New York: Random House, 1995), 108. Frances Fukuyama then added, "a million Taiwanese certainly would." Fukuyama, "Immigrants and Family Values," in Nicolaus Mills, *Arguing Immigration: The Debate Over the Changing Face of America* (New York: Touchstone, 1994), 166.

51. Patrick Buchanan, "What Lesson for the U.S. in Canada," *Washington Times*, June 27, 1990, F1; Patrick J. Buchanan, *A Republic, Not an Empire: Reclaiming America's Destiny* (Washington, D.C.: Regnery, 1999), 371.

52. Brimelow, *Alien Nation*, 272.

53. *See* Richard Brookhiser, "Others, and the WASP World They Aspired To," in Richard Delgado and Jean Stefancic, eds., *Critical White Studies: Looking Behind the Mirror* (Philadelphia: Temple University Press, 1997), 366.

54. Arthur M. Schlesinger Jr., *The Disuniting of America* (Knoxville, Tenn.: Whittle Communications, 1991); Todd Gitlin, *The Twilight of Common Dreams: Why America Is Wracked by Culture Wars* (New York: Henry Holt, 1995); Peter D. Salins, *Assimilation, American Style* (New York: Basic Books, 1997); Roy Beck, *The Case Against Immigration: The Moral, Economic, Social, and Environmental Reasons for Reducing U.S. Immigration Back to Traditional Levels* (New York: W. W. Norton, 1996); John J. Miller, *The Unmaking of Americans: How Multiculturalism Has Undermined America's Assimilation Ethic* (New York: The Free Press, 1998); Georgie Anne Geyer, *Americans No More: The Death of Citizenship* (New York: The Atlantic Monthly Press, 1996); Richard D. Lamm and Gary Imhoff, *The Immigration Time Bomb: The Fragmenting of America* (New York: Truman Talley, 1985); H. Fuchs, *The American Kaleidoscope: Race, Ethnicity, and the Civic Culture* (Hanover, N.H.: Wesleyan University Press, 1990); Nathan Glazer, *We're All Multiculturalists Now* (Cambridge, Mass.: Harvard University Press, 1997); Robert Hughes, *Culture of Complaint: The Fraying of America* (New York: Oxford University Press, 1993); Walter Benn Michaels, *Our America: Nativism, Modernism, and Pluralism* (Durham, N.C.: Duke University Press, 1995); and Michael Piore, *Beyond Individualism* (Cambridge, Mass.: Harvard University Press, 1995). I also have consulted the following regarding moral pluralism: Isaiah Berlin, *The Proper Study of Mankind* (New York: Farrar, Straus & Giroux, 1997); Robert A. Dahl, *Dilemmas of Pluralist Democracy: Autonomy vs. Control* (New Haven, Conn.: Yale University Press, 1982); John Kekes, *The Morality of Pluralism* (Princeton, N.J.: Princeton University Press, 1993); Gregor McLennan, *Pluralism* (Minneapolis: University of Minnesota Press, 1995); J. Donald Moon, *Constructing Community: Moral Pluralism and Tragic Conflicts* (Princeton, N.J.: Princeton University Press, 1993); Nicholas Rescher, *Pluralism: Against the Demand for Consensus* (New York: Oxford University Press, 1993); Michael Stocker, *Plural and Conflicting Values* (Oxford: Clarendon Press, 1990); Iris Marion Young, *Justice and the Politics of the Difference* (Princeton, N.J.: Princeton University Press, 1990).

55. Peter D. Salins, *Assimilation, American Style* (New York: Basic, 1997), 179.

56. John Higham, *Strangers in the Land: Patterns of American Nativism 1860–1925* (New Brunswick: Rutgers University Press, 1998), 198.

57. Thomas G. Dyer, *Theodore Roosevelt and the Idea of Race* (Baton Rouge: Louisiana State University Press, 1980), 140.

58. I have relied on the edition of Wilson's papers prepared by Albert Shaw. Albert Shaw, ed., *The Messages and Papers of Woodrow Wilson* (New York: Review of Reviews, 1924), 1114, 1120. The same text appears in the complete edition of Wilson's work as well. *See* Arthur S. Link, *The Papers of Woodrow Wilson*, vol. 63 (Princeton, N.J.: Princeton University Press, 1990), 500–13.

59. Arthur S. Link, *Wilson: Confusions and Crises* (Princeton, N.J.: Princeton University Press, 1964), 36.

60. Will Herberg, *Protestant, Catholic, Jew: An Essay in American Religious Sociology* (Garden City, N.Y.: Doubleday, 1955).

61. George Steiner, "Our Homeland, the Text," in *No Passion Spent: Essays 1978-1995* (New Haven, Conn.: Yale University Press), 319–20.

62. Gerald Early, ed., *Lure and Loathing: Essays on Race, Identity, and the Ambivalence of Assimilation* (New York: Penguin, 1993).

63. Anthony Day, "A Shift in Composition; Asian and Asian American Musicians Increasingly Can Be Found Playing in U.S. Symphony Orchestras. 'This Is a Manifestation of a Normal Cycle in American Musical Life,' Says Joseph Polisi, President of Juilliard," *Los Angeles Times Calendar* section, April 3, 1994, 7. As is true of the arguments about immigration control, discussed in Chapter 3, Stern relies on racial memory. As an individual, of course, he has not lived with Western music "for hundreds of years" either. *See also* Paula Yoo, "Asian Classical Musicians Still Face Stereotyping," distributed by Gannett News Service, May 9, 1994.

64. Sheryl WuDunn, "Japanese Are Making Great Deal of Music," *New York Times*, May 15, 1996, A10.

65. Day, "A Shift in Composition."

66. James R. Oestreich, "The Sound of New Music Is Often Chinese: A New Contingent of American Composers," *New York Times*, April 1, 2001, B1. In China, Dun belongs in the more ambiguous category of "overseas Chinese."

67. Tracy Wilkinson, "The Sound of Cultures Clashing; When the Venerable Vienna Philharmonic Voted Last Week to Admit Women, It Quieted a Global Furor. But to Many in Austria, the Orchestra's Tradition of Sexism Is But One Aspect of a Society That Abhors Change," *Los Angeles Times*, March 4, 1997, A1.

68. Blyden Jackson, "Langston Hughes," in M. Thomas Inge, *Black American Writers: Bibliographical Essays: The Beginnings Through the Harlem Renaissance and Langston Hughes*, vol. 1 (New York: St. Martin's Press, 1978), 187.

69. Quoted in Valerie Wayne, "*Shakespeare Wallah* and Colonial Specularity." in Lynde E. Boose and Richard Burt, eds., *Shakespeare: The Movie, Popularizing the Plays on Film, TV, and Video* (New York: Routledge, 1997), 95.

70. Brimelow, *Alien Nation*, 272.

71. Ibid., 270.

72. Horace M. Kallen, *Culture and Democracy in the United States: Studies in the Group Psychology of the American Peoples* (New York: Boni & Liveright, 1924), 42.

73. Ibid., 124.

74. Ibid., 122–23.

75. Ibid., 176.

76. Ibid., 174.

77. Louis Menand, *The Metaphysical Club* (New York: Farrar, Straus & Giroux, 2001), 394. I have found helpful Sarah Schmidt, *Horace M. Kallen: Prophet of American Zionism* (Brooklyn, N.Y.: Carlson Publishing, 1995).

78. Menand, *The Metaphysical Club*, 394.

79. Kallen, *Culture and Democracy*, 184–85.

80. Francis Fukuyama, *The End of History and the Last Man* (New York: Bard, 1998).

81. Francis Fukuyama, "Culture Vulture," *National Review*, May 1, 1995, 77.

82. Francis Fukuyama, "Immigrants and Family Values," in Mills, *Arguing Immigration*, 156.

83. Francis Fukuyama, "Great Planes," *New Republic*, September 6, 1993, 10.

84. Randolph Bourne, *The Radical Will: Selected Writings, 1911–1918*, edited by Olaf Hansen (New York: Urizen Books, 1977), 248–64. I have consulted Bruce Clayton, *Forgotten Prophet: The Life of Randolph Bourne* (Baton Rouge, La: Louisiana State University Press, 1984).

85. John Dos Passos, *U.S.A.* (New York: Literary Classics of the United States, 1996), 447–49.

86. Bourne, *The Radical Will*, 248.

87. Ibid., 249.

88. Ibid.

89. Ibid., 249.

90. Ibid., 254.

91. Ibid., 255–56.

92. Ibid., 257.

93. Menand, *The Metaphysical Club*, 404.

94. Horace M. Kallen, "Democracy Versus the Melting-Pot: A Study of American Nationality, Part Two," *Nation*, February 25, 1915, 219.

95. W.E.B. Du Bois, *Writings* (New York: Literary Classics of the United States, 1986), 363.

96. Ibid., 365.

97. Ibid.

98. Shelby Steele, *The Content of Our Character: A New Vision of Race in America* (New York: Harper Perennial, 1991), 95.

99. Ibid.

100. Ibid., 95–97.

101. Ibid., 102.

102. Michael Novak, *Unmeltable Ethnics: Politics and Culture in American Life* 2d ed. (New Brunswick, N.J.: Transaction Publishers, 1996).

103. Ibid., xvi–xviii.

104. *See* "In Alabama, Secessionists Rally Ahead of Clinton Visit; President Set to Mark Selma's 'Bloody Sunday'," *Washington Post*, March 5, 2000, A11; Michael Hill and Thomas Fleming, "The New Dixie Manifesto: States' Rights Shall Rise Again," *Washington Post*, October 29, 1995, C3.

105. C. Vann Woodward, *The Burden of Southern History* (Baton Rouge, La.: Louisiana State University Press, 1960). Ever since W. J. Cash wrote *The Mind of the South*, many students of the region have marshaled copious evidence to show that Southern culture is distinct, and how it was formed by a combination of European and African cultures, along with the interaction of blacks and whites through the institution of slavery. *See, e.g.,* Mechal Sobel, *The World They Made Together: Black and White Values in Eighteenth Century Virginia* (Princeton, N.J.: Princeton University Press, 1987).

106. Craig Timberg, "Va. Rescinds White History Declaration; Separatists Sought Salute," *Washington Post*, May 11, 2001, B1.

107. Peter Applebome, *Dixie Rising: How the South Is Shaping American Values, Politics and Culture* (New York: Times Books, 1996).

108. Susan Moller Okin, *Is Multiculturalism Bad for Women?* ed. Joshua Cohen (Princeton, N.J.: Princeton University Press, 1999). For a critique of Okin, *see* Leti Volpp, "Feminism Versus Multiculturalism," *Columbia Law Review* 101 (June 2001): 1181–1218.

109. Menand, *Metaphysical Club*, 388.

110. Helen Zia, *Asian American Dreams: The Emergence of an American People* (New York: Farrar, Straus & Giroux, 2000), 228.

111. For a critique of such multicultural conservatism, *see* Angela D. Dillard, *Guess Who's Coming to Dinner Now?: Multicultural Conservatism in America* (New York: New York University Press, 2001); Angela D. Dillard, "Multicultural Conservatism: What It Is, Why It Matters," *The Chronicle of Higher Education*, March 2, 2001, B7.

112. Geoffrey Wheatcroft, "The Friends of Salman Rushdie," *Atlantic Monthly* (March 1994): 22–43.

113. Henry Pratt Fairchild, *The Melting Pot Mistake* (Boston: Little, Brown, 1926).

114. *See* Bellah et al., *Habits of the Heart*, 142.

115. Lee Ross and Richard E. Nisbett, *The Person and the Situation: Perspectives of Social Psychology* (Philadelphia: Temple University Press, 1991).

116. Charles Taylor, *Multiculturalism: Examining the Politics of Recognition*, ed. Amy Gutmann (Princeton, N.J.: Princeton University Press, 1994), 32–37.

117. Richard Rorty, "Review of Richard E. Flathman, *Willful Liberalism: Voluntarism and Individuality in Political Theory and Practice*," *Political Theory* 22, no. 1 (1994): 190–94. 118. Kwame Anthony Appiah, "Cosmopolitan Patriots," *Critical Inquiry* 23 (Spring 1997): 617. Another version of the essay appears in Martha Nussbaum et al., *For Love of Country: Debating the Limits of Patriotism*, ed. Joshua Cohen (Boston: Beacon, 1996), 21–29.

118. David Hollinger, *Post-Ethnic America* (New York: Basic Books, 1995). Other key works on multiculturalism that must be considered in any discussion of the topic are Will Kymlicka, *Multicultural Citzenship: A Liberal Theory of Minority Rights* (New York: Clarendon Press, 1995); Will Kymlicka, ed., *The Rights of Minority Cultures* (Oxford: Oxford University Press, 1995); Will Kymlicka, *Liberalism, Community and Culture* (New York: Clarendon Press, 1991); Charles Taylor, *Multiculturalism: Examining the Politics of Recognition*, ed. Amy Gutmann (Princeton: Princeton University Press, 1994); and Iris Marion Young, *Justice and the Politics of Difference* (Princeton: Princeton University Press, 1990).

119. Compare the complaints of Victor Davis Hanson and John Heath, *Who Killed Homer? The Demise of Classical Education and the Recovery of Greek Wisdom* (New York: Free Press, 1998) with Neil Postman, *Amusing Ourselves to Death: Public Discourse in the Age of Show Business* (New York: Viking, 1985).

120. Allan Bloom, *The Closing of the American Mind: How Higher Education Has Failed Democracy and Impoverished the Souls of Today's Students* (New York: Simon & Schuster, 1987).

Chapter Seven

1. *Loving v. Virginia*, 388 U.S. 1 (1967).

2. David Greenberg, "White Weddings," *Slate*, June 14, 1999.

3. Jeanne Wakatsuki Houston, *Beyond Manzanar: Views of Asian American Womanhood* (Santa Barbara, Calif.: Capra Press, 1985), 20. This essay is reprinted in Russell Endo et al., *Asian Americans: Social Psychological Perspectives*, vol.. 2 (Palo Alto, Calif.: Science and Behavior Books, 1980), 17–25.

4. James Weldon Johnson, *Along This Way* (New York: Viking, 1934).

5. Ibid., 170.

6. Gunnar Myrdal, *An American Dilemma: The Negro Problem and Modern Democracy* (New York: Harper & Row, 1944), 60–61.

7. Sidney Kaplan, "The Miscegenation Issues in the Election of 1864)" in Werner Sollors, ed., *Interracialism: Black-White Intermarriage in American History, Literature, and the Law* (Oxford: Oxford University Press, 2000), 219.

8. Michae Lind, *The Next American Nation: The New Nationalism and the Fourth American Revolution* (New York, Free Press, 1995), 291.

9. Theodore G. Bilbo, *Take Your Choice: Separation or Mongrelization* (Poplarville, Miss.: Dream House Publishing Co., 1947).

10. Ibid., frontispiece.

11. Ibid., 198.

12. Ibid., 201.

13. Ibid., appendix A.

14. Tom Brady, *Black Monday* (Winona, Miss.: Association of Citizens' Councils, 1954), 88.

15. Ibid., 89

16. Charles Herbert Stember, *Sexual Racism: The Emotional Barrier to an Integrated Society* (New York: Elsevier, 1976), 24-25.

17. Norman Mailer, *Advertisements for Myself* (New York: G.P. Putnam's Sons, 1959), 332. Mailer also says in his famous "White Negro" essay that "the deeper issue is not desegregation but miscegenation." Ibid., 356.

18. Richard Wright, *Native Son* (New York: Literary Classics of America, 1991), 525–26, 667–68.

19. Lind, *Next American Nation* , 290.

20. Robert E. Kuttner, "Race Mixing: Suicide or Salvation," *American Mercury* (Winter 1971): 45–48.

21. Paul R. Spickard, *Mixed Blood: Intermarriage and Ethnic Identity in Twentieth-Century America* (Madison, Wis.: University of Wisconsin Press, 1989), 25.

22. William D. Zabel, "Interracial Marriage and the Law," in Sollors, *Interracialism*, 54.

23. Sollors, *Interracialism*, 13.

24. Darryl Fears and Claudia Deane, "Biracial Couples Report Tolerance; Survey Finds Most Are Accepted by Families," *Washington Post*, July 5, 2001, A1.

25. Flavia Tam et al., *Inter-Generational Paper on Asian American Attitudes Towards Family Values, Interracial Dating and Marriage* (Washington, D.C.: Organization of Chinese Americans, 1998). *See also* Betty Lee Sung, *Chinese American Intermarriage* (New York: Center for Migration Studies, 1990).

26. Timur Kuran, *Private Truths, Public Lies: The Social Consequences of Preference Falsification* (Cambridge, Mass.: Harvard University Press, 1995).

27. Tilden G. Edelstein, "*Othello* in America: The Drama of Racial Intermarriage," *in* Sollors, *Interracialism*: 361.

28. David Lister, "RSC Actors Beaten in Racist Attack," *The Independent*, May 22, 1998, 5.

29. Spickard, *Mixed Blood*, 3.

30. Edgar M. Bronfman, *Good Spirits: The Making of a Businessman* (New York: G. P. Putnam's Sons, 1998), 187.

31. I have relied on three accessible accounts of evolutionary psychology written for lay readers: Matt Ridley, *The Red Queen: Sex and the Evolution of Human Nature* (New York: Macmillan, 1994); Matt Ridley, *The Origins of Virtue: Human Instincts and the Evolution of Cooperation* (New York: Viking Penguin, 1997); and Robert Wright, *The Moral Animal: Why We Are the Way We Are: The New Science of Evolutionary Psychology* (New York: Pantheon Books, 1994).

32. Arnold Rampersad, ed., *The Collected Poems of Langston Hughes* (New York: Alfred A. Knopf, 1995), 305. The "tragic mulatto" was a recurring theme of Hughes's; he later turned "Cross" into a play.

33. Fawn M. Brodie, *Thomas Jefferson: An Intimate History* (New York: W. W. Norton, 1974); Annette Gordon-Reed, *Thomas Jefferson and Sally Hemings: An American Controversy* (Charlottesville: University Press of Virginia, 1997).

34. Leef Smith, "Tests Link Jefferson, Slave's Son; DNA Suggests a Monticello Liaison," *Washington Post*, November 1, 1998, A1. The scientific data were reported in Eugene A. Foster et al., "Jefferson Fathered Slave's Last Child," *Nature* 396 (November 5, 1998): 27–28 and Eric S. Lander and Joseph J. Ellis, "Founding Father," *Nature* 396 (November 5, 1998): 13–14.

35. Joseph J. Ellis, *American Sphinx: The Character of Thomas Jefferson* (New York: Knopf, 1997), 20. For an example of the pre-genetic testing debate, *see* Edwin McDowell, "Jefferson Liaison Is Disputed Again," *New York Times*, June 2, 1981, C7.

36. Itabari Njeri, "The Challenge of Diversity in an L.A. Cultural Crucible; In Crenshaw Neighborhood, Japanese-Americans, Blacks Have Forged a History of Complex Relationships," *Los Angeles Times*, May 2, 1990, E1.

37. John Updike, "Metamorphosis," *New Yorker*, August 9, 1999, 66–70. The title alludes to Franz Kafka's short story of the same name in which Gregor Samsa awakes to find himself transformed into a giant cockroach.

38. Terry McMillan, *Waiting to Exhale* (New York: Viking Productions, 1992).

39. Ibid., 329.

40. Ibid., 29–30.

41. Poppy Cannon, *A Gentle Knight: My Husband, Walter White* (New York: Rhinehart & Co., 1956), 12–13. The O.J. Simpson murder trial, in which he was acquitted of the murders of his ex-wife Nicole and her friend Ronald Goldman, also focused attention on the complexities of interracial marriages. *See* Jacqueline Adams, "The White Wife," *New York Times Magazine*, September 18, 1994, 36–38.

42. Cannon, *Gentle Knight*, 14.

43. Walter White, *A Man Called White: The Autobiography of Walter White* (New York: Viking Press, 1948), 338.

44. Juan Williams, *Thurgood Marshall: American Revolutionary* (New York: Times Books, 1998), 244.

45. Lynn Norment, "The Best Weddings of the Last 50 Years," *Ebony* (June 1995): 82.

46. Robert Suro, "Mixed Doubles," *American Demographics* (November 1999): 58.

47. Novelist James Michener profiled such an interracial couple, Frank and Sachiko Pfeiffer, in "Pursuit of Happiness by a GI and a Japanese: Marriage Surmounts Barriers of Language and Intolerance," *Life*, February 21, 1955, 124–41. For personal reflections on the racial aspects of such marriages by the daughter of such a couple, *see* Debbie Storrs, "Like a Bamboo: Representations of a Japanese War Bride," *Frontiers* 21, nos. 1–2 (January 2000): 194–224.

48. Yuh Ji-Yeon, "Out of the Shadows: Camptown Women, Military Brides and Korean (American) Communities," *Critical Mass* 6, no. 1 (Fall 1999): 13–33.

49. Venny Villapando, "The Business of Selling Mail-Order Brides," in Asian Women United of California, ed., *Making Waves: An Anthology of Writings By and About Asian American Women* (Boston: Beacon, 1989).

50. Lise C. Ikemoto, "Male Fraud," *Journal of Gender, Race & Justice* 3 (Spring 2000): 511–43.

51. The racial and gender aspects of intermarriage are reflected in the technical social term "hypergamy," "marrying up," which social scientists define as a woman, not a man, whose spouse is of a higher social status.

52. F. James Davis, *Who Is Black: One Nation's Definition* (University Park: Penn State University Press, 1991), 37.

53. Ibid., 62.

54. Patricia Hill Collins, *Black Feminist Thought: Knowledge, Consciousness, and the Politics of Empowerment*, 2d ed. (New York: Routledge, 2000).

55. Ibid., 162.

56. Rampersad, *Collected Poems of Langston Hughes*, 305.

57. The effects of these stereotypes are discussed in David L. Eng, *Racial Castration: Managing Masculinity in Asian America* (Durham, N.C.: Duke University Press, 2001); Yen Le Espiritu, *Asian American Women and Men* (Thousand Oaks, Calif.: Sage, 1997); Karen Ma, *The Modern Madame Butterfly: Fantasy and Reality in Japanese Cross-Cultural Relationships* (Rutland, Vt.: Charles E. Tuttle Co., 1996); Noy Thrupkaew, "Going Geisha," *Sojourner: The Women's Forum* (November 2000): 25–28; and Gina Marchetti, *Romance and the "Yellow Peril:" Race, Sex, and Discursive Stratgies in Hollywood Fiction* (Berkeley: University of California Press, 1993). The same images affect Asian American gay men. *See* Richard Fung, "Looking for My Penis: The Eroticized Asian in Gay Video Porn," in David L. Eng and Alice Y. Hom, eds., *Q&A: Queer in Asian America* (Philadelphia: Temple University Press), 115–38.

58. Esther Pan, "Why Asian Guys Are on a Roll," *Newsweek*, February 21, 2000, 50.

59. Shoko Ieda, *Yellow Cab* (Tokyo: Koyu Shuppan, 1991).

60. Lloyd Grove, "A Member of the Wedding; Stallings Takes Bride at Group Ceremony in New York," *Washington Post*, May 28, 2001, C1; Lloyd Grove, "The Reliable Source," *Washington Post*, May 18, 2001, C3; Lloyd Grove, "The Reliable Source," *Washington Post*, May 15, 2001, C3.

61. Marguerite Duras, *The Lover*, translated by Barbara Bray (New York: Pantheon, 1985).

62. Julie A. Su, "Heed the Call of the Dreamer," *Crosscurrents* (Fall/Winter 1996): 9. Su's published account discussed only the "American" hero aspect of the conversation; she related the "American" love interest aspect in an August 2001 telephone interview with the author.

63. David Henry Hwang, *M. Butterfly* (New York: Plume, 1989), 17.

64. Yoko Yoshikawa, "The Heat is on *Miss Saigon* Coalition: Organizing Across Race and Sexuality," in Karin Aguilar-San Juan, ed., *The State of Asian America: Activism and Resistance in the 1990s* (Boston: South End Press, 1994), 275–94. *See also* Urvashi Vaid, *Virtual Equality: The Mainstreaming of Gay and Lesbian Liberation* (New York: Anchor, 1995), 304.

65. Timothy Fong, *The Contemporary Asian American Experience: Beyond the Model Minority* (Upper Saddle River, N.J.: Prentice Hall, 1998), 1997; Helen Zia, *Asian American Dreams: The Emergence of an American People* (New York: Farrar, Straus & Giroux, 2000), 274–75; Ben Fong-Torres, "Why There Are No Male Asian Anchors," *San Francisco Chronicle*, July 13, 1986, Datebook, 51.

66. Steve Sailer, "Is Love Colorblind?" *National Review*, July 14, 1997, 30.

67. "Who Would 'See the Asian in Me'?" *Time*, May 5, 1997, 35.

68. Barbara Kantrowitz, "The Ultimate Assimilation," *Newsweek*, November 24, 1986, 80.

69. Eric Liu, *The Accidental Asian: Notes of a Native Speaker* (New York: Random House, 1998).

70. Ibid., 182–83.

71. The issue of exit is critical for the deaf. Almost all deaf individuals are born to hearing parents; most deaf couples have hearing children. Except among the deaf born of deaf parents, then, the deaf generally must choose between being minorities within a hearing community and belonging to a minority community. Whatever their choice, their roles within either community will probably be different than those of their parents and their children.

72. Alan M. Dershowitz, *The Vanishing American Jew: In Search of Jewish Identity for the Next Century* (Boston: Little, Brown, 1997); Samuel G. Freedman, *Jew vs. Jew: The Struggle for the Soul of American Jewry* (New York: Simon & Schuster, 2000); Barry Rubin, *Assimilation and Its Discontents* (New York: Times Books, 1995). A memoir that addresses the tensions is Eli N. Evans, *The Provincials: A Personal History of Jews in the South*, rev. ed. (New York: Free Press, 1997).

73. Freedman, *Jew vs. Jew*, 74.

74. *Plessy v. Ferguson*, 163 U.S. 537 (1896).

75. Spickard, *Mixed Blood*, 268.

76. Stephen Budiansky, "The Truth About Dogs," *The Atlantic* (July 1999): 39.

77. Associated Press, "Hate Mail Costs Donor an Honor," *Chicago Tribune*, February 18, 1988, A3. Even after his identity was revealed, he was intransigent, having found his calling. According to the most recent accounts, he has sent more than 100,000 letters. Doug Grow, "Elroy Stock's Mission Cost Him More Than Just Stamps," *Star Tribune*, April 15, 1994, B3.

78. C. B. Davenport, "Effects of Race Intermingling," *Proceedings of the American Philosophical Society* 56, no. 4 (1917). 367, *reprinted in* S. T. Joshi, *Documents of American Prejudice: An Anthology of Writings on Race from Thomas Jefferson to David Duke* (New York: Basic, 1999), 83.

79. Everett V. Stonequist, *The Marginal Man: A Study in Personality and Culture Conflict* (New York: Russell & Russell, 1961), 25.

80. Quoted in Henry Yu, "Mixing Bodies and Cultures: The Meaning of America's Fascination with Sex between 'Orientals' and 'Whites,'" in Martha Hodes, ed., *Sex, Love, Race: Crossing Boundaries in North American History* (New York: New York University Press, 1999), 455. *See also* Stanley Sue and Derald W. Sue, "Chinese-American Personality and Menthal Health," *Amerasia Journal* 1, no. 2 (1971): 42.

81. James Chapman, *Licence to Thrill: A Cultural History of the James Bond Films* (New York: Columbia University Press, 2000), 77–78.

82. *See* Sheng-Mei Ma, *The Deathly Embrace: Orientalism and Asian American Identity* (Minneapolis: University of Minnesota Press, 2000), 36–37.

83. Brant T. Lee, "Liars, Traitors, and Spies: Wen Ho Lee and the Racial Construction of Disloyalty," *Asian American Policy Review* 10 (2000): 8.

84. Ishmael Reed et al., "Is Ethnicity Obsolete?," in Werner Sollors, ed., *The Invention of Ethnicity* (New York: Oxford University Press, 1989), 227.

85. Gregory Howard Williams, *Life on the Color Line: The True Story of a White Boy Who Discovered He Was Black* (New York: Plume, 1996).

86. Judy Scales-Tent, *Notes of a White Black Woman: Race, Color, Community* (University Park, Penn State, 1995); Kevin R. Johnson, *How Did You Get to Be Mexican? A White/Brown Man's Search for Identity* (Philadelphia: Temple University Press, 1999). *See also* Jane Lazarre, *Beyond the Whiteness of Whiteness: Memoir of a White Mother of Black Sons* (Durham, N.C.: Duke University Press, 1996); James McBride, *The Color of Water: A Black Man's Tribute to His White Mother* (New York: Riverhead, 1996); Edward Ball, *Slaves in the Family* (New York: Farrar, Straus & Giroux, 1998).

87. Abigail Van Buren, "Booklet Tells All About Dealing with Anger," *Chicago Tribune*, June 24, 1991, C9.

88. Soraya Sarhaddi Nelson, "An Ethnic Strategy on the Census; Population: Campaign Urges African Americans to Retain Clout by Defining Themselves as Only Black, Even if Heritage is Mixed," *Los Angeles Times*, April 17, 2000, B1.

89. Thomas Ginsberg and Nita Lelyveld, "For Minorities, Census Presents Deep Conflicts With More Than an Accurate Count at Stake," *Philadelphia Inquirer*, April 2, 2000, A1.

90. Charles Paul Freund, "The New Face of Betty Crocker; Her Portrait As Drawn by Adam Smith's Invisible Hand," *Washington Post*, April 14, 1996, C5.

91. Jon Michael Spencer, *The New Colored People: The Mixed-Race Movement in America* (New York: New York University Press, 1997).

92. Kathy Russell, Midge Wilson and Ronald Hall, *The Color Complex: The Politics of Skin Color Among African Americans* (New York: Doubleday, Anchor Books, 1992).

93. William Hannibal Thomas, *The American Negro: What He Was, What He Is, and What He May Become: A Critical and Practical Discussion* (New York: Macmillan, 1901). *See also* John David Smith, *Black Judas: William Hannibal Thomas and the American Negro* (Athens: University of Georgia Press, 2000).

94. Mezz Mezzrow, *Really the Blues: An Autobiography* (New York: Random House, 1946).

95. Associated Press, "Slave Descendant Fights Race Listing," *New York Times*, September 15, 1982, A1; Calvin Trillin, "American Chronicles: Black or White," *New Yorker*, April 14, 1986, 62–78.

96. Lauren Kessler, *Stubborn Twig: Three Generations in the Life of a Japanese-American Family* (New York: Random House, 1993).

97. Woods ultimately decided on cheeseburgers and French fries, an historic first. Thomas Bonk, "It's Food That's Fit for This Golf King; The Masters: Wood's Choice for the Traditional Tournament Dinner Includes Cheeseburgers and Fries," *Los Angeles Times*, April 7, 1998, C1.

98. Hal Bock, "The Inside Track; Say What You Mean, Mean What You Say," *Los Angeles Times*, April 27, 1997, C2.

99. Gary Smith, "The Chosen; Tiger Woods Was Raised to Believe That His Destiny Is Not Only to Be the Greatest Golfer Ever, But Also to Change the World. Will the Pressures of Celebrity Grind Him Down First?" *Sports Illustrated*, December 23, 1996, 28.

100. Claudine Chiawei O'Hearn, *Half and Half: Writers on Growing Up Biracial and Bicultural* (New York: Pantheon Books, 1998), xxxiv.

101. Lucy M. Cohen, *Chinese in the Post Civil-War South: A People Without A History* (Baton Rouge, La.: University of Louisiana Press, 1984); James Loewen, *The Mississippi Chinese: Between Black and White* (Cambridge, Mass.: Harvard University Press, 1971).

102. Karen Isaksen Leonard, *Making Ethnic Choices: California's Punjabi Mexican Americans* (Philadelphia: Temple University Press, 1992).

103. Darby Li Po Price, "Mixed Laughter," in Paul Spickard and W. Jeffrey Burroughs, eds., *We Are a People: Narrative and Multiplicity in Constructing Ethnic Identity* (Philadelphia: Temple University Press, 2000), 179.

104. Leef Smith, "A Powhatan Princess in Their Past; Disney's 'Pocahontas' Inspires Virginians to Shake the Family Tree," *Washington Post*, July 3, 1995, B1. Regarding Indian identity, *see generally* Joane Nagel, *American Indian Ethnic Renewal: Red Power and the Resurgence of Identity and Culture* (New York: Oxford University Press, 1986).

105. For a discussion of these issues, *see* William S. Penn, *As We Are Now: Mixblood Essays on Race and Identity* (Berkeley: University of California Press, 1997).

106. For a contemporary account of Indian life, *see* Ian Frazier, *On the Rez* (New York: Farrar, Straus & Giroux, 2000).

107. Kieu-Linh Caroline Valverde, "From Dust to Gold: The Vietnamese Amerasian Experience," in Maria P. P. Root, ed., *Racially Mixed People in America* (Newbury Park, Calif.: Sage, 1992), 144–61.

108. Norman Podhoretz, "My Negro Problem—And Ours," *Commentary* (February 1963): 93–101. He wrote a postscript to this famous essay thirty years later. *See* Mark Gerson, ed., *The Essential Neoconservative Reader* (Reading, Mass.: Addison-Wesley, 1996), 18–22.

109. Ibid., 101.

110. Hannah Arendt, "Reflections on Little Rock," in Sollors, *Interracialism*, 492-502. Sollors's account of the reaction to Arendt's article is in Werner Sollors, *Neither Black Nor White Yet Both: Thematic Explorations of Interracial Literature* (Cambridge: Harvard University Press, 1997), 316.

111. Robert William Fogel, *The Fourth Great Awakening and the Future of Egalitarianism* (Chicago: University of Chicago Press, 2000), 96.

112. Michael Ignatieff, *Blood and Belonging: Journeys into the New Nationalism* (New York: Farrar, Straus & Giroux, 1993).

113. Kevin Phillips, *The Cousins' Wars: Religion, Politics, and the Triumph of Anglo-America* (New York: Basic, 1999).

114. Alissa Quart, "The Lost Emperors: Japanese Scholars Struggle to Unearth the Past," *Lingua Franca* (December 2000/January 2001): 55–59.

115. Benjamin DeMott, *The Trouble with Friendship: Why Americans Can't Think Straight About Race* (New York: Atlantic Monthly Press, 1995).

116. Race has been dead for some time as a serious concept in the hard sciences. For a recent survey of the literature, I have relied on Joseph L. Graves Jr., *The Emperor's New Clothes: Biological Theories of Race at the Millennium* (New Brunswick, N.J.: Rutgers University Pres, 2001).

Chapter Eight

1. Edward W. Said, *Orientalism* (New York: Random House, 1978). An important development of the thesis is found in Robert G. Lee, *Orientals: Asian Americans and Popular Culture* (Philadelphia: Temple University Press, 1999).

2. Quoted in Douglas Coupland, "Los Angeles 90049," *New Republic*, December 19, 1994, 18.

3. Interview with author, May 2000.

4. Fadiman, *The Spirit Catches You and You Fall Down: A Hmong Child, Her American Doctors, and the Collision of Two Cultures* (New York: Farrar, Straus & Giroux, 1997), 128–29.

5. Christopher Lasch, *Culture of Narcissism: American Life in an Age of Diminishing Expectations* (New York: Norton, 1978).

6. P. J. O'Rourke, "Seoul Brothers," *Rolling Stone*, February 11, 1988, 93. The essay is reprinted in J. O'Rourke, *Holidays in Hell* (New York: Vintage, 1989), 44–57.

7. Bob Drury, "Outrageousness Is His Calling Card," *Newsday*, October 20, 1988, 85.

8. The article appears as an essay in Stan Yogi, ed., *Highway 99: A Literary Journey through California's Great Central Valley* (Berkeley, Calif.: Heyday, 1996), 394–96, published in conjunction with the California state humanities council.

9. Ibid.

10. The works written and edited by Lynn Pan exemplify this worldview. *See* Pan, *Sons of the Yellow Emperor* and Pan, *Encyclopedia of Overseas Chinese. See also* Daniela Deane, "Chinese in U.S. as Diverse as Opinions of Jiang," *USA Today*, October 27, 1997, A1.

11. The same sentiment was expressed by Keith Richburg, an African American foreign correspondent posted in Africa, in Keith B. Richburg, *Out of America: A Black Man Confronts Africa* (New York: Basic, 1997).

12. The emergence of Asian Americans is described in detail in three books: Yen Le Espiritu. *Asian American Panethnicity: Bridging Institutions and Identities* (Philadelphia: Temple University Press, 1982); Juanita Tamayo Lott, *Asian Americans: From Racial Category to Multiple Identities* (Walnut Creek, Calif.: Alta Mira, 1998); and William Wei, *The Asian American Movement* (Philadelphia: Temple University Press, 1983). A documentary history of Asian Americans during the civil rights era has been recently published, Steve Louie and Glenn K. Omatsu, *Asian Americans: The Movement and the Moment* (Los Angeles, Cal.: UCLA Asian American Studies Center, 2001).

13. David Hollinger, *Post-Ethnic America* (New York: Basic Books, 1995), 19.

14. Melissa Nobles, *Shades of Citizenship: Race and the Census in Modern Politics* (Stanford: Stanford University Press, 2000), 80.

15. Ibid.

16. *See* Vijay Prashad, *The Karma of Brown Folk* (Minneapolis: University of Minnesota, 2000), 157–83.

17. For information about Asian Americans and political participation, *see* Chang, ed., *Asian Americans and Politics: Perspectives, Experiences, Prospects*. *See also* Pei-Te Lien, *The Making of Asian America Through Political Participation* (Philadelphia: Temple University Press, forthcoming). Also useful are the annual Asian American Political Almanacs produced by the UCLA Asian American Studies Center.

18. For a sampling of Asian America experiences, I have examined Maria Hong, ed., *Growing Up Asian American* (New York: Avon Books, 1993); Garrett Hongo, ed., *Under Western Eyes: Personal Essays from Asian America* (New York: Anchor, 1995); and Lawrence Yep, ed., *American Dragons: Twenty-Five Asian American Voices* (New York: HarperCollins, 1993). For a recent account of learning to be a racial minority by a young Asian immigrant, *see* Shu Shin Luh, "Learning a Role I Didn't Choose," *Washington Post*, Aug. 8, 999, B1.

19. David Mura, *Turning Japanese: Memoirs of a Sansei* (New York: Atlantic Monthly Press, 1991).

20. Amy Tan, *Joy Luck Club* (New York: G. P. Putnam's Sons 1989).

21. Bernard Weinraub, "Turning the Tables on Race Relations," *New York Times*, February 6, 1995, C11.

22. A book length assault on critical theory in legal reasoning is Daniel A. Farber and Suzanna Sherry, *Beyond All Reason: The Radical Assault on Truth in American Law* (New York: Oxford University Press, 1997). *See also* Stephen L. Carter, *Reflections of an Affirmative Action Baby* (New York: Basic, 1991) and Randall L. Kennedy, "Racial Critiques of Legal Academia," *Harvard Law Review* 102 (1989): 1745–1819.

23. Cornel West, *Race Matters* (Boston: Beacon, 1993), 25.

24. For the perspective of a white professor at a predominantly black university, *see* Karl Henzy, "Finding Connections: A White Professor at a Black University," *Chronicle of Higher Education*, October 10, 1997, B6.

25. Genna Rae McNeil, *Groundwork: Charles Hamilton Houston and the Struggle for Civil Rights* (Philadelphia: University of Pennsylvania Press, 1983), 84.

26. *See, e.g.,* Tamar Jacoby, "In Asian America," *Commentary* (July-August 2000): 21–28.

27. Peggy McIntosh, "White Privilege and Male Privilege: A Personal Account of Coming to See Correspondences through Work in Women's Studies," in Richard Delgado and Jean Stefancic, eds., *Critical White Studies: Looking Behind the Mirror* (Philadelphia: Temple University Press, 1997), 291–99.

28. Barbara J. Flagg, *Was Blind, But Now I See: White Race Consciousness and the Law* (New York: New York University Press, 1998).

29. Clint Bolick, *The Affirmative Action Fraud: Can We Restore the American Civil Rights Vision?* (Washington, D.C.: Cato Institute, 1996), 20.

30. This is a central claim of critical race theory and its allied field of whiteness studies. I have relied on several anthologies for an overview of the research: Karen Brodkin, *How Did Jews Become White Folks and What Does That Say About Race in America?* (New Brunswick, N.J.: Rutgers University Press, 1998); Kimberle Crenshaw et al., eds., *Critical Race Theory: The Key Writings That Formed the Movement* (New York: The New Press, 1995); Delgado and Stefancic, *Critical White Studies*; Richard Delgado and Jean Stefancic, eds., *Critical White Studies: The Cutting Edge*, 2d ed. (Philadelphia: Temple University Press, 2000). I also have found the following studies especially helpful: Theodore W. Allen, *The Invention of the White Race: The Origin of Racial Oppression in Anglo-America*, vol. 2 (London: Verso, 1997); Ian F. Haney Lopez, *White by Law: The Legal Construction of Race* (New York: New York University Press, 1996); Grace Elizabeth Hale, *Making Whiteness: The Culture of Segregation in the South, 1890–1940* (New York: Vintage Books, 1998); Matthew Frye Jacobson, *Whiteness of a Different Color: European Immigrants and the Alchemy of Race* (Cambridge: Harvard University Press, 1998); Noel Ignatiev, *How the Irish Became White* (New York: Routledge: 1995); Noel Ignatiev and John Garvey, eds., *Race Traitor* (New York: Routledge, 1996); George Lipsitz, *The Possessive Investment in Whiteness: How White People Profit from Identity Politics* (Philadelphia: Temple University Press, 1998); Michael Omi and Howard Winant, *Racial Formation in the United States: From the 1960s to the 1990s*, 2d ed. (New York: Routledge, 1994); David R. Roediger, *Black on White: Black Writers on What It Means to Be White* (New York: Schocken, 1998); David R. Roediger, *The Wages of Whiteness: Race and the Making of the American Working Class*, rev. ed. (London: Verso, 1991); Alexander Saxton, *The Rise and Fall of the White Republic: Class Politics and Mass Culture in Nineteenth-Century America* (London: Verso, 1990).

31. *See* Herbert J. Gans, "Symbolic Ethnicity: The Future of Ethnic Groups and Cultures in America," *Ethnic and Racial Studies* 2 no. 1 (1979): 1.

32. Beverely Daniel Tatum, *Why Are All the Black Kids Sitting Together in the Cafeteria: And Other Conversations About Race*, rev. ed. (New York: Basic, 1999).

33. *See* U.S. Department of Labor, Federal Glass Ceiling Commission, *A Solid Investment: Making Full Use of the Nation's Human Capital* (Washington, D.C.: U.S. Printing Office, 1995) *and* Federal Glass Ceiling Commission, *Good for Business: Making Full Use of the Nation's Human Capital* (Washington, D.C.: U.S. Printing Office, 1995). *See* Richard L. Zweigenhaft and G. William Domhoff, *Diversity in the Power Elite: Have Women and Minorities Reached the Top?* (New Haven, Conn.: Yale University Press, 1998). The effects continue to this day. *See* Johnathan D. Glater, "Law Firms Are Slow in Promoting Minority Lawyers to Partnerships," *New York Times*, August 7, 2001, A1. A well-known case study concerning an African American attorney at an elite law firm who failed to make partner, who was not only well-qualified but also politically conservative, is Paul M. Barrett, *The Good Black: A True Story of Race in America* (New York: Dutton, 1999).

34. Once the fourth largest city in the country, Detroit has declined to become one of the poorest. Continuing to experience population loss, the number of white residents dropped from more than 1.5 million in 1950 to fewer than 225,000 in 1990. Despite modest integration elsewhere, over time segregation has become more pronounced in Detroit. *See generally* Reynold Farley et al., *Detroit Divided* (New York: Russell Sage Foundation, 2000) and Thomas J. Sugrue, *The Origins of the Urban Crisis: Race and Inequality in Postwar Detroit* (Princeton, N.J.: Princeton University Press, 1996). (Gary, Indiana is as segregated, or more segregated, but does not compare in scale to Detroit and its metropolitan area.)

35. Among its first students were the white children of the white trustees. It did not have a black president until Mordecai Johnson took the helm in 1926.

36. Stanley Coren, *The Left-Hander Syndrome: The Causes and Consequences of Left-Handedness* (New York: Free Press, 1992). Nor are other means of discriminating among people, some of which we still accept, the same as discriminating by race. Birth order discrimination, which was once severe, does not carry with it the same stigma as racial discrimination. Age discrimination, which continues against both the young and the old, cannot have the same permanence as racial discrimination, for the simple reason that everyone ages at the same rate and passes through each phase of life.

37. The clinical literature on Asian Americans has developed significantly in recent years. I have consulted Evelyn Lee, ed., *Working with Asian Americans: A Guide for Clinicians* (New York: Guilford Press, 1997); Lee C. Lee, ed., *Handbook of Asian American Psychology* (Thousand Oaks, Calif.: Sage, 1998); Daya Singh Sandhu, ed., *Asian and Pacific Islander Americans: Issues and Concerns for Counseling and Psychotherapy* (Commack, N.Y.: Nova Science, 1999); Laura Uba, ed., *Asian Americans: Personality Patterns, Identity, and Mental Health* (New York: Guilford Press, 1994); and Nolan W. S. Zane et al, ed., *Confronting Critical Health Issues of Asian and Pacific Islander Americans* (Thousand Oaks, Calif.: Sage, 1994). Two older compilations of work remain valuable resources: Stanley Sue, *Asian Americans: Psychological Perspectives* (Palo Alto, Calif.: Science and Behavior Books, 1973) and Russell Endo et al., *Asian Americans: Social Psychological Perspectives*, vol. 2 (Palo Alto, Calif.: Science and Behavior Books, 1980).

38. Christopher Shea, "White Men Can't Contextualize," *Lingua Franca* (September 2001): 44–51. The work may turn out to be similar to Harvard psychologist Carol Gilligan's research which suggests that men and women have different cognitive styles. *See* Carol Gilligan, *In a Different Voice: Psychological Theory and Women's Development* (Cambridge, Mass.: Harvard University Press, 1993). *See also* Jon Entine, *Taboo: Why Black Athletes Dominate Sports and Why We Are Afraid to Talk About It* (New York: Public Affairs, 2000).

39. Ibid.

40. Richard E. Nisbett et al., "Culture and Systems of Thought: Holistic Versus Analytic Cognition," *Psychological Review* 108, no. 2 (2001): 291–310. *See also* Hazel Rose Markus and Shinobu Kitayama, "Culture and the Self: Implications for Cognition, Emotion, and Motivation," *Psychological Review* 98, no. 2 (2001): 224–53.

41. Deborah Tannen, *The Argument Culture: Moving from Debate to Dialogue* (New York: Random House, 1998); Deborah Tannen, *You Just Don't Understand: Women and Men in Conversation* (New York: William Morrow, 1990).

42. Robin D. G. Kelley, *Yo' Mama's Disfunktional!* (Boston: Beacon Press, 1997).

43. Kazuo Ishiguro, *The Remains of the Day* (New York: Knopf, 1989).

44. Kochiyama said this during a speech at the Japanese American Citizens League headquarters in San Francisco in summer 1993. A selection of her works is available in Russell Muranaka and Tram Nguyen, *Discover Your Mission: Selected Speeches and Writings of Yuri Kochiyama* (Los Angeles: UCLA Asian American Studies Center, 1998).

45. Grace Lee Boggs, *Living for Change: An Autobiography* (Minneapolis: University of Minnesota Press, 1998).

46. Harold H. Koh, "We Are a Nation of Refugees," *Asian Week*, April 2, 1993, 3.

47. Ibid.

48. Anna Deavre Smith, *Twilight: Los Angeles, 1992; On the Road: A Search for American Character* (New York: Anchor, 1994).

49. Ibid., xxiv–xxv.

50. Ibid., 244–49.

51. There are several works that address the same concerns within the American Jewish-African American context. The estrangement of American Jews and African Americans is even more agonizing to former colleagues from the civil rights movement. Paul Berman, ed., *Blacks and Jews: Alliances and Arguments* (New York: Delacorte, 1994); Michael Lerner and Cornel West, *Jews and Blacks: Let the Healing Begin* (New York: G. P. Putnam's Sons, 1995). These recent books

revisit an issue raised in the 1960s. *See* James Baldwin et al., *Black Anti-Semitism and Jewish Racism* (New York: R. W. Baron, 1969).

52. Nicolaus Mills, *Arguing Immigration: The Debate Over the Changing Face of America* (New York: Touchstone, 1994), 97–100.

53. *See* Edward T. Chang and Russell C. Leong, *Los Angeles —Struggles Toward Multiethnic Community: Asian American, African American, and Latino Perspectives* (Seattle: University of Washington Press, 1993); Eui-Young Yu and Edward T. Chang, *Multiethnic Coalition Building in Los Angeles* (Claremont, Calif.: Regina Books, 1995). Three books that can be recommended on such efforts are Deborah A. Prentice and Dale T. Miller, *Cultural Divides: Understanding and Overcoming Group Conflict* (New York: Russell Sage Foundation, 1999); Bill Piatt, *Black and Brown in America: The Case for Cooperation* (New York: New York University Press, 1997); and Eric Y. Yamamoto, *Interracial Justice: Conflict and Reconciliation in Post-Civil Rights America* (New York: New York University Press, 1999).

54. The very title of this book, of course, commits this error. I recommend Prashad, *Karma of Brown Folk*, (Minneapolis, Minn.: University of Minnesota Press, 2000) as a thoughtful counterpoint. *See also* Lavina Dhingra Shankar and Rajini Srikanth, *A Part, Yet Apart: South Asians in Asian America* (Philadelphia: Temple University Press, 1998).

55. Farai Chideya, *The Color of Our Future: Race for the 21st Century* (New York: Quill, 2000).

56. Ibid., 258.

57. This sense of beleaguered whites is documented in Dale Maharidge, *The Coming White Minority: California's Eruptions and America's Future* (New York: Times Books, 1996). *See, e.g.,* Ron Unz, "California and the End of White America," *Commentary* (November 1999): 17–28.

58. Patrick J. McDonnell and Paul Jacobs, "Fair at Forefront of Push to Reduce Immigration; Population: Group's Roughts Are in the Environmental Movement. It Is Now An Influential Player in Border Issues," *Los Angeles Times*, November 24, 1993, A1; Zita Arocha, "Dispute Fuels Campaign Against 'Official English'" Foes say Memo Shows Racism's Behind Plan," *Washington Post*, November 6, 1988, A20.

59. Orlando Patterson, "Race By the Numbers," *New York Times*, May 8, 2001, A27.

60. Glenn Kessler, "Black Group Seeks Repeal of Estate Tax; Businessmen Say Levy Increases Disparity in Wealth Among Race," *Washington Post*, April 2, 2001, A4.

61. John B. Christiansen and Sharon N. Barnartt, *Deaf President Now! The 1988 Revolution at Gallaudet University* (Washington, D.C.: Gallaudet University Press, 1995); Jack R. Gannon, *The Week the World Heard Gallaudet* (Washington, D.C.: Gallaudet University Press, 1989).

62. James I. Charlton, *Nothing About Us Without Us: Disability, Oppression and Empowerment* (Berkeley: University of California Press, 1998); Lennard J. Davis, *Enforcing Normalcy: Disability, Deafness and the Body* (London: Verso, 1995); Lennard J. Davis, ed., *The Disability Studies Reader* (New York: Routledge, 1997); Martha Minow, *Making All the Difference: Inclusion, Exclusion, and American Law* (Ithaca, N.Y.: Cornell University Press, 1990); Carol Padden and Tom Humphries, *Deaf in America: Voices from a Culture* (Cambridge, Mass.: Harvard University Press, 1990); Johnathan Ree, *I See a Voice: Deafness, Language and the Senses—A Philosophical History* (New York: Metropolitan Books, 1999); Joseph P. Shapiro, *No Pity: People with Disabilities Forging a New Civil Rights Movement* (New York: Random House, Times Books, 1993).

63. *See* Lucy Grealy, *Autobiography of a Face* (Boston: Houghton Mifflin, 1994).

64. Even the earliest accounts of assimilation treat academe as its own subculture. *See* Milton M. Gordon, *Assimilation in American Life: The Role of Race, Religion, and National Origins* (New York: Oxford University Press, 1964). The unique aspects of military culture have been instrumental in its anti-discrimination programs. *See* Charles Moskos and John Sibley Butler, *All That We Can Be: Black Leadership and Racial Integration the Army Way* (Princeton, N.J.: Princeton University Press, 1998).

Epilogue

1. *See* Michael Walzer, *Thick and Thin: Moral Arguments at Home and Abroad* (Notre Dame, Ind.: University of Notre Dame, 1994), regarding "thick" and "thin" arguments.

2. *Essays and Lectures* (New York: Literary Classics of the United States, 1983), 67, 65, 70.

3. Ibid., 386, 259, 262.

Acknowledgments

This work is possible only because of others. I have many more collaborators than are aware of their status. All errors, of course, are my own.

My parents have come to support my dilettante pursuit of writing and they appear as important figures in this book. My younger brothers, Carson and Nelson, have become writers themselves; Carson published books well before I did, and Nelson edits a newspaper. My in-laws, the Mitoris, Rolls, and Steeles, also support my endeavors. My nephews and nieces by marriage, who make cameo appearances in these pages, have critiqued early drafts.

My teachers and editors have pointed me in the right direction to discover my subject, develop my thoughts, and improve my technique. Ruth Zoe Ost provided me with the passion to write, along with a copy of Rainer Marie Rilke's *Letters to a Young Poet*. Fiction writer Stephen Dixon supervised my work in the Johns Hopkins Writing Seminars program and conducted an invaluable workshop. The late Kenneth Lynn and Terrance Sandalow, two professors who led seminars that challenged me and who were principled in mentoring students whose views differed with theirs greatly, showed me how to conduct academic research and prepare rigorous arguments. Yale Kamisar, a professor who always knew the hard questions to ask, assisted me in becoming a law professor. Joe Stroud, editor of the *Detroit Free Press*, hired me as an intern while I was still in college and gave me the opportunity to write thirty-two editorials representing the opinion of the paper over the course of a summer. Much later, James Fang and James Carroll, the publisher and the editor of *Asian Week*, and then Jeff Yang and Dina Gan, the publisher and the editor of *A. Magazine*, introduced me to a regular audience of Asian Americans. The Progressive Media Project of Knight Ridder Tribune Wire Services has distributed my opinions to newspapers throughout the country, as did the New America News Service of the New York Times Syndicate.

The diverse individuals who joined forces in Californians United Against Proposition 187, notably Robert Rubin of the Lawyers' Committee for Civil Rights Under Law, taught me about progressive politics. The students who intervened in the University of Michigan affirmative action lawsuit helped me renew a commitment to their cause.

The Asian American law professors of the "yellow pearl" e-mail listserv have provided crucial support. They have used technology to create a new type of cybercommunity. My collaborators on other projects—Gabriel Chin, Sumi Cho, Jerry Kang, Maggie Chon, Eric Yamamoto, Ted Wang, and Francey Lim Youngberg—have been especially important. Together, we have tried to demonstrate that "publish or perish" need not make peers unwilling to cooperate.

The president of Howard University, H. Patrick Swygert, has led the institution through an ongoing renaissance, promoting its leadership role in civil rights and its commitment to high intellectual standards. The former dean of Howard University Law School, Henry Ramsey, hired me, and the current dean, Alice Gresham Bullock, has always offered support for research. On the faculty, Homer La Rue and Andrew Taslitz have been key among many senior colleagues. Reference librarians Stephanie Dyson and Luis Acosta have been vital to providing ideal service on a multitude of requests, ranging from tracking down obscure sources in nineteenth-century American literature to looking for the latest websites on transnational adoption. My several research assistants, among them Andrea Ritchie, Melissa Holder, and Diara Andrews, Jonathan Goins, and Lynn White have found sources, organized materials, and proofread. Research assistants Lynden Steele and John Wornell also helped tremendously with last-minute fact-checking. The staff of the Howard University Clinical Law Center—Lisa Bruce, its office manager, and Mary Sirleaf and Marilyn Toran, its secretaries—have ensured that the office operates while I write.

My editors at Basic Books, initially Tim Bartlett and then Jo Ann Miller, have persevered and ensured that my ideas were committed to paper. Freelance editor Mary Pastis provided invaluable comments. Without them, this book would not exist.

Above all, the many people I have been privileged to meet over the years at many venues when I speak on the topics of this book have given me the insights that are what democratic deliberations are all about. It is to return the favor and stimulate dialogue that I have written.

Some of the material in this book has appeared in earlier form and different versions in *Asian Week*, *A. Magazine*, op-ed articles, and various law review articles.

The dust jacket photograph was shot by Lynden Steele.

My wife, Carol L. Izumi, has been a partner in every respect; this book is as much hers (except for the errors) as it is mine.

Index

About the Author

Frank H. Wu is an Associate Professor of Law at the Howard University School of Law. His writings have appeared in such periodicals as the *Washington Post*, the *L.A. Times, Chicago Tribune, Chronicle of Higher Education, National Law Journal, Legal Times, Nation, Progressive, Asian Week,* and *A. Magazine.* He lives in Washington, D.C.